Our Caribbean

Our Caribbean

A GATHERING
OF LESBIAN AND GAY WRITING
FROM THE ANTILLES

Edited and with an Introduction by
Thomas Glave

DUKE UNIVERSITY PRESS Durham & London 2008

Designed by Jennifer Hill
Typeset in Carter and Cone Galliard
by Keystone Typesetting, Inc.

Library of Congress
Cataloging-in-Publication Data
appear on the last printed
page of this book.

To all those
above the water
and beneath it,
still silent

CONTENTS

ACKNOWLEDGMENTS

I extend sincere thanks to the editor for this project, Ken Wissoker, without whose generosity and insight this gathering, in its present form, would not be a reality. My thanks also to all the staff at Duke University Press who ensured that this collection received the best possible care while in their midst. Particular thanks to the ever-meticulous Molly Balikov.

I cannot thank enough all the writers, scholars, colleagues, and friends — several of whose work appears here — who provided the names and locations of more writers, possibilities, suggestions, and a generally inestimable amount of truly invaluable information. I am particularly grateful to Maureen T. Reddy, Charles H. Rowell, Lisa Li Shen Yun, and Leo Wilton for their advice, support, and friendship. I am honored to know them also as colleagues. I am also extremely grateful to my esteemed colleagues Juanita Díaz-Cotto and Lawrence La Fountain-Stokes for so generously helping this gathering to realize a wider Caribbean.

Thanks to the translators who made it possible for some of the works in this collection to be published: Dick Cluster (with extra gratitude for his *paciencia tan fuerte!*), Dolores M. Koch, Harry Morales, Mark Schafer, Gilberto Lucero, and Michael Ray.

Special thanks to Ina Brownridge at the State University of New York, Binghamton, for her technical and technological support and suggestions, all of which made the ultimate process of dealing with a book-in-progress of this size both more manageable and less stressful.

My appreciation to the English department and administration of SUNY Binghamton for providing me with leave time during which I was able to work extensively on this book.

Special thanks to those in my family who, when they heard about my interest in this project, said, "Yes."

Very special thanks to Anne Higginbottom.

Desire through the Archipelago

As a child of Jamaican immigrants to the United States, and one who regularly spent extended time with family in Jamaica, I couldn't know how much, over the accumulating years, a book like this would someday mean to me. It is both fair and accurate to say that this anthology — this gathering, as it is titled, which makes its own contribution to an ever increasing conversation — is a book that I and others have been waiting for and have wanted for all our lives. It is in no way an exaggeration to say that this gathering originated as an idea born out of the most extreme longing: the desire to know finally, and with complete certainty, that a book such as this one actually existed and could exist. Could exist in spite of thundering condemnation from Christian fundamentalist ministers and, from those in churches, mosques, and other places, sidelong disapproving — and sometimes baleful — glances. Could exist despite proscriptions, banishments, ostracisms, and, in more than a few cases, extreme violence.[1] Could exist: a book like this that, though some — including a number of our most renowned, if not always most generous, Caribbean minds — might wish to ignore or dismiss it, none would ultimately be able to deny or wish away. Numerous writers whose work I have long admired have consistently expressed a sentiment similar to the one that motivated this collection, also centered in desire; they wrote the books they did, they said, because they wished deeply to read those texts, texts that up until the moment of that writer's yearning had not been written. Those writers wanted to know that the stories they committed to paper actually existed — indeed, could exist. Exist for the passing along, the making known from consciousness to uttered word to the next watchful, waiting eye.

I wouldn't be truthful if I didn't admit that this gathering also owes its genesis to the most painful, inexpressible loneliness: one that, as the years passed me from childhood to adolescence to adulthood, grew increasingly agonizing, made more so by the sorts of intransigent silences I fervently hope the voices in these pages will unsettle. That loneliness stretched through every hour of the silent and silenced wondering one couldn't possibly dare, when young, to ever express out loud to anyone else, or — perhaps most dangerously, terrifyingly — to oneself. Wondering: could there somewhere "out there" be others like me? Wherever "out there" was, I knew it to be a place beyond the supposed safety of family (which was not always so safe) — a place where I was despised, even hated, by those who ranted that hatred publicly and shouted it joyously in church. Were there others in Jamaica and other parts of the Caribbean who also pondered "unspeakable" things and thought, in the depths of their own silences, "unmentionable" thoughts? Were there others immobilized and cowed by silence and mired in the same shame that colluded with that silence and its creeping shadows? Shadows that, like the heavily weighted silence, invariably led to rage, self-loathing and desperation. Desperation backed the thoughts: *I hope someday I can get out of here. I hope I survive long enough not to walk, for the last time, with open eyes and open mouth into the swirling sea. I hope that star-apple trees and bougainvillea blooms never learn my secrets — no, not any of them — and that the hummingbird that adores scarlet hibiscus never penetrates my dreams. I hope that this silence doesn't kill me or make me kill myself, because* (some of us thought and continue to think) *it doesn't seem as though I can possibly be myself, my fullest truest self, the self that everyone would love to know and hug and laugh with, greet with open hands and arms, if I remain here . . . remain here.* Some of us, myself included, thought those things. Some of us, in spite of those thoughts, did not leave the Caribbean, and will not leave it still. Although some opted to stay, many had — and continue to have — no choice. Green cards are not always easy to secure, nor are visas, for those who need them most. And families, families often are in need of help. The desire for Home or "home" often abides in the traveler. Our history — perhaps especially the history we find most intolerable to remember, that began for some of us with harsh voyages across the sea, but never ended there — is about nothing if not movement, memory. Dis-placement. This book began, crept to its knees, and shakily, then more assuredly, began to walk through all of that and more.

Walking, though slowly, and increasingly aware of its flesh taking shape, the book began to ask questions — pester, even. Through all the hours of its more groggy, wobbly-kneed state, it wanted to know the same things I did: things about the people like me whom I longed so much to know (and who, it seemed, were so often impossible to find) in Jamaica, Martinique, St. Lucia, Trinidad. People whose eyes would say something recognizable, friendly even, in the Dominican Republic, Sint Maarten, and Guyane Fran-

çaise. People "out there" who also gazed across that water that simultaneously divided and united us all and who dreamed — yearned their way
through those emotions and all that desire: women for women, men for
men, women and men for women-men. That erotic-emotional desire for
people of our own gender that it seemed no one — not anyone at all — ever
spoke about, much less wished to hear about unless in the realm of "scandal"
and "disgrace."

Those people, yes. The people of "out there" and, as I would later learn,
nearer. But where did they live? How did they dream?

What colors would their stories have taken, if one could have seen them?
Read them? How would they have sounded?

Who, through love and desire, loneliness and pleasure, were we hoping
to be, imagining ourselves to be, and becoming through our many Antilles?
Our Antilles of Creole and English, Kréyol and French, and Spanish, Papia-
mentu, Dutch. Our many Caribbeans of cricket and *béisbol*, soccer and *fútbol*,
and Carnival, jouvert, crop-over. Our islands and memories of *zonas colo-
niales*, *ciudades viejas*, a very well known Soufrière, and Basse-Terre, Grand-
Terre — all traversed by mountains, rivers, ghosts, *diablesses*, duppies, soucouyants, jumbies, and more.

And all of our music! Zouk. Salsa. Rara. Bouyon. Reggae. Rumba. Calypso. Ska. Son. Tumba. Biguine. Bomba. Dancehall. Soca. Merengue. And
still so much more.

What would it be like to attend — to truly hear, for once — the many
conversations that we have had with each other and still need so very much
to have? What would it be like to listen to and now, by way of a gathering of
voices like this one, actually observe those conversations between ourselves?

What would it be like to bear witness to the conversations between *mati*,
women-loving women, in Suriname and their distant sisters and brothers in
St. Eustatius, Saba, and Bonaire?

But then close your eyes, a certain tree tells you, in order to hear better the
words of those two: two women together, or two men, or two women-men
or men-women. They are in Haiti — yes, in Jérémie, this time. There, in that
near-darkness, overlooking the sighing shoals and what remains of the ever-
entangled mangroves, they are holding each other, those two. Holding,
caressing each other's most secret parts, and whispering things into each
other's neck — things, the tree says, that their brethren and sistren in Fort-de-
France, Marie-Galante, and even all the way over in Cayenne, Guyane, would
like to hear. We too would like to hear it, the tree tells us. (In its own, old way,
it is one of us, that tree. Of course. It always has been.) We would like to hear

all of it, for the expansion of our imaginations and our very lives—our survival. It is so very important for us each to know that we are not, no matter what anyone tells us, throughout the archipelago and beyond it, alone.

INCIPIENT CHALLENGES: NOTES ON "NARROW" AND "A SLICE OF A SLICE"

When I first conceived of this gathering as a viable project, I was taken aback—though in the increasingly corporate-minded publishing world, sadly not entirely surprised—by the opinion of a few myopic editors and one remarkably uninsightful literary agent, who felt that an anthology like this one would be a "narrow" book: "a slice of a slice," as one extremely market-minded editor put it; that is, the (non-Latino) Caribbean "market" as perceived by some continental North American editors was a "slice," and a lesbian and gay text within that category an even more selective "slice." (Prompting the question of who or what was looking down from somewhere, holding the determining slicing knife?)

After hearing this editor's words—an assessment that instantly struck me as informed mostly by ignorance and prejudice—I immediately lost faith in her judgment. Fortunately for this book's ultimate existence, I eventually made contact with a more broadminded editor—one in possession of the imagination and generous vision the naysayers lacked, who not only decided to take on this project but from the very start voiced his unstinting support for it and belief in its importance.

This gathering's blessed fortune in that regard notwithstanding, I remained deeply troubled by those people's summary dismissal of Caribbean lesbian and gay lives. How, I wondered, could they feel so confident in their arrogance? Confident enough to use the dismissive word "narrow" about our very complex and, to them, unknown and unseen lives? What, I wondered, did they in their continental North American worlds—contexts rife with spurious images and conjurings of the Caribbean as a fetishized "paradise" for tourists—really know about our lives? The Caribbean, as packaged globally for tourists, purposely obscures quotidian (and often poor) Antillean lives—existences rendered as of scant importance beyond obsequious servitude in the generally consumer-directed packaging. Lesbian and gay lives generally do not enter into this truncated representation at all, unless they surface in some momentary wink of sexual tourism. The naysayers, editors and agent, were not Caribbean themselves. None among them, as far as I knew, self-identified as lesbian or gay (although I remain uncertain even today that an editor from either group would have seen things any differently). If they considered a book containing texts about our lives "narrow," what would they have considered the opposite? An anthology containing work by U.S., Canadian, or European heterosexuals?

I recount these challenges in order to bring to light the very difficult, *un*welcoming context out of which this anthology fought — and was required to fight — for its right to exist; to point out how, in that context, many in the "global north" or "first world" think little of those in the "global south" or "third world" and frequently have no problem in saying so; and to briefly delineate the reprehensible attitudes (narrowness, actually) of some publishers (including, in this case, more than one very respectable university press) who retain the power to decide which ideas achieve visibility under their aegis and which do not — including books by and about people whose life (and death) experiences are continually rendered invisible, or silent, or both.

ORIGINS: GATHERING

Sometime during the late winter to early spring of 2002, when I realized, startled, that my longstanding wish to see and hear Caribbean lesbian and gay voices in conversation could actually be a book, I began to speak with and write to people who I very much hoped might be interested. Whatever else occurred, I knew from the beginning that I wanted this project to move, as much as possible, as a grassroots effort: one that reached out to people across and through the varying Caribbean communities I had known and of which I had been a part, as well as those unknown to me, but viable. These communities included women-loving women and men-loving men, all of whom were in one way or another aware of and affected by the issues that have always weighed heavily upon us: racism, xenophobia, sexual and gender violence, economic stresses, the need for voluntary or forced migration (as in the case of political asylum seekers), the erasing or silencing of ourselves (and, in some cases, the murdering of ourselves) because of our sexualities, and more. The book I yearned to read was one that would disclose *how* we wrote and continued to write. And why. And where. That book would suggest questions like: writing and thinking as we did, did we remain in the Caribbean? Was that decision ours to make, or someone else's? Could we remain in that place — the place we might have called home — as the people we were and continued to become? That is, as our fullest, most realized selves? Would those places we thought of as home provide a welcome for us whomever we turned out to be and whatever we decided to do or say in artistic, creative, and intellectual response to those places and to ourselves as people ancestrally, imaginatively, and culturally part of them? For whatever else happened, we were part of those places and their people (our people) in just about every way. We remained connected to them, even as — perhaps especially as — members of an enormous diaspora. What effect would the decisions we made and the actions we took — artistically, intellectually, politically — extend not only to our literal movements, but also to our internal ones in the realm of our imaginations where, as people involved with language and words, we think in each of our very different locales about the ways in which we might not only express ourselves, but also challenge ourselves and others? How might a journey to our particular diaspora, a settling in that diaspora, and a return to "home" from that "foreign" place affect or not affect our choice of literary topic and the way we chose to imagine it, shape it, inhabit it?

As same-gender-interested people, what was and will be our relationship to the colonial powers that impressed their languages upon us and convinced us that their tongue was not only the "correct" one, but the word of the Almighty (Christian) God? Such questions arose for me and for many other writers featured here as the collection developed.

It was not my intention to focus on any one piece of writing in this gathering, but partly in response to some of the questions above and others to come, and also for additional amplification, I wish to draw attention to the rarely seen, little known essay "Of Generators and Survival: Hugo Letter," by the U.S. born, Caribbean descended author and activist Audre Lorde. This work, though written by someone who constantly, energetically identified herself as a lesbian — indeed, as a black, feminist lesbian — concerns itself not at all with matters explicitly lesbian or gay, but with the devastation wreaked by a Caribbean hurricane in the "developing" world and its lingering, dire effects of poverty, colonialism, racism, and imperialism: realities beneath which all Caribbean peoples, especially the poorest, suffer, and which a natural disaster, in its damage of infrastructures and vital resources, horrendously highlights. In this regard, Lorde's essay strikes me as bearing particular relevance to all Antilles-connected people, including those of us — perhaps especially those of us — erotically and romantically inclined toward those of our own gender. "Of Generators and Survival," as all of Lorde's lifelong writing and activism, reveals to us that even in the most integrated, humane world possible, none of us can afford to indulge in single-focus politics, irrespective of how we name ourselves or are named by those who have the power to do so. For the majority of us, the practice of single-focus politics is essentially always impossible, given that virtually none of us on this planet occupies a single-focus existence. Lorde's blackness, womanness, and lesbianness, though barely discussed in political terms in "Of Generators and Survival," nonetheless occupy center stage in the black, female, lesbian body she physically moved to help her fellow citizens in St. Croix after Hurricane Hugo. Like Lorde's essay, the works in this book demonstrate their authors' concern with the varying issues that impact on the lives of Antilles-connected people. These issues, which originated in our labyrinthine history, still have neither been completely confronted nor fully understood by many Caribbean peoples; by the empires that conquered, enslaved, and transformed us; or by the tourists and wider public who think of us (when they think of us at all) as people of "the islands."

With this book's emergence, I anticipate that the voices collected herein will provoke radically different interpretations of all of these considerations and of innumerable others. Above all, I hope that each reader will journey through this gathering and garner much pleasure along the way from the questions and possibilities that not only will loom but also will deepen, widen.

GATHERING / LANGUAGE

Language itself posed one of the most vexing questions at the center of this project's development, principally in the consideration of a title. What title might appeal to and invite into the collection as many as possible, especially those most in need of it, while representing as generously as possible all our vastly different ways of being Caribbean, as well as our reflections on our experiences as same-gender-interested people? What words could evoke and, if possible, encapsulate the nuances, complexities, and powers of these gathered works?

At first, quite ethnocentrically and with the blithe naïveté that some ethnocentrism brings, I considered a title that would have used Jamaican Creole words. If any tongue were to represent the collection, I reasoned, surely a Creole or "patois" language would be the most appropriate offering, given the often rancorous debates among Caribbean people about Creole languages and the outright contempt frequently expressed for those tongues as dialects and "broken" or "bastardized" versions of a more "proper" language. I thought that I would choose a Creole language that, like many of the people who routinely used it, was regularly overlooked, disdained, trivialized, and regarded with irritated amusement and condescension, if not outright disgust: a tongue developed out of the mouths and memories of slaves and others whose presence had made possible the Caribbean of our lives today. Fortunately, I quickly realized that given this gathering's pan-Caribbeanness, my working as a Jamaican "supremacist" in this regard would be an inexcusable act of nationalism thickened by naive nostalgia.

That said, not long afterward, I threw up my hands in resignation at the realization that, for a variety of reasons, I could see no way around the decision — an editorial decision, entirely my own — to make English the book's representational language, with all of the texts originally written in other languages produced in these pages in translation. In respect to my Caribbean sistren and brethren whose first tongue is not English, including those in English-speaking Antillean nations, I remain uncomfortably aware of the difficult and problematic realities surrounding my decision, especially given the English language's controlling force in the world at large and its potential to erase, here and elsewhere, the tongues of those who do not (and do not necessarily have any wish to) write, speak, think, dream, or imagine in English. For many reasons, this particular language dilemma was one that I could finally bring to no truly satisfactory conclusion. Yet with the supreme importance of our diverse tongues acknowledged and grasped, I am glad — at least in this incipient moment, though some of us speak here through the scrim of translation — that we are in this gathering truly present: speaking and listening to each other as the neighbors we are and have always been. It is this speaking and listening that I am certain will lead us closer to what one poet long ago imagined out loud as the dream of a common language; as we acknowledge the fierce reality that (to paraphrase the title of another poem, one featured in this gathering) no language — not any language — can ever be neutral.[2]

For me, this collection's title remains partly vexing for its use of the words *lesbian* and *gay* — for what exactly, I wondered along the way and wonder ever more today, is — can be — "lesbian and gay writing"? Is it writing with "lesbian" or "gay" (or "queer"?) content? Writing by those who consider themselves to be lesbian or gay? By those who consider themselves to be simply not heterosexual? But there are several individuals whose work is featured here who would most definitely not identify themselves as lesbian, gay, bisexual, *zami,* "that way," *así,* "so," or — as presently heard among some in the English-speaking areas of North America and Europe — queer. What of those who write about erotic and romantic same-gender interests, but who would refuse to consider naming in any "lesbo" or "homo" way their erotic inclinations and ideals—those who might say about themselves, if they said anything at all, that they were women interested in other women, men focused on other men, and leave it at that? How, if only for the purposes of a project like this one, to define or place their work? I use the words "a project like this one" not at all lightly. For if anything, the works in this book are deeply concerned with, rooted in, the efficacies and intricacies of a variety of different languages and words that have historically been forbidden, taboo. If some of us choose to name ourselves with the more defining (or at least, in many quarters, familiar) words *lesbian* and *gay*, and speak of our writing in such terms, we face the challenge put forth by those whose self-naming desires differ from ours of bumping straight up against a language that, like most if not all languages, simply will not, cannot, serve nor satisfy everyone. Yet this frustrating fact has a potentially productive conflict at its center and can make possible for all of us new, greatly unsettling journeys. At the very least, it illustrates our enormous diversity. Contrary to the opinion of some, we are not—cannot possibly be—all the same.

And so, to complicate matters further, what exactly is—can be—"Caribbean lesbian and gay writing"?

The words *lesbian* and *gay* in the title lost this gathering at least two writers: one a woman of Caribbean background who, while erotically interested in other women, has long refused to call herself a lesbian and, as she told me, wished not to have her work involved with any text that would categorize her writing as either lesbian in content or as authored by a lesbian. In the other instance, the word *gay* in the title gave pause to the executors of the estate of Severo Sarduy, the marvelous Cuban writer whose work I have long admired for, among other things, its formidable experimentation with form and content. I wished very much to include his work here, and would have done so but for objections raised by those who, now overseeing his work, did not wish any of it to be associated with a gay volume. Such objections—by the woman writer mentioned, and others—are real, enduring, and, for an editor working on a project like this one, both painful and frustrating, even enraging; yet the very powerful unwillingness of some people to be associated with anything lesbian, gay, or "queer" illustrates dramatically and often sadly the very great need for this book. If it is impossible to know how many people might steer clear of this collection because of its subject matter, we know that it is simultaneously possible to dream, in the most lustrous colors imaginable, of all those who will be drawn to these pages precisely *because of* their contents.[3] Such dreams bring great pleasure. All pitfalls and initial concerns considered, I am finally very pleased with the title, and especially with its claiming of the Caribbean as "our" place — for in whichever Caribbean we originate (including those we ourselves invent, re-invent, and re-imagine), it all remains ours, irrespective of what those who would rather pretend that we do not exist or who actually would wish us harm have to say.

GATHERING, BEGINNING: OUR CARIBBEAN

It is a great pleasure to present this book to readers — readers everywhere and, I hope, as many in the Caribbean and of Caribbean background as possible. For all of us, wherever we may be and however we may ultimately decide to identify ourselves and pursue our lives, an ending of silences and invisibilities begins here. In the pages that follow, the conversations that began long ago in imagining and desire continue. For as you surely know, and as I have learned and am still learning, the coming together that is this one, and others like it, widens, deepens, and — as far as I can see — has no end.

No end, like the sea: that sea not far from which this all began. Its water still stretches a broad, restless belly out to the sky; just now, the sun meets it, gently wetting first its chin in those waves, then its wide brow; palms flanking the shore murmur as seabirds dip, scolding but more weary at the day's end; cane stalks rustle in the breeze, insects wither, and the evening's peepers commence their choral chants. The water continues to gaze calmly, as it has always enjoyed doing, at the light-speckled shorelines suddenly retreating beneath dusk's quiet step. Quite soon the moon, lumbering up over those hills in the east, will have something to say about all this. But for now, over all that glistening water and beneath it, gathered voices are rising. Rising as they call *Now*, as they call *Here*. As they utter, so softly, *Listen*.

THOMAS GLAVE
Kingston, Jamaica
June, 2006

NOTES

1 By "extreme violence" I refer to the violence and rage enacted against same-gender-interested people in a place which I know well, vividly remember, and to which I continue to return: Jamaica. As an additional note against the cruelty and indifference of forgetting, coupled with the desire to avoid demonizing any locale, I also wish to make clear that extreme violence continues to be visited upon same-gender-interested people throughout the entire world, including nations whose populations consider themselves "first world" and "developed."

2 "The dream of a common language" comes from Adrienne Rich's poetry collection of the same title; "no language . . . can ever be neutral" borrows, in paraphrase, from Dionne Brand's poetry collection *No Language is Neutral*.

3 As I acknowledge the joy that this anthology's publication brings me and the pleasure I know it will bring others, I also wish to state here my deep regret in not being able, for a variety of reasons, to include so many other writers' work that really should have appeared here, and which will perhaps loom in future anthologies that will continue the critical work this collection has begun. Foremost among those authors is the magnificent Cuban novelist José Lezama Lima, without question one of the Caribbean's and Latin America's — and the world's — greatest literary artists. His novel *Paradiso* remains a supreme masterpiece, appropriately revered by those fortunate enough to have encountered it. In spite of his absence here, I would like to think that Lezama Lima's towering presence — the fierce intelligence, style, and precision manifest in all his work — moves through this book, even if his actual prose does not.

JOSÉ ALCÁNTARA ALMÁNZAR

Lulú or the Metamorphosis (1995)

When night falls everything grows confusing, there are no precise contours or defined faces, nothing but blurry edges, formless masses, shadows gliding from place to place. Lulú is aware of this as she prepares for this big carnival night, on this impatiently-awaited February, long anticipated in minute rites, minuscule savings, restrained impulses, the zealous selling of sweets, and the singsong with which she hawks her merchandise. There's the basket, on the table covered by a flowered tablecloth, still bearing traces of pine nut candy, guava crystals in cellophane half melted from the sun, and other leftovers from her daily work trekking from office building to office building, starting early in the morning, delivering her candied oranges in syrup to the chubby secretary at the Municipal Hall, the ever-yearned-for bread pudding to the Corporation archivist, the plum mini-tarts to the peroxide blonde at Internal Revenue, the nuts-and-honey nougat to the cutie-pie of a chauffeur at Bagrícola, the one who always croons at her with a voice ripe with inspiration: "Lulú, honey, no one makes these sweets better than you." And she glances at him, melting, incredulous, an impish hand on her smiling lips, and sighs, warbles, flutters her curly eyelashes. She leaves swinging a tiny ass imprisoned in tight blue jeans, and saying, no longer looking at him: "Oh, what a lying rascal this Guelo is!," heedless of the bursts of laughter behind her.

As she went out she felt the hot breeze laden with humidity, dragging along heavy clouds, hoisting dust and papers off the street, tickling her legs, and making her wonder once again if it was worth going to the park and risk ruining under a rain shower what she had put such an effort into creating. She locked her door and started walking with awkward steps. As she walked she displayed the fruits of her labors for all to see, making herself deaf to stupid comments, smiling at those who appreciated the rosiness of her cheeks, the exuberance of her dress, the sparkle of her glittery tinsel jewelry. The streets, swarming

with carousers, had become an extension of a grand fiesta, a frolicking revelry
spilling drunk and dusky men and women, with their flamboyant masks and
costumes and their contagious shrills of happiness, onto the sidewalk. She went
on, falsely majestic, betrayed by trips and burps, by the convulsive swishing of her
hips, the agitated flailing of her excessively bejeweled arms, the nervous contor-
tions of her head, the troubled and searching eyes.

Now the ceremony must begin. It doesn't matter how long this transformation into the carnival's most fabulous rumba dancer takes. Her ironed
dress, ready, pleased as punch in its court of festoons and ruffles, hangs on
the clothes rack, almost dancing with the sling-back high-heeled shoes, the
scintillating bracelets, the necklaces of iridescent bijouterie, the long earrings
of deceptive sparkle, and everything that adorned the famous dancers that
Lulú never grows tired of going to see at the Julia Cinema, the very same
ones that she used as models in making her dress, the flame-colored turban
that will cover her head, the plastic roses she has sewn to her shoes, the tones
of that exuberant makeup she has reserved for today.

The park was packed with people, with hawkers of every sort of tidbit to satisfy
the carnival revelers' every possible whim as they swaggered in the park's inner
paths, watching the performance of the municipal band. From the gazebo
wafted the strains of a danzón *that invaded the reveries of the old, making them*
yearn for an era decidedly dead. She made her entrance with an undisguisable
awkwardness which seemed to increase as the effects of the three beers she had
drunk intensified. She walked down the center of the main path, shaking the
festoons of her slithering multicolor train. From the benches flanking the path,
now occupied by strange characters, she began to hear insidious taunts and
catcalls that prompted her to raise her head too high, exposing her to tripping on
the mosaics dislodged by the tree roots.

Lulú is lying on the bed like a wet and porous leaf. She is soothing herself
before initiating the beautification ritual. Although seemingly at peace, her
body quivers on the bed, her skin vibrates as it makes contact with the clean
white cotton of the bedclothes. She picks up the hand-held mirror and looks
at herself. Her face betrays the apprehension that perturbs her. She drops the
mirror, turns on the radio, and instantly the honey-and-molasses voice of an
announcer explodes into the room, counseling brief rests between household chores, touting the importance of relaxation for remaining young and
beautiful, my dear homemaker, the benefits of that cleansing cream you
bought to keep your face smooth like that of a porcelain doll, even though it
may not lighten your dark skin. That's why she won't be dressing up as a
sassy Spaniard or a little Dutch girl. Who has ever heard—Lulú says it

herself — of black Europeans, thick-lipped, with straightened hair and meat-ball noses? What Dutch and Spanish women lack is her slender wasp waist, the long strong legs she exercises every day, walking from office to office, up and down stairs and hallways, asking leave to drop off orders, bending to put her basket down somewhere to sell a macaroon to a busy passerby, placing it again on the *babonuco* of rolled-up rags crowning her head before going on her way with an old Lola Flores song on her lips.

Despite the laughter from the crowd, she advanced to the gazebo, trying with discombobulated steps to climb up to the platform for a chat with the band leader. The catcalls increased with each stride on the worn-out steps. The initial uproar gave way to cruel and provoking taunts. A young boy almost made her fall down by stepping on her train. She turned around and, goaded by anger, spat a phrase at him that was drowned out by the cymbals and drumbeats of the song's final crescendo. She raised a menacing fist against the mob, grabbed her train, wrapped it around her arm and continued her climb to the gazebo.

She picks up the razor, lathers up her arms and legs and starts to shave off the growth of the last few days. There can't be a trace of hair left on the skin. The razor glides down the arm to the beat of a piercing salsa coming from the radio. The hairs slide down the drain and the arm glistens, silky, still streaked with mentholated foam. The legs are a more difficult terrain. They resist the blade's depilatory action, proffering obstacles that bog the razor down, causing tiny sharp cuts that sting like scratches from a cat's claws. She replaces the blade on the razor and the new edge removes the stubborn hairs, vanquishing their stiff resistance. Now they are two sleek and pliant legs, speckled with white foam, legs that can slide easily into the net of a pair of nylon stockings.

The band leader glanced at her from head to toe and couldn't repress a smile in which mingled derision and compassion. He nodded his agreement, promising her that after the pasodoble his boys would play the rumba she was request-ing. She thanked him by extending a limp hand and making a long and ceremonious bow. Then the band leader turned to his musicians, raised his hands, and launched into the next selection of the concert program. She climbed down the steps to the martial strains of an operatic march.

She goes to the refrigerator, takes out a beer, opens it, introduces the opening of the bottle into her mouth, sips the golden liquid, drinks it in until the cold stuns her and makes it impossible for her to continue swallowing. The melody of a romantic bolero pierces through her body, making her forget momentarily the razor and what remained of the procedure. Lulú closes her eyes and thinks of Ciro. He will be at the park selling peanuts when she appears in her rumba dancer costume, joining the phony ladies and the gentlemen decked out in suits rented for the occasion. She will provide the sorely needed spice. She will go to the gazebo and ask the director of the band to play something hot and then she will dance — and she will steal the show. If Ciro approaches her she will offer to buy him a drink, and she knows he will accept, as she knows he will go home with her because he needs both the money and the affection, and who but she could give them to him, as she always has.

During the pasodoble *she saw her man in the throng. He was carrying on his daily work, oblivious to the bustle of the crowd and the roar of the cars climbing the hill on the broad avenue, stopping at the park entrance or blowing their horns at the distracted pedestrians. The alcohol rushed to her head, she felt her legs giving way and shuddered at the thought of an encounter with him. She hesitated for an instant. It would be better if he tried to make his way towards her first. She took a powder case from between her breasts and looked in the tiny mirror at her own face covered with wee beads of sweat that were beginning to make her makeup run. She dusted fresh powder on her face with the small puff.*

The indecisive razor moves down her underarm, detaching a clump of hard bristles. More lather, more water, another blade, the third. The hairs give way, the body is becoming as hairless as that of a fifteen-year-old girl, only the belly remains before everything looks like the surface of polished mahogany, without scratchy or rough patches that could lead to rejection, that could discourage caresses from robust hands or betray the scandalous contradictions of her body.

The rumba burst as she was putting the powder case away. She immediately ran to the gazebo and started to dance, surrounded by the crowd that had gathered to watch the spectacle. Her body was moving without restraint; the feet drew sparks from the mosaics; the legs, lengthened by the high heels, dashed to and fro furiously, as if deranged; the hips contorted; the bracelet-laden arms whirled, tracing circles in the air; the head gaily followed the rhythm of the music. In the midst of the frenzied uproar, she danced with eyes closed, seemingly enthralled in a brutal trance. She advanced and retreated, shook the bare shoulders, got down on her knees and up again, now completely barefoot. Her two massive feet, finally liberated from the high heels, took hold of the pavement, zigzagging, filling her with pleasure.

The eyebrows are more used to the punishment of the tweezers. The coarse hairs wrench themselves from their root systems following the jittery progress of the small metallic jaws. Each plucked hair wrings a tear out of Lulú. Her watery eyes watch how the recently bared flesh swells, and the line of black dots that used to be her eyebrows disappears, leaving a clear smooth surface for a perfect stroke of an eyebrow pencil.

She continued to move, totally possessed by the madness of the dance. Then the pirates burst in, vociferating, pushing their way through the crowd. The group was captained by a Francis Drake too dwarfish and pot-bellied to be convincing. They hurled fierce curses at the crowd, threatening it with wooden swords, tin knives, cudgels, and toothless mouths with sewer breath. The dancer, furious at their stealing her audience's attention, pounced on the intruders with a savage cry. The rumba was coming to an end, precipitated by the band leader, who sensed the chaos of the approaching brawl.

Lulú spreads the lotion over her body, and the dusky, chocolate-colored skin glistens, thirstily absorbing the oil from the cleansing substance. Her flexible body quivers under the warmth of the massage, the epidermis throbs as it is stroked by the caresses from her own hand, now descending to her groin and stopping, hesitatingly, anxiously, at the edge of an immense appendage which the hand squeezes and abandons in sudden bursts, intermittently, going as if from fury to repentance. Lulú lies on the bed, gulps down the rest of the beer, closes her eyes, and buries her head in the pillow. Her temples pulsate, she gropes for air, the rebellious hand continues its task, Ciro's face emerges from the bottom of a river, his body covered with drops of water, but he's not dead, just playing with the liquid, and he waves goodbye with a victorious hand. He dives in again for an instant, the hand goes up and down, slides on the slippery phallus. Ciro returns to the surface and this time signals to Lulú to dive in after him, he wants her to accompany him. Lulú dips her foot in the warm water, then drops her body in, and the river swallows her. It seems to her as if she were going to die, but Ciro rescues her, he lifts her up in the air as if he could not hold her for long or find a foothold under water. Then he takes her to a safe place. Up and down, charging forcefully, the member bulges to its utmost, nearing the climax. Lulú feels Ciro's warm body next to her, looks at his face in the sunlight, their breaths mingle, she holds on to the man's equine neck and then she feels his hand on the penis which her hand now grabs convulsively, and Lulú explodes in obscene cries which the pillow silences so that only she can witness the volcano's eruption.

From every corner of the park emerged frenzied characters joining the fray. In jumped little devils with rubber pitchforks, followed by Death chasing an almost naked Lothario, a carioca band which materialized from another corner, several gladiators carrying shields and spears, Don Quixote mounted on a donkey, and a multitude of magicians, soldiers, and peasants. The witches appeared at the most unexpected moment, brandishing brooms that they wielded as clubs. The dancer clung to Drake's tangled locks, digging her teeth into the corsair's flabby neck. They had fallen to the ground, circled by a crowd egging them on. From time to time others also fell, spurred by the example of the dancer and the corsair. Not very far from them, a goblin strangled two ape-men, and a harlequin, decked in jingling bells, ribbons, and bit and pieces of mirror, attempted to finish off a manly nun growling in a thicket.

She is immediately overtaken by an inescapable slackness, her tendons go limp, the muscles yield to a compulsory lethargy which yearns to be infinite. Suddenly the flesh slackens, the extremities slump, the skin oozes the effluvium of fulfilled desire, the fires that fed her fantasy die out. The image of Ciro in the river also fades, replaced by an immediate and more humdrum reality. Lulú's head emerges from the depths of the pillow: there's the table with its flowered tablecloth, the basket encircled by a line of gluttonous ants, the refrigerator with its voiceless hum, the alarm clock, the sink still leaking, the battery-operated radio still turned on, the landscapes cut out of old calendars, and an armoire with its doors open where the regal carnival dress still hangs, imperturbable. Lulú drops her head back on the pillow while she wipes away the jelly-like remains of the eruption and bit by bit reinitiates the inventory of what has already been done and calculates what's still left to do. She jumps to her feet and opens a drawer in the lower half of the armoire. She rummages through the contents and takes out a pair of panties into which she introduces her long legs. The sex is reduced to a mound that she compresses further with a pair of pantyhose. Her vital problem resolved, her androgynous figure moves from one end of the room to another. She takes out her makeup implements and finally settles down on a stool before the armoire's mirror.

Her dress torn, her turban gone, her eyelashes unglued, the dancer still hangs onto the corsair. The band has dispersed. The musicians fled the gazebo, their instruments above their heads, protecting them from irreparable harm. The band leader had tried to calm tempers down and break up the fight, but two mischievous harlequins prevented him, holding him by the arms and leading him on a dance through the park.

She's dazzled by the resplendent layer of cream that her fingers spread on her cheeks, jaws, and forehead. The mutations of her face bring forth memories that are like electrical charges, remote and undesirable. As in a dream, Lulú recalls the sweet singsong of Guelo's voice when he says to her, "Honey, nobody makes these sweets better than you," before he takes the nuts-and-honey nougat and smiles at her with his gold-capped teeth. A few brushstrokes of rouge on her cheekbones. Or the day she tripped and the basket rolled down the staircase to the landing, and the sweets spilled all over the steps. Two fine lines on the tired eyelids, a trace of blue shadow right along the lash line, higher up a broad though brief silvery stroke arching up to the brows. Or that afternoon when she was on her way home, dead tired, and ran into Ciro, and, although he saw her, he wouldn't return her greeting, wouldn't or was ashamed to, since he looked the other way and went on selling his peanuts, ignoring the cashew nut paste she had made just for him. The firm movements of the lipstick over the thick lips, furious movements like the ones she used when she threw the cashew paste in the garbage for the flies and the rats to eat, movements that leave her lips red and creamy. Or the day she was chased by some thugs yelling "faggot," "queer freak," throwing orange rinds and food scraps at her and all because she had not agreed to let them have some sweets on credit, yelling at them that "no son of a bitch is going to live at my expense." A thick layer of mascara coats her lashes, turning them into two long, dark brushes. And she locked herself in her room, a knife at hand in case one of them dared force the door. The mirror reflects the gaily colored face the occasion requires. "I'll gut the son of a bitch who dares come in here." The face of a tropical rumba dancer. "I swear by my blessed mother." A very coquettish face. And then the crowd dispersed amidst guffaws and threats. The face of an ecstatic Latin dancer. Now she gets up, opens another beer, gulps down the bubbling foam that makes her forget the bad times.

The folding chairs flew from the gazebo to the crowd, catapulted by some buccaneers and several men wearing goat masks. The confusion grew when the patrons of the Atenas Cinema started coming out of the movie house. The blows and the punches turned into a rocks-and-bottles battle waged by three or four ferocious gangs. The dancer tried to disentangle herself from Drake's hands, which were closed tightly around her slender seagull neck. She dug her fingernails into the diminutive corsair's eyes and was finally able to extricate herself from the large hands trying to choke her.

She adjusts the false breasts on the thoracic expanse, trying to place them right where they belong. She shifts the mounds of foam from left to right, fixing them at the precise point that she judges equidistant from the center of the chest. The third beer leaves her shuddering, tottering awkwardly up and down the room, searching for shoes and bracelets for the culmination of the ritual. She unhangs the dress, coils it up her body like a boa, from her feet to her waist and from there to her shoulders. She is enraptured by the corolla of flounces that engirdles her body as the teeth of the zipper are welded together in a seemingly eternal embrace.

The crowd roared. The gangs carried on their volleys of rocks and bottles. The black helmets emerged from the police station and, in a matter of seconds, crossed José Martí Avenue and entered the park. She tried to find her man in the midst of the melee, but the commotion was such that she saw only the hysterical masked fugitives fleeing from the pacifying billyclubs. A few thick drops of rain began falling, turning quickly into a downpour. She felt a blow on her back and tried to escape, but the policeman grabbed her by the arm as he continued hurling blows at the dancer's soaked body, thrusting her into the line of prisoners heading for the station in a forced march.

"That's it," Lulú says in front of the mirror, raising her voice so she could be heard, "there's no resisting this flair and this style. I'd just like them to show me a queen that could be compared to me, let them bring her to me." And she hides a powder case between her falsies, perfumes herself, and exits the room with a joyous expression on her face that makes her look radiant, as if she were floating in space.

Translated by Lizabeth Paravisini-Gebert

ALDO ALVAREZ

Property Values (2001)

1

There wasn't anything short of a shantytown shack that Claudia Ferrier had not scouted as a property that could benefit from her skills as a realtor. That some of these dwellings had people still living in them who had no intention of relocating was another matter altogether. Such were her ambitions that, at a wake for an acquaintance's mother, she asked the bereaved if the departed's lovely four bedroom house was going to be up for sale.

In that booming year of 1988, Claudia operated out of Mireya, the medium-sized city that served as a hub to the west coast of Puerto Rico. Her mother rode shotgun as she drove around the nicer neighborhoods of the area, and around neighborhoods with major gentrification potential, often late into the night. They looked for For Sale and For Rent signs the way some people look for guavas in other people's backyards — with stealth and no intention to be neighborly. Of course, she was all pulpy sweetness when she called the phone numbers posted on oak or mahogany doors, or on the steel grillwork that enclosed most self-respecting, upper middle class porches. And people always took her calls. This was how she came to represent other people's properties. Sometimes buyers contacted her before she had a suitable property available. She would do her fieldwork and find them one.

Her wardrobe was never short of style or brand-name designers, for this hustling of buyer and seller, in a seller's market, made for more than a decent living. Especially since she charged a fee to both buyer and seller. Claudia Ferrier had not heard of any regulation of this practice in the Common-wealth of Puerto Rico, and nobody had openly questioned her business methods. Before she swooped onto the scene, most people had handled real estate issues without a middleman. By the time she attempted to discourage Dean Rodriguez from acquiring a home, Claudia had gained a reputation among the *cognoscenti* of Mireya as a relatively harmless nuisance whose greed and malfeasance were tolerable. Harsher opinions saw her as the ambulance chaser of real estate agents.

2

The old-landed-gentry-turned-professional-money women's auxiliary — the *cognoscenti di tutti cognoscenti*, really — met for breakfast once a week. Three times a month, lavish breakfasts were held in the privacy of one of the social club members' houses. Thick potato and onion omelettes, guava or mango jelly-filled confections dusted with the finest powdered sugar, crisp yet flaky pastry fingers filled with sweet cheese would accompany conversation whose intimacy and warmth belied the snobbery accorded to the group's members by the larger social whirl of the town. Gossip did pass between the ladies, of course, but it wasn't all frivolous. The group had a hand in all kinds of fundraising for worthy causes, got involved in library drives and literacy campaigns, and took care of the housebound elderly and infirm who had no extended family to look after them. They played canasta with Spanish playing cards; they had an unspoken, ongoing "top-this!" competition involving breakfast comestibles. They wished their children to marry into one another's families, and always planned major social events around their core group. But they were, actually, very sweet and conscientious in a cautiously progressive way. They tried to better themselves and their town, and they were sincere.

Once a month, though, the breakfast club met in a restaurant or a coffee shop. Claudia, knowing that these people were the shapers of good taste and public opinion, desperately wanted to become a member of this elite. After all, the group included the wife of the town's most prestigious architect of luxurious houses and apartment buildings, the wife of the most reliable and well-liked appraiser of land value and property, the wife of the financier who approved most of the loans that went into the large-scale building of homes, besides the wives of doctors, lawyers, and sundry professionals at the top of their fields, all of whom invested in real estate. A lot of business was done inside this group. Claudia wanted to be part of it. But she knew that a baldfaced request to be invited to the group would lack propriety. So, on Thursday mornings — their usual meeting time — she would check all the possible breakfast venues, hoping to casually pop in to say hi at the table, be invited to sit down, and stay in all morning. And then, pop in often enough to feel she had arrived and invite them to breakfast at her place the next week.

On this momentous morning, she finally found the group breakfasting at the coffee shop of the chichi department store in town, the place with the best teeny-tiny cupful of strong, bitter coffee.

"What a coincidence!" Claudia said, hovering over the table, to the few who looked up from the group to acknowledge her presence. "I was just coming over here for a quick bite to eat before showing a house to a very nice couple . . . and I find you all gathered here!"

"Well, it was just a matter of time," said Olivia, the wife of the reliable and well-liked appraiser. Claudia had had the opportunity to become acquainted with Olivia when her husband did a small appraisal job for her. "The world is a handkerchief, isn't it? How is your mother?"

"Fine, fine," Claudia said, still hovering, her hand suggestively holding onto the back of an unoccupied chair. "With her usual aches and pains. But she's such pleasant company, not a burden at all. She makes my life so much easier, truly. She really helps out with my business."

"Well, it's nice to hear your mother's doing well," Olivia said. "So nice of you to stop and say hello." Olivia smiled politely but not widely, and turned to speak to another member of the party.

Claudia hovered over the table, at last reaching the point where she could no longer bear the embarrassment of being ignored, when another voice rose up to her from the coop.

"Actually — Claudia, isn't it? — maybe you could sit down for a bit and give me a little help with something."

Luisa, the doctor's wife. . . . What an opportunity, what an opening! Claudia quickly swept to her side.

"How could I serve you?" Claudia asked.

"I've been looking for a house for my son, and I am at a loss as to how to help him."

"But you, you know so much about houses! Surely you don't need any help from an *arriviste* like myself!"

"Oh, but Dean is so fussy. He was a fussy eater as a child," Luisa said.

"Was he?" Claudia said. "Poor thing."

"You see, his tastes are . . . extravagant and specific, and I haven't been able to locate something he'd like. He's looking for a castle in the air, and I haven't been able to please him. And I'm going on a trip to Europe very shortly, and won't come back for two weeks or so, and Dean wants to move in before Christmas. . . . Could he call you for help? He doesn't like stucco. Everything I've seen has stucco."

"Something *must* be wrong," Claudia said to her mother while driving around in the middle of the night. They were driving through San Sebastián, a small town to the northeast of Mireya, on their hunt for signage. "Luisa could not possibly need any help from me. Luisa, the wife of the head surgeon of, at last count, three hospitals in the county, is a canny investor. She must make as a landlord at least as much as her husband. And she's sold locations downtown to fast-food concerns, and owns parking lots and houses on the best locations in town."

"Who gave you this information?" asked her mother.

"Town records, registered deeds and such," she said. "It's all written down in paper, if you care to find it. Anyway, I just don't get it. What would she need me for? All the signs indicate that I'm being taken advantage of."

"Maybe she's doing you a favor, out of kindness."

"Hah! I don't need her *noblesse oblige*," Claudia said. "But at least she's giving me business. . . ."

"That's all that matters, doesn't it — Stop!" her mother said. "I think I saw a sign."

They backed up.

The house had a few patches of faded paint which had once been a rather fetching kingfisher blue. A cement base held up a wooden structure, two floors high. The long, wide porch ran from the side of the house that opened to the side street and around a rounded corner to the side that faced the main thoroughfare of the town. The porch was framed by lovingly fluted columns and intricate, leaf-shaped lattice work, some of which had fallen sideways onto the floor. The front doors had wooden slats that opened and closed to let light and air in, and on the second floor the windows that faced the side street were made in a similar manner. The top story opened up to a small balcony above the porch. The roof was flat, like most roofs in the tropics, but the edges curved out slightly, embroidered with sinuous, florid arabesques, joining at the corner of the street to meet a horn of plenty that poured forbidden fruit.

There was no stucco on the house. No stucco whatsoever.

"What a trashy little house," Claudia said.

"Shall I write down the number?" her mother asked, pen and paper ready.

"No," she said. "Who'd want this? Only to tear it down. And who wants to live near the center of town anymore? To live near the transvestites who hang around the plaza at night? Forget it. This has no potential. Let's go near the mall, property values are higher there."

The next morning, she got a call from Dean, Luisa's son.

"Thank you so much for taking my call," Dean said. "I don't want to impose on you and on your friendship with my mother, but I need help finding a house for myself."

Claudia was properly flattered by the fact that he called her his mother's friend. All that worry for nothing! "I am here to serve you," she said. "Where are you calling from?"

"Upstate New York."

"Oh! Maybe you can help me improve my English. I've always wanted to be a polyglot. Shall we speak English?"

"Sure," Dean said, switching tongues.

"What an enchanting young man!"

"I'm not so young, Doña Claudia."

"Call me Claudia," she said. "Well, your mother tells me that you are looking for a home."

"Not just any home," Dean said. "I've driven Mom crazy. You see, I've made my living in antiques and collectibles, and I'm . . . retiring, so I want to keep some of the things I really like . . . and I can't just place all my things in a place that doesn't *go* with them. My mother sent me snapshots of these houses that, well . . . they're a bit *too* modern."

"Something traditional?"

"Not exactly. I'd love a townhouse with a turn-of-the-century feel. You know, classy yet exuberant. Like . . . how do I explain it to you? You know, like an Aubrey Beardsley illustration."

"I am not familiar with her."

"Him," Dean said, "I guess. Anyway . . . you know Art Nouveau? Toulouse-Lautrec?"

"Oh, yes! I can see it now. Art Nouveau. Very decorative."

"That's it. I want a house with that feel."

"That's going to be difficult."

"But oh so worth it . . . I don't know, I'm very picky with details."

"It's going to be difficult to find a propriety like that."

"It's the kind of *property* I'm looking for. Price is no object. But I am a little short of time, and I'd like to move down to the island as soon as possible."

"A townhouse, though? Maybe it is too large a place for one person."

"Don't worry, I'm going to share it with someone. We both need lots of space. And I expect to have lots of houseguests over from the States, and have my family stay over for weekends. . . ."

"Ooh, a friend? You have someone living with you?" What a piece of gossip! She hadn't heard that Luisa's son was living with someone. Maybe a wedding was in the offing? Surely she would be invited now.

"Well . . . yeah. My partner. . . . He used to restore houses on the side, so if the house needs a lot of work, not to worry. Mark likes a challenge."

"Partner?" That killed the wedding idea.

"Yeah. We met when I was buying pieces for a house, and he was restoring it. We've been . . . business partners and friends since. He's gone back to the music business — he's a record producer — but he still does a little rebuilding work here and there. Me, I just buy things, but he makes them."

"Maybe your friend can do some work for me . . . for some of my clients. You maybe have not heard, but the Luna section of Mireya is being redeveloped. You know, it was once a nice neighborhood . . . well, the latest is, the wealthy young, they take these old houses and remake them to their taste. So now it's becoming a nice neighborhood again, though, for *my* taste, it is too close to the university. . . ."

"Maybe you can find me something of that sort?" Dean asked.

"Let's see what I can do," she said. "Anything else you have in mind?"

"I want a nice big porch, and please, no stucco!"

5

The first thing that Claudia noticed when she saw Dean was how thin and sickly he looked. Then she saw how tenderly Dean and Mark argued about who would carry a small piece of luggage out of the baggage claim area. And she noticed how they touched, casually flaunting their desire for each other.

As she stood by the Plexiglas divider which separated the arriving from the receiving, she decided to pretend she was waiting for someone else. Dean had homosexual AIDS! And he brought his fornicator with him! She didn't know how to hide herself and wished she could make herself invisible. However, she forced herself to continue smiling and looked at a young couple who had arrived on the same flight as if they were the ones she was waiting for. She kept looking at them while the plot came to her in a flash: Luisa was giving her what she herself did not want to deal with. A homosexual son! Of course, no one would like to sell or buy from degenerates. That's why Luisa dropped him on her. *She* wouldn't look like she approved or abetted him; her reputation would be clean. But Claudia wasn't about to do Luisa a favor that would dirty her reputation. Look: Claudia sells houses to degenerates. Look: Claudia brings down property values. Look: Claudia brings the horses of the apocalypse to your neighborhood—

"Doña Claudia?"

Claudia pretended not to hear.

"Excuse me, Doña Claudia?"

Claudia had never been put in such a situation. Yes, life had ugly things, but she thought she left them behind when she left South America.

"Doña Claudia, it's me, Dean."

"Call me Claudia," she said turning around, a wide toothy smile on her face.

Before her stood Dean, in a white long sleeved shirt, gray slacks, and wing-tips. He held in the crook of his arm a winter jacket lined with the most amazing and unidentifiable fur. He looked as if a wind could lift him away. His friend Mark had the mien of yet another unremarkably cornstalk-tall American man: jeans, blue jersey shirt, Converse canvas shoes. And a ski jacket.

"It's me, Dean Rodriguez," he said, and he held a hand out in peace.

She shook it, practically trembling. She resisted the urge to wipe her hand in horror.

"This is Mark Piper," Dean said. Mark mumbled a hello and shook her hand coldly, keeping his scary grimace. "He's kinda shy," Dean whispered.

As if that mattered to her.

Now she faced the indignity of having to force herself to speak to the homosexuals while looking at them in the eye.

"Where did you get those shoes?" Claudia said.

"Schenectady," Mark said.

6

Claudia had had a few properties in mind before their arrival. She did not show them to the couple. While she shifted her comfy seat cover to the shotgun seat, with the pretense of making Dean comfortable—she could burn the seat cover later and avoid contamination—she wondered what to do. She would subtly discourage the dregs from buying anything by showing them dregs. But where would she take them? This question did not remain unanswered for long, for Claudia had a prodigious memory for properties. She recalled the house in San Sebastián. Genius! she thought. Who'd buy that filthy thing? Meanwhile, there was the matter of preparing them for a disappointment.

"Oh, it was so hard to find something to suit you!" Claudia said, practicing her English. "I am afraid that houses like the ones you like have been torn down."

"What a pity," Dean said. "I've always wanted to live in one. My grand-mother had one. When I was five years old, she hired someone to wreck it and build a cement thing in its place."

"Funny how your mother couldn't find you one," she said. "She buys so many houses. . . ."

"Yeah," Dean said. "My mother collects houses like I collect cookie jars. But well, my mother's tastes run to the conventional, and I just couldn't live in something like that."

"If you pardon me asking," she said, "why do you wish to move to the island?"

"Can I speak with you in the strictest confidence?"

"Not a problem," she said. Her curiosity was stronger than her distaste. Besides, this would be great currency in the gossip exchange.

"Well, I'm going to pass away, so I hope to spend my last few years in my native land. Mark here agreed to take a year or two off and move here with me. . . . So it's a matter of finding the perfect place for me and all of my things."

"Oh, you are deadly sick?"

"Don't I look it?"

"Not at all! I just thought you were a vegetarian or something."

Mark, in the backseat, somehow found this awfully funny. Why, she was just being nice.

They drove by the main plaza of San Sebastián. It was a late Tuesday afternoon. Sadly, Claudia noted, there was no suggestion of the town loon-ies, drug addicts, drag queens, and indigents that would congregate there at nightfall.

"Here we are," she said, with a slight sigh, as if this house was the best she could find. She stepped out of the car. Mark stepped out and opened the door for Dean. Now those two, Claudia thought with piercing irony, are perfect little gentlemen. . . .

She stood in front of the house with absolute stillness and gravity, as if she were pondering a great injustice, noticing that the For Sale sign had fallen onto the floor of the porch. Mark and Dean soon joined her, looking at the house in silence.

A queer breeze flew through the shutters of the front door.

"It's perfect," Mark said.

What? She turned in shock to look at Mark smiling shyly, putting his arm around Dean.

"But . . . but . . . it is badly in need of disrepair!" she said.

"Mark likes a challenge," Dean said. "You should see what he did to our house in Ithaca. Shall we go in?"

Oh Sainted Mother, she did not have the keys. It wasn't even her house to represent. She did not know to whom the house belonged. Now her charade fell apart.

She made a show of looking through her purse. "My Lord, I forgot to bring the keys with me—"

"The door's open, I think," Mark said. "May we go in?"

"Ah, well, ah . . . why not?" Claudia smiled, rictus-like.

Mark and Dean climbed up the steps to the porch. With a slight push, Mark jostled the thin doors open. Inside, ceilings rose to great heights, wallpaper fell and folded over the floor, dust accumulated. Mark felt the walls and the beams of the house like a doctor palpating for unseemly bumps in glandular regions. Dean followed his own path into the house, going straight to the kitchen in the back. Claudia followed Dean, hoping to help him find something he didn't like. From the backyard there emanated the smell of guavas rotting on moist ground. In the bare and dirty cupboard, Dean found a ceramic cookie jar in the shape of a log cabin.

"An omen . . ." Dean said, inspecting the jar with an expert's eye. "You know they haven't made these in God knows how long. And this is in perfect shape. People just don't know what they're throwing away." He put the jar down, leaned on the countertop, and swept his eyes over the expanse of the kitchen.

"We'll take it," Dean said.

"I'll . . . I'll call you tomorrow to sign on the propriety," she said.

"Fabulous," Dean said. "Fabulous property."

"Property," she repeated. Fabulous, my foot.

Mark walked into the kitchen, an aw-gosh smile on his face, holding a player-piano roll in hand as if it were a treasure.

"Found this upstairs," Mark said, and showed it to Dean. "Does this mean something, or what?"

7

Claudia started a bonfire in her backyard with her mother's help, and threw the car-seat comforter, and the coffee cup she offered to Dean out of social obligation, into the flames. How could have she missed those signs? "Partner"? "Antiques"? "Upstate New York"? Dead giveaways. It could have not been clearer. And she was so desperate for a sale that she did not listen to her reason and patch those pieces of information together to figure out that he was a pervert. She couldn't shake off the feeling of being violated somehow, even after scrubbing herself raw with a brush, á la Karen Silkwood, to make sure there was no risk of contamination. Maybe all he wanted was to move back home to torture his family with shame. Yes, revenge, the revenge of the perverse; now that he was sick with the filth of his desires, he was rubbing it in the face of his family and making them watch him die slowly. No wonder his mother couldn't find him a home! And Claudia was caught in the web of that family's intrigue.

But no, she would not embroil herself in this. She would not lower herself to help those two find a home in her adopted country. Or would she? Could she could find a way of selling them the house, and let Luisa and her clan suffer the indignity? What would other people say! Look: what a bad mother, she had a homosexual child. Look: how her child pays her for not raising him well. Look: now she brings death and decay to our tropical paradise —

But at what cost! Claudia's reputation would look even worse. No, she would not bother to call the owners of that ugly house. She would call the couple the next morning and say the deal could not go through. Better yet, that the owners had already accepted another offer. She would call Mark and Dean at the hotel where she'd dropped them off. The whole thing had so perturbed her that she had driven home with the fur-lined jacket on the backseat. She almost threw it in the fire with her things. But the fur, whose origin she couldn't place — was it fox? sable? degenerate, for sure — was too beautiful to throw into the purifying flames. She put on dishwashing gloves and stuffed it into the thickest plastic bag she could find. Maybe she would return it to Luisa as a sign that she washed — scrubbed, really — the whole dirty affair off her hands.

The next morning, Claudia called Dean with the terrible news.

"What a sad day!" she exhaled.

"So, are we closing the deal?" Dean asked.

"Ah, I am afraid that the people who own the house, well, they are already in negotiations to sell the house."

An odd silence occurred.

"Really." Dean sounded completely unconvinced.

"Yes," she said. "A fast-food thing, you know, has been getting clearance to build there. And just yesterday they got a permit from town government."

Another, odder silence occurred.

"And there is nothing else available that I know of — to your taste, of course . . ." she added. "Maybe you could return home, and I could call you when I find something. . . ."

Last night's bonfire still smoldered in the backyard. The bag stuffed with the jacket lay in a cupboard in her laundry room, near and dear to bottles of bleach.

Dean took a deep breath on the other side of the phone. "Can I tell you a quick story, Miss Claudia? It just so happens that I called my mother as soon as I got to the hotel. I told her I was delighted with the house. She told me she knew the house, that a family her family was friends with not long ago owned the house, and that a bachelor uncle of theirs lived there until he died forty years ago. And that nobody had been able to sell the house since then, that someone had said the house was jinxed, or that it had a ghost or something. Now, Mom keeps contact with everyone she's ever met, and she told me to call her friends and say hi for her."

"Heh, the world is a handkerchief," Claudia mumbled.

"I phoned them up. They were delighted that someone wanted the house, and that it was someone that they knew personally. You see, I had dinner at their table and played with their kids when we were very young. They said they had fond memories of me. They said they would be, to use the Spanish term, *encantados* to have me over for dinner tonight and sign the papers."

"How . . . ?"

"The thing is—did I hallucinate this? Or are you lying? And if you are lying, let me tell you, I'm going to get the house no matter what."

Claudia was *incensed* that he should dare question her integrity. "The house is mine to sell, not for you to take from me!"

"By the way, I mentioned that you showed us the house, and they had absolutely no knowledge of your existence."

"It is not proper for you to go behind my back like this! The propriety is mine to sell!"

"Propriety is theft," Dean said.

Claudia heard the line go dead, and she was *furious*.

8

Claudia immediately called Olivia, the appraiser's wife, hoping to smear things up as much as she could with the high-grade dirt she had on Luisa's son. If she put Luisa in enough trouble, maybe she would be shamed into seclusion . . . and perhaps her place in the social order might need to be filled. . . .

"Ay, Olivia," Claudia said. "I know something so terrible . . . so terrible . . . I cannot possibly keep it secret any longer. Oh, the shame. . . ."

"What is it?"

"You know, the Rodriguezes' youngest son . . ."

"Dino?"

"He calls himself Dean now."

"I know."

"Well. . . . He came over to do some business with me . . . and, well. . . ."

"Yes?"

"Dean is homosexual. And he is sick with AIDS! Can you imagine, Luisa letting her son have a lifestyle like that! How could a mother let a child do that to himself?"

Today was evidently the day for odd silences.

"You heard?" Claudia said.

"No, no . . . I hadn't heard," Olivia said.

"Terrible, isn't it."

"Very sad," Olivia said. "Everyone embarks on a sad journey."

"Speaking of journeys, we must go on a shopping trip to the capital. I found the quaintest shoe store in the old city center. It's adorable; it's no bigger than a living room but their stock is imported and exclusive to the shop."

"That sounds very interesting. But right now I'm all set for shoes."

"We wouldn't just buy shoes. There's much we can talk about. Share. How about tomorrow?"

"Tomorrow we're having breakfast at my place."

"Really!"

"Yes. We're organizing a fundraiser, and we're going to have an expert come in to help us out. He's raised funds for this cause before, and he's well known in the community, so we're looking forward to breakfasting with him."

"Has . . . has a chair been decided for this committee?" Claudia asked, the intricate machinery in her head spinning, spinning plots.

"Why, would you like to run it?"

"My organizational skills, if I may say so, could be an asset to the group."

"Perhaps you should offer your help tomorrow?"

"It would be my great pleasure!"

"Fabulous," Olivia said. "I'm sure you'll fit right in. . . ."

9

Within the idiom of casual daytime wear for the tropics, Claudia Ferrier dressed to impress at the breakfast. The outfit she wore cannot be fully described without naming a designer or two. It consisted of a blue-green silk blouse, the slacks that came along with it as a set, accessorized with a big,

dark blue belt with a silver buckle, matching shoes with not-too-high heels, silver-mounted aquamarine earrings and necklace (her emeralds would have been *too* flashy), and a tiny little handbag that hung and swung from her shoulder by a silver chainlet. Elegant yet colorful, composed yet casual, classy yet friendly, serious yet fun: why, the outfit stood for how she wanted to be seen. She showed up slightly late to make an entrance, and be noticed, and be introduced to everyone as the glittering new member of the family.

An entrance she sure did make. The room fell into silence as the group, one by one, turned to glare at her.

Dean sat on the center seat of the table, holding up a cheese pastry in the air, Mark leaning over and whispering into his ear.

How could she save this situation? Talk, quickly!

"Dean . . ." she said, running over to his side, "Dean . . . I am so sorry, you left your beautiful coat in my car. . . ."

"And?" Dean asked.

"Ah. . . . What brings you here?"

"I'm organizing an AIDS benefit. And you, what kind of mischief are you up to?"

Dean smiled, a wide, toothy smile. Mark looked at her like he was about to throttle her. Claudia looked around to see that all eyes were upon her.

"Oh, you know Dean, how pleasant," said Olivia, from her corner of the table. "I'm so sorry Luisa is not here to see you as well."

Claudia kept trying to ingratiate herself with Dean. "Uh. . . . Uh. . . . What kind of animal fur is your coat?" asked Claudia.

"It's cretin," said Mark.

Claudia visibly amused herself with Mark's remark. "Oh, what a funny American —"

"You have no power here," Dean said. "Begone, before a house falls on you too."

10

Claudia left the party soon after, bursting in tears and agony. What would she tell her mother?

Eroticism (1992)

(from *Before Night Falls*)

Sometimes our adventures did not end as we would have liked. I remember that traveling on a bus one day Tomasito La Goyesca grabbed at the fly of a very handsome young man. The young man had actually signaled Tomasito several times and had touched his own evidently erect penis. When Tomasito grabbed it, the man reacted violently, beat him up, and called him, and all of us, queers. The driver opened the door of the bus and we ran across Revolutionary Square while a crowd of "chaste" men and women followed us yelling insults. We took refuge in the National Library, through a back door, and hid in María Teresa Freyre de Andrade's office.

Tomasito's face was swollen, and Hiram Prado discovered that the wallet Tomasito was holding was someone else's. In the melee, he had grabbed the wallet thinking it was his own; it actually belonged to the man who had beaten him, an official of the Ministry of the Interior, no less. Tomasito had lost his identification card, and now it was in the hands of the aroused man who had hit him. A few hours later, the man came to the National Library in a rage, looking for Tomasito. Since Tomasito did not want to come out of his hiding place, Hiram and I talked with him. He told us to bring the wallet to his home at midnight or he would have us all arrested.

At midnight the three of us arrived at his house, trembling. The young man had been taking a shower and came out naked and drying himself with a towel, which he then wrapped around his waist. He had drawn up a long, strange affidavit for us to sign, stating that we had returned all his documents and that he had returned ours. While we read and signed the affidavit, he was touching his penis, which again was giving signs of life. At the same time, he was insulting us, calling us immoral. In questioning us, he found out that Hiram had been in the Soviet Union, and he wondered how one could be gay after having been in that country. He also said that he would do everything in his power to have us expelled from the National Library. When he found out that I was a writer, he looked at me indignantly. But his penis was still erect, and every now and then he touched it.

He finally asked us to sit down and tell him about our lives. The towel gave us ever-increasing evidence of the man's excitement. We exchanged glances among ourselves, astonished, wishing to reach out and touch the promising bulge. We left at around four in the morning; the man dismissed us with his penis still in a state of arousal under the towel. We did not dare touch that wonderful area. We feared that it might be a trap, that the house could be full of cops to catch us in the act. But this was probably not the case. The man, who was persecuting us for being gay, probably wanted nothing more than for us to grab his penis, rub it, and suck it right then. Perhaps this kind of aberration exists in all repressive systems.

I remember another adventure with a young soldier. We met in front of UNEAC;[1] I gave him my address; he came by and sat on my only chair. There was no need for much talk; we both knew what we were after, because at the Coppelia urinals he had already given signs of urgent desire. We tangled in a pretty memorable sexual battle. After he had ejaculated and fucked me passionately, he dressed quietly, pulled out his Department of Public Order ID, and said, "Come with me. You are under arrest for being queer." We went to the police station. All the officers there were young, like the one who had fucked me. He declared that I was gay, that I had made a grab at his dick. I told them the truth, and that I still had his semen in my body. We were accusing each other face-to-face. Perhaps he thought that by being the active partner he had not done anything wrong. Or perhaps he saw himself as having lost his virginity to a sexually depraved person. The fact is that he had enjoyed himself like a real bastard and now wanted to put me in jail. The officers were amazed at the confession; the offense was too blatant. They ended up saying it was a shame that a member of the police force would engage in such acts, because I, after all, had my weakness, but for him, being a man, there was no excuse for getting involved with a queer. I believe a record of the proceedings was drawn up and he was expelled from the police, or at least transferred to another station.

I had other such problems with army officers. Once I went into the Barreto Woods in Miramar with a soldier. We were open with each other from the beginning. He was aroused and so was I. When we found a convenient place he said, "Kneel down and touch me here," and pointed to his belly. I tried to touch his penis, which he had taken out of his pants, but he moved my hand farther up to his waist, and what I touched was a pistol. He took the pistol out and said, "I'm going to kill you, you faggot." I bolted, heard some shots, yelled out and threw myself into the bushes. I stayed there the whole day. I heard patrol cars; the police were looking for me. Evidently the soldier, once his sexual arousal was under control, was trying to hunt me down, fortunately to no avail.

At dawn I returned to my room in Miramar. There was a terrific-looking boy waiting for me, one of my many lovers at the time who would come back again and again. He had waited for me all night. We went up to my room and between his legs I found refuge, as I had done before among the bushes when the soldier was searching for me.

My friends also had disappointments in love and with their erotic encounters. During a really dazzling carnival celebration in Havana, Tomasito La Goyesca entered one of the portable urinals set up on Prado Boulevard. Nobody went there to pee, except perhaps those who had been drinking and needed to go. They then became excited and ended up entangled with other men; there were dozens of men standing around while others sucked their cocks; some were being fucked right there. At first you could not see anything; then you could make out the bright penises and the sucking mouths. When Tomasito walked in he felt someone caressing his buttocks and his legs; he felt hands rubbing and touching him all over. Finally, completely sated and unable to bear it any longer, he went out to the street, only then realizing that someone in the bathroom had picked up shit and smeared it all over his body. It was an incredible scene to watch; a queer, full of shit from head to toe, right on Prado Boulevard, in the midst of the carnival and surrounded by thousands of people. Actually, he had no trouble making his way through the crowd; the stench coming from him was so bad that as he ran, a breach opened up to make way for him. He got to the Malecón and plunged, fully clothed, into the ocean. He swam beyond El Morro and, following him closely, I lost sight of him and feared a shark might have finished him off. He swam for hours and did not come ashore until daybreak, when he no longer smelled of shit.

Walking back to Prado Boulevard, we made up for all this. We picked up two fabulous sailors and went to the house where Tomasito lived with his mother. She was a tolerant old lady who did not mind if he came home with men, provided he did it quietly. We enjoyed those young men as much as they enjoyed us.

Pepe Malas also had numerous tragic encounters when he tried to satisfy his erotic urges. Once he was infatuated with a great example of masculine beauty who worked the night shift at the pharmacy. Pepe liked to stick his head through the small window that was left open at night, and then order ten cents' worth of aspirin while he stared at the pharmacist's fly. One night the man, tired of this game, yelled that he did not have any aspirin and yanked the window down with such force that Pepe's head got caught as if in a guillotine that had jammed at the crucial moment. People walking by on the street were somewhat astonished to see a man stuck in the little window, while the pharmacist slept peacefully on the other side.

Another one of his adventures turned out to be a little more costly. He took a hoodlum to his room on Monserrate Street, which was on the fifth floor of an old building and had a balcony above the street. The hoodlum told Pepe to take his clothes off and then pushed him onto the balcony, locking him out. The hoodlum filled a suitcase with the queer's belongings and left. Pepe, naked on the balcony above the street, did not know what to do. It would have been ridiculous to call the police; there was no way Pepe could explain how that delightful hoodlum was able to walk away with all his clothes, including the ones he had been wearing.

Hiram Prado always got into trouble in theaters. He had been sent to the Soviet Union as a young communist student, but was expelled after he was caught sucking the cock of a young Russian during a Bolshoi Theater performance.

Some time later, on one of our literary and erotic excursions to the Isle of Pines, Hiram Prado met a young man who was part of a grapefruit picking brigade. At the height of their erotic encounter, while Hiram was sucking the young man's penis behind a theater curtain, the curtain was suddenly pulled open and there they were, on center stage. The response to their performance was not exactly applause; rather, it was a deafening roar. The young man was only sixteen years old. Hiram was arrested, shaved to the scalp, and jailed. For a week I roamed the Isle of Pines trying to find out which jail he had been taken to. When I was finally about to catch the boat back to Havana, I saw Hiram and behind him the beautiful boy, who had also been arrested, being led under guard to a ship. Hiram was deported from Havana and sent to a farm in Oriente, his place of birth. We kept writing to each other for quite some time.

Once in a while our lovers had criminal intentions or mental quirks that made them commit acts of unjustified violence. The case of Amando García is a good example. He met a beautiful young judoka and took him home. The young man told him to lie down, and then he looked at Amando García and said, "You have such a beautiful neck. Stretch it out a little more." Then the beautiful Adonis ordered, "Now, close your eyes." Amando, his neck outstretched and eyes closed like a swan in ecstasy, was desperately awaiting the caress, when the young man gave out one of those terrifying judo yells, pounced on Amando, and with open hand struck him on the neck. The young man was actually trying to break Amando's Adam's apple and kill him. Amando, a very strong queer, screamed so loud that his neighbors at the boardinghouse came to his assistance. They took him immediately to the hospital, spitting blood. The young man had disappeared, shouting insults.

Several of Amando's erotic adventures ended in the hospital. I recall one occasion when I introduced him to one of my regulars, a recruit. I had a sort of special army; I would meet a recruit and the next day he would bring one of his friends, who in turn would bring one of his, so at times there were fifteen or twenty recruits in my room. This was too much of a surplus. And besides, we were generous and would share our lovers with our friends, who would also feel stimulated by meeting new guys. So I took this recruit to Amando. The man was really beautiful but his penis was smaller than Amando expected. Unsatisfied, he asked the recruit to stick a baseball bat (which he kept for such purposes) up his anus. The recruit went too far and shoved almost the entire bat into Amando, causing intestinal perforation and peritonitis. For a long time he had to live with an artificial anus. (His nickname changed then from Glugú to "Double Ass.")

We would also become victims of the jealousies of those buggers, as they called themselves. Sometimes they were jealous of one another. Once I got a very good-looking youth into one of the changing booths at La Concha Beach, and another guy, apparently in love with him, called the police, saying that two men were fucking in the booth. Needless to say, all homosexual acts were illegal and punishable, and to be caught in the act could mean years in jail. But that malicious guy brought the cops right to the booth where we were, naked and sweaty. They demanded we open the door; from above they had already seen us coupled. It seemed there was absolutely no escape: two naked men, inside a booth and sexually involved — there was just no way of justifying this to the police. I quickly wrapped my belongings in my shirt, making a tight little bundle, then opened the door, and before the police could lay hands on me, gave out a yell and ran at top speed down the stairs at La Concha, jumped into the ocean, and started swimming away. That day nature was my ally; suddenly there was a tropical downpour. It was almost a miracle; I saw the police looking for me in a patrol boat along the shore, but the rain was so heavy they lost sight of me. I was able to swim, naked, to Patricio Lumumba Beach, which was one or two miles from La Concha. It had stopped raining, and there were three boys jumping from the diving board. They were beautiful. In their full view I climbed up the diving board and put on my bathing suit. Then I started talking with them. I don't know if they noticed something odd about me, but they did not ask any questions. We swam awhile, and a few minutes later they were already with me in my room, which luckily was a short walk from Patricio Lumumba Beach. They really made up for my distressing experience at La Concha. For several months I had to stop going to that beach; there were so many men wanting to fuck other men. But La Concha had been famous since the days of the Republic as a place where everybody went to fuck; you could lock yourself in those booths and do whatever you wanted. Besides, whether naked or in bathing suits, all those men were truly irresistible.

Men would go to the beach with their wives, and sit on the sand to relax; but sometimes they would go to the changing booths, have erotic adventures with other young men, and then return to their wives. I remember a particularly good-looking man playing with his son and wife in the sand. He would lie down, lift his legs, and I could see his beautiful testicles. I watched him playing with his son for a long time, lifting his legs and showing me his testicles. Finally he went to the changing booth building, took a shower, and went up to get dressed. I followed him; I think I asked him for a cigarette or a match, and he invited me in. For five minutes he was unfaithful to his wife in the most astonishing way. Later I saw him again with his wife on his arm and his son, a beautiful family picture. I think that image prompted the idea for my novel *Otra vez el mar* [The sea once again, published in the United States as *Farewell to the Sea*], because the sea really provided us with the greatest sexual excitement, that tropical sea full of extraordinary young men who swam either in the nude or in bikinis. To be by the ocean and look at the sea was always a wonderful feast; we knew that somewhere in those waves an anonymous lover would be waiting.

Once in a while we made love underwater. I became an expert at this. I managed to get a face mask and flippers. It was wonderful to dive and swim underwater and be able to feast my eyes on all those bodies. Sometimes I would make love underwater with someone who also had a face mask. Occasionally he was not alone, and while he was up to his neck in the water, I would suck his penis powerfully until he ejaculated, and would then swim away with the help of my flippers. The person he was talking to at a little distance would notice no more perhaps than a deep sigh at the moment of ejaculation.

We usually had to stand in long lines to get a booth at La Concha, but if we were unsuccessful, we would perhaps make love up in the almond trees that surrounded the beach. These were luxuriant tropical trees of dense foliage; adolescents could easily climb them and then, up there amid the warbling of birds, we would perform erotic maneuvers worthy of professional tightrope walkers.

Our greatest joy, though, was being able to rent a house at Guanabo Beach, always a difficult proposition. Nevertheless, during the sixties one friend or another would usually manage to get one. He would not rent the house himself; it would have to be a woman or a married man. But somehow we would get a house for the weekend or, at times, for the whole week. It was a great feast. We would all bring our notebooks and write poems or chapters of our books, and would have sex with armies of young men. The erotic and the literary went hand in hand.

I could never work in pure abstinence; the body needs to feel satisfied to give free reign to the spirit. In the afternoons I would lock myself in my little room in Miramar, and sometimes write until late into the night. But during the day I roamed all the beaches, barefoot, and enjoyed unusual adventures with wonderful guys in the bushes, with ten, eleven, twelve of them sometimes; at other times with only one, who would be so extraordinary he would satisfy me as much as twelve.

Many of the guys would come back to me, but the problem was that the house was not mine; I lived in the maid's room of my aunt Agata's house. She was, moreover, an informer for State Security, and therefore it was dangerous for those young men to pay me a visit, especially if I was not home and they started pounding on the door. My aunt had many cats. I told my lovers not to enter through the front door but through the patio, and to do this they had to jump a wall on the ocean side. Unfortunately, they would sometimes land on one of my aunt's numerous cats. The cat would let out incredible howls and my aunt would scream louder. On many occasions, the youths were so terrified that they did not come to my room as we had agreed. Others were more daring and would climb in from the roof or onto the balcony on the street side. Sometimes there were four or five, and while I fucked one the others would masturbate, awaiting their turn. At times we had group sex, which was like having a party.

I would tell Lezama about my adventures. As soon as María Luisa left to prepare tea, he would ask me how I was doing and how my love life was going.[2] I was doing all right, although occasionally I suffered from the violence of some of my lovers, an experience shared by all of us.

I remember once, getting off the bus, I approached a muscular adolescent. We didn't waste words. One of the advantages of a pickup in Cuba was that not much talk was needed. Things were settled with a look, asking for a cigarette or saying you lived nearby and would he like to come with you. If he accepted, everything else was understood. The young man accepted, and once inside my home, surprisingly asked me to play the role of the man. Actually that gave me pleasure too, and the man went down on me. I fucked him and he enjoyed it like a convict. Then, still naked, he asked me, "And if anybody catches us here, who is the man?" He meant who fucked whom. I replied, perhaps a little cruelly, "Obviously, I am the man, since I stuck it into you." This enraged the young man, who was a judo expert, and he started to throw me against the low ceiling; thank God, he would catch me in his arms on the way down, but I was getting an awful beating. "Who? Who is the man here?" he repeated. And I, afraid to die on this one, replied, "You, because you are a judo expert."

Two blocks away from my aunt's house there was a huge school called INDER.[3] Thousands of young men on scholarship trained there in cycling, boxing, pole vault, and other sports. Almost all the students went through my room — sometimes a number of them, sometimes only one. Once a professor and a student met by coincidence; they looked at each other in surprise. The professor belonged to the Communist Youth Organization, and when he arrived and knocked at my door, I did not open it because I had the student in my room. He climbed onto the balcony, however, pushed the window open and came in, finding his naked student there. How could he explain to that student why, at three in the morning, he was bursting into a queer's room? The truth is, I don't know how he managed it. He left that night and returned the following day when, fortunately, the student was not there.

My erotic adventures were not limited to beaches and military camps; they also occurred in universities and university dorms where hundreds of students slept. Once I met a student whose name was Fortunato Granada. He was Colombian and had come to Cuba in the hope of studying medicine. In those years the Revolutionary government had invited many young people from all over Latin America to study at Cuban universities. Once enrolled at the universities, they were subjected to political indoctrination, and finally they were told that their country had to be liberated, that it was a victim of U.S. imperialism, that they had to return home as guerrillas.

Fortunato told me all this while we were making love on a bunk mattress in the dorm basement. He wanted to be a doctor — his reason for coming to Cuba — not to go back as a guerrilla. When he refused, his passport was taken away, and now they were threatening to expel him from the university. He was trying desperately to figure out what to do in Cuba after being expelled from the university and deprived of any ID.

We continued making love for a year; he finally had to enlist as a guerrilla fighter. I don't know if he got killed, because I never heard from him again. When I wrote *El palacio de las blanquísimas mofetas* [*The Palace of the White Skunks*], I wanted to pay tribute in a small way to this great lover of mine; the hero's name in my novel is Fortunato.

The guerrillas who were lucky returned to Cuba. One of them, Alfonso, had met Fortunato. One day Alfonso knocked at my aunt's door asking for me, and he identified himself as Fortunato's friend. I realized right away what he wanted. We became good friends and excellent lovers. He had belonged to the guerrillas and now worked for the Ministry of the Interior in Cuba. He had an official role at diplomatic affairs attended by Fidel Castro, as part of his security guard. Perhaps his homosexual inclination was forgiven because he was a foreigner; or perhaps the government didn't find out about it. He kept coming to me for years. Of course, he came only now and then and, frankly, behaved in a very masculine way. Then suddenly he disappeared; maybe he was transferred to another country on a special mission. God knows where he is now.

In addition to the pickups during the day, which generally took place at the beaches, there was another powerful homosexual scene in Havana, underground but very visible. There were pickups at night all over La Rampa, at Coppelia, on Prado Boulevard and along the Malecón Shore Drive, and at Coney Island in Marianao. These areas were full of recruits and students, single men who were locked up in barracks or schools and went out at night eager for sex. They were willing to settle for the first thing that came along. I always tried to be one of the first they met in these places. Hundreds of them ended up in my room. Sometimes they did not want to go that far, in which case we had to risk going downtown, to Old Havana, where we would walk up some stairway to the top floor and lower our pants. I think that in Cuba there was never more fucking going on than in those years, the decade of the sixties, which was precisely when all the new laws against homosexuals came into being, when the persecutions started and concentration camps were opened, when the sexual act became taboo while the "new man" was being proclaimed and masculinity exalted. Many of the young men who marched in Revolutionary Square applauding Fidel Castro, and many of the soldiers who marched, rifle in hand and with martial expressions, came to our rooms after the parades to cuddle up naked and show their real selves, sometimes revealing a tenderness and true enjoyment such as I have not been able to find again anywhere else in the world.

Perhaps deep down they realized they were breaking into the realm of the forbidden, the dangerous, and the damned. Perhaps that is the reason why, when that moment came, they showed such fullness, such radiance, and enjoyed every instant in the awareness that it might be their last, that it could cost them many years in jail. There was, moreover, no prostitution. It was pleasure for pleasure's sake, the craving of one body for another, the need to find fulfillment. Sexual pleasure between two men was a conspiracy, something that happened in the shadows or in plain daylight, but always forbidden; a look, a wink, a gesture, a sign, was enough to start the sequence that resulted in such full enjoyment. The adventure in itself, even if fulfillment did not come with the desired body, was already a pleasure, a mystery, a surprise. To enter a movie theater was to figure out whom we would sit next to, and whether that young man over there would stretch out his leg toward us. To reach over slowly with one hand and touch his thigh, and then to dare a little more and feel the part of his pants where that penis wanted to break through the fabric; to masturbate him right then and there during an old American movie, to see how he would ejaculate, and then leave before the movie ended; and perhaps I would never see him again, after having seen his face only in profile. What does it matter, he was surely a wonderful guy.

People would really get sexually aroused on interstate trips. If you took one of those buses crowded with young men, you could be sure that some erotic games would take place during the trip. The driver would turn out the lights, and the bus would be moving on those highways full of potholes; with each lurch of the vehicle one had the opportunity for contact, for touching an erect penis, a young thigh, a strong chest; hands could move over a body, feel for the waist, unbuckle the belt, and then, cautious and eager, reach for the spot where that terrific member lay hidden. Those adventures, and the people with whom one had them, were great. Those men enjoyed their roles of active males; they wanted to be sucked and even to fuck right on the bus.

Later, in exile, I found that sexual relations can be tedious and unrewarding. There are categories or divisions in the homosexual world. The queer gets together with the queer and everybody does everything. One sucks first, and then they reverse roles. How can that bring any satisfaction? What we are really looking for is our opposite. The beauty of our relationships then was that we met our opposites. We would find that man, that powerful recruit who wanted desperately to fuck us. We were fucked under bridges, in the bushes, everywhere, by men who wanted satisfaction while they penetrated us. Either conditions here are different, or it is just difficult to duplicate what we had there. Everything here is so regulated that groups and societies have been created in which it is very difficult for a homosexual to find a man, that is, the real object of his desire.

I do not know what to call the young Cuban men of those days, whether homosexuals who played the male role or bisexuals. The truth is that they had girlfriends or wives, but when they came to us they enjoyed themselves thoroughly, sometimes more than with their wives, who often would refuse to suck or had inhibitions that made lovemaking less pleasurable.

I remember an extraordinary mulatto, married and with several children, who escaped his family once a week to fuck me on the iron chair in my room. I never saw a man enjoy sex so much. He was, nevertheless, an excellent father and exemplary husband.

I think that the sexual revolution in Cuba actually came about as a result of the existing sexual repression. Perhaps as a protest against the regime, homosexuality began to flourish with ever-increasing defiance. Moreover, since the dictatorship was considered evil, anything it proscribed was seen in a positive light by the nonconformists, who in the sixties were already almost the majority. I honestly believe that the concentration camps for homosexuals, and the police officers disguised as willing young men to entrap and arrest homosexuals, actually resulted in the promotion of homosexual activities.

In Cuba gays were not confined to a specific area of a club or beach. Everybody mingled and there was no division that would place the homosexual on the defensive. This has been lost in more advanced societies, where the homosexual has had to become a sort of sexual recluse and separate himself from the supposedly nonhomosexual society, which undoubtedly also excludes him. Since such divisions did not exist in Cuba, the interesting aspect of homosexuality there was that you did not have to be a homosexual to have a relationship with a man; a man could have intercourse with another man as an ordinary act. In the same way, a real gay who liked another gay could easily go out and live with him. But the gay who liked real macho men could also find one who wanted to live or be friends with him, without in any way interfering with the heterosexual life of that man. It was not the norm for one queer to go to bed with another queer; "she" would look for a man to fuck "her" who would feel as much pleasure as the homosexual being fucked.

Homosexual militancy has gained considerable rights for free-world gays. But what has been lost is the wonderful feeling of meeting heterosexual or bisexual men who would get pleasure from possessing another man and who would not, in turn, have to be possessed.

The ideal in any sexual relationship is finding one's opposite, and therefore the homosexual world is now something sinister and desolate; we almost never get what we most desire.

That world, of course, also had its dangers. Along with other homosexuals, I was robbed and blackmailed a number of times. Once, after I received my monthly pay from the National Library, just ninety pesos, which was not much but had to cover all of my expenses for the month, I was foolish enough to go straight to the beach. I met a marvelous youth who had caught a crab, tied it to a string, and was walking it on the sand as if it were his dog. I praised the crab while looking at the legs of the youth, who then quickly came with me to my booth. He was wearing a tiny bathing suit. I don't know how he did it, but during his sexual gymnastics, which he handled with practiced skill, he managed to steal all my money from my pants pocket and hide it in his small bathing suit. The truth is that after he left I realized that I had been cleaned out; I did not even have a nickel for the bus fare home. I looked for him all over La Concha Beach. In one of the open booths I found a smashed crab. He was evidently a violent person. The carapace was all that was left of the crab. The beautiful adolescent had disappeared without leaving a witness: not even a crab.

That afternoon I walked home. Once in my room, I continued writing a long poem. I entitled it "Morir en junio y con la lengua afuera" [To die in June, gasping for air]. A few days later I had to stop working on the poem, because somebody had entered my room through the window and stolen my typewriter. This was a serious theft; to me that typewriter was not only the one object of value in my possession but also the thing I treasured the most. To me, sitting down at the typewriter was, and still is, something extraordinary. I would be inspired (like a pianist) by the rhythm of those keys and they would carry me along. Paragraphs would follow one another like ocean waves, at times more intense, at others less so; sometimes like huge breakers that would engulf page after page, before the next paragraph. My typewriter was an old iron Underwood, but to me it was a magical instrument.

Guillermo Rosales, then a good-looking young writer, lent me his typewriter and I finished the poem.

Some time later a mulatto police officer, rather handsome in fact, showed up at my home. He told me my typewriter was at the police station. The thief had been caught burglarizing another home, and his house had been searched. They found many stolen items, my typewriter among them. Apparently the thief himself told the police that the typewriter was mine. After many bureaucratic formalities, it was returned and I had to carry it home in a bus full of people; it seemed to weigh a ton, but I got it back where it belonged. I was afraid it would be stolen again, and my friend Aurelio Cortés had the bright idea of bolting it to its metal table.

A number of times hoodlums — that is, the boys with whom I had made love — entered my room and tried to steal the typewriter, but to no effect; it was impossible to carry both typewriter and metal table. From then on I felt safer, better able to continue my love life without endangering the rhythm of my literary production. That rhythm has always been part of me, even during periods of the most intense lovemaking or of the greatest police persecution. Writing crowned or complemented all other pleasures as well as all other calamities.

There were three marvelous things that I enjoyed in the sixties: my typewriter, at which I sat as a dedicated performer would sit at his piano; the unique youth of those days, when everybody wanted to break away from official government policies and be free and make love; and lastly, the full discovery of the sea.

As a child, I had already been in the town of Gibara for several weeks with my aunt Ozaida, whose husband, Florentino, worked there as a bricklayer. I was able to get into the water then but not to experience the magic of the sea as much as I could later, at twenty-something. During the sixties I became an expert swimmer. I would swim out into the open sea in those crystal-clear waters, look back at the beach as if it were something very remote, and enjoy being rocked by the ocean waves. It was marvelous to dive in and behold the underwater world. The views are incomparable, no matter how much you have traveled and how many other undoubtedly interesting places you have seen. The island platform surrounding Cuba is a world of rock and coral, white, golden, and unique. I would come up glistening, smooth, full of vitality, toward that dazzling sun and its immense reflection in the water.

The sea was then my most extraordinary source of pleasure and discovery; to see the raging waves in winter; to sit looking at the sea; to walk from my home to the beach and there to experience the sunset, the twilight. Those late afternoons by the sea are unique in Cuba, particularly in Havana, where the sun falls into the sea like a giant balloon; everything seems to change at dusk, cast under a brief and mysterious spell. There is the smell of brine, of life, of the tropics. The waves, almost reaching my feet, ebbed and left a golden reflection on the sand.

I could not live too far from the sea. Every morning when I woke up, I would go to my little balcony to look at the blue, scintillating expanse reaching to infinity, at the lavishness of that extraordinary glittering water. I could not feel despair, because no one can feel despair when facing such beauty and vitality.

Sometimes I would get up at night to look at the sea. If the night was dark, the thundering of the surf would comfort me; it was the best company I ever had, then and always. In me the sea reverberated with erotic resonance.

While sitting at Patricio Lumumba Beach one day, I watched a teenager walk toward the wall and then disappear behind it. I followed the youth; he had lowered his bathing suit and was masturbating, looking at the sea.

I was familiar with all the nooks and crannies of the seashore around Havana, the places where a sudden deepening would attract fish of unexpected colors, the areas covered with red coral, the big rocks, the huge sandbanks where one could stand to rest. After my swim I would return home and take a shower. I generally ate little and not well. Rationing was very severe, and besides, I was registered in my aunt's rationing book. She gave me only part of my share, and usually the worst part. I once heard her say to my uncle, "I told him the chicken was spoiled so that there would be more for us." Chicken was available once a month and my aunt had a husband and three children, in addition to various lovers; because of that, I suffered more than others under the rigorous rationing quotas imposed by Castro. But after taking a shower or, rather, after dumping a bucketful of water over me (there was not enough pressure for the water to rise to my shower), I would go to UNEAC feeling so alive that all those hours of bureaucratic work seemed bearable. I had to check galleys of horrendous publications like the UNEAC magazine, where I was supposed to be an editor but was actually only a proofreader, allowed to have neither an opinion nor the right to publish. But after my ocean swim I could imagine all of it was only a nightmare; real life started near the shore in the glittering sea that would be waiting for me the next day, and into which I could vanish, at least for a few hours.

Even to own a diving mask and flippers was a privilege in Cuba. I had them thanks to Olga, the French wife of a friend of mine. Those flippers and face mask were the envy of all the young men around me at that beach. Jorge Oliva trained with them many, many times, until one day he was able to swim to the Guantánamo Bay Naval Base, and freedom. La Nica, Jorge Oliva's girlfriend, trained with my swim fins too and was also able to leave Cuba secretly, via the U.S. naval base.

One day an adolescent, a really splendid creature, asked to borrow my flippers. I saw no danger in this and gave them to him. I don't know how he managed to disappear the way he did; he must have come out of the water several miles from there. The fact is that I never saw that young man or my beloved swim fins again.

Hiram Prado, who was with me and knew the youth, said that we could pay him a visit. I did not hesitate and ventured with Hiram into one of the most dangerous neighborhoods in Havana. It was known as Coco Solo, and was not far from Marianao. When we knocked at the young man's door he was so confused that he asked us to wait for him at the corner, where he showed up with more than twenty-five hoodlums armed with sticks and stones. We had to retreat at top speed.

All we could hope for was that Olga would bring us a new pair of flippers on her next trip to France. Olga was an incredible woman; she liked gays and found it impossible to have sex with anyone else. I assume that her life was unfulfilled, but I have met many women with such a preference. Her husband was always on the prowl for gays; they had to be passive gays who would also want to possess Olga, indeed a beautiful woman. Many heterosexuals were eager to possess her, but to no avail; she wanted to go to bed only with passive and openly gay men. Miguel asked all of us to make love to Olga and I think we all made love to his wife, out of friendly loyalty.

Miguel, however, claimed to be heterosexual, although his friends were monuments of masculine beauty. One afternoon at the beach a fierce storm broke out and Miguel and two of his friends, José Dávila and a very handsome judo expert, who I think was a member of State Security, had to take shelter in my room. Night came and they stayed over. Around midnight the judoka had an enormous erection; I had never seen a man with such a powerful penis. Miguel and José Dávila were sleeping or pretending to be asleep. The judoka, who according to Miguel and José was one of the most womanizing men they had ever met, engaged me in a memorable encounter.

A few days later Miguel came to visit and could not believe it when I told him. In any case, he soon told me that he felt the need to be possessed and prodded me to do it; I had to comply. He came to my house several times with the same request, and I always obliged. After getting dressed, he would say, "I don't do it for the pleasure; I just need a prostatic massage, which is most important to maintain a healthy equilibrium."

This kind of thing happened quite often. I remember a tanned, charming young man, very masculine, who would come to my room wanting to get laid. I confess I enjoyed possessing the type of youth who appeared to be very masculine. Even if one eventually got bored, at the beginning it was an adventure. That young man, after being possessed and enjoying himself more than I did, would get dressed, give me a strong handshake, and say, "I've got to go, I have to see my girlfriend." And I really don't think he lied; he was a handsome guy and his girlfriends were lovely too.

My friends and I always liked to get together by the sea. Hiram Prado would wait for me under some pines, near the surf. Whenever we could, our group would go to Guanabo, Santa María, and Varadero Beach near the Bay of Matanzas, or to the most remote beaches in Pinar del Río. But our destination was always by the sea. The sea was like a feast and forced us to be happy, even when we did not particularly want to be. Perhaps subconsciously we loved the sea as a way to escape from the land where we were repressed; perhaps in floating on the waves we escaped our cursed insularity.

An ocean voyage, practically impossible in Cuba, was a major pleasure. Just to cross Havana Bay on the ferry to Regla was a marvelous experience.

Those times spent near the ocean inspired my novel *Otra vez el mar.* Like ocean waves, the manuscripts of this novel, which I had to write three times, kept vanishing and later landing, for various reasons, in the hands of the police. I imagine all those lost versions of my novel must be taking up a lot of shelf space in the Department of State Security in Cuba. Bureaucrats are very systematic and for that very reason, I hope my manuscripts have not been destroyed.

By the year 1969 I was already being subjected to persistent harassment by State Security, and I feared for the manuscripts I was continually producing. I packed all my manuscripts and the poems I had written earlier—that is, everything I had not been able to smuggle out of Cuba—in an empty cement bag, and visited all my friends in order to find one who could hide them for me without arousing the suspicions of State Security. It was not that easy to find someone willing to risk having those manuscripts; anyone found with them could spend years in prison.

Nelly Felipe kept them for me. For months my manuscripts were hidden in her house. One day she started to read them and was very honest with me: "I do like the novel but my husband is a lieutenant in State Security, and I don't want him to find those manuscripts at home." Again I found myself walking along Fifth Avenue with my cement bag full of scribbled papers and no place to take them.

I finally took them back home. In my room there was a small closet, which I was able to camouflage by wallpapering it just like the rest of the room with pages from foreign magazines, surreptitiously obtained. The closet disappeared; it was now part of another wall in my room, and all those sheets of paper I had scribbled over the years were perfectly hidden.

Translated by Dolores M. Koch

NOTES

1 Unión de Escritores y Artistas de Cuba (National Union of Writers and Artists).
2 Lezama is José Lezama Lima, the renowned Cuban novelist, who was also homosexual and an important mentor of Arenas's. María Luisa Bautista was Lezama Lima's wife and a friend of his family.
3 Instituto Nacional de Deportes y Recreación [National Institute of Sports and Recreation] (author's note).

RANE ARROYO

Three Poems

SATURDAY NIGHT IN SAN JUAN WITH THE RIGHT SAILORS (2004)

I'm younger than the calendar. We like this
floating on bar stools, mermen amazed by
our miraculous sea legs. Apocalypse has

nothing to offer, upstaged as it is by this
jukebox playing Shakira as if noise staves off
dawn. They rub against me for I'm the shore

of their shore leaves. It's just before the heat
leads to choices, and we like this competition
between beers and our fate lines, the risks.

ALMOST A REVOLUTION FOR TWO IN BED (2004)

You're still the island of the holy
palm tree. What can I offer to the man
married first to God and then soon to
the wrong rib? Here, it's shining outside,
a spy stirred by the colors between us.
The sea is never rhetorical and asks
about your nakedness, that theft.

*

You weep because your clothes
drag you back to vows. I will not
comfort you, not be another goddamn
mosquito net for Adam's innocents,
not shave this dawn's whiskers of
whispers. Coconuts look like balls
of angels refusing perfection.

Our bed floated on a floating
miracle humble with spectacle.

*

You leave. I stay. We fall off
the bed, this time as ghosts.
Winds steal words from books.
In the mirror, I see verbs,
read Arenas' Arenas, discover
love letters inside my irises,
rediscover Homer's honesty:
we return to our leaving.

TROPICAL FEVER (2003)

The Puerto Rico inside Puerto Rico,
my shadow's shadow. Think of how a skull

is generic even while wearing
the grace of astonishment — and yet

when it's the skull of one's beloved,
the specific yields to the spiritual.

The man outside of my male self,
call and response with genitalia.

The map of skin and the skin of maps.
Sailor as port, the unimportant nights

on shore. Drowning inside arms
while flying, while looking down at

our upscale Eden. Bring your own
serpent and apples, naked light

provided by geography, grace.
Sharing razors, the shine of godliness

far from commandments. Body hair
speaks *tide* and means *fire*. Adios

brief pause, sunset's eternity.
The nakedness after the nakedness.

Island inside island, the sea inside
tears, tears lost inside the sea.

JESÚS J. BARQUET

Three Poems

TRANSACTIONS (2001)

I have been in jails, in refugee
camps, in sterilized airports where
by showing voiceless documents
there was no need to say who I was not.
I have been in cities where no one
— even after making love to me many times —
knew who I was, in trains crowded with young men
grabbing each other until getting off at the next station,
in ruins, palaces, gardens, gas chambers filled with tourists
scared of missing the last bus back to their hotels.
I have bought my clothes at top-drawer department stores,
had lunch in buffet restaurants,
driven for hours on freeways
open like one-way tunnels.
I have slept listlessly and without worries
with strangers that a transatlantic stewardess
placed beside me without previous consultation.
I have made love in bathrooms, in the back seats of buses,
on the edge of any interstate highway, and still I am not sure
if I have come to discover on my skin
the traces of true given,
the marks — even shreds —
of any identity which belongs only to me,
even if returned for being useless and defective
at any international exchange
office.

Translated by Gilberto Lucero and the author

SAN FRANCISCO—NEW ORLEANS (2001)

For manolo, on departure

This,
that
which I fly over
from the hostile Pacific to the welcoming Gulf
right now
— not yesterday, perhaps not tomorrow — is
                    my country:
mountains, deserts, pillaging snow, immense rivers
demanding endless bridges, the mirage of big cities
but no fire, unstoppable objects and machinery, diverse
colors to reformulate every day
                    do not succeed
in replacing
— not even as a cheap imitation —
a brief Havana night escaping from rain
and kissing each other, ominously perhaps,
at every platform.

Translated by Gilberto Lucero and the author

THE IMAGE SAVES (1994)

For rei, eye witness

My gaze fails to wake him.
He knows — or does he? — that I exist, that I penetrate
pore by pore his lineage, his sleeping
insolence, his indifference towards me.

        Suddenly
he moves and the Dogana
wind seizes its opportunity,
not my accomplice, but rather my rival, and opens
his blue t-shirt, caressing him,
back and forth, and there he is, absent, letting his
        anonymous somnolence
be caressed.

(My eyes

manage to catch sight of only a few more inches of that skin

that seems to go on forever.)

      Once more,

he moves, uncooperative, with brief indecisive gestures,

and now I'm a cubist with a myriad of new angles

glimpsed yet unattainable.

            (My sight

— which understands the impossible —

tries to adjust precisely to each new vision:

        chest,

                back,

      thighs,

              he turns again,

      the knee

that rises creating a dimension that didn't exist, his lips far-off in

  dream . . .)

      My eyes shoot arrows

at each of his forms, and they bounce off

making more of a nick in me than in him who sleeps or aspires

not to be, but to simply exist: He is

Venice. I am

my eyes. My eyes

anchored on him. My eyes

that will never be able to wake him

nor should they . . .

      CLICK!

      He wakes. With one hand he searches for

his external possessions, with the other he adjusts

his pants. He gathers his things

— now is the true cubist revelry —, he doesn't spit, he gets up

and leaves.

               (The towers of San Marco, the distant arcs

                     of the Palazzo Ducale

                           take

                       his place,

                poor substitutes.)

But I'm not finished: I come back to the empty space,
perhaps to the waves left by his departure, I demand of the air a
    possible
peculiar aroma, perhaps some object of his
intentionally left behind smack dab in the end-of-2oth-century:
        As if from another era
I lay claim stone by stone, to his heat,
his dew

                  — the Piazza San Marco
                        insists,
          the Grand Canal pounds the shore —

but what
does it matter . . .

Now all that's left is to reveal the photo that replaced him.

Author's Note: The photo exists, and is in my exclusive possession.
He must be older now.

                              Translated by Michael Ray

MARILYN BOBES

Somebody Has to Cry (1998)

DANIEL

She's almost in the middle, smiling. Really she's the most beautiful, though she didn't know it then. She didn't even dare imagine it. Her nose bothers her; maybe it's too big for a girl of fifteen. With time, her face will arrange itself and nothing will be out of proportion, nothing to mar it. But right now the present is all she cares about.

On her right, Alina, who has already got a pair of enormous breasts. She's the *criollita,* the curvaceous prize that all the junior high boys desire and incessantly pursue. Cary envies her a little, not knowing that twenty-four years later all that will remain of the imposing Alina is a woman who is fat, flabby, and sad. Alina doesn't know it either and maybe that's why, in the year 1969 that's frozen in the photo, she's standing on tiptoe above the others, proud of all her volume, her splendor, usurping the space of the rest, relegating them to second best.

On the far left, fuzzy from the back lighting, it's hard to make out Lázara: thin thighs, graceless figure, mousy face. Her chest is still flat and innocuous. She raises her eyes to the camera as if begging pardon for her existence. That's Lázara a few months before the tragedy. Afterward she dropped out of school. She couldn't stand the looks, the laughter, the reputation that came along with an unsanctified pregnancy in junior high in those years. The flight of The Old Man topped it off — he was the guy in his forties who used to wait for her outside the school in the little park, and with whom she would trustingly disappear into The Woods. Next to Cary, also to the left, two unidentified girls. They look alike; you'd almost call them twins. Short, round, with dolls' eyes, they're present only so that behind them, rising over their bangs and their heads and their small happy destinies, Maritza can appear. Her powerful frame, rising over the group, is an aggressive presence in the portrait.

Time, working on the photo, has turned Maritza's eyes transparent. She already seems marked for death. She doesn't look at the camera. She doesn't smile. She's the only one not putting on a birthday face. Her broad shoulders reveal the athlete, the champion in freestyle for four straight seasons. She's also beautiful, although in a different way. Her face was perfect and mysterious, like no other in the photo, like there may never be in Havana again.

CARY

They found her drowned. Like a character in an ephemeral soap opera: an overturned glass and a half-empty bottle of rum on the bathroom floor, an inch or two away from the hand that hung over the edge of the tub. The remains of the pills in the mortar, still there on top of the sink, and the wrinkled wrappers in the trash.

At the wake, a man whose face seemed familiar said that it didn't seem like a woman's suicide. Except for the pills. It seemed too rational: predicting the deep sleep from the barbiturates, the downward slide until her back rested on the bottom and water irreversibly filled her lungs. I suspect what bothered him was the idea of Maritza's nude body exposed to the eyes of a dozen curious onlookers waiting for the Forensic Medicine technicians to arrive.

But Maritza never had any sense of modesty like that. She would be the first to arrive at the sports complex and, before opening her locker, she'd yank off her blouse, step out of her skirt, and start doing knee bends and sit-ups in an explosion of uncontrollable energy. Her legs and torso, their muscles strong and well-knit, whirled compulsively before our eyes. I remember that once she'd finished her exercises, she'd put a stretch cap over her short hair and, completely nude, disappear into the showers with the stride that was so much her own: long, confident, slow.

Unlike us, she didn't care much about her image. Now that time has gone by and I see things differently, it occurs to me that she cultivated her body for its use-value.[1] All the rest of us, even if we devoted ourselves to gymnastics or swimming, were preparing ourselves for a future auction; one way or another, we were always on display.

Lázara, Alina, and I tortured ourselves daily with cinched-up belts and tight pants. Maritza was happier; she disguised herself with loose outfits, slightly strange ones, as if stubbornly trying to come in last. We scolded her more than once for her laxness and, sometimes, for her lack of modesty too: when she sat down she'd never pull at the hem of her miniskirt or strategically locate her pocketbook on her thighs as the rest of us did. I don't even remember her carrying a pocketbook. She'd leave the house with a beat-up wallet, made by some anonymous artisan, that would barely hold her identity card and some cash. Lots of times, as we walked, she'd ask Alina to keep it in her shoulder bag full of perfume, tissues, lipsticks, eyeliners, and all the other makeup imaginable.

ALINA

She always had it inside her. Always. More than once it occurred to me and I was on the point of warning Cary. That nerviness about going around naked, those indecent theories, that mania about controlling her . . . I don't know why we didn't discover it in time. We were normal, we dressed well, we thought the way women think.

That thing with my husband, she didn't do it just to bother me, but for God knows what other dirty reasons. Nonetheless, she paid for it. You pay for those things.

He couldn't manage anything with her. He told me this morning in the funeral parlor. There was something strange in the way she took off her clothes, something brazen. And afterward, she humiliated him. She got dressed again as if it were nothing, she didn't want explanations, she said goodbye with a nasty look and even dared to crack a cynical joke: And now, what are you going to do if I decide to tell Alina about this?

He confessed all that in an attack of sincerity and rage, so I wouldn't be moved, so I wouldn't get sucked in by Lazarita's weakness and put my name on the wreath. No, I won't allow it. Maybe Caridad and Lázara don't care what people say, but we do. We did enough by coming to the wake. We're not going to the funeral. Politeness has its limits.

It's true that I let myself go. The childbirths did me in, they ruined me, it's true. But how could I think about my figure? The woman who doesn't have children never feels fulfilled. Lots of them, like Maritza, like Cary, stay in better shape because they don't give birth. I was brought up differently, to have a family. I'm not sorry. I love my children very much, and nothing could have replaced the joys they've given me. That's what completes a woman: a family.

I decided that they were sacrificing all this because they liked to show off. If they'd had to cook, wash, iron, and take care of a house, they would have had trouble finding the time to read books and daydream. Cary figured that out. She's spent her life divorced. But Maritza . . . Now it's clear why she wasn't interested in marriage or stability. In her case, the answer was much simpler.

I was dumb. If they surprised me at a bad moment, I'd let it all out, telling them things I didn't even think. I was still young and immature. I didn't have to tell them what went on between me and my husband. Maritza didn't have to see me crying. Why should I have given them that pleasure? Over time, I came to understand that it's normal. It happens in all marriages, that passion turns into companionship, into peaceful and lasting affection. Even if they need a little affair once in a while, a wife is a wife. The woman they chose to marry. The question of sex becomes secondary when one matures.

Nonetheless, it hurt me. Maritza always tried to compete with me, to outdo me in some way. In '72, on a voluntary work brigade, she managed to be a finalist in the Tobacco Queen contest. Of course, it was me who won. The head of the rural Plan, three farmers, and the high school principal were the judges. The principal and one of the farmers voted for her. But the rest of the judges and the public were on my side from the beginning. She could never be my equal. In spite of her pretty face and that reputation she cultivated by playing hard to get. She knew it was the mystery that made her interesting, and she managed to keep it going for a long time. In our junior year at the university she was still a virgin. Or at least, that's what people said.

I had to put up with her day after day at the university too. When she knew I wanted to study architecture, that's where she went and enrolled. So I know her better than anyone. I put up with a lot from her. Especially her envy. The only thing I wouldn't accept was her attempt to dominate me. She didn't like that, and the friendship ended then and there. We had a falling out.

I feel like I can still see her, acting humble but really being so arrogant underneath. That little voice, syrupy and halfway hoarse, and her affected vocabulary. She wore herself out with interviews, letters, and meetings, thinking that someone was going to take an interest in her thesis: alternative building styles. She was a snob. So many people needed houses and she worried about diversity, about reconciling functionality, available resources, and aesthetics. She ruined a whole New Year's Eve with that litany. I don't know why we invited her. It was Lazarita's idea, or Cary's.

Everybody trying to enjoy themselves, and her sitting in the easy chair like an English lady, monopolizing their attention. And Cary kept giving her more and more rope, so she'd keep talking. Even Lázara was taken in by her nonsense. Something Maritza said seemed to her like the height of genius: that getting up every morning and looking at identical buildings makes people intolerant, predisposes them against differences. Poor stupid Lázara was impressed by that foolishness. She always had a complex about the supposed intelligence of Maritza and Cary. The two of them, especially

Maritza, filled her head with pretensions when she was still a girl. And now what? She can't keep a man. Not just because she's ugly, but because she's dumb. I've seen many uglier than her who are married now. It's because she doesn't learn. She chases them, and then right away she opens her legs. She confesses that she wants to marry them. Nothing scares a man more than the feeling that you want to trap him. That's why The Old Man left her high and dry. He left her burdened with a fatherless daughter, to this day. I got really tired of repeating myself. What you've got to do with men is show them indifference, drive them to distraction and make them think they're the ones making the decisions. I'm not going to waste more breath on her. Let her keep being led by Cary, she'll see. Cary has been married three times and has had as many boyfriends as she's wanted, but poor Lázara . . . nothing happens for her. And at forty, not even Marilyn Monroe can get a guy to marry her.

DANIEL

I met Lázara at work. I knew from the way she looked at me that she'd put out easily and that later it would be easy to get rid of her as well. She had too low an opinion of herself to become one of those stubborn, clinging women who refuse to accept the fact that when they cross paths with a man by chance, their condition is going to be volatile, ephemeral, and without roots. In her sad flirtation without charm or pride, there was a resignation to the fleeting nature of any bond she might make. I liked that about her. That and the harebrained idea that she might be good in bed.

Sometimes not-very-attractive women can be really surprising when you get intimate with them. As if they want to make up for what they lack with daring and imagination. Besides, I was alone and bored, and New Year's was coming up.

That New Year's Eve, Lazarita was invited to a party. When I agreed to go too, her face lit up with a joy that seemed excessive. It was clear that she'd spent too many New Years' alone, and to show up with me (at that house where "her lifelong friends" would be), was a coup, a boost for her self-esteem.

We'd already gone out two or three times before. I'd found her drab, trembling body to be pleasant, but I could see it wouldn't amount to more than that. In the middle of January I was scheduled for a trip to the provinces and I was planning to leave Lázara for good then, without hurting her too much, taking advantage of the forced separation plus other pretexts, postponements, and pious white lies.

But that New Year's Eve I met what Lázara called "her lifelong friends." Among them was Alina, whose house it was: a fat housewife with three children and of no interest to me. But there was also Maritza, who was an impressive woman: something like a Pallas Athena in the middle of that silly room crammed with macramé. She gave the impression of being untouched and, nonetheless, seemed experienced too. And, above all, there was Cary. Cary, on the far end of the sofa, attentively following Maritza's explanations — about architecture, I think. She was holding a glass of rum in one of her thin, aristocratic hands, while she indolently surrendered the other to a man I instantly disliked. Cary: her fine, angular face, her eyelids always blinking because of her lenses, her delicate mouth, her body, her skin. All meticulously crafted by a goldsmith: for love, to be kissed, touched, and sipped inch by inch.

CARY

We went to movies, cafeterias, and parties, but Maritza preferred the beach. Any time of year, even winter. I was the only one who would go with her on those cold, gray days. We enjoyed a very pleasant privacy that you could never find in August.

On the deserted reefs we'd undo our bikini tops and each anoint the other's back with the mixture of cooking oil and iodine which we used to cope with the lack of store-bought tanning cream. Along a stretch of the coast which we called La Playita, Maritza and I talked a lot. With a sincerity I never felt with the others, I told her all about the setbacks in Alejandro's and my engagement, which I shed so many useless tears for. She listened with a careful attention that I've never found in anybody else since.

Maritza understood me. Nonetheless, it irritated her that I should waste so much time and energy analyzing in such detail — obsessively, she said — something so insubstantial. She had a hard time accepting that I could convert my relationship with Alejandro into something central and decisive, that this pastime was so absorbing as to erase the interest and satisfaction of all others — writing, for example. She was sure I'd become a writer, especially after I told her about my diaries. Since I was a girl, every night before going to sleep, I've written my impressions of the day in a notebook. I'm still surprised that one of those afternoons I let Maritza read a few pages — the ones I thought were the best-written and most intense.

Maybe, without knowing it, I had been looking for a reader. Maritza seemed so interested, she encouraged me so much, that I couldn't resist the temptation to show her those entries in spite of the fact that, until then, I'd considered my diary sacred and inviolable. I kept it hidden under my pillow.

I remember that she praised my facility for description and the supposed keenness with which I presented details. The only thing she didn't like was that (there too) the leading character was Alejandro. Because her criticisms hurt, I defended myself by trying to undercut her argument with my experience: maybe she would understand when she fell in love. And then she told me that she too had once thought she was in love. But love, she told me, is too uncertain and changeable a sentiment. We shouldn't give it the central role that only the most essential things deserve.

At seventeen, Maritza already thought that the more fulfilled a person felt, the less she needed another person in order to be happy. Love, she insisted, is an arrangement between losers. That's why it's almost always we women who are most in love. Because women by nature are the ones who lose.

We've been brought up, she told me once, to facilitate the triumph of men: look at you, with all your talent, and all you talk about is them.

Maritza always broached those subjects very naturally, without any dramatizing, and avoiding solemnity. Suddenly, as if the conversation no longer interested her, she would jump up and, after refastening her bikini straps, she'd give me a complicitous tap on the shoulder and dive into the sea. From there she'd begin joking about Alejandro and making fun of my sufferings with so much wit that, many times, they'd seem ridiculous and false even to me.

ALINA

Maritza could talk you into anything. She had this tricky, lawyerish quality that Cary never did. Nobody high up listened to her, but other people, even intelligent ones like my own husband, looked at her as if they were seeing an extraterrestrial. It's true that, on that night, she came very well dressed. When she began working, she started to enjoy dressing up. She made herself up like a queen and she had that bronzed skin that you only see in magazines. She always managed to seem prettier than she really was.

I'm sure that on that New Year's Eve she came with the intention of taking my husband away. And then I had to hear her complain that men never listened to her: they invited her to lunch, supposedly because they were interested in her project, and ended up inviting her to sleep with them. That's not the way I see it. She provoked them herself. Maybe if she'd said yes to just one of them, Havana would be full of alternative buildings. I mean, if she was able to do it to my husband, why not one of those functionaries too?

That's what she was into in '83 or '84. I think those were her best years. Because we have to be honest: she didn't seem like what she was. You would have had to be very suspicious to notice those few details. For instance, I never liked her manner of dragging out her *s*'s — the way they do.

The indications are that sometime after we stopped seeing each other, she started to drink a lot. Not in public, but in private. At the wake, her neighbor said that Maritza would go into the apartment every day with a bottle of wine or Havana Club in her shopping bag.

In the afternoons, after her bath, she'd sit on the terrace in a pair of shorts and a little white top to listen to Brazilian music and drink. Alone. Completely alone.

They never saw her with any men. When the other woman moved in with her, everybody thought it was a relative or a very close friend. The woman had a child. That boy must have been the reason she decided to go back to her husband. Poor thing. I can't imagine how people can sacrifice their children to go indulge their deviant behavior.

Maritza fell into a deep depressive state. She stopped greeting the neighbors and she quit her job.

I didn't see her again until today: old and blue, through the glass of the coffin. It was a very unpleasant spectacle. Caridad seemed like a zombie, completely transformed. I had never seen her like that, not even over men, which is the problem that destabilizes her most. When they took the body away she blanched, and if my husband hadn't held her tight, I think she would have fainted right there. Right in front of everyone, giving people grounds to think badly of her. And by association, of us. I had to speak to her harshly to get her to react. Finally, I said: a woman like Maritza, with no children, no man, and her pathology, what does she have to live for? It's like if you give birth to an abnormal child — even though it's yours, it's better if it dies, right? She made a decision and she had reasons to commit suicide. Cary, don't you see that?

LÁZARA

Now that they've taken her away, and now that Alina has left with all the hate she's got inside her that turns a person evil like Odette or like Fatima or like Justina, the maid in the other soap opera, now I'm going to cry as much as I want. Because I don't believe that Maritza liked women that way. And if she did, it was her business. She didn't hurt anybody, being like that. But no. I know perfectly well that she wasn't attracted to women. It's just that she was so good. She shared everything. She didn't keep anything for herself. I remember that when her father brought her those orange patent leather shoes from Hungary, she gave them to me. I didn't have any good shoes. But I didn't want her to deprive herself. I was ashamed. Then Maritza told me: you're going to enjoy them more than me. And I think that was true. She didn't care about things, but about people's happiness. She got so happy when my girl would say, Aunt Maritza, take me to the aquarium. She would take her, she'd explain the habits of the fish, she'd tell her that story about the lonesome seal that she made up. I even liked it myself. It hurts Cary a lot too, that she should kill herself. Just like that, overnight, as if she were a bad person who didn't deserve to live. Everybody knows Maritza didn't make trouble for anyone. And if she wanted to build those houses, that wasn't for herself but for other people. For me, too. Wouldn't you like to live in one of these, she asked me once, showing me a drawing she had made for her job. She didn't need those houses. She lived very well. In a very pretty apartment, elegant, full of plants and paintings, and with decorations outside. I never saw her look at us with any improper intentions or anything like that. On the contrary.

Even Daniel, that strange man who went out with me for about two months, liked her a lot. He behaved very well. He stayed at the funeral parlor all day. He was always very well-mannered. He spent all that time taking me to museums. He was a little boring and had a real temper, but I would have married him if he asked me to. He never married. He's a loner. Days and days shut up in the house and I couldn't even call him. Not because he was with other women. What he did was write in big notebooks and ask me about my life and my girlfriends' lives. Especially Maritza and Cary. We went to Alina's house together one New Year's Eve, and he spent a lot of time looking at Cary. Now I remember that he kept my picture of her *Quinceañera* party. (Cary gave one copy to Alina, one to Maritza, and one to me.) But he didn't flirt with her at all, he danced with me all night, and even put his arm around me while Maritza was talking about those pigeon lofts. It's true. Everytime I see them, I remember. Gray, ugly, and all the same. I'm happier being in my little room in Old Havana and seeing different buildings, so I can notice that people are very different too. Not like mice, pigeons, and cats. They're different colors, yes, but basically they're all the same. If they didn't have stains, or those colors, who could tell them apart? In Havana all the houses are different, even if they're crumbling, while Alamar seems like a Russian movie I don't know. They don't even build *barbacoas* there.[2] It was Maritza who helped me build mine. She got the truck and even nailed the boards. It's true that she did a lot of men's things, but to jump from there to saying that she liked women, that's a long stretch. I don't believe it. I really don't. Just because a friend came to live with her? And if that woman didn't have a house, or if her husband beat her up? Maritza didn't like to see her friends mistreated. She was very advanced. Very liberated. That's why Alina was green with envy. She couldn't stand it that Maritza could be happy without a man. Just staying at home, reading, listening to nice music, classical things. If only I could have been like her. I would have gotten a degree at night instead of spending time in cabarets with guys who didn't know how to respect me or be my friend.

Cary too has wasted time with a lot of people. She's run into lots of jerks who didn't respect her. But that's different; she's famous and writes those novels. It's true that no one reads them, but that doesn't matter, once in a while she gets interviewed and she's been on TV.

CARY

One afternoon at the beach, as dusk came on, Maritza was very sad. Only that day did I understand that she too could be fragile, that inside her strong body there might be a weak girl like any other. It was the first time, and the only time if I remember right, that she spoke to me about something personal.

The person she was attracted to, Maritza confessed, was in love with another. She didn't see any way that a relationship was possible, because, even if her feelings were noticed, Maritza was prepared to sacrifice herself. She wasn't going to make herself into a problem for someone she regarded so highly. She assured me that she only believed in pleasure, because love, as most people understand it, is something complex, responsible, and in a certain sense representative: a social commitment.

It was a strange conversation. I didn't dare ask who the person was. Maritza's sentiments seemed noble, but the ideas were too intricate for me. Also I felt a little afraid. The sun was setting, and conversation is transformed at that time of day. For me, they always take on a tragic tinge.

I remember: I stayed silent and, a little nervous, collected some of our things that were scattered on the rocks and began to put them in my bag. I kept myself busy that way for a while. When I looked at her again, her eyes had a devastating expression. They reflected a bitterness so great that I felt sorry for her. I thought of trying to help her, but I didn't know what was happening or understand very well what we were talking about. I ended up asking her whether the pleasure that we gave, what we gave to others, wasn't important too.

She said yes, very much. But pleasure is loaded with guilt. Many people get married — she said — believing they're in love when really they're seeking approval. Love doesn't exist, it's an invention, she repeated with the stubbornness of someone who is convinced they know the whole truth. I assured her she was wrong, that I for one did believe in love. I knew very well the difference between desiring someone and falling in love. I accepted the possibility of confusing these feelings, but to turn this confusion into an absolute seemed to me a simplification, absurd.

Then Maritza said, raising an eyebrow, that if this was how I thought, I was lost: You'll end up as a toy or something much worse, a slave.

I tried to follow Maritza, her logic. But in that moment I felt unable to grasp her message. She insisted I had to write, that writing would free me from the need to cling to some man who would represent me. You can't allow them to make you suffer, she told me. If somebody has to cry, let it be them.

I remember that after saying this she bounded up and started joking, pressing her hands against her chest and repeating in the affected tone of a radio announcer: Somebody has to cry, original script by Caridad Serrano, performed by Maritza Fernández.

That afternoon we parted, dying of laughter, without yet knowing that for many years we would go on having fun with her idea. Somebody has to cry, Maritza would say to me when she arrived at my house and divined my sadness over the failure of some casual relationship. Well, if somebody has to cry, let it be him, I would answer, being ironic about my sufferings and writing off the cause of my distress.

LÁZARA

I wouldn't exchange Cary's life — what do I mean Cary's life, I wouldn't even trade my own sad and insignificant one — for Alina's, her and that vain little pretty boy she got married to. He doesn't respect her. Now he doesn't even bother to hide when you run into him with some tramp at the bus stop, at a restaurant, at the most unexpected place, never with Alina but always with someone else. It seems like he's ashamed of her. Now. Because before, when Alina was young and pretty, he would introduce her boastfully: "My wife," he'd say. "Let me introduce my wife." One day, to make fun of him, Maritza said: your wife who just happens to be named Alina. He looked at her as if he wanted to swallow her and Maritza stuck out her tongue at him, right there in front of everyone. He didn't have any choice but to laugh along with the rest. But I noticed something strange, morbid. It seemed to me he wanted something with her. I could follow it in his eyes when Maritza stood up or crossed her legs. I remember that in those years when they were first married, Alina invited us to that house at the beach, and I came into the kitchen where Maritza and he were mixing the drinks. I could see it out of the corner of my eye when she pushed him away. They laughed, but she made it crystal clear: cut out the monkey business. Poor Alina in the living room, hands full with the kids, and this man fooling around with her girlfriends. Because Cary told me he made passes at her too. She asked me not to even think of telling Alina, and much less Maritza, because Maritza would call him on the carpet and throw it in his face. He's shameless. Later he didn't even want us to put Alina's name on the wreath. Maritza always said better to commit suicide than to be married to a guy like that. And now look, the one who committed suicide was her, poor thing, who was the smartest and the best of us. That's why they make up things to discredit her. That's what always happens to people who stand out. You notice that not even her friend, the one with the problem, has had the decency to show up around here. Maritza's good deeds have always been paid back that way. But I don't think she was unhappy—just the opposite. I can't explain why she did it. Cary told me something I didn't understand about the need to fulfill herself. Fulfill what, I asked. But Cary was in very bad shape. She didn't cry. It was like she couldn't do it, and I told her: It's bad for you not to cry, you have to let it out. What's it to you if Alina doesn't cry? She's very hard. But you're not, you have to cry. What we have to do now is order another wreath so that poor Maritza can have more flowers on her grave. The flowers are nice. We can ask her father —that shy man who sat in his chair and didn't even hear us when we told him our regrets—to tell us the name of the flowers so we can order another . . . Cary doesn't want me to cry, she says I'm getting hysterical. But I don't know any other way to cry. Since I was little, I've gotten these attacks of sobbing with whimpers and all. In front of Alina and her husband I made an effort to control myself. But now I can't. Why should I control myself? Maritza used to say that you have to act from your heart, and my heart is telling me to cry. I'm going to cry as much as I want and I'm going to scream too. Somebody has to cry for Maritza, somebody has to show that she wasn't this pervert they're saying she was, and so I sure am going to cry and I'm going to scream and I'm going to tell the world that she was my friend. Because somebody has to cry for her.

DANIEL

We buried her in a pitiless downpour and people ran to take shelter underneath the roofs of the mausoleums. When the gravediggers lowered the coffin, three of us were left: Lazarita, Caridad, and I. Cary's dry eyes reflected horror and doubt. Looking at her close up, I wondered what was left of that verdant skin, that shining body that had me lying in wait so many years, powerless but hopeful.

I kept on seeing Lazarita once in a while, just to be a little close to her. And to Maritza. Although they never looked at me. Cary always had someone, one of those men who helped her feel like everybody else. And Maritza . . . who knows? Both of them lived in worlds quite different from this one, even if they seemed to inhabit ours. To really get to know those worlds would have required great audacity, and perhaps a different sense of freedom.

I know that my comments at the funeral parlor bothered Cary. I spoke about Maritza's suicide that way to attract her attention. But she didn't remember me. She just gave me a hard stare. Then I realized that her eyes had lost their shine, that the skin around them had started to wrinkle, inevitably so.

She shifted her gaze back to the coffin: gray, absurd like the death that it hid, like Lazarita's sobbing, like the whole ritual. I knew that Cary's thoughts were headed elsewhere, to some uncertain time, perhaps, some private time — someplace where I too, together with Maritza and together with her, would have liked to be.

Until yesterday it was still possible to dream about that. Not any more.

Translated by Dick Cluster

NOTES

1 Marxist economics makes a distinction between use-value (what a good or service is worth in terms of utility) and exchange-value (the price at which it can be bought or sold).
2 Alamar is a large bedroom community outside of Havana, made up mostly of five-story, concrete apartment buildings constructed according to a single basic design. *Barbacoas* are extra rooms made by building a loft within a single high-ceilinged room, especially common in Old Havana and Central Havana.

Elizete, Beckoned (1996)

(From *In Another Place, Not Here*)

Grace. Is grace, yes. And I take it, quiet, quiet, like thiefing sugar. From the word she speak to me and the sweat running down she in that sun, one afternoon as I look up saying to myself, how many more days these poor feet of mine can take this field, these blades of cane like razor, this sun like coal pot. Long as you have to eat, girl. I look up. That woman like a drink of cool water. The four o'clock light thinning she dress, she back good and strong, the sweat raining off in that moment when I look and she snap she head around, that wide mouth blowing a wave of tiredness away, pulling in one big breath of air, them big white teeth, she, falling to the work again, she, falling into the four o'clock sunlight. I see she. Hot, cool and wet. I sink the machete in my foot, careless, blood blooming in the stalks of cane, a sweet ripe smell wash me faint. With pain. Wash the field, spinning green mile after green mile around she. See she sweat, sweet like sugar.

I never wanted nothing big from the world. Who is me to want anything big or small. Who is me to think I is something. I born to clean Isaiah' house and work cane since I was a child and say what you want Isaiah feed me and all I have to do is lay down under him in the night and work the cane in the day. It have plenty woman waiting their whole blessed life for that and what make me turn woman and leave it I don't know, but it come. Bad spirit they say, bad spirit or blessed, it come, what make me notice Verlia' face spraying sweat in the four o'clock heat.

Because you see I know I was going to lose something, because Verl was surer than anything I see before, surer than the day I get born, because nothing ever happen to me until Verl come along and when Verl come along I see my chance out of what ordinary, out of the plenty day when all it have for a woman to do is lie down and let a man beat against she body, and work cane and chop up she foot and make children and choke on the dryness in she chest and have only one road in and the same road out and know that she tied to the ground and can never lift up. And it wasn't nothing Verl do or say or even what Verl was or what Verl wanted because even now I can't swear but is just that I see Verl coming, like a shower of rain coming that could just wash me cool and that was sufficient and if God spite me for this, is so things is.

I abandon everything for Verlia. I sink in Verlia and let she flesh swallow me up. I devour she. She open me up like any morning. Limp, limp and rain light, soft to the marrow. She make me wet. She tongue scorching like hot sun. I love that shudder between her legs, love the plain wash and sea of her, the swell and bloom of her softness. And is all. And if is all I could do on the earth, is all.

She would say, "Open your eyes, I want to see what you're feeling": I don't know what she see in my eyes but she stare into me until I break. Her look say, "Elizete, you is bigger than me by millennia and you can hold me between your legs like rock hold water. You are wearing me away like years and I wonder if you can see me beyond rock and beyond water as something human that need to eat and can die, even as you dive into me today like a fish and want nothing or so you say." Something say to me, Elizete, you is not big enough for nothing you done live and Verlia is your grace.

Isaiah gone mad catching me lying underneath Verlia, and even the sure killing in him couldn't sweep me away from the sweetness of her. I didn't even raise my head. I finished loving Verlia taking she face and she skin black as water in my hand so I was to remember what I lose something for. I never see him after that. They say he sit under a fishing net in Las Cuevas now and he talk to himself, they say he don't remember me but call out the name of the Venezuelan woman what first was his wife and what make him carry she fishing one night and when day break she was not there. They say he is like a jumbie, and is best for me and he to leave that way for it have too much between we, and is vindication what make him open the door. Isaiah was a hard man, a hard man down to his skin. Is best I didn't kill him as I plan, is best I didn't pour the milk of buttercups in his eyes and blind him, is best I didn't sling his neck off, is best I didn't rub his head with killing root. Is best I see this woman when I raise up in my swing, when the sweat was falling like rain from she. I say is grace the way it happen and is grace.

He and me story done right there, one time. It have nothing to say else about it.

Everything make sense from then the way flesh make sense settling into blood. I think to myself how I must be was sleeping all this time. I must be was in a trance because it was as if Verl wake me up to say, "Girl, put on your clothes. Let we go now." It have ways of trancing people and turning them against they very self and I suspect Isaiah now with his prayer book and his plait hair but I have no time with him. I suspect the woman I grow with and she hands that can't stop growing things. I suspect the cane. I suspect Moriah. I suspect my life. I suspect the moon. Everything. What don't meet you don't pass you.

Verl was sure. Sure of everything. And sure like that was not something in my life. I was sure that I would wake up each day, I was sure that I had to work cane, I was sure that the man they give me to was Isaiah Ferdinand. I was sure that he would illtreat me. I was sure that each night I would dream of miles of cane waving. Things like this. I was sure iguana would be thirsty enough to cross the road if the dry season was too long, I was sure birds would fly across the house in the morning. I was sure of what anybody would be sure of. Spite, hunger, rain. But Verl is sure of what she make in her own mind and what she make didn't always exist.

I like it how she leap. Run in the air without moving. I watch she make she way around we as if she was from here, all the time moving faster than the last thing she say. It come so I know where she standing in the field without looking for she. Because she moving, moving, moving all the time without moving. If I didn't like it she would frighten me.

There is a heat that looks like glass waving if you make your eyes look far. Everybody didn't like that moving but everybody eyes was on she the first time she come. She was walking in that heat and we was all in the shed eating. Some was laying down for the while and she reach and start busy busy giving out papers. She look like the transport drop she by the junction and she walk in. People get up and start going but the old ones listen to she. I know why they listen. Is not often that some young one with soft hands and skin smelling of the kind of sweat they make in the town come talking to them. They touch up she clothes and she hands and she face and say, "Who child is you?" They play with she and kiss she up. And it give them a softness like how they might have been if they live in town and if they had money and if their life was different. They give she water and they give she fry fish. They tell she don't drink fast. They love it when she just eat as if she don't scorn them but they laugh when she say what she want. They laugh long. And then they hush.

Nobody here can remember when they wasn't here. I come here with Isaiah. He show me the room and he show me the washtub and he show me the fire and he show me the road. He tell me never let him catch me at the junction. I didn't believe him but I find out soon when I catch the end of his whip. That was long time now. No need to remember. I don't even remember when I stop trying to run away, stop trying to make that junction. It was long. He would always be at that junction when I get there. I tried for a long time. I think to myself one day he is going to miss, one day. One day when he think I train, he is going to miss. But I stop. He get his way. When I see that it was his play, I resign. He stop watching me but then I could not remember why I was trying to get there. Didn't have no place to go anyway when I think of it. Trying to get to the junction so much I forget where I was going. I know every track leading to it but when I get there and see Isaiah, it come like he was the end of it. I used to have some place in mind I know but . . . One time, I plotting my way through the mangle, one of these old ones I never expect ask me, "Where you running running so all the time?" The spite of the thing hit me and it take me by surprise, and I suppose I didn't have nowhere in mind except not here. Cold water just run in my feet then. You trust old people to know better. Why they wouldn't want good for me? If you can't see a way for yourself, see it for somebody else nah? So all of that is how I wear away.

Not a bone in she like that. Verlia. Hatred and anger, but not spite. Spite is loving to see people suffer. She say to me that you could get used to suffering. She say is what curve we back to the cane. Is all we know. Hatred you could out and out deal with, and anger, but not spite. It was her speed though, the way she could make the junction still standing in front of you, the way she could move fast in she head. People say this is not people to trust, people who know what you saying before you say it, people hurrying you up to move, them kinda people busy busy going someplace soon but I was ready for Verlia. She get send for me.

She was burning. You could see she burning bright. Before you know it they making sweet bread for she, before you know it washtub full of ice cream done plan. Before you know it she invite for Sunday. I suppose not only me see rescue when she reach.

I used to wonder who she went home to; watch she walk to the junction in the evening half dead and wonder if her quickness fall away on the transport, wondered if she was the same in town, what she kitchen smell like, and if she plant okra and what she think. Soon I was only wondering about she. I watch she disappear up the junction and I wait for she to break it in the mornings. Is nothing that draw me to she but that and the way she want nothing from me and the way she brand new and come from another life.

After the woman I lived with die on me I was given to Isaiah. She passed on when I was not yet a young lady. It seem to me that one day I wake up under

Isaiah. Isaiah ride me every night. I was a horse for his jumbie. His face was like the dead over me on the floor when he cry out for the woman who leave him as he ride me to hell. Each night I hear him say these words as if I should pity him. "When I meet that Venezuelan woman it was the last day of my life. She sail me like a ship. That woman could tell stories. It was through one of her tales that I arrived at this sandpit with my back breaking and my eyes burning with this sweat, with her fine clothes and her fine ideas; I laid every brick on that stone house where she take man in front of me. My hair turn red and I never scream in this place yet." With that he ride me again. These times I wander, I turn my head to the wall and travel in the dust tunnels of wood lice. I cover my self in their fine, fine sand, I slide through the tunnel and I see all where I have to go, and I try to reach where they live and I try to be like them because try as I did when I was little I never see one of them yet only the rifts on the walls. Is so they work in secret and in their own company. Is so I travel the walls of this room catching hell and Isaiah' advantage till morning. I dream every day to break a shovel over his head which he plait in braids for he read in the Bible that he should not cut his hair. Every evening when they was in season he would climb the land above the quarry to pick cashew fruit and nuts. I would stand at the bottom looking at him hoping that the bitter juice from the fruit burn him to death for I know that it is poison. I carried a mountain inside of me. The thought of him and his hardness cut at the red stone in me from sun-up to sundown. I went in the evenings after work to the sand quarry while he sleep. The salmon dank sides rise up around me and I was silent there. It was a place where I had peace, or I wouldn't call it peace but calm, and I shovelled, the sweat drizzling from my body as I think and think of escaping him. I did not sympathize with him, no matter what he said that red woman do to him. What she make him eat, how she tie his mind. It could not compensate for what he do to me. There in the damp, it make me calm, calm, calm and hollow inside me. If I dig enough it cool me and take my mind off the junction. I feel my body full up and burst. All my skin split. Until I was so tired I could not run. I dream of running though, to Aruba or Maracaibo. I hear about these place. Yes, Maracaibo. I love the sound of it yet I have never seen it. I dream of taking his neck with a cutlass and running to Maracaibo, yes. I imagine it as a place with thick and dense vine and alive like veins under my feet. I dream the vine, green and plump, blood running through it and me too running running, spilling blood. Vine like rope under my feet, vine strapping my legs and opening when I walk. Is like nowhere else. I destroying anything in my way. I want it to be peaceful there. The air behind me close thick as mist whenever

I move and Maracaibo open rough and green and dense again. I dream I spit milk each time my mouth open. My stomach will swell and vines will burst out. I dream it is a place where a woman can live after she done take the neck of a man. Fearless. I dream my eyes, black and steady in my black face and never close. I will wear a black skirt, shapely like a wing and down to my toes. I will fly to Maracaibo in it and you will see nothing of me but my black eyes in my black face and my black skirt swirling over thick living vine. I dream of flying in my skirt to Maracaibo. I want to go to Maracaibo if it is the last thing I do. This black skirt will melt like soot if it get touched. And my face too. One day I will do it, for Isaiah don't know my mind in this. He too busy in his own mind now. He make his heart too hard to know anyone else. One day I will done calculate him.

The time in between as I say I don't remember but it must have been there because by the time I recognize myself I was a big woman and the devil was riding me. How I reach here is one skill I learn hard. The skill of forgetfulness. So I shovel in this pit from morning till night, cut cane when it in season and lie under this man at night until one day I see this woman talking, talking like she know what she is saying and everybody around listening. I walk past because I have no time for no woman talking. It don't mean nothing. It don't matter what woman say in the world, take it from me. This woman with her mouth flying . . . cheups. I hear something about cooperative. Black people could ever cooperate? This little girl too fast again. Her mouth too fast, she tongue flying ahead of sheself. Face plain as day, mouth like a ripe mango and teeth, teeth like a horse. I en't talk to she then. They tell me she is for the revo, that she is for taking all the land and giving it to people who work it all their life. Revolution, my ass. Let foolish old people believe she. Is only them have time to sit down and get wrap up in her mouth and think Oliviere and them will let go any land. Is only one thing will fix Oliviere and them and is the devil because them is the devil' son self. I pass by her going my way and didn't that woman skin she big teeth for me and look at me so clear is as if she see all my mind clear through to Maracaibo. Her look say, "I know you. I know you plan to sling off a man' neck and go to Maracaibo." I brazen she look and I pass she straight. Smelling vetiver and salt, fresh ironed clothes I pass she. Nobody from no town coming to look me in my face so. Nobody coming here to tell me what I done know. Anything she do could help me? Who she think she is come preaching here? Revolution, my backside. Then, she say "Sister." And I could not tell if it was a breeze passing in that heat-still day or if I hear the word. "Sister." I know I hear it, murmuring just enough to seem as if it was said but not something that only have sense in saying. I know I hear it silver, silver clinking like bracelets when a woman lift her arm to comb hair. Silvery, silvery the wind take it. It hum low and touch everything on the road. Things in me. I feel it cuff my back. I have to take air. A spirit in the road. It make a silence. It feel like rum going through my throat, warm and violent so the breath of her mouth brush my ear. Sweet sweet, my tongue sweet to answer she and it surprise me how I want to touch she teeth and hold she mouth on that word. I keep walking. I don't answer. But I regret every minute until I see she next.

The next time she come playing she trying to swing cutlass with she mouth moving as fast as you please about strike. Strike and demand a share in the estate. Well, look at bold face. We navel string bury here, she say, and we mother and we father and everybody before them. Oliviere use it up like manure for the cane, and what we get, one barrack room and credit in he store until we owe he more than he owe we, and is thief he thief this place in the first place. The people listen to she and smile because they know she make sense but she don't know what a hard people these Oliviere is. Is not just people navel string bury here is their shame and their body. They churn that up in the soil here too. It have people they just shoot and leave for corbeau to eat them. What left make the cane fat and juicy. She come from town and God knows where light, light and easy so. She not ready yet. One for she, she work hard. She body en't make for this, well who body make for it, but she do it.

She break my swing. It was the quiet. When I get used to she talking as I bend into the cane, when I done add she up for the swing so I wouldn't miss doing how much I need to do to make the quota, when I make she voice count in the stroke, I don't hear she no more. I swing up. What she doing now, like she tired talk at last. Good Lord! I say to myself, God wasn't joking when he make you girl. She was in front of me, staring my way, sweating as if she come out of a river. She was brilliant. I could see she head running ahead of we, she eyes done cut all the cane, she is not here, she dreaming of things we don't dream. I wanted to touch the shine of her, to dry off she whole body and say, "Don't work it so hard," show she how to swing, how to tie up she waist so that she back would last, shield she legs so that the sheaf would- n't cut. That is the first time I feel like licking she neck. She looked like the young in me, the not beaten down and bruised, the not pounded between my legs, the not lost my mother, the not raped, the not blooded, the not tired. She looked like me fresh, fresh, searching for good luck tea, leave my house broom, come by here weed. It ease me. It sweet sweet. A woman can be a bridge, limber and living, breathless, because she don't know where the bridge might lead, she don't need no assurance except that it would lead out with certainty, no assurance except the arch and disappearance. At the end it might be the uptake of air, the chasm of what she don't know, the sweep and soar of sheself unhandled, making sheself a way to cross over. A woman can be a bridge from these bodies whipping cane. A way to cross over. I see in she face how she believe. She glance quick as if unimportant things was in she way, like Oliviere, like fright. She eyes move as if she was busy going some-where, busy seeing something and all this cane all this whipping and lashing was a hindrance. Then like a purposeful accident she eyes rest on me, and she face open, them big teeth push out to laugh for me, sweat flying, she fall again to the cutlass.

TIMOTHY S. CHIN

"Bullers" and "Battymen":
Contesting Homophobia in Black Popular Culture and Contemporary Caribbean Literature (1997)

The recent controversy surrounding Buju Banton, the Jamaican dancehall "don" — which, like so many contemporary debates about race, gender, and sexuality, has been played out in the theater of popular culture — demonstrates the high ideological stakes as well as the discursive limits that determine current discussions of gay and lesbian sexuality and Caribbean culture. Occasioned by the circulation over North American airwaves of Banton's popular dancehall tune "Boom Bye Bye," the controversy provides a prime example of the cross-cultural conflicts and contradictions that are often generated by the increasingly globalized markets of the culture industry. The debate, as it was staged in the pages of the popular press (*New York Post*, *Village Voice*) and periodicals associated with the music industry (*VIBE*, *Billboard*), concerned the alleged homophobia displayed in the lyrics of Banton's song.[1] According to an article that appeared in the *Village Voice*, two groups — GLAAD (Gay and Lesbian Alliance Against Defamation) and GMAD (Gay Men of African Descent) — joined forces in 1992 to "decode Buju Banton's bullet-riddled patois" and "embarked on a media campaign to have 'Boom Bye Bye' removed from the playlists of radio stations WBLS and WRKS." Peter Noel and Robert Marriot, the co-authors of the *Village Voice* article, applauded GLAAD for boldly defining the meaning of *diversity* and *tolerance* for Banton. Insisting on a literal reading of Banton's lyrics, Noel and Marriot state that the song "advocates the execution of gay men" and, consequently, reflects the especially virulent forms of homophobia that are rampant in Caribbean culture generally and Jamaican culture specifically.[2]

Interestingly enough, the critics who have — to varying degrees — defended Banton also tend to rely primarily on culturally based arguments. However, these critics typically assert that Banton's lyrics should be understood metaphorically and that metropolitan critics have therefore misread both Banton's song and the "indigenous" culture from which it springs. For example, in a piece written for *VIBE*, Joan Morgan criticizes certain North American reviewers for their "ignorance of Jamaican street culture" and their inability or unwillingness to "grasp the metaphoric richness of Jamaican patois."[3] In addition, Morgan contends that Buju Banton's refusal to apologize for "Boom Bye Bye" "makes the most sense" given his first and ultimate commitment to the "hardcore dancehall audience" to whom Banton owes his success. According to Morgan, Banton's loyalty to this (cultural) constituency has been rewarded — unlike what is conversely seen as Shabba Ranks's capitulation to the powers that be — with an even greater adulation from his "true" fans.[4]

Carolyn Cooper, a well known Jamaican literary and cultural critic, has likewise insisted that Banton's gun is essentially a "lyrical" one that is meant to illustrate "the function of metaphor and role play in contemporary Jamaican dancehall culture."[5] Consequently, Cooper argues that critics who are unfamiliar with the metaphorical qualities of the Jamaican vernacular have misread Banton's song by taking his words all too literally: "Thus, taken out of context, the popular Jamaican Creole declaration, 'aal bati-man fi ded,' may be misunderstood as an unequivocal, literal death-sentence: 'all homosexuals must die.' " In contrast, Cooper suggests that Banton's "lyrical gun" should be understood primarily as a "symbolic penis" and, therefore, "in the final analysis, the song can be seen as a symbolic celebration of the vaunted potency of heterosexual men who know how to use their lyrical gun to satisfy their women."[6]

Although critics like Cooper and Morgan have rightfully exposed the ethnocentrism that typically informs dominant accounts of the controversy — which often suggest, for example, that North American culture is more advanced and therefore less homophobic than its Caribbean counterpart — their arguments, nevertheless, tend to reinforce a notion of culture that relies on certain fixed oppositions between native and foreign, indigenous and metropolitan, us and them, and so on. Even if we concede that their arguments do not seek "to legitimate homophobia on so-called cultural grounds," as one response to Morgan's *VIBE* piece alleges,[7] these critics have nevertheless missed a crucial opportunity to challenge the deeply rooted homophobia that is unmistakably reflected in Banton's lyrics and that, more importantly, pervades Caribbean societies, as it does most third and first world cultures. In contrast to the reactive or defensive postures implied by such arguments, it is necessary — especially given the complex ideological issues currently surrounding the question of black cultural production — to formulate modes of cultural criticism that can account for the differences within as well as between cultures. In addition, our contemporary situation calls for a cultural politics that can critique as well as affirm — a politics that recognizes, in other words, the heterogeneous and contradictory (as opposed to homogeneous and monolithic) nature of all cultural formations. In the words of Jamaican anthropologist Charles V. Carnegie, "Even as we seek to restore 'indigenous' knowledge' systems, we must simultaneously seek to sharpen an 'indigenous' criticism."[8]

Despite the limitations that currently define the terms in which the debate has been carried out, the Banton controversy — as Cooper ironically notes — nevertheless opens a critical space for talking about questions of gay and lesbian sexuality and homophobia as they pertain to Caribbean culture.[9] Using this critical space as a point of departure, I would like to continue and extend this dialogue by exploring the representation of gay and lesbian sexuality in contemporary Anglophone Caribbean narratives. Such an exploration implicitly assumes that the texts in question inevitably reflect and, indeed, participate in (by reinforcing or contesting) the sexual ideologies that pervade the wider culture.

If the Buju Banton controversy represents a manifestation of how such questions have recently erupted in the realm of the popular, Caribbean literary production has traditionally maintained a conspicuous silence around issues of gay and lesbian sexuality. In this case, the absence of representation is perhaps the most telling factor, especially when we consider the earlier decades of literary activity. Nevertheless, there are writers — like Claude McKay and Paule Marshall, for instance — for whom gay and lesbian sexuality or "homosexuality" remains an important subtextual issue, and one that is intimately and inextricably intertwined with other, more explicit narrative preoccupations. In addition, there are more recent writers — emerging particularly within the last three decades — who have broken the taboo that has previously surrounded the question of gay and lesbian sexuality and homophobia in Caribbean culture. These writers have vigorously challenged the patriarchal and heterosexual ideologies that have resulted in the marginalization of women and gay men at the same time that they have continued to expose the social and political structures that serve to perpetuate the region's colonial legacy. Consequently, these writers have made the critique of homophobic and sexist ideologies an integral component of what we might call a decolonized Caribbean discourse.

CLAUDE MCKAY AND THE CONSTRUCTION
OF (UN)NATURAL SEXUALITIES

A pioneering Jamaican writer who migrated to the United States in 1912, Claude McKay was, needless to say, a product of his time. In his biography of McKay, Wayne Cooper notes that although there is ample evidence to confirm his homosexuality, McKay never publicly identified himself as a homosexual and "like many homosexual writers of his day, did not seriously challenge the rule that such subjects were not to be discussed openly in creative literature."[10] Therefore, it is not surprising that McKay's most successful narratives — *Home to Harlem* (1928), *Banjo* (1929), and *Banana Bottom* (1933) — do not deal, at least in any explicit way, with the subject of homosexuality or contain any overt homosexual characters. On the contrary, *Home to Harlem* and *Banjo* both feature swaggering, good-natured, hypermasculine protagonists, who are emphatically and unequivocally heterosexual. Passionate, sensual, and instinctive, Jake and Banjo embody the African American folk spirit that the narratives celebrate, representing what Bernard Bell calls "romantic prototypes of the rootlessness, creativity, and spiritual resilience of the common people of the race."[11]

Nevertheless, *Home to Harlem* and *Banjo* construct what is, in effect, a "homosocial" world of men interacting predominantly with other men.[12] This exclusively male domain is defined by the gamblers, musicians, hustlers, sailors, soldiers, Pullman porters, cooks, and waiters who typically populate McKay's novels. Although women are frequently objects of the protagonists' sexual desire — Jake's "tantalizing brown" in *Home to Harlem,* for example — the values and codes of this masculine domain are the ones that Jake and Banjo must strive to uphold and that the novels ultimately reinscribe and celebrate. Despite the vitality and passion with which McKay typically imbues his protagonists, the forms of masculinity that the narratives inscribe do not ultimately depart from traditional notions of maleness and masculine behavior. Indeed, McKay's folk heroes reflect and even reinforce dominant sexual ideologies by asserting a masculinity that is predicated on both sexism and homophobia. For example, during one of his stints as a cook working in a railroad dining car, Jake encounters a waiter reading a "French" (clearly a code for homosexual) novel. While questioning the waiter about the book — a story by Alphonse Daudet entitled *Sappho* — he begins to hum a tune that makes explicit the link between the novel's particular figuration of masculine identity and the sexist and homophobic values on which it depends: "And it is ashes to ashes and dust to dust, / Can you show me a woman a man can trust? / And there is two things in Harlem I don't understan' / It is a bulldycking woman and a faggotty man."[13]

McKay's participation in a discourse of primitivism that prevailed in both black and white literary circles of the era resulted in the replication of certain essentialist notions about blackness and black sexuality in particular. Reflecting tendencies that were more or less prevalent in the major literary and cultural movements that distinguished the period — the Harlem Renaissance in the United States and Négritude in Africa and the Caribbean, for example — McKay's texts constructed a notion of blackness that reinscribed a racial binary in which blacks were once again associated — albeit in a positive sense — with the realm of instincts, emotions, and passions, with sensuality, sexuality, and all that was considered "natural."

McKay's depictions of black urban life undoubtedly worked to disrupt class-bound notions of appropriateness and respectability — a fact that the negative response of certain black intellectuals to his work only serves to confirm.[14] In addition, his novels broke new ground in the sense that they challenged the taboo surrounding the representation of black sexuality. At the same time, however, his reinscription of a racial binary — especially one that depends so crucially on a category of the "natural" — implicitly articulates the very terms that have historically been used not only to devalue black cultures but also to marginalize gay and lesbian sexualities. The Caribbean feminist scholar M. Jacqui Alexander has demonstrated, for example, how the "naturalization" of heterosexuality as state law has traditionally depended on the designation of gay and lesbian sex as "unnatural." Furthermore, Alexander points out that "there is no absolute set of commonly understood or accepted principles called the 'natural' which can be invoked definitionally except as they relate to what is labelled 'unnatural.' "[15]

The reinscription of this category of the natural and its implicit corollary the unnatural is implicated even more explicitly in McKay's third novel, *Banana Bottom,* which is set in his native Caribbean. McKay's narrative is structured around a series of oppositions that include the native versus the European, Obeah versus Christianity, the primitive versus the civilized, instinct versus intellect, folk culture versus high culture, spontaneous warmth versus cultivated refinement, natural growth versus artificial growth, and so on. Within this schema, the female protagonist, Bita Plant — a name which is clearly meant to suggest the character's rootedness in the "native" soil of Jamaican folk culture — represents the triumph of "indigenous" cultural values over the metropolitan ones that have been imposed upon her. Consequently, Bita maintains an inherent and "instinctive" connection to the language, culture, and folkways of the rural peasantry from which she springs, despite her European education and the "seven years of polite upbringing" provided by the Craigs, the British missionary couple who adopted Bita and sent her to England.

Moreover, McKay's valorization of indigenous culture also entails the affirmation of a "native" sexuality, specifically coded as natural and therefore necessarily counterposed to the possibility of an unnatural or "aberrant" sexuality. Bita's marriage at the end of the novel to Jubban the drayman—instead of to Herald Newton Day, the Craigs's choice for Bita—signals the triumph of this natural sexuality as much as it represents the affirmation of an indigenous Jamaican folk culture. Like Jordan Plant, Bita's father—over whose literal dead body Bita and Jubban consummate their love—Jubban "possessed a deep feeling for the land" and he was "a lucky-born cultivator."[16] Jubban's sexual desires for Bita—and hers for him—are thus associated with the natural cycles of birth and death, growth and decay that determine the rhythms of peasant life. Furthermore, the sexuality that their union affirms is consequently linked to the reproductive laws that supposedly govern nature as well as humankind.

In contrast to Jubban's "natural" sexuality, Herald Newton Day, the promising young deacon who tragically "defiled himself with a nanny goat," represents the epitome of an "unnatural" sexuality. Whether explained as an "aberration" within nature as Teacher Fearon suggests or "the result of too much exclusive concentration on sacred textbooks and holy communion" as Squire Gensir conjectures (176–77), Herald's behavior constitutes a deviation from the (reproductive and heterosexual) norm that defines the "instinctive" sexuality of the black peasantry. In addition to reinforcing notions about racial atavism that circulate throughout the text, Herald's "aberrant" behavior also serves to confirm the novel's premise of the potentially degenerating effects of an overcivilized, sexually repressed, Western (European) civilization that privileges intellect over instinct, reason over emotions.

McKay's construction of a dichotomy between "natural" and "unnatural" sexualities consequently fixes "native" sexuality within certain narrow terms —restricting it to an exclusively reproductive function, for example—at the same time that it seems to link aberrant or unnatural sexual behavior (bestiality, rape, and presumably other forms of non-procreative sex) to the effects of either miscegenation or foreign "decadence and degeneracy."[17] Indeed, McKay's depiction of Squire Gensir—the eccentric Englishman who befriends Bita—prefigures, to a certain extent, the representation (in Paule Marshall's *The Chosen Place, The Timeless People* [1969], for example) of homosexuality and the homosexual as products of foreign "contamination."

As Cooper points out in his biography, Squire Gensir represents the "fictional prototype" for Walter Jekyll—the eccentric Englishman who served as one of McKay's literary patrons. Although Cooper acknowledges Jekyll's homosexuality, he cautiously asserts that in all probability "Jekyll's admiration and love . . . expressed itself wholly in his role as mentor and friend."[18] Given the unspoken taboo that in McKay's time precluded the explicit representation of homosexual characters, it is certainly not surprising that Jekyll's homosexuality is sublimated in the portrayal of Squire Gensir. Nevertheless, the traces of this repressed homosexuality are discernible in Gensir's so-called "eccentricity," his life-long bachelorhood, and his admission that he was "not a marrying man."[19] Indeed, the complete desexualization of Gensir within the novel underscores—by way of its conspicuous absence—what the narrative is unable to name. According to the text, Gensir "lived aloof from sexual contact" and was, as Mrs. Craig often remarked, "a happy old bachelor with . . . not the slightest blemish upon his character —a character about which nothing was whispered either *naturally* or otherwise" (emphasis added; 92). To the extent that Gensir remains an outsider whose appreciation of Jamaican folk culture is ultimately "merely cerebral" (85), the homosexuality (however latent) implied in his characterization is likewise encoded as non-native and therefore "foreign."

(NEO)COLONIALISM AND (HOMO)SEXUALITY
IN PAULE MARSHALL'S
THE CHOSEN PLACE, THE TIMELESS PEOPLE

In an exchange that in many ways echoes the cultural politics of the Buju Banton controversy, Hortense Spillers takes issue with Judith Fetterley's claim that Paule Marshall's novel, *The Chosen Place, The Timeless People*, is "homophobic." Fetterley's allegation is presumably based on her reading of the brief lesbian affair that takes place between Merle, the novel's protagonist, and a wealthy white woman who serves as her "London patroness." In an attempt to account for the divergence between her interpretation and that of Fetterley, Spillers suggests that the disagreement represents "an illustration of the sorts of conflicts that arise among discontinuous reading and interpretive communities." In addition, Spillers argues that Merle's lesbian encounter is not "a major thematic issue in the novel" and suggests instead that Marshall is more concerned in the episode with "the particular dynamics of colonial politics and its involvement on the intimate ground of feeling."[20]

Although Spillers's reading of the ways in which the relationship between Merle and her London patroness reflects the inequities of the colonial relation is certainly astute, the question of the novel's "homophobia" is not (or should not be) so easily dismissed. Rather than choosing between readings that emphasize either colonial *or* sexual politics, I would argue that the two are inextricably linked in Marshall's text and that Merle's encounter with the white lesbian functions as a trenchant critique of colonialism at the same time that it reinscribes certain dominant sexual ideologies. In fact, I would argue that this particular conjunction of the sexual and the colonial in Marshall's novel reflects the terms in which anti-colonial arguments were often constructed in certain "Afrocentric" or black nationalist discourses that characterized the period. Consequently, Marshall's formulation demonstrates how such discourses — especially insofar as they rely on notions of family or "race" as family — are always already gendered, always already, in Stuart Hall's words, "underpinned by a particular sexual economy, a particular figured masculinity [or femininity], a particular class identity," and so on.[21]

Although the "lesbian episode" may not appear to occupy a central place in the thematic scheme of the novel — Spillers points out, for example, that the encounter is only retrospectively recalled by Merle — it can (and should) be read alongside other episodes where the question of homosexuality is either implicitly or explicitly raised. A pattern of representation might, thus, be established in terms of the recirculation of certain ideologies of gender and sexuality within the narrative. These ideologies have to do not only with positioning gay and lesbian sexuality as foreign and/or unnatural but also with prescribing normative boundaries for male and female gender identity in general.

The affair between Merle and her London patroness is clearly meant to signify the asymmetries of the colonial relationship itself. This link between sexual and imperial motives is made explicit when Merle recalls her patroness's preference for "foreigners": "During the time I lived there I met people from every corner of the globe: India, Asia, Africa . . . all over the place. The sun, you might say, never set on the little empire she had going in her drawing room."[22] In addition, Merle's account of the indebtedness and dependency that the wealthy white woman would deliberately and strategically encourage exposes one of the primary mechanisms by which post-independence Caribbean states — like the fictitious Bourne Island — are kept under the crush of the neocolonial heel. However, at the same time that the portrayal of Merle's encounter with the English woman enacts an insightful critique of (neo)colonial politics, it simultaneously reinscribes a rhetoric that positions gay and lesbian sexuality as unnatural and foreign. Describing the "wild crowd" she fell in with, Merle states that they (the English) were "experts at making anything they do seem perfectly *natural,* and getting you to think so, too." In addition, she describes her patroness as "one of those upperclass types you hear of over there who don't seem to mind having produced a *degenerate* or two" (emphases added; 327–28).

This association of gay and lesbian sexuality with the unnatural also informs Marshall's characterization of the gay tourists who frequent Sugar's, the local nightclub. Like Merle's patroness, the gay men are portrayed as predators; their exploitation of "native" sexuality serves as an emblem of the economic exploitation that defines the neocolonial regime. Pointing out this group of affluent gay white men to Saul Amron, the white protagonist and later Merle's lover, Merle exclaims: "As for that bunch out on the balcony . . . Not a boy child over the age of three is safe since they arrived on the island" (87). Nevertheless, at the same time that it reflects an acute and subtle understanding of the way that the colonial dynamic permeates all levels of indigenous life—including what Spillers calls "the intimate ground of feeling"—this characterization also reinforces certain stereotypical notions about the unnaturalness of gay sexuality. The narrator states that these men "had the overstated gestures of their kind, as well as the *unnaturally* high voices that called attention to themselves and the laugh that was as shrill and sexless as a eunuch's, and which never ceased" (emphasis added; 88).

As M. Jacqui Alexander points out, these narrative figurations that position gay and lesbian sexuality as unnatural also serve to naturalize heterosexuality as an implicit norm.[23] In addition to ensnaring her in a cycle of debt and dependency, Merle's liaison with the English lesbian has the effect of destabilizing her identity as a woman. Merle admits that the "business between her and myself . . . had me so I didn't know who or what I was." And she confesses to Saul that when she finally decided to sever the ties with her patroness it was because "most of all . . . I was curious to see if a man would maybe look at me twice."[24] In other words, Merle's recuperation of a stable black female identity seems to hinge on her ability to attract the sexual attentions of a (heterosexual) male. In fact, Merle is eventually "saved" from the corrupting influence of the white lesbian not only by a man, but also through marriage and motherhood—in other words, the type of sexual relationship that epitomizes the heterosexual norm, what Alexander calls "conjugal heterosexuality."[25] Recalling her brief marriage to Ketu—the committed Ugandan nationalist she met in London—Merle states that "most of all, he made me know I was a woman. . . . After years of not being sure what I was, whether fish or fowl or what, I knew with him I was a woman and no one would ever again be able to make me believe otherwise. I still love him for that."[26] In the novel, Merle's lesbian affair represents a betrayal not only of her "true womanhood"—the "great wrong" that Ketu finds it impossible to forgive—but also of her anti-colonial politics, her family, and ultimately her "race." Afraid that Merle's touch might somehow "contaminate" their child, Ketu eventually abandons Merle and returns to Africa, taking their daughter with him. Demonstrating the degree to which she has internalized the supposed naturalness of the heterosexual norm, Merle herself is convinced that Ketu's actions are entirely justified. From another perspective, one might convincingly argue that Ketu leaves primarily because the knowledge of Merle's lesbian affair threatens his own sense of masculinity.

Similarly, Marshall's portrait of Allen Fuso, Saul's young assistant, implicitly assumes the universality or "naturalness" of a normative heterosexual masculinity. Although Allen's (latent) homosexuality is more complexly delineated than that of Merle's London patroness or the gay men at Sugar's, the resolution (or the lack thereof) of his "identity crisis" ultimately reveals the narrative's refusal to imagine anything other than a heterosexual solution to his "problem." Allen's crisis is precipitated by the homosexual feelings that are occasioned by his growing friendship with Vere, the "native son" who has returned home to Bourne Island after a brief stint on a labor scheme in the United States. Moreover, Allen's homosexuality is represented in the narrative as a kind of arrested development that is the consequence of an unresolved castration anxiety. Allen is unable to perform (hetero)sexually with Elvita—the date that Vere arranges for him during Carnival—not only because he finds women's bodies which "lacked purity of line with the upjutting breasts and buttocks" distasteful, but also because of "his fear, borne of a recurrent phantasy of his as a boy, that once he entered that dark place hidden away at the base of their bodies, he would not be able to extricate himself" (309).

Alone on the settee, with Vere and Milly making love on the other side of the screen, Allen performs a solitary sexual act that signifies in the text not only a substitute for intercourse but also a parody of the (heterosexual) sex act itself. As Allen masturbates to the sounds of the unseen lovers, the image of Vere looms large in his imagination: "The girl was faceless, unimportant, but he saw Vere clearly: his dark body rising and falling, advancing and retreating, like one of the powerful Bournehills waves they sometimes rode together in the early evening" (312). Allen, in effect, erases Milly from the scene and puts himself in her place, thus becoming what he has subconsciously longed to be—namely, Vere's lover. "His cry at the end, which he tried to stifle but could not, broke at the same moment the girl uttered her final cry, and the two sounds rose together, blending one into the other, becoming a single complex note of the most profound pleasure and release" (312).

Given the ambiguity of the text—especially where issues of gay and lesbian sexuality are concerned—it is difficult to determine the extent to which Allen is aware (consciously, at least) of his own homosexuality. Nevertheless, he admits to Merle—in an attempt to explain the deep depression that had overtaken him since the events of Carnival and the subsequent death of Vere—that he longs for "something that wasn't so safe and sure all the time" or even "something people didn't approve of so they no longer thought of me as such a nice, respectable type." The obvious inadequacy of Merle's response —she recommends "a nice girl and some children"—is not surprising, given the guilt she has internalized as a result of her own lesbian affair (378–81). However, her response also reflects the novel's investment in and recirculation of an ideology that naturalizes heterosexuality while it positions gay and lesbian sexuality as deviant or unnatural. Furthermore, Merle's inability to imagine anything other than a conventional heterosexual (and reproductive) solution to Allen's "problem" not only defines the limits of the novel's discourse on questions of homosexuality, it also exposes one of the consequences —inherent in certain black nationalist discourses, for example—of uncritically conflating race with notions (especially naturalized ones) of family.

MICHELLE CLIFF, H. NIGEL THOMAS, AND THE CONTRADICTIONS OF REPRESENTING THE "INDIGENOUS" GAY/LESBIAN SUBJECT

> We are always in negotiation, not with a single set of oppositions that place us always in the same relation to others, but with a series of different positionalities. Each has for us its point of profound subjective identification. And that is the most difficult thing about this proliferation of the field of identities and antagonisms: they are often dislocating in relation to one another.— STUART HALL, "What Is This 'Black' in Black Popular Culture?"

In an essay in which he attempts to map the critical challenges presented by the current historical conjuncture, Stuart Hall suggests that "it is to the diversity, not the homogeneity, of black experience that we must now give our undivided creative attention." Hall argues that, given the emergence of what he refers to as "a new kind of cultural politics," it is necessary now more than ever to "recognize the other kinds of difference [those of gender, sexuality, and class, for example] that place, position, and locate black people."[27] Two recent Caribbean writers — Michelle Cliff (Jamaica) and H. Nigel Thomas (St. Vincent) — have produced texts which reflect the way anti-colonial/imperial discourses need to be conceptualized in the context of the present historical and cultural situation. Attending to the differences that operate within as well as between cultures, these texts simultaneously critique the sexist/homophobic and colonial/neocolonial structures that continue to pervade contemporary Caribbean societies. By posing an implicit challenge to the binary oppositions that often define discussions of "native" sexuality, writers like Cliff and Thomas have cleared a discursive space for the articulation of an "indigenous" gay/lesbian subjectivity.

In contrast to these binary structures — which often imply the mutually exclusive choice of an either/or — these writers frequently deploy narrative strategies that privilege ambiguity and the ability to negotiate contradictions. For example, in an essay entitled "If I Could Write This in Fire, I Would Write This in Fire," Michelle Cliff relates an incident that underscores the contradictions generated by a Caribbean lesbian identity — contradictions that illustrate, in Hall's terms, how the multiple "positionalities" that inevitably constitute such an identity "are often dislocating in relation to one another." Cliff becomes justifiably enraged when she and Henry, a distant cousin who is "recognizably black and speaks with an accent," are refused service in a London bar. Although she is light-skinned enough to "pass" for white, Cliff states that she has "chosen sides." However, the lines suddenly become blurred — and allegiances begin to shift — when her cousin joins his white colleagues in a "sustained mockery" of the waiters in a gay-owned restaurant.[28] The conflicting feelings of anger (at Henry's homophobia/sexism) and solidarity (because he is also a victim of racism and colonial oppression) that exemplify Cliff's response to Henry mirror the profound ambivalence she feels towards Jamaica itself — the "killing ambivalence" that comes with the realization that home (especially for the "lesbian of color") is often a site of alienation as well as identification.[29]

This ambivalence is also reflected in the dual strategy that informs Cliff's first novel, *Abeng* (1984). On one hand, the narrative affirms the value of an indigenous Jamaican culture — especially the oral traditions and folk practices that embody the island's long history of anti-colonial resistance. On the other, the novel elaborates an incisive critique of the oppressive ideological structures that continue to pervade the postcolonial state—a deeply entrenched color-caste system, homophobia, and sexism, for example. Exemplifying the formal and stylistic innovations that are characteristic of her work, Cliff deliberately disrupts the narrative continuity of *Abeng* by intercutting the story of Clare Savage—the novel's young female protagonist—with fragments of history, myth, and legend. In her attempt to reconstruct what the critic Simon Gikandi calls a "repressed Afro-Caribbean history,"[30] Cliff inscribes a revisionary account that challenges not only the Eurocentric premises of conventional historiography but also its phallocentric and heterosexist assumptions as well. In other words, in addition to representing a female-centered tradition of resistance, *Abeng* also attempts to posit a historical or "genealogical" precedent for an indigenous lesbian/gay subjectivity.

Although it would perhaps be a historical misnomer to label Mma Alli—the mythical figure who plays a part in the novel's reconstruction of Caribbean slave resistance—a lesbian character per se, she clearly represents the possibility of an indigenous or even Afrocentric precedent for a non-heterosexual orientation:

> Mma Alli had never lain with a man. The other slaves said she loved only women in that way, but that she was a true sister to the men—the Black men: her brothers. They said that by being with her in bed, women learned all manner of the magic of passion. How to become wet again and again all through the night. How to soothe and excite at the same time. How to touch a woman in her deep-inside and make her womb move within her.[31]

Descended from a line of "one-breasted warrior women," Mma Alli is spiritually if not biologically related to Maroon Nanny—the slave leader who, according to local legend, "could catch a bullet between her buttocks and render the bullet harmless" (14)—and all the other female figures who function as historical precursors in a tradition from which Clare ("colonized child" that she is) has become tragically disconnected.

In addition to inscribing a proto-lesbian figure within the reconstructed mythology of an Afro-Caribbean past, Cliff exposes the homophobia that results in the marginalization and persecution of lesbians and gay men within contemporary Jamaican culture. These deeply ingrained homophobic attitudes—which reflect a fear of "difference"—represent one of the primary means by which a normative heterosexuality is consolidated and, indeed, enforced. For example, the story of Clinton, the son of "Mad Hannah," demonstrates what can happen if one is even suspected of being homosexual.

When Clinton is "taken with a cramp while . . . swimming in the river," he is left to drown while "shouts of 'battyman, battyman' echoed off the rocks and across the water of the swimming hole" (63). Likewise, the fate of an uncle who was rumored to be "funny" serves as an implicit warning to Clare against the dangers of transgressing the boundaries of what is culturally sanctioned as acceptable or "normal" sexual behavior. Although Clare was "not sure what 'funny' meant," she "knew that Robert had caused some disturbance when he brought a dark man home from Montego Bay and introduced him to his mother as 'my dearest friend.'" Stigmatized and ostracized by his family, Robert finally "did what Clare understood many 'funny' 'queer' 'off' people did: He swam too far out into Kingston Harbor and could not swim back. He drowned just as Clinton — about whom there had been similar whispers — had drowned" (125–26).

In Cliff's second novel, *No Telephone to Heaven* (1987), the ambivalence of the Caribbean gay/lesbian subject is literally embodied by the character Harry/Harriet — the "boy-girl" who serves as the friend, confidant, and alter ego of an older Clare Savage. In the very indeterminacy of his/her name, Harry/Harriet reflects the unresolved (and perhaps unresolvable) contradictions that are inevitably generated by an indigenous gay or lesbian identity. Constantly transgressing the boundaries that supposedly separate male from female, upper from lower classes, insider from outsider, self from "other," natural from unnatural sexuality, Harry/Harriet inhabits an "interstitial" space — designated by the conjunction "both/and" rather than "either/or" — that, as he/she asserts, is "not just sun, but sun and moon."[32] In addition, Cliff clearly disrupts the discursive positioning of homosexuality as a "foreign contamination" by de-allegorizing the rape of Harry/Harriet when he was a child by a British officer. Although Harry/Harriet admits to Clare that he/she is often tempted to think "that what he [the officer] did to me is but a symbol for what they did to all of us," he/she asserts that the experience was not the "cause" of his ambiguous sexuality. Instead, Harry/Harriet insists on the concrete and literal brutality of the rape: "Not symbol, not allegory . . . merely a person who felt the overgrown cock of a big whiteman pierce the asshole of a lickle Black bwai" (129–30).

In his first novel *Spirits In The Dark* (1993), H. Nigel Thomas deploys a narrative construct that functions — especially in its utopian gestures — much like the band of "revolutionaries" that Clare joins in *No Telephone to Heaven*. Jerome Quashee, the protagonist of Thomas's narrative, is initiated into an obscure and vaguely Afrocentric religious sect known as the Spiritualists. As a consequence, Jerome undergoes a ritual experience during the course of the novel that ultimately transforms and redeems him. Moreover, this redemptive experience becomes a way for Thomas to imagine and represent what might be called a decolonized Caribbean reality. In his attempt to articulate the ideological conditions of this decolonized Caribbean reality, Thomas insists on the need to dismantle not only oppressive political structures but restrictive sexual ones as well. Demonstrating an implicit understanding of how, as Stuart Hall puts it, "a transgressive politics in one domain is constantly sutured and stabilized by reactionary or unexamined politics in another,"[33] Thomas simultaneously confronts the patriarchal, heterosexist, and Eurocentric ideologies that constitute the particular legacy of the Caribbean colonial experience. Jerome's descent into "madness"—he suffers a series of "breakdowns" prior to his initiation—consequently reflects his unstable status as both a colonial subject and a homosexual.

Jerome's initiation entails a period of self-imposed isolation and sensory deprivation that enables him to reflect on and thereby come to terms with his experiences with a deeply flawed colonial school system, the expectations and disappointments of his parents, and his sexual feelings for other men. Assisted by Pointer Francis, who serves as his spiritual guide, Jerome emerges with a newfound understanding of his "African heritage" as well as an acceptance of his homosexuality. Jerome finally realizes that he had "put the sex part of [his] life 'pon a trash heap just fo' please society" and that "madness" was the price he paid for "hiding and sacrificing [his] life like that."[34]

However, if Jerome's spiritual rebirth constitutes a utopian gesture that reflects Thomas's desire to inscribe a decolonized indigenous gay subject within his text, that gesture is necessarily tempered by the pervasive homophobia that the novel also exposes. Although Pointer Francis tells Jerome that there is "nothing sinful 'bout sex" even if Jerome is "a case of a pestle needing a pestle" (as opposed to a pestle needing a mortar or vice versa), he nevertheless reminds Jerome that he is "going back to live in the real world, with real people" and that "most o' the brethren ain't grown enough fo' understand why you is how yo' is and fo' accept yo' as yo' is" (198, 212–13). In the course of his spiritual journey, Jerome recalls various incidents that were decisive in terms of his subconscious decision to repress his homosexuality. Chief among these are his memories of Boy Boy, the gay cousin who "was a constant point of reference for what the society would not accept" (94). The ridicule and humiliation that Boy Boy was forced to endure confirmed the unacceptability of Jerome's homosexual feelings. In addition, the fate that Boy Boy suffered when he "arranged with a young man to meet him in one of the canefields" demonstrated how physical violence was often used by the community in order to enforce a normative heterosexuality: "When he [Boy Boy] got there, there were ten of them. They took turns buggering him; one even used a beer bottle; then they beat him into unconsciousness and left him there. He'd refused to name the young men. But everyone knew who they were because they'd bragged about what they'd done — everything but the buggering" (199).

Jerome also recalls a more recent incident that illustrates how the community often acted in complicity with such violence by condoning or at least refusing to challenge these virulent displays of homophobic behavior. Jerome remembers that when Albert Brown, a cashier in the post office where he worked, was slapped by a coworker because he dared to offer a strikingly effective riposte to the mail sorter's crude homophobic insult, "no one, not even Jerome, reprimanded Brill." Moreover, when Jerome is called as a witness, the postmaster seems almost unwilling to believe his account, which leads Jerome to wonder if "perhaps the postmaster would have preferred that he lie and save him from having to take action against Brill" (200). Despite the postmaster's apparent reluctance, Brill is eventually dismissed — it seems he was on probation at the time for "telling a female clerk that he didn't have to 'take orders from a cunt.'" Nevertheless, many of Jerome's coworkers were "angry with Albert, saying that he did not know how to take a joke as a man, that he had caused Brill to lose his job, and didn't he know that Brill had a wife and two children to feed?" Jerome is likewise criticized for not knowing "how to see and not see and hear and not hear" (200). The obvious implication is, of course, that homophobia and sexism are not considered serious offenses — since they uphold an apparently "natural" order — and therefore hardly warrant such severe censure. From this perspective, it is unimaginable that Brill would lose his job simply because "he slap a buller."

However, at the same time that it exposes the complicity of the community, Thomas's text, like Cliff's, demonstrates an acute sensitivity to the ambiguous and sometimes contradictory spaces that inevitably exist in any culture. These sites of ambiguity and contradiction — which often reflect how "differences" are actually lived and negotiated — are, paradoxically perhaps, the ones that can potentially enable new forms of social and cultural relations. For example, at one point in his meditations, Jerome finds himself contemplating an episode that reveals the surprising capacity for tolerance that also exists alongside the homophobia pervading all levels of Caribbean society. Jerome recalls that among the female food vendors who plied their trade in the open-air market, there was also "a man whom the buyers and non-buyers said was the biggest woman of the lot. They called him Sprat."

Because he "got more customers than the women," Sprat often became the target of homophobic insults in the quarrels that frequently broke out as a result of the fierce competition among the vendors. However, despite the caustic nature of these exchanges, Jerome observes that Sprat nevertheless "loaned Melia [a vendor with whom he had previously argued] ten dollars to buy some ground provisions somebody was selling at a bargain." Noting Sprat's absence on another occasion, Jerome learns that he had the flu and that "three of the women had been to see him. One said he would be out the next week and she was buying supplies for him that day" (21–22). What Jerome comes to understand, then, is that there are relations of professional and personal reciprocity binding Sprat and the other vendors together — existing social relations which pose a contradiction to the homophobic ideologies that serve to position him as other.

Indeed, Thomas's novel seems to suggest that the willingness to accept the indeterminacy associated with such contradictions — the opposite of rigid binary thinking, in other words — is often the first step in undoing the homophobia that continues to marginalize lesbians and gay men in contemporary Caribbean cultures. For example, Pointer Francis reminds Jerome that it "is only when most people have a son or a daughter that is like that [that] they stop ridiculing and start thinking" (213). Once again, it is particularly within the context of concrete affiliative social relations that the potential for negotiating these contradictions can exist. Consequently, Jerome singles out his brother, Wesi, as the one "he would tell . . . everything about himself," mainly because Wesi "was the first person he knew that understood and accepted contradictions" (156). In fact, one of the central insights that Jerome gleans from his initiation has to do precisely with the importance of this "non-binary" mode of thinking: "Jerome knew that by the time the spirit called you, you knew that life itself was a contradiction" (177).

In the context of an indigenous criticism, the need for non-binary modes of thinking that resist the totalizing impulses implicit in both the "universalist" and "nativist" positions — the impasse between which the Buju Banton controversy so clearly exemplifies — is equally urgent. Given the alarming persistence of anti-gay violence in contemporary Caribbean societies and the reproduction in literature and popular culture of ideologies that condone or legitimate such violence, we clearly need a critical practice that goes beyond simple dichotomies — us/them, native/foreign, natural/unnatural — a practice that can not only affirm but also critique indigenous cultures in all of their varied and inevitably contradictory forms.

NOTES

1 "Boom Bye Bye," written by Mark Myrie, *Buju Banton: The Early Years 90–95* (Kingston, Jamaica: Penthouse Record Distributors, 1992). See Ransdell Pierson, "'Kill Gays' Hit Song Stirs Fury," *New York Post,* October 24, 1992; Joan Morgan, "No Apologies, No Regrets," *VIBE,* October 1993, 76–82; Peter Noel and Robert Marriott, "Batty Boys in Babylon: Can Gay West Indians Survive the 'Boom Bye Bye' Posses?" *Village Voice,* January 12, 1993.

2 Noel and Marriott, "Batty Boys in Babylon," 35, 31.

3 Morgan, "No Apologies, No Regrets," 76.

4 Ibid., 82.

5 Carolyn Cooper, "'Lyrical Gun': Metaphor and Role Play in Jamaican Dancehall Culture," *Massachusetts Review* 35, no. 3–4 (1994): 437. Cooper borrows the notion of the "lyrical gun" from Shabba Ranks's dancehall tune, "Gun Pon Me."

6 Ibid., 438.

7 "Open Letter," *VIBE,* October 1993, 82. This letter was published alongside Morgan's *VIBE* piece and collectively signed by many prominent "lesbians, gay men, and transgendered persons of African, Afro-American, Afro-Caribbean, and Afro-Latin descent."

8 The quote is taken from an unpublished paper that the author was kind enough to share with me: "On Liminal Subjectivity" (paper presented at the National Symposium on Indigenous Knowledge and Contemporary Social Issues, Tampa, Florida, March 3–5, 1994).

9 According to Cooper, plans for a protest to be led by a group of "local homosexuals" failed to materialize because "on the day of the rumoured march, men of all social classes gathered in the square, armed with a range of implements — sticks, stones, machetes — apparently to defend their heterosexual honor." Nevertheless, Cooper states that the aborted attempt paradoxically generated a public discourse on homosexuality when, in the wake of the non-event, "numerous callers on various talk show programs aired their opinions in defence of, or attack on the homosexual's right to freedom of expression" ("Lyrical Gun," 440). In addition, Isaac Julien's film, *The Darker Side of Black* (Arts Council of Great Britain, 1993), explores these very issues in relation to rap, hip-hop, and African American popular culture in general, as well as its diasporic counterpart in the Caribbean, the culture of the dancehall.

10 Wayne Cooper, *Claude McKay: Rebel Sojourner in the Harlem Renaissance* (Baton Rouge: Louisiana State University Press, 1987), 75.

11 Bernard Bell, *The Afro-American Novel and Its Tradition* (Amherst: University of Massachusetts Press, 1987), 118.

12 I am indebted to my colleague, Charles Nero, for helping me to clarify this concept of the homosocial in McKay's novels.

13 Claude McKay, *Home to Harlem* (New York: Harper and Brothers, 1928), 129.

14 For example, see Wayne Cooper's discussion of the critical reception — especially on the part of black American intellectuals like W. E. B. Du Bois — of McKay's *Home to Harlem* (*Claude McKay,* 238–48).

15 M. Jacqui Alexander, "Not Just (Any) *Body* Can Be A Citizen: The Politics of Law, Sexuality and Postcoloniality in Trinidad and Tobago and the Bahamas," *Feminist Review*, no. 48 (1994): 9.

16 Claude McKay, *Banana Bottom* (1933; New York: Harcourt, Brace, Jovanovich, 1961), 291.

17 Early in the novel, Bita is raped by Crazy Bow Adair, a third generation descendant of a "strange Scotchman who had emigrated to Jamaica in the eighteen-twenties." Although the narrator states that the mixed-race progeny of this "strange liberator" were, for the most part, "hardy peasants," he nevertheless admits that there are those who believe "the mixing of different human strains" had less salutary effects (2–4). In addition, the novel suggests that Patou, the "cripple-idiot" son of the missionary couple, Priscilla and Malcolm Craig, is both a product and a reflection of the repressed sexuality that is associated with their Englishness.

18 Cooper, *Claude McKay*, 32.

19 McKay, *Banana Bottom*, 126.

20 In a footnote to her essay, Spillers states that Fetterley discussed parts of the novel with her, and in Fetterley's opinion, "the work is homophobic." Spillers cites Fetterley's book, *The Resisting Reader: A Feminist Approach to American Fiction* (Bloomington: Indiana University Press, 1978), as an example of work done on the "evaluative dynamics of critical reading and the formation of reader communities." Hortense Spillers, "Chosen Place, Timeless People: Some Figurations on the New World," in *Conjuring: Black Women, Fiction, and Literary Tradition*, ed. Marjorie Pryse and Hortense Spillers (Bloomington: Indiana University Press, 1985), 172–74 n. 6.

21 Stuart Hall, "What Is This 'Black' in Black Popular Culture?" in *Black Popular Culture*, ed. Gina Dent (Seattle: Bay Press, 1992), 31. See also Paul Gilroy's article, "It's a Family Affair," in the same anthology, 303–16; and Anne McClintock's essay, "Family Feuds: Gender, Nationalism and the Family," *Feminist Review*, no. 44 (1993): 61–80.

22 Paule Marshall, *The Chosen Place, The Timeless People* (1969; New York: Vintage, 1992), 328.

23 Alexander, "Not Just (Any)*Body* Can Be A Citizen," 5–6.

24 Marshall, *The Chosen Place*, 329.

25 Alexander, "Not Just (Any)*Body* Can Be A Citizen," 10.

26 Marshall, *The Chosen Place*, 332.

27 Hall, "What Is This 'Black' in Black Popular Culture?" 30.

28 See p. 68 in Michelle Cliff, *The Land of Look Behind* (Ithaca, N.Y.: Firebrand Books, 1985), 57–76.

29 Ibid., 103.

30 Simon Gikandi, *Writing in Limbo: Modernism and Caribbean Literature* (Ithaca, N.Y.: Cornell University Press, 1992), 233.

31 Michelle Cliff, *Abeng* (1984; New York: Penguin Books, 1991), 35.

32 Michelle Cliff, *No Telephone to Heaven* (1987; New York: Vintage, 1989), 171.

33 Hall, "What Is This 'Black' in Black Popular Culture?" 31.

34 H. Nigel Thomas, *Spirits In The Dark* (1993; Oxford: Heinemann Publishers, 1994), 198.

MICHELLE CLIFF

Ecce Homo (2002)

Dream . . . on black wings . . . you come whenever sleep . . . sweet god, truly . . . sorrow powerfully . . . to keep separate . . . I have hope that I shall not share . . . nothing of the blessed . . . for I would not be so. — SAPPHO, no. 63

The story as I was told it begins in Rome.

There is a man who is a linguist. He is accomplished in several languages. Western and non-western. He gets a job as a translator in the U.S. embassy. He translates for Italians who clamor for visas. Jews among others.

His is a low-level position for a man of his qualifications.

He is black, which is of concern to his country.

He is homosexual, but they seem unaware.

He counts his blessings beside the Trevi Fountain.

All in all he has been comfortable in Rome.

His is an adopted country.

He was brought to America when he was fourteen. His are a nomadic people. Strivers, always in search of a better place. His mother and father — he was blessed with both — settled in Philadelphia. He did well in school, near the top of his graduating class.

He availed himself of Lincoln, the Black Princeton.

One evening in the Piazza Navona he is sitting at an outdoor restaurant. He has ordered a glass of Pinot Grigio — Campanile '36 — and is lighting a Muratti cigarette. The restaurant — the storyteller cannot recall the name — is located at the south end of the piazza, and from his table the linguist can see Bernini's *Il Moro* and takes heart.

That very evening he meets a man, an Italian.

A simple meeting: the Italian stops by the linguist's table, asks for a cigarette, a light.

They stroll the Roman streets, light at the Italian's apartment.

They become lovers.

On the weekends they spend time in a hilltown beyond the hills of the city the Italian knows from childhood.

They speak freely.

The storyteller says that was when they fell in love.

But too soon Americans have to leave. The linguist — like it or not — is a naturalized American. As such he must go.

But the linguist does not want to abandon his beloved. The linguist — the Negro who speaks in tongues — of rivers — unlike the tongues of the women back home (home the place that is unAmerica) in the pocomania shacks — twirling their spirituous tongues — was once tongue-tied —

"What's the matter, boy?"   "Wha' do you, bwai?"

"Is Cat got you tongue?"

"Don' mek me give you one tongue-lashing."

Now his tongue is the most skilled part of him.

He works with his tongue. He makes love with his tongue.

He knows when to hold his tongue.

The linguist tries to arrange a visa but the beloved is a known quantity and the application is denied.

He will not leave.

And that — the storyteller says — is the beginning of the end.

One night the fascists descend on the rooms the two men share in the Piazza della Repubblica. They are removed suddenly, without incident, but for the incident of their removal.

When he was a boy, before the family left for America, he read in a newspaper about two men apprehended because they were found together. A laborer, a casual laborer, the paper had reported, and a bank clerk. They were discovered in "an obscene condition" — a child, he did not know what this meant. When the two men were arraigned on a charge of public indecency (they'd been discovered under a pier near the Myrtle Bank Hotel) hundreds packed the courtroom — including mothers and their children. Later the two men were given twelve strokes of the Cat and five years hard labor.

The police take the two men to the nearby train station where they are loaded on a car bound for a camp.

Do you remember the end of *The Garden of the Finzi-Continis*? The film, this does not happen in the book. The schoolroom where the deportees are taken to be sorted and shipped. The train station in this story has a similar feel right now. There are still the stalls selling bottles of Acqua Mia and San Benedetto, bunches of grapes in white paper, newspapers, magazines, paper-bound libretti — the air smells of cigarette smoke and oranges and damp — the ordinariness of it all — strikes them — commerce, train travel — the schoolroom smelling of chalkdust — and people who have been tagged.

The two men arrive at the camp together. Thank God they have not been separated. But they will do well to ignore one another. To ignore one another while looking out for the other — that is their task.

They mask their longing.

They are assigned forced labor. Breaking rocks. Drawing the rocks, wagonload by wagonload, up the side of the quarry, stacking them in pyramids. The guards, wielding sledgehammers, smash the pyramids; the prisoners return to the pit of the quarry and break more stones, draw them to the lip of the quarry, stack them.

The two men are mocked, called names only the linguist understands.

Outside the windows of the storyteller's flat the sun is going down over the Pacific, beyond the Golden Gate.

The storyteller does not know how the two managed to escape. We will have to bring our imaginations to bear.

It must be night. Under cover of night they drift to the edge of the camp. In the darkness they burrow out under the barbed wire. Something like that. An opportunity has presented itself and they take it.

They find their way into some woods.

They live in the heart of the woods in the heat of a war as lovers. They live on mushrooms and lamb's quarters and wild birds the Italian traps. And the storyteller knows this is romantic, but let's let them have it. They make a place to sleep in a tree trunk heavy with moss and shelved with lichen.

A decayed, decadent nest.

The gunfire which seems to encircle them is coming closer to them. They whisper about which course to take. They sleep with their legs wrapped together. One man's penis nestles against the other's flank. When it rains, the rain draws a curtain around them.

They decide they will try to find Switzerland. They laugh. At least they have a plan. The linguist will pretend to be the Ethiopian servant of the Italian: "A spoil of war," the linguist whispers.

Now they're getting somewhere.

Suddenly luck finds them. They stumble upon a company of American troops — Negro soldiers encamped nearby. The linguist explains — omitting the triangle — now a ghost on his chest.

Time passes. Switzerland is forgotten.

The Negro soldiers get orders to move north and drop the men at a way station where displaced people wait.

The two are processed.

The linguist is returned to his adopted country.

The Italian is made a prisoner of war.

The linguist says, "When this is all over I will send for you."

This is a slender thread.

In the end it is no use.

The beloved hangs himself shortly after he is taken prisoner.

The linguist, this being postwar New York City, gets a job in the kitchens of The Waldorf-Astoria. He translates for the Hungarian chef.

When he hears of the Italian's death he breaks down.

He is committed to the Metropolitan State Hospital where he will die.

A man is seated under a silk-cotton tree in the Blue uniform of the mad.

There are no silk-cotton trees anywhere near this place.

Epiphytes — plants that live on air — disport themselves above his head. Brom-eliads whose sharp pink blooms last months.

The rainforest just beyond the man in mad dress reminds him of the forest where they hid, two men trying to be safe. But his mind's eye moving closer he notes the difference.

In a contest — in a fancy dress parade of Green — the rainforest would win: a dead heat between the iguana and the breadfruit.

Home.

He places the beloved on the bench beside him. They face the Green impenetrable, listen to its suddenness of sound: shrieks, howls, echoes from within brick walls.

The constrictors would tie with the man in mad dress for silence.

He holds his tongue.

WESLEY E. A. CRICHLOW

History, (Re)Memory, Testimony, and Biomythography: Charting a Buller Man's Trinidadian Past (2004)

There comes a time when silence becomes dishonesty. The ruling intentions of personal experience are not in accord with the permanent assaults on the most commonplace values. For many months my conscience has been the seat of unpardonable debates. And the conclusion is the determination not to despair of man, in other words, of myself. The decision I have reached is that I cannot continue to bear a responsibility at no matter what cost, on the false pretense that there is nothing else to be done. — FRANTZ FANON, *Black Skin, White Masks*

INTRODUCTION: LAYING OUT ETHICAL CONCERNS

The story that you are about to read is not exclusively a story of oppression; it does, however, express a considerable amount of pain and humiliation. The process of articulating so as to ask other men, or bullers, to make public their stories is an attempt to assert and broaden the reality of black male same-sex existence in Trinidad and Tobago and other parts of the Caribbean.[1] In this project the phrase "buller man" will be used to talk about men who have sex with men, for two reasons. One, it is a term I grew up with culturally, hence it resonates a specific set of historical events in charting my past; two, I feel it is necessary to reclaim the term in today's culture to share that past.

Same-gender sex, sexuality, and sexual orientation still represent a very taboo subject area, which too many people in the Caribbean, for far too long, have tried to erase and by proxy avoid. The absence of dialogue on same-sex practices between black heterosexual communities and black male same-sex communities is central to this exploration. Both bell hooks and ,Audre Lorde have urged dialogue within black communities to unearth black epistemological claims to truth and knowledge.[2] Dialogue, in this case, takes place when bullers and heterosexuals meet to talk about and reflect on their lived experiences and create social ties. Yet dialogue seems almost impossible — at least for now. The assertion and representation of a buller man's existence in Trinidadian communities are essential to facilitating more humane and human social relationships.

But this essay will be limited to the history and memory of a buller man's past from the 1970s to the early 1990s. I recognize that in reading my story of pain and humiliation, the readers may become voyeurs of the exotic other. This process may objectify my life and present my experiences as entertainment. This inevitable danger raises a number of questions: Does the academic and political project of this work justify the public presentation of this pain? How can readers work to overcome the possibility of becoming voyeurs?

I urge readers to reflect on these questions and to ask themselves consciously how they might be complicit with my story. The problems of voyeurism and objectification become greater whenever someone presents excerpts of his own or other people's lives and codes them into data. The presentation of this material to people who have not experienced how bullers live raises a number of ethical concerns. The researcher and the reader should adopt an ethical stance in their analytical practices and in their reading. They must be willing to analyze critically the ways in which their failures to challenge heterosexist oppressive practices affect the lives of bullers or gay men.[3] All of us should attempt an analysis of personal complicity with the oppression that I experienced every day while living in Trinidad and abroad.

Academic writers have an obligation to account for the type of framework that they use. Because of my social location and my professional and personal commitment to social justice, I must as a buller man work for positive change. When we engage in work to which we are personally committed, our academic contributions are more likely to come out of a creative, politically engaged self, one that adds social to academic purpose.[4] In pondering how to narrate my gay life in Trinidad and how to make connections with others, I decided to engage in a history and memory testimony of my gay youth while in Trinidad, employing the framework of Audre Lorde's biomythography. I hope this approach will allow me to elucidate similarities and differences with other men who share and have shared a similar location, towards the goal of social change. As Trinh Minh-ha has put it, "The place of hybridity is also the place of [our/]my identity."[5] Identity is never fixed; that is, it is fluid and continuously changing, hence suspect. My awareness of the complex issues involved when I make my life public has, I believe, informed my ethical approach to this project.

In Gayatri Spivak's terms, I see myself as subaltern, representing self and relating to other similar, yet unique experiences in a developmental exploration of other bullers' lives and identities. All representation is constructed and hence partial; it will never be virtual, will never fully reproduce "reality." It is always interpreted by a particular system of thought — typically, by a hetero-sexist structure of dominance. Trinidad's nationalistic, hegemonic, heterosexist community contains structures of dominance in which heterosexism and "morality" prevail. Thus as a subaltern I speak from a contested place. This project shows how I made sense of my life within the confines of black nationalism, Trinidadian communal living, black families, and the church. It analyzes how I and possibly others suffer at the hands of a hegemonic compulsory heterosexism that, I argue, is paralyzing Trinidadian black and other communities.

THE GENRE OF BIOMYTHOGRAPHY

I am a black buller man,[6] born in Trinidad to Caribbean parents. It is from within this ethnically rich cultural heritage — imbibed from grandparents, parents, relatives, and friends — that I begin my journey. I use *biomythography*, as coined by Audre Lorde — meaning life story, or representation of self — to translate my experiences of heterosexist oppression into this project.[7] The genre elucidates Lorde's interest in using her life story to create a larger framework for other zamis.[8] For her, the individual becomes the collective, as she recognizes the women who helped give her life substance: "A hybrid group of friends, family, lovers, and African goddesses: Ma-Liz, Delois, Louise Briscoe, Aunt Anni, Linda, and Genevieve; Ma-wu Lisa, thunder, sky, sun, the great mother of us all; and Afrekete, her youngest daughter, the mischievous linguist, trickster, best-beloved, whom we must all become."[9] In this sense Lorde enables the move from the singular (I) to the collective (we) in black autobiographical writing. Anne McClintock argues that "Lorde's refusal to employ the prefix 'auto' as the single, imperious sign of the self expresses a refusal to posit herself as the single, authoritative, engendering voice in the text. Instead, her life story is the collective, transcribed life of a community of women — not so much a perfect record of the past as a fabulated strategy for community survival."[10]

Marlon Riggs, too, in his documentary film *Black Is . . . Black Ain't*, links his individual identity with that of his grandmother's "gumbo" — a metaphor for the plurality and rich diversity of black identities.[11] He brings us face to face with black people — grappling with numerous, often contested definitions of black life, black oral inscriptions, and black identities. Identity here is represented as coming into being through black communities.

In a similar vein, my sense of writing, as influenced by others in the community, continues the tradition of Lorde's biomythography and Riggs's gumbo. The absence of frameworks for bullers in the Caribbean made it imperative that I incorporate the biomythography as used by Lorde and the gumbo analysis as used by Riggs as a starting point for this project, to assist me in developing a framework to write and talk about Trinidadian gay men's lives. I do not posit myself as a single, authoritative voice. For me biomythography has been invaluable, because I am living proof of some of the experiences that some men in the Caribbean face in coming out and coming to terms with their sexual orientation.[12] To truly "question is to interrogate something from the heart of our existence, from the centre of our being."[13] As a black intellectual and buller man, I find that this genre provides greater legitimacy to my project in relationship to my community.

Yet the questions that arise are not superficial, nor do they disappear merely because I am a member of the community or am given space to write about the experience. According to Antonio Gramsci, an *organic intellectual* can experience and be experiencing the consequences of living from a certain social position, and can articulate a set of problems associated with the lives of himself or herself and others. Gramsci's essay, "The Formation of Intellectuals," describes organic intellectuals: "Every social class, coming into existence on the original basis of an essential function in the world of economic production, creates within itself, organically, one or more groups of intellectuals who give it homogeneity and consciousness of its function not only in the economic field but in the social and political field as well."[14]

Quite simply, one must "connect" to oneself, each other, and "those others" in order to become, in the Gramscian sense, an organic intellectual.[15] The organic intellectual is one who is positioned to have experienced — and is experiencing — the particular consequences of living from a certain social position, and has articulated a set of problems associated with one's own life and other people's lives. As a result, one develops a relationship of familiarity with people and has the opportunity to think through issues in order to effect change in the oppressive heterosexist structures of dominance. For too long the silence of bullers has been deafening in its support of systemic inequalities. Struggle and the repositioning of identities are essential, especially for heterosexuals who have long enjoyed the benefits of homophobia and heterosexism. It is critical to locate myself in this project, to bring into being a self-conscious buller, within a particular set of experiences and social history, to make clear the experiences and ways of understanding that inform my theoretical framework.

There is an integral relationship between myself and other men of similar experiences to those described in this project. According to Lila Abu-Lug-hod, there is a "discourse of familiarity": "Others live as we perceive our-selves living not as automatons programmed according to 'cultural' rules or acting out social roles, but as people going through life wondering what they should do, making mistakes, being opinionated, vacillating, trying to make themselves look good, enduring tragic personal losses, enjoying others, and finding moments of laughter."[16] The varied, complex experience of other bullers has inspired my research and provided a forum for articulating the strength, pride, and dignity required to negotiate black communal living. In charting my biomythography, I locate myself in my childhood memories of schooling and community living, family, religion, popular culture and mass media, sports and trades, and girlfriends. In short, as a young black man in the Caribbean, I found a desperate assurance in my hypermasculinity through religion, sports, aggressiveness, loudness, having many intimate women friends, and practicing occupations or trades constructed as "manly" in my family and the community at large.

FAMILY

I am of mixed race from parents of black, Indian, and Chinese ancestral backgrounds, raised in a heterosexual nuclear family with fourteen siblings — five sisters and nine brothers. I am the fourteenth child and the youngest boy. My oldest brothers and sisters left home and immigrated to North America early in my life. As a result, the youngest five of us formed a close relationship. I grew up with my elder brothers but had very little in common with them. I felt that I could never compete with them in the arenas of sports and masculinity, so I avoided these contexts. I was very close, however, to my elder sisters, as well as to the youngest.

Within my family, discussions on same-sex relationships came up only in private and between adults. My parents raised us to embrace constructs and values that were inherently heterosexist. We were told what "pure and clean" sexuality was and which member of the opposite sex we would marry and go on to form a nuclear family with. My parents would often ask me, during my teenage years, about the girls in my life: "Do you have a girlfriend yet?" "I have never seen you bring home any girls." "Are you okay?" These questions were a way for them to assure themselves that I was "normal," and to signal a warning to me if something was wrong. It was always acceptable for us to talk about having more than one young woman in our lives, but if we failed to mention any young women, our parents would suggest potential girlfriends.

Most of the time our parents suggested girls who were Indo-Caribbean, light skinned, and well educated. They often told us that blacks were not a progressive group and that if we wanted to succeed in life we should avoid them. We had a black neighbor and very good friend who would compare blacks to crabs in a pan of pitch oil — as one tries to climb out, the other pulls him or her down. Parents often spoke in parables to pass messages to children, and if we did not know what they meant, they would say, "If you doh want to hear, then you would have to feel."

Needless to say, my parents never once asked if I was interested in same-sex relationships, and would not speak about or allow any other sexual identities or options beyond heterosexuality. This situation imprisoned me within compulsory heterosexuality and constructed same-sex relationships as sinful, traitorous, and deviant. Lorde writes, "As a forty-nine-year-old Black lesbian feminist-socialist mother of two, including one boy, and a member of an inter-racial couple, I usually find myself part of some group defined as other, deviant, inferior, or just plain wrong."[17] Within my family the naturalization of heterosexism and its cultural norms about sexuality produced and defined same-sex practices as unwelcoming and unnatural. Caribbean feminist scholar M. Jacqui Alexander has demonstrated, for example, how the "naturalization of heterosexuality as state law has traditionally depended on the designation of gay and lesbian sex and relationships as 'unnatural.'" She further points out that there is no absolute set of commonly understood or accepted principles called "the natural" which can be invoked definitionally, except as they relate to what is labeled unnatural.[18]

This typical, unwelcoming family environment, along with the resulting private nature of homoerotic sexuality, is a reality for most bullers in the Caribbean. My family assumed that I, like my father, would marry someone of the opposite sex and have a family and maintain the family name and identity through paternity, even though I had fourteen siblings. As bell hooks has argued, black men are expected to reproduce and maintain the black family.[19] Part of this pressure also stemmed from my close relationship with my father and his expectations of me. In many respects my father was like an elder brother to me — he trusted me, and we did a lot of things together.

When I was eight he showed me how to drive his motor vehicles and how to do basic auto repairs, something that he never did for my older brothers. He also taught me basic welding, plumbing, and masonry repair, and he would often call on me when repairs needed doing around the house or at the homes of my brothers and sisters. We also had some friends in common and socialized in some of the same places. I accompanied him to the grocery store, did market shopping with him, and paid the bills. He would often let me drive him, and was very proud of me when with his friends. When going places we would talk about local and international politics, social issues, and relatives, and each of us had very vocal opinions on most subjects. We played cards together with his adult friends, many of whom I highly respected. In Trinidad, playing cards, especially "all fours" at the competitive level, is a popular sport among males, especially on the block (a street corner) or in village competitions. My father and I were often partners at cards. I was only a teenager, and this meant a great deal to me, especially because it helped to disguise the signs of my being a buller.

Overall I thoroughly enjoyed my relationship with my father, and yet there was a sense of shame, betrayal, dishonesty, and distance that I felt because I was hiding my sexuality from him, and it caused me great pain. Despite our shared activities I never felt comfortable enough to let him know about my same-sex feelings and desires. This produced a deep ambivalence within me. I grew hesitant about working closely with him and yet had no way of refusing. I also knew that my masculinity was secure when I was with him, because his friends would often say, "Your son is so nice; he will grow into a good man." I felt that the tasks that I performed with him were "manly enough" to hide the signs of my emerging sexuality. Hence, I constructed a hyper-masculinized persona within the family to cover up my confusion and remain in the closet.[20]

My relationship with my mother was very different. It mattered greatly to her that we got an education, had three meals a day, and were healthy and happy. She was a very busy woman who listened to everyone's problems and managed the family finances. I would often turn to her for permission to go places or for money to buy clothes or food or to socialize, but she and I did not talk much about other people, political issues, or my life. She was very private, very cautious about what she said in front of us, always reminding us that if we could not say good things about someone then we should say nothing. She hated any form of gossip and was always ready to remind us that we should not keep bad company. She had instilled in me a very rigid hyper-male gender prison, which meant that I had a slightly different type of gender-raising structure, and I was often even more cautious around her than around my father. I never wanted to give her any signs or raise suspicions of my same-sex attraction for men, so I acted hyper-masculine to exhibit the persona she expected of me.

It was my mother who would chastise my behavior when she thought it stereotypically feminine; "Stop acting like a girl," she would say. She had very clearly defined gender roles for her children, which decided the chores that she would assign us. We boys always did the field or yard work, and the girls the housework. While our mother considered food shopping feminine, her sons had to do most of it, because it meant lifting heavy baskets or boxes of food to feed a large family. Physicality avoided signs of tenderness or femininity. The only "soft" tasks for the boys were polishing and whitening shoes for school, cleaning fish from Saturday market, shelling peas, and cleaning sorrel. Such discourses demonstrate how roles in families are always gendered, always already, in Stuart Hall's words, underpinned by a particular sexual economy, a particular figured masculinity or femininity, a particular class identity, and so forth.[21] The term "discourse" is used here to describe how knowledge, behavior, and practices are institutionalized in social policies and in family as an extended institution of the state. Discourses are located within relations of power and organized positions and places in the field of power. In Foucauldian theory, discourse is not just another word for speaking, but denotes historically situated material practice that produces power relations. Discourses are thus bound up with specific knowledges. My family is an example of how social knowledge about gender norms and attitudes about gays and lesbians as deviant, sick, and immoral are organized through a particular heterosexist discourse.

I always felt that my mother knew that I was a buller, and I hoped that religion or a heterosexual relationship would cure me, so that I could hide it from her. She was very particular about where I went, who called for me, and my clothes and hairstyle. For her some of these codes were central to defining appropriate male behavior. I never imagined that I could fool her, and I therefore always felt great pressure in her presence, which reminded me of her religious beliefs and their attitude towards same-sex practices.

RELIGION

It is sad indeed that we as a church have more often than not turned our back on a significant portion of God's people on the basis of their sexual orientation. We have inflicted on gay and lesbian people the tremendous pain of having to live a lie or to face brutal rejection if they dared to reveal their true selves. But oppression cuts both ways. Behind our "safe" barriers of self-righteousness, we deprive ourselves of the rich giftedness that lesbian and gay people have to contribute to the whole body of Christ. — ARCHBISHOP DESMOND TUTU, letter to a gay and lesbian Episcopal ministry in California, December 20, 1995

Christianity is the dominant religion of most Caribbean islands, a relic of colonial rule. When community members object to same-sex relationships, they often invoke religious discourse to condemn those relationships as immoral and sinful. In Trinidad, Christian congregations have traditionally viewed and continue to view same-sex practices as sinful and, as a result, have sought to regulate these practices.

While growing up in Trinidad, I went to church every Sunday, and the pastors often referred to biblical passages condemning same-sex relation-ships — for example, Genesis 19; Leviticus 18:22 and 20:13; Romans 1:18–32; 1 Corinthians 16:9; and 1 Timothy 1:10. The passages in Leviticus are the most explicit: "You shall not lie with a male as with a woman; it is an abomination" (18:22), and "If a man lies with a male as with a woman, both of them have committed an abomination; they shall be put to death; their blood is upon them" (20:13). My mother always mentioned these teachings when she saw a buller man or heard about someone thought to be a buller. I was uncomfortable when pastors spoke about marriage and "family values," for they always found a way to talk about men having sex with men. Thus in church services and Sunday school I felt confused and ashamed, because I was aware of my sexual feelings and tendencies. However, I continued to attend services, hoping for a "cure" for my desires.

The sense of duality articulated by W. E. B. Du Bois takes on a particularly painful and specific meaning for bullers who experience powerlessness, rejec-tion, alienation, and shame in black communal living. Although Du Bois analyzed the concept of "the Negro" in the United States, his ideas are equally applicable to black men who engage in same-sex practices and are seeking agency, acceptance, and approval within black and Trinidadian com-munal life.

Du Bois wrote about double consciousness, or the two-ness of being — the sense of always looking at oneself through the eyes of others.[22] I always looked to family, the parish priest, and friends for approval. As a buller man I found that my double consciousness hampered my ability to make up my mind on significant issues such as same-sex sexuality, gender construction, and identity politics, or to speak out in support of buller men. Du Bois argued that with a strong cultural sense of self and a commitment and connection to African people, blacks would move beyond double conscious-ness. He urged us to look at the duality of conflict produced by living in an oppressive or racist society. Being both black and a buller meant harboring "two warring souls": "A sort of seventh son, born with a veil and gifted with second-sight in this American world — a world which yields him no true self-consciousness, but only lets him see himself through the revelation of the other world. . . . One ever feels his two-ness, . . . two unreconciled strivings; two warring ideals in one dark body, whose dogged strength alone keeps it from being torn asunder."[23]

The longing to attain self-consciousness, deny my same-sex desires, and merge into a heterosexual, sexualized manhood was a source of psychological confusion and moral regulation that existed inside me, two souls forever torn asunder in Trinidad.

Dennis Altman, in his classic text, *Homosexual: Oppression and Liberation,* maintains "that societies impose upon humanity a repressive regime that channels our polymorphous eroticism into a narrow genital-centered, procreative-oriented heterosexual norm."[24] This confining of sexuality manufactures the illusion of sexual liberation as its social foil. It forces the subordinated to bear the social anxiety concerning repression.[25] Gayle Rubin calls this the "erotic pyramid" of sexuality, which has heterosexual procreative masculinities at the top:

> Modern Western societies appraise sex acts according to a hierarchical system of sexual value. Marital, reproductive heterosexuals are at the top of the erotic pyramid. . . . Individuals whose behavior stands high in this hierarchy are rewarded with certified mental health, respectability, legality, social and physical mobility, institutional support and material benefits. As sexual behaviors or occupations fall lower on the scale, the individuals who practice them are subjected to a presumption of mental illness, disrespectability, criminality, restricted physical and social mobility, loss of institutional support and economic sanctions.[26]

The idea that the sexual impulse exists solely for procreation, not for pleasure, is rooted in the Bible, the Qur'an, and the *Bhagavad-Gita,* which have fostered religious interpretations and hegemonic practices that exclude same-sex relationships. Religious debates and the ongoing debate about respectability, cleanliness, and decency take on social forms — such as church, school, and family — which individuals rely on and live their lives through. These institutions mediate the many ways in which people might view sex, sexual practices, and same-sex relationships. Within these institutions and discourses, state and non-state organizations control sexuality, sexual identity, and communal cultural identity. As M. Jacqui Alexander points out, these institutions which narrate and position gay and lesbian sexuality as unnatural also serve to naturalize heterosexuality as an implicit norm.[27]

Because of religious and moral regulation of the body and its practices, I always felt that my identity was deployed against the subjective grounds of the dichotomies of good and evil, moral and immoral, sinful and non-sinful. In this scenario the core of consciousness, as espoused by the various black communities in the Caribbean and as instituted by schools, communal living, churches, the state, and the black family, erases the realities of gay people's lives.

SCHOOL AND COMMUNITY LIVING

School represented a crucial phase for me in dealing with sexuality and coming to terms with manhood. As a teenager I listened as my schoolmates and friends expressed their hatred towards bullers. I can recall conversations with friends, both in school and in the community, that proposed violent acts such as stoning — with the intent to kill — against men whom they suspected were bullers. As Peter Noel and Robert Marriott write of violence against batty bwoys in Jamaica,[28] "hunting batty bwoys is as instinctive as the craving for *fry fish an' bammy*, a national dish. The mere sight of them can trigger the bedlam of a witch hunt. When the toaster (rapper) Hammer Mouth discovers two gay men in a garage — 'hook [hug] up an' ah kiss like . . . meangy dog' — he hollers: 'Run dem outa di yard.' Murder them, advises another toaster . . . 'Kill dem one by one. Murder dem till dem fi change dem plan.'"[29] Likewise, as a teenager I frequently witnessed verbal and physical harassment of bullers or effeminate men in Trinidad as they walked past gatherings of men standing on the street corner. In Kingston, Jamaica, write Noel and Marriott, between 1983 and 1988 many suspected homosexuals were stabbed or shot dead. My friends and others who disliked and targeted bullers often attacked them violently. Witnessing these acts provoked the type of psychological and emotional fear I lived through as a teenager in Trinidad.

I often heard my older brothers, when we had arguments or fights, tell me to stop acting like "ah she or Reginald." Reginald was a man whom many in the community suspected of being a buller. The reference was dismissive and reinforced the obvious fact that I was younger, not quite a man yet, and needed to be warned or policed about what not to become. When his name came up in arguments, it substituted for heterosexist oppressive language, induced guilt, and encouraged shame and emasculation. I consciously resisted arguing with my brothers, for fear that they would call me Reginald in front of my parents or friends.

Anger towards zami queens seldom surfaced, because most people expected women to carry themselves in traditional ways. Women played highly feminized gender roles, raising children, cleaning house, cooking, washing, dressing, and behaving in ways that excluded the labels "lesbian," "manly," or "zami." According to Judith Butler, gender is a corporeal style, a way of acting the body, a way of wearing one's flesh as a cultural sign.[30] That is, it is a sign, a signifier of an underlying biological sex and a discernible sexual orientation.

Women wearing men's overalls, or doing physical work traditionally constructed as masculine, did not challenge women's traditional gender roles. If anything, some of the clothes that women wore reflected poverty, and it was acceptable to use them until they could afford something new. Here clothes function as visible signs of identity, subject to disruption and symbolic theft, which challenge the role of clothes as a ground for gender. Furthermore, acts such as physical aggressiveness, when a woman was fighting for her male partner, children, girlfriend, or a good friend, were reconfigured and represented as very womanly — the act of a strong woman and at the same time a girlish thing to do. Observers never assumed that a woman protecting another woman from male violence had a sexual interest in her, or that women who listened to each other's problems had same-sex attractions. Rather, women supported one another in response to violence and shared communal experiences.

M. Jacqui Alexander calls this a "gendered call to patriotic duty. Women were to fiercely defend the nation by protecting their honour, by guarding the nuclear, conjugal family, 'the fundamental institution of the society,' by guarding 'culture' defined as the transmission of a fixed set of proper values to the children of the nation."[31] Or, as patriarchal black nationalists have argued, a woman's role "is omnipresent as the nurturer of Black children, the cultural carrier . . . and the teacher of the community."[32] Such public practices and gender expectations of black women do not correlate protective or caring behavior with sexual preference. There are very strong stereotypical roles enforced for women, but they are also blurred for women in ways that they are not for men. Within a Trinidadian community, some codes of women's behavior allowed women to go unmarked, less rigorously policed in terms of a regulated notion of gender behavior and its connection to sexuality. The notion of what it meant to look and to be zami was not as overtly marked as what it meant to look and act as a buller man.

The stability of a male's sexual identity would be interrogated if he wore the wrong clothes or colors, failed to participate in particular sports, or did not protect his female partner or show an interest in events constructed as "boyish" or "mannish." The sexual identity of men who stepped outside their traditional masculinized or mannish roles was always in question. Yet many bullers had very good relationships with older women in the community. Some women, mostly housewives, had no problem forming close relationships with bullers, as long as the males displayed laughable, gossiping, stereotypical, flamboyant, feminine characteristics, presenting themselves less as maligned than as humorous.

Bullers have been and still are objects of contempt in Caribbean culture. They are part of a communal setting with teachings and practices that involve the policing of same-sex relationships, grounded in religious canons. Today same-sex relationships and homosexuality are still illegal in most Caribbean islands,[33] subject to the long line of oppressive "-isms" in society. These "-isms" have not created, for Caribbean folks, any new spaces, but continue the tradition of oppressive thinking. Heterosexism, like racism, classism, and ableism, denies people their human agency to be fully who they are. It further creates a hierarchy of heterosexual categories. In essence, heterosexism starts and operates from a paralyzing position that everyone is heterosexual, while denying the human sexual or emotional existence of those who engage in same-sex practices, identifying these practices as deviant, sick, and abnormal, as well as religiously and morally wrong.

During my teenage life, in an effort to temporarily secure my masculinity or hyper-masculinity and hegemonic heterosexuality, I participated in events such as stealing (sugar cane, cocoa, coffee pods, plums, mangoes, and other fruits), breaking bottles with slingshots or stones on the street, engaging in physical fights, and "hanging on the block" with the boys until late at night. These heterosexist, hyper-masculinist constructions were ways for me both to assert and test my physical strength and to attest to my heterosexuality.

During my childhood these physical acts secured my masculinist persona. For me heterosexuality was, as Judith Butler puts it, "a normative position intrinsically impossible to embody and the persistent failure to identify fully and without incoherence with these positions revealed heterosexuality not only as a compulsory law, but as an inevitable comedy . . . a constant parody of itself."[34] For many of us these forms of hyper-masculinity were like walking with or having a permanent "hard-on" — necessary performances that bought our way into the communal construction of a normative masculinity, constructed through the prism of heterosexuality. Our fights usually indicated an "overt disdain for anything that might appear soft or wet . . . more 'a taboo on tenderness' than a celebration of violence," a "matter of learning to identify being male with these traits and pieces of behaviour."[35] Young women aided young black men in maintaining this form of behavior, and sometimes ascribed status to them for being able to do all these things and not get into trouble. Furthermore, these activities demonstrated "power" to parents, women, teachers, and friends, who were proud to see that a young man was not a buller, a sissy, or a coward.

In school young men often called me "buller man" if I refused to talk about any sexual encounters with young women, harass young women, laugh at the clothing of economically disadvantaged students, play sports after school, or break *l'école biche* (skip classes). My associates saw these qualities as feminine and believed that they had the right to call me a buller. Many days I felt unsafe going to school but was afraid to let my parents know why. Homophobic violence in school and homophobia within my family left me with nowhere to turn for help or advice. On several occasions I left for school but never arrived. Throughout high school I lived in fear of men who wanted to beat me because they thought that I was a buller man. For me, acting macho was a product of what I now see as masculinized resistance, and I presented myself as tough, independent, loud, aggressive, and in control — attributes of traditional dominant gender constructions and of their definitions of manhood — in order to erase all signs of being a buller or shirley.

I also negotiated heterosexist violence by forming relationships with men who had sex with other men, who did not self-identify as bullers or bisexual, and who were constructed as heterosexuals in the community. These men were tough, big, masculine, and aggressive. No one dared to cross their paths. They were considered heterosexual because of their large frames, their hyper-masculine actions, and their heterosexual relationships. They were the "cool guys" on the block. Many young men "hung out" with them when they were going to the movies, smoking pot, going to the river to "make a cook," playing cards on the block, or going to football and cricket matches. Most of these men also had blue-collar jobs in the auto industries, stove and refrigeration industries, or sugar cane factories — showing their masculinity, providing for the family, and forestalling questions about their sexuality. Their masculinized fronts made them appear heterosexual — true men and real brothers.

I associated with these men and confided in them in order to avoid or mitigate violence, verbal or physical. My contact with them secured me against frequent violent attacks on bullers by gangs of young men, always ready to protect their gender and hyper-masculinity. I often heard my friends talk about the beatings that they had given to men whom they caught at the river during the day, or in the savanna at night,[36] having sex with other men. These acts of violence often had police support, leaving the victims without recourse to state or community.

These men also exposed me to a culture of same-sex sexuality through magazines and books. They confirmed and provided an avenue for my self-recognition and acceptance of myself as a buller. They also told me secrets about other men with whom they had sexual encounters or who they knew were doing it "the other way" or were swinging. My ongoing association with these men reduced my ambivalence by affirming my sexuality, and protected me from heterosexist violence. Yet they were also friends with my brothers, although I never heard my brothers interrogating their sexuality — they perfectly represented my brothers' social construction and understanding of heterosexual masculinity. Knowing these men facilitated my understanding of my same-sex sexual desires and made me feel a bit more comfortable. I was not alone.

Despite this enabling self-recognition and my growing knowledge of my sensibilities and possibilities, my constant fear of heterosexist violence prevented any form of public expression. There was an emerging self-identification as a result of my feelings and understanding and of the way in which other people were naming me and subjecting me to violence. Violence against "queers," argue Bill Wickham and Bill Haver, is "installed . . . in that ideological, lived relation termed daily life itself, as well as in the objectification, thematization and valorization of everydayness."[37] Compulsory heterosexuality denies many the possibility of positive self-identification. To avoid violence I embraced forms of a heterosexual identity, constructed and regulated within family, school, religion, and popular culture. As a young teenager I was able to position myself as a buller but adopted, as I show next, the appropriate heterosexist type of dress to escape violence.

CLOTHING

The 1960s, 1970s, and early 1980s saw rigid gender-based restrictions on clothing color in Trinidad. As a man I was not allowed to wear pink, red, yellow, or any color that appeared too "flamboyant" or "bright," for these hues were viewed as weak, feminine, "uncool" — usually worn by women, bullers, or white boys. The socially coded buller man's body is stereotyped as "flamboyant," "effeminate," "flashy," "crazy-acting," and in some cases loud and childlike. The flamboyant buller who became friends with older black women could braid his hair, wear headbands and bright clothing, and speak with a feminine voice, as long as he allowed others to laugh at him and make him the village clown. As gay historian Jeffrey Weeks writes, "The male homosexual stereotype of effeminacy and transvestism has had a profound yet complex impact on men who see themselves as homosexual. No automatic relationship exists between social categories and people's sense of self and identity. . . . The most significant feature of the last hundred years of homosexual history has been that the oppressive definition and defensive identities and structures have marched together."[38]

Black men who contravened these codes were always marked as bullers within our culture and community. As Eve Kosofsky Sedgwick states in "How to Bring Your Kids up Gay," in Michael Warner's *Fear of a Queer Planet*, "Indeed, the gay movement has never been quick to attend to issues concerning effeminate boys. There is a discreditable reason for this in the marginal or stigmatized position to which even adult men who are effeminate have been relegated to the movement."[39]

For black men generally, effeminophobia has always been a real threat to (their) masculinity, while for some bullers it is another way of reclaiming parts of their identity that they were taught to hate and despise. For many bullers effeminacy is "undesirable," "blightful," or "sinful" because black society condemns it. Yet some bullers employ it to challenge misogynist and sexist practices in black cultures, performing drag or cross-dressing to express themselves. Sedgwick writes about appositional forms of sexual self-expression that challenge the traditional norms and values that imprison black masculinity and black communal living. It certainly is dangerous to resist traditional notions of masculinity. As Sedgwick writes:

> A more understandable reason for effeminophobia, however, is the conceptual need of the gay movement to interrupt a long tradition of viewing gender and sexuality as continuous and collapsible categories — a tradition of assuming that anyone, male or female, who desires a woman must by the same token be masculine. That one woman, as a woman, might desire another; that one man, as a man, might desire another: the indispensable need to make these powerful, subversive assertions has seemed, perhaps, to require a relative de-emphasis of the links between gay adults and gender nonconforming children.[40]

It is not surprising, then, that fear of violence, actual or psychological, affects the lives of men who define themselves as bullers. My actions and my fears of communal and family violence emerged from this psychological trauma of same-sex practices, which I attempted to erase through activities such as sports and trades.

SPORTS AND TRADES

My involvement in competitive sports such as football and cricket was a means of survival. Sports offered an accepted arena in which young men could exercise their masculinized personhood and erase same-sex suspicion. Parents and teachers strongly encouraged sports. It was common to hear parents and coaches talk about how big and muscular the boys were becoming, and to hear schoolgirls scream at the display of black bodies in competitive boys' sports.

Once while I was playing football in the savanna with my male friends, a young man walked by. My fellow players yelled out, "Look ah buller man, check she how she walking nah. Leh we go beat and kill de man nah." As the young man walked in fear and hope that the harassment would stop, he did not respond. My friends went up to him and insisted that he fight. His refusal led to more name-calling and physical attacks, which left him bruised and alone. I stood and watched and did nothing.

This experience made me question my own safety and wonder how I would publicly affirm a same-sex identity and inform others of it. I started to think about how lonely my life might be if I did inform family and friends about my sexual orientation, and about the potential effects on my family and associates. I did not want to lose my male friends, who would call me "buller" as a put-down, or further risk the violent attacks that I feared in school on a daily basis, so I continuously constructed my gender and acted in a hyper-masculine way to negotiate the homophobic and violent conditions of my daily existence. Here I am reminded of Michel Foucault, who "argued that the emergence of homosexuality as a distinct category is historically linked to the disappearance of male friendship." As Lynne Segal writes, Foucault thought that "intense male friendships were perceived as inimical to the smooth functioning of modern institutions like the army, the bureaucracy, educational and administrative bodies."[41]

Even more disturbing for me, there was no protection from the state, nor were there organizations that supported bullers. My friends called me a buller when we played sports. They thought that I put too much emphasis on being clean, on getting home on time, and on resisting fights. I also remember the mother whose house stood near where we played cricket in the streets. She would tell her sons and the other young men not to pick me on their team because I did not like to get dirty, would bat and then go home, or was not strong enough, since I was a buller man. If I was selected, I tried to act like a "really tough man" and to avoid her name-calling and her children.

All my older brothers played excellent football and cricket and were very good athletes. I never mastered sports but immersed myself in them to erase all signs of femininity and possible suspicions about my sexuality. When I played football, men often made fun of me, because I could not kick the ball as hard as my brothers or because I did not score as many goals as they did. I was mostly excluded from playing except as a substitute — a position with which I became all too familiar.

It was useful to learn trades such as welding, plumbing, carpentry, and masonry in school, to be able to do basic repairs and simple construction at home. Most communities called on members for help with building a community project or a house. Men would do the physical labor, and women the cooking. The person or group being helped was expected to supply large amounts of food for the workers. Sometimes those who could afford to pay for the work did so, in addition to serving food. For many men, including me, there was pride in having helped a family to build their new house by mixing cement, welding fences, or laying bricks. It also allowed men to project their masculinized selves to the community, which earned them popularity. Especially when women were around, men would often show off their strength by hauling heavy loads and comparing their accomplishments to those of others. As Ray Raphael wrote, "Our competitive initiations tend to exaggerate rather than alleviate male insecurity and the greater our insecurity, the more prone we are to overcompensating for our weakness by excessive and aggressive male posturing."[42]

Sports and trades were — and are — valued by Trinidadian men more than academic achievement. Many young men in Trinidad still argue that academic subjects such as mathematics, physics, and English are for bullers and women, while trades are for men. This embrace of a physical form of knowing — displaying dexterity and knowledge of one's own body — was and is a means for young men to graduate into their black male coolness, machismo, and masculinity. Hence school, family, male communal pressure, and popular culture form and maintain social values. Raphael adds "that macho, or cool, as constructions of masculinity, is just one more indication of insecurity."[43]

Fathers, older brothers or uncles, neighbors, friends, and relatives reminded us of how big, strong, and tough they were and how hard they worked to provide for and protect their families. They boasted about the many women in their lives. Someone who did not have as many women as they did was "sick," suspected as a buller or not "the average young black male." My father, however, never fit these stereotypical constructions of manhood. He was very gentle and never worried about the chores that he did in the home. Nor did he have more than one female in his life. But these stereotypes continue to frame judgments of black men.

POPULAR CULTURE AND MASS MEDIA

The mostly American movie genres that appeared in Trinidad in the 1960s, 1970s, and 1980s typically portrayed violence, stereotypes, a colonial and sexist mentality, and American heterosexual family values. Racist and colonial representations of cowboys and Indians, the black rapist, the black macho stud, or the black comedian inundated the market. Evil was invariably equated with "blackness." We watched television shows such as *Bonanza*, *The Brady Bunch*, *Dark Shadows*, *Days of Our Lives*, *Lassie*, *Flipper*, *The Lone Ranger*, *Lost in Space*, and *Tarzan*, and movies such as *The Million Dollar Man* and *Planet of the Apes*. Then came the "blaxploitation" genre of the 1960s, 1970s, and 1980s, depicting black machismo and black language / slang in movies like *Black Belt Jones*; *The Black Godfather*; *Cleopatra Jones*; *Coffee*; *Hell up in Harlem*; *Sheba, Baby*; *Shaft's Big Score!*; and *Urban Jungle*.[44] Kobena Mercer and Simon Watney argue, "The hegemonic repertoire of images of Black Masculinity, from docile 'Uncle Toms' to the shuffling minstrel entertainer, the threatening native to superspade figures like Shaft, has been forged in and through the histories of slavery, colonialism and imperialism."[45]

Many black Caribbean men imitated the representation they saw in the blaxploitation films, adopting codes of machismo and "black" masculinity to recoup some power over their conditions. This depiction of manhood, masculinity, and hyper-masculinity transformed the ways in which black men in the Caribbean acted and how they treated women and gays. Most of them started to wear big Afro-hairstyles, plaid pants, and high-heeled platform shoes, to adopt American and not-so-American accents, and to claim an identity that they interpreted as cool and popular. This adoption of style and politics was also partly influenced by the Black Power movements of the time; again, these were mostly driven by black American male activists. For Richard Majors and Janet Mancini Billson in *Black Manhood*, "cool" is "the presentation of self many Black males use to establish their identity . . . it is a ritualized form of masculinities that entails behaviors, scripts, physical posturing, impression management and carefully crafted performances that deliver a single, critical message: pride, strength and control."[46]

Parents caught up in the Hollywood dream started to name their children after black movie stars. This seemed to suggest that black male babies would grow up to be bodies without brains, insecure and animalistic, without feelings or compassion. This representation reinforced existing insecurities and racist stereotypes already facing black men in the Caribbean, which had originated with slave masters who defined, labeled, racialized, and sexualized black men and women as "other" without understanding, valuing, or respecting them.

In 1970 Trinidadian and Caribbean popular television culture saw the birth of a new form of sexual politics. From NBC's New York studios came the first black male cross-dressing character on television. A black American male named Flip Wilson played the role of Geraldine,[47] in the first successful black hosted variety show in television history, *The Flip Wilson Show Tonight*. Watching him was painful, for my family and friends directed derogatory and heterosexist remarks at him during the show. Some of my friends said that they wished that they could pull him out of the television screen and "put ah good lash and beating upon him and straighten him out." My parents would caution us about the program and insist that we not watch it unattended, or would recommend that we do school work while it was on. People would often express disbelief that a buller man was on television and wonder why he would embarrass black people by acting so stupid. This show came at a time when the North American feminist movement was beginning the struggles for women's liberation, and at a time when women within the black consciousness movement were questioning their roles and places in society. Forced upon us through American cultural hegemony, popular culture became a contested site upon which the Trinidadian, through comedy and music, entered (in a more public or open fashion) the gender, sex, and sexuality debate; hence, the resistance at the time was constructed around social change. Wylie Sypher reminds us, "The ambivalence of comedy reappears in its social meaning, for comedy is both hatred and revel, rebellion and defense, attack and escape. It is revolutionary and conservative. Socially, it is both sympathy and persecution."[48]

Redd Foxx's big-screen movie *Norman . . . Is That You?* (1976) was a little more controversial, playing with sex, sexuality, and the heterosexual sexual revolution.[49] *Norman . . . Is That You?* is based on a Broadway play by Ron Clark and Sam Bobrick, about a young man who is black and gay. Redd Foxx's character, after not seeing his son Norman for over ten years, pays Norman a surprise visit. Norman at first hides his effeminate white boyfriend, Garson, who tries to persuade him to tell his father that they are lovers. In Norman's absence, Garson returns to pick up his clothes and opens the closet door by packing a dress in his suitcase in front of Norman's father. The father attempts to convince his son that he is not gay by asking him to walk and to say "Mississippi," and by reminding him that he never dropped the ball when they used to play football. He even tells Norman to go to a physician for help, which is not an uncommon suggestion from many parents who see homosexuality as a sickness.

For the first time a black American movie televised in the Caribbean depicted a same-sex relationship involving a black man, just when most people in the Caribbean were denying the existence of such a thing. For many Trinidadians, however, the decadence of whiteness explained Norman's status as a buller. According to their heterosexist logic, whites infiltrate day-care centers, prisons, and schools, turning black males into sissies, bullers, and weak traitors to their race.

Many calypsonians, mostly men, sang about Norman that year, and the next. It is common for calypsonians engaging in musical competitions to make fun of buller men, village women, or public figures. Such music often appropriated sexist, homophobic, and misogynist themes in a society where hyper-masculinity is the key to manhood. Calypsonian Dennis Williams (a.k.a. Merchant) captured Trinidadian pop culture with his 1977 hit "Norman Is That You." His calypso launched a debate — in communities, on television and radio, in the broadsheet and tabloid newspapers — about same-sex relationships. Many other calypsonians, especially those without record labels in their calypso tent, continued during Carnival seasons to sing and make fun of bullers in the most hostile and violent way.

That year people started to identify some mas bands as buller-men mas bands and some as heterosexual.[50] Hecklers on the street or within my family would call a male who walked, spoke, or acted in a feminine manner "Norman." The graphic, violent, and homophobic calypso "Pepper in the Vaseline" — a threatening reference to sexual practices — reflected prevailing attitudes towards bullers and batty bwoys. Another calypsonian's song said, "Come out at your own risk."

Then came calypsonian Edwin (a.k.a. Crazy) Ayoung's popular song titled "Take ah Man," a controversial song that became a private anthem and a way of reclaiming power for many gays in Trinidad, who enjoyed the double meaning of the song. His most empowering words for some bullers were "If yuh cyar get ah wooman, take ah man." Under the cover of discotheques and private parties in Trinidad, this song was loved and played often by bullers. The same experience was played out among Caribbean bullers and lesbians living in Canada.

As a buller, I found the calypso and the debates about the mas bands illuminating. I started to learn about places and people in Trinidad that had a culture of bullers. I discovered how they created their space for survival, their geographies and sites of pleasure. Although I did not attend their events or visit their homes, at least I knew that I was not alone and that there was an emerging culture of bullers that I would be able to embrace someday. If you were an out buller man, everybody called you Norman, buller, anti-man, panty man, shirley, or "she," and you dared not respond because physical and verbal violence would follow, with no police protection. Buller men both challenged and confirmed heterosexist norms, but could not offer a transformative challenge.

The movie *Norman . . . Is That You?* became a great concern for pastors. They reminded the congregation about the evils of same-sex relationships. There was a moral panic about men becoming bullers. Our parents warned us not to become a buller like Norman. I saw two options for myself: be silent or join in the slander of bullers. Most of the time I joined in the slander, because it helped me to erase guilt and provided privileged membership in the hyper-masculinized heterosexist club.

There was also a paucity of reading material on same-sex issues. The Bible, traditional psychology and psychiatry, and the local newspaper condemned bullers. Trinidadian weekly tabloids such as the *Bomb* and the *Punch,* and the daily newspaper, the *Express,* slandered men and women suspected of being in same-sex relationships. They would often publish a picture and write about someone in the most destructive and belittling way, sometimes urging that person to leave the community or even the country. The *Bomb* and the *Punch* reported the first known buller-man wedding in Trinidad, in 1982; the reports exposed the names of the two grooms and their families, which forced both men to quit their jobs and move to Canada, where they now live. Through this irresponsible reporting I learned a great deal about other bullers and zamis, and about the violence to expect if I decided to come out. I often hid from family members when I read these stories.

In reading rooms or libraries the subject of homosexuality appeared only in the sections about law, medicine, psychiatry, psychology, or sociology, under the topics of deviance, immorality, or mental illness. After discovering this pathology I ceased my search for reading material on same-sex issues. Eventually I turned to texts by black writers such as Stokely Carmichael, Eldridge Cleaver, Angela Davis, Bobby Seal, and Eric Williams, hoping to find a paragraph or two on black same-sex relationships. Instead, most of the ideologues of the 1960s and 1970s had negative views or had ignored the subject; their writings remained focused on the historical and often-virulent presence of racism. For brevity's sake, I will not develop further an analysis of the Black Power movement and its impact on homosexuality in Trinidad. However, black literary works, consciousness, ideology, and nationalism, and the discourses of black activists, have sought to present the race in the "best light," often depicting blacks with qualities, values, and beliefs admired by white, patriarchal right-wing society. Many black writers have felt great anxiety about presenting sexuality, same-sex desire, or feminist politics. In the words of bell hooks, black nationalism has been constructed as a "dick thing."[51] Henry Louis Gates Jr. has written, "That is not to say that the ideologue of Black Nationalism in this country has any unique claim on homophobia. But it is an almost obsessive motif that runs through the major authors of the Black aesthetic and the Black Power movements. In short, national identity became sexualized in the sixties and seventies in such a way as to engender a curious subterranean connection between homophobia and nationalism."[52] Nonetheless, these texts continue to help shape black culture, communal solidarity, and identity.

GIRLFRIENDS AND EXPLORING THE EROTIC

Social pressures and family and community values made me feel that I had to have a few "girlfriends" with whom I was intimate. This pressure was a combination of two forces: the normative prescriptions of family and community, and my own internalized fear and guilt about an attraction to men. Thus I sought out intimate relationships with women. These relationships, I hoped, would cure my same-sex erotic feelings and attach me to the rules of a heterosexist cultural masculinity within family and community. Being intimate with girlfriends, or having multiple sexual partners, was another way to exhibit my toughness and masculinity and to erase public suspicion about my being a buller man. However, my relationships with women did not last long, because I was never fully comfortable or satisfied with the resulting exploration of my erotic, emotional, and physical feelings.

I use the term "exploration of the erotic" in a broad sense, as Lorde has defined it: "Our deepest knowledge, a power that, unlike other spheres of power, we all have access to and that can lessen the threat of our individual difference."[53] A form of Caribbean state-ordained nationalism and religious hegemonization has discouraged such exploration by creating a "dualism central to [Caribbean/]Western thought, finding parallels in distinctions between good/evil, man/woman and a range of other binarisms, which have shaped the glass through which institutionalized Christianity (religion) has viewed the world: either/or; good/bad; us/them; soul/body."[54]

It is within these religious binarisms that I judged my same-sex attraction, often leading to a sense of shame, unhappiness, sinfulness, and dirtiness, while being torn apart inside.

The gender system (or prison), as Steven Seidman argues in "Identity Politics in a Postmodern Gay Culture," "is said to posit heterosexuality as a primary sign of gender normality. A true man loves women; a true woman loves men. Sex roles are a first, and central, distinction made by society."[55] The gender performance, as constructed for black manhood, has been both heterosexist and sexist. Marcel Saghir and Eli Robins state that "a majority of gay people irrespective of race [over half of gay men and more than three-quarters of gay women] have had heterosexual experiences."[56] This practice is common to many people in the Caribbean, although not unique to that region. Michael Warner calls this heteronormativity "the domination of norms that supports, reinforces and reproduces heterosexual social forms." For Warner, a reproductivist conception of the social institutions of hetero-sexual reproduction, institutions of socialization, and heterosexual hege-mony supplements this heteronormativity.[57]

As a social construct heteronormativity permeates what Gayle Rubin has called the "sex gender system," which codes everything from social class to race into a particular set of sexualized and gendered identities that constitute and reproduce the social system in which we live.[58] Clearly most bullers have accepted heterosexuality as the norm and have viewed homosexuality as abnormal, deviant, or different. Perhaps this explains why for bullers, ac-cording to Saghir and Robins, "the most frequently encountered emotional reaction following heterosexual involvement is that of indifference. It is not an aversion, nor a conscious fear of heterosexuality, for most homosexual women and men find no emotional aversion and feel no trepidation in becoming involved heterosexually. The determining factor in the subse-quent avoidance of heterosexual involvement is the lack of emotional grati-fication and true physical arousal with opposite sex partners."[59]

These norms invade same-sex practices by feminizing some black men who, when engaging in same-sex practices, act hyper-masculine in order to secure their heterosexuality and masculinity. Black nationalists and black individuals embracing stereotypical constructions of masculinity and black self-expression have sought to regulate and control the masculinity and sex-ual practices of bullers, and thereby to discourage all same-sex sexuality. As bullers, if we attempt to deconstruct and reconstruct the traditional black, nationalist, male, heterosexual gender "norms," we encounter great hostility and in some cases violence. Nevertheless, I resist the myopic definitions of "black masculinity" and "manhood." I do so to free myself from the black gender prison imposed on us by white racist constructions of black masculinity, which go hand-in-hand with the black ideologue's construction of family and black masculinity.

WITHOUT CONCLUSION

> And my brother's back at home, with his Beatles and his Stones. / We never got it off on that revolution, / What a drag, / Too many snags.
> — DAVID BOWIE, "All the Young Dudes" (performed by Mott the Hoople)

For me this debate is ongoing, hence "without conclusion" correctly captures the stage of our struggle for same-sex recognition and equal protection in law. I also want to say that although I have focused on my struggles as a Trinidadian, these struggles are common in other Caribbean islands. For example, a homophobia-fueled protest was staged in Jamaica in anticipation of a concert by the Village People in March of 2002 (their appearance was cancelled). In addition, when the Jamaican government suggested condom distribution in the prisons to the guards and inmates alike, the insulted (and, one might add, homophobic) guards walked off the job, setting off a series of riots in which prisoners killed sixteen of their fellow inmates believed to be batty bwoys or bullers. In the Bahamas, a cruise ship was turned back by the Bahamanian government when they found out that the cruise was filled with gay men from the United States. These are just a few examples of recent stories and issues that have plagued other Caribbean islands.

It would indeed be an understatement, from both a historical and a contemporary perspective, to say that Caribbean culture has been unkind to men and women who engage in same-sex practices and relationships. This is obvious in the policing of bodily practices, institutionalizing of hegemonic laws, acts of violence, compulsory heterosexist practices, and other borders that set bullers apart from heterosexuals through the denial of our human rights and dignity.

When Louis Althusser wrote that ideology represents "not the system of the real relations which govern the existence of individuals, but the imaginary relation of those individuals to the real relations in which they live" (and which govern their existence), he was also describing exactly, to my mind, the functioning of sexuality and sexual orientation.[60] An engendered space is negotiated within Althusserian Marxism, one of the most humanistic branches of Marxist thought. Here "negotiation" describes the process of including a formerly excluded, taboo, marginalized, or policed concern. So if, for example, many in Trinidad and the Caribbean do not see the struggle for same-sex recognition and human rights protection to be an important area for consideration, it is our responsibility as those who carry the burden and have a stake in social-justice work to always be vigilant, and to speak to issues of human rights concerns for men and women who have and are in same-sex relationships. The failure to do so leaves me to ask myself: Where has the passion for Left politics disappeared to, if no one is bringing this struggle to the forefront in Trinidad? Such passion does exist, as has been seen with Black Power movements in Trinidad. For example, who ever would have thought that we would have a Black Power revolution in the 1960s and another attempt to overthrow the ruling government on July 27, 1990, shutting down the country for almost two weeks?[61] Change is inevitable, and a sexual revolution is boiling and it will boil over soon, as it has started to boil over slowly in Jamaica.[62] It is hoped that other Caribbean islands, like Jamaica, will gain the confidence and garner the support for social activism on the issue of same-sex protection.

I have always been driven by the desire to serve my community and my people, and I believe that those who live in that community understand its problems. Some of those intelligent, sensitive, understanding, and resourceful people are women, buller men, and batty bwoys. I am frequently told that I can support and be active in heterosexist black organizations, attend sit-ins and street demonstrations, fight against police injustice, and work with homeless youths and their families. But I must not "flaunt" my "sickness," because it runs counter to black unity, black family values, and black collective consciousness.

Positing a split between being a good black person and Trinidadian and being gay can be dangerous, because of the inherent dangers of denying differences within our black communities. As Cornel West concludes in Marlon Riggs's documentary *Black Is . . . Black Ain't*, "We have got to conceive of new forms of community. We each have multiple identities, and we're moving in and out of various communities at the same time. There is no one grand Black community or Black male identity."[63] Stuart Hall, too, has called for a new kind of politics, based on the diversity of the black experience and recognizing black people's historically defined black experiences. Hall's plea for "a new kind of cultural politics" insists that we "recognize the other kinds of difference (those of gender, sexuality, race and class, for example) that place, position, and locate Black people."[64]

In summary, the lack of support in the Caribbean context for people engaging in same-sex practices, the violent attacks on people who seek same-sex agency or identities, and family, community, and religious oppression have made it impossible for people to engage in same-sex practices and be open about it. The Caribbean context has policed desire along lines of good and bad, clean and unclean, and has imposed stereotypical roles and expecta-tions on men and women, hence constructing at all times a heterosexual identity. We did not have a Stonewall riot in the Caribbean to give rise to a black same-sex politics that would support bullers politically, economically, and socially. However, I do foresee change in the Caribbean, due to North American hegemony, in this millennium. Just as many things have changed, we will see a change in the policing of peoples' attitudes in the Caribbean, in particular when women join the struggle for sexual liberation, and I do believe that the collective will is there and that the time is soon.[65] State and cultural power will shift in their policing of differences. As the Chicana poet Gloria Anzaldúa writes:

> Borders are set up to define the places that are safe and unsafe, to distinguish us from them. A borderland is a dividing line, a narrow strip along a steep edge. A borderland is a vague and undetermined place created by the emo-tional residue of an unnatural boundary. It is in a constant state of transition. The prohibited and forbidden are its inhabitants. *Los atravesados* live here: the squint-eyed, the perverse, the queer, the troublesome, the half-breed, the half-dead; in short, those who cross over, pass over, or go through the confines of the "normal."[66]

And these borders we will cross!

NOTES

1 "Buller man" is an indigenous derogatory epithet that I grew up with in Trinidad and Tobago, used to refer to men who have sex with other men. It is also widely used in some English-speaking Caribbean islands such as St. Lucia, St. Vincent, and Barbados. For more information on the term, see Richard Allsopp, *The Dictionary of Caribbean English Usage* (London: Oxford University Press, 1996), 120. Future references to Trinidad and Tobago will be abbreviated to "Trinidad."

2 See hooks, *Talking Back: Thinking Feminist, Thinking Black* (Boston: South End Press, 1988); Lorde, *Sister Outsider: Essays and Speeches* (Trumansburg, N.Y.: Crossing Press, 1984).

3 "Heterosexist" refers to characteristics of an ideological system that denies, deni-

grates, and stigmatizes non-heterosexual forms of behavior, identity, relationship, or community. The end result of this dynamic is oppression, intolerance, and daily acts of violence.

4 Karen Olson and Linda Shopes. "Crossing Boundaries, Building Bridges: Doing Oral History among Working Class Women and Men," in *Women's Words: The Feminist Practice of Oral History,* ed. S. Berger Gluck and D. Patai (New York: Routledge, 1991), 200.

5 Minh-ha, *The Framer Framed* (New York: Routledge, 1992), 129.

6 While I am attempting to use or restore indigenous sexual terms or knowledge specific to Trinidad, I am also at the same time echoing Jamaican anthropologist Charles V. Carnegie, who argues that "as we seek to restore indigenous terms and knowledge systems, we must simultaneously seek to sharpen an 'indigenous' criticism." Charles V. Carnegie, "On Liminal Subjectivity" (paper presented at the National Symposium on Indigenous Knowledge and Contemporary Social Issues, Tampa, Florida, March 3, 1994).

Hence the use of the term "buller man" is not without criticism due to North American hegemony in Trinidad, but it is important to employ this concept because this move signifies a break with the white hegemony of lesbian and gay politics and the recent development of queer theory. Finally and importantly, when I was in Trinidad it was the term I knew.

7 Lorde uses the term *biomythography* to describe her work *Zami: A New Spelling of My Name* (Trumansburg, N.Y: Crossing Press, 1982).

8 Lorde, reaching back into the past, remembering her Grenadian mother's history in a small island called Carriacou, tells us that *zami* is "a Carriacou name for women who work together as friends and lovers." The word comes from the French patois for *les amies*, lesbians. For more on this, see Lorde, *Zami*, 255.

9 Ibid.

10 Anne McClintock, *Imperial Leather: Race, Gender and Sexuality in the Colonial Context* (New York: Routledge, 1995), 315.

11 Gumbo is a traditional Southern black American dish made from a combination of seafood, poultry, meats, sausages, and other ingredients. For Riggs, "gumbo" as metaphor expresses who we are as black people: "Some are light skin, dark skin, Christian, atheist, men, women, women who love women, men who love men, a little bit of everything that makes whole Black communities." Riggs, *Black Is . . . Black Ain't* (San Francisco: Independent Television Service/California Newsreel, 1995).

12 Sexual orientation, according to Bonnie Simpson, "refers to an individual's predisposition to experience physical and affectional attraction to members of the same, the other or both sexes. Established early in life, it is the result of a little-understood but complex set of genetic, biological, and environmental factors" (Simpson, *Opening Doors: Making Substance Abuse and Other Services More Accessible to Lesbian, Gay, and Bi-sexual Youth* [Toronto: Central Toronto Youth Services, 1994], 5).

13 Max van Manen, "Practicing Phenomenological Writing," *Phenomenology + Pedagogy* 2, no. 1 (1984): 45.

14 Gramsci, *The Modern Prince and Other Writings* (1957; New York: International Publishers, 1990), 118.

15 Gramsci, *Selections from the Prison Notebooks* (New York: International Publishers, 1971).

16 Abu-Lughod, *Writing Women's Worlds: Bedouin Stories* (Berkeley: University of California Press, 1993), 27.

17 Lorde, *A Burst of Light: Essays on Sexuality and Difference* (Toronto: Women's Press, 1992), 47.

18 Alexander, "Not Just (Any) *Body* Can Be a Citizen: The Politics of Law, Sexuality and Postcoloniality in Trinidad and Tobago and the Bahamas," *Feminist Review*, no. 34 (1994): 9.

19 hooks, *Black Looks: Race and Representation* (Boston: South End Press, 1992).

20 The metaphorical term "closet" is used to talk about persons who are aware of their same-sex attractions and identities, but choose not to declare them to the public, family, friends, community, or coworkers. To "be in the closet" results in others assuming that you are "heterosexual," or repressed and living in social isolation.

21 Hall, "What Is This 'Black' in Black Popular Culture?" in *Black Popular Culture*, ed. Gina Dent (Seattle: Bay Press, 1992), 31.

22 Du Bois, *The Souls of Black Folk* (Chicago: National Urban League, 1903).

23 Ibid., 16–17.

24 Altman, *Homosexual: Oppression and Liberation* (New York: Outbridge and Dienstfrey, 1971), 74.

25 Barry Adam, *The Survival of Domination: Inferiorization and Everyday Life* (New York: Elsevier, 1978), 44.

26 Rubin, "Thinking Sex: Notes for a Radical Theory of the Politics of Sexuality," in *Pleasure and Danger: Exploring Female Sexuality*, ed. Carole Vance (Boston: Routledge and Kegan Paul, 1984), 279.

27 Alexander, "Not Just (Any) *Body* Can Be a Citizen," 5–6.

28 Batty boy/bwoy/man is a derogatory term indigenous to Jamaica, but it is also commonly used in Antigua and Guyana to describe sexual practices between men who have sex with other men (Allsopp, *The Dictionary of Caribbean English Usage*, 84). I have not been able to discover its etymology as I have been able to do with buller man, but an adequate history of the genesis of the term might help to enable its use in contemporary Caribbean theories in the area of study on sex and sexuality.

29 Noel and Marriott, "Batty Boys in Babylon: Can Gay West Indians Survive the 'Boom Bye Bye' Posses?" *Village Voice*, January 12, 1993, 30.

30 Butler, *Gender Trouble: Feminism and the Subversion of Identity* (London: Routledge, 1989), 256.

31 Alexander, "Not Just (Any) *Body* Can Be a Citizen," 13. While the nuclear, conjugal family may be the "ideal," it is not the norm for most in the Caribbean. But some Caribbean parents still push for that ideal to protect class image and identity.

32 Wahneema Lubiano, ed., *The House that Race Built: Black Americans, U.S. Terrain* (New York: Pantheon, 1997), 241.

33 In Trinidad, the Sexual Offences Act or Sodomy Laws of 1986, sections 13 and 16, and the Immigration Act of 1986, article 8 (18/1), prohibit and regulate

sexual activity between consenting adults and declare homosexuality illegal in the country.

34 Butler, *Gender Trouble*, 122.

35 David Morgan, "It Will Make a Man of You: Notes on National Service, Masculinity and Autobiography," *Studies in Sexual Politics,* no. 17 (1987): 48, 82.

36 The savanna is the grounds used for sporting, political, and cultural activities.

37 Wickham and Haver, "Come Out, Come Out, Wherever You Are: A Guide for the Homoerotically Disadvantaged" (typescript, 1992), 36.

38 Weeks, "Discourse, Desire, and Sexual Deviance," in *The Making of the Modern Homosexual,* ed. Kenneth Plummer (London: Hutchinson, 1981), 117.

39 Sedgwick, "How to Bring Your Kids up Gay," in *Fear of a Queer Planet: Queer Politics and Social Theory,* ed. Michael Warner (Minneapolis: University of Minnesota Press, 1993), 72.

40 Ibid., 72–73.

41 Lynne Segal, *Slow Motion: Changing Masculinities, Changing Men* (New Brunswick, N.J.: Rutgers University Press, 1990), 139.

42 Raphael, *The Men from the Boys: Rites of Passage in Male America* (Lincoln: University of Nebraska Press, 1988), 138.

43 Ibid., 3.

44 Blaxploitation films involved black actors being trapped in the racist, stereotypical "other" position, while white actors were cast as heroes and smart people. Blacks were always thieves, shiftless, lazy, and unintelligent; often the first to be killed, they sometimes acted in stereotypically humorous ways to gain acceptance.

45 Mercer and Watney, "Imagining the Black Man's Sex," in *Photography/Politics: Two,* ed. Patricia Holland, Jo Spence, and Simon Watney (London: Commedia/Methuen, 1988), 136.

46 Majors and Billson, *Cool Pose: The Dilemmas of Black Manhood in America* (New York: Lexington, 1992), 4.

47 Geraldine was created, according to Flip Wilson, because while he was working, white men would often come up to him and invoke the age-old racist and sexist stereotype, asking, "Hey, can you get me a girl?" He took offense to this and wanted to erase white society's racist stereotype by creating a proud, independent and dignified black woman, so he created Geraldine. See Mel Watkins, "The Whole Cookie," *AFP Reporter* 3, no. 1 (1979): n.p., http://www.aliciapatterson .org/APF0301/APF0301.html.

48 Sypher, "The Social Meanings of Comedy," in *Comedy: "An Essay on Comedy," by George Meredith, and "Laughter," by Henri Bergson,* ed. Sypher (Baltimore: Johns Hopkins University Press, 1980), 242.

49 George Schlatter, *Norman . . . Is That You?* (Los Angeles: Metro Goldwyn Mayer, 1976).

50 I had many male friends who had sex with other men and also played in mas bands, such as Peter Minshall, Wayne Berkley, Stephen Lee Young, and Harold Saldenah. They informed me that these were the bands to play with, or that I should attend these bands' launching parties in order to meet other bullers. They also stressed that this was an ideal opportunity to meet tourists who were bullers and who came to play mas — in particular Peter Minshall's band. Minshall's band,

they argued, had the most whites (tourists or locals) who were bullers. These bands and mas tents often got my undivided attention, because I saw this as a way to seek out men like myself, but I was afraid to get close to them or let any of my hyper-masculinist friends or family know that I found these bands interesting, or that I liked them. I felt that if I mentioned any of these bands to my friends, it would make me the target of suspicion, a suspicion I could not deal with or defend myself against at the time.

51 hooks, *Feminist Theory: From Margin to Center* (Boston: South End Press, 1984).

52 Gates, "The Black Man's Burden," in *Fear of a Queer Planet*, 79.

53 Lorde, *Sister Outsider*, 53.

54 Sedgwick, *Espistemology of the Closet* (Berkeley: University of California Press, 1990), 123.

55 Seidman, "Identity and Politics in Postmodern Gay Culture: Some Historical and Conceptual Notes," in *Fear of a Queer Planet*, 114.

56 Saghir and Robins, *Male and Female Homosexuality: A Comprehensive Investigation* (Baltimore: Williams and Wilkins, 1973), 92.

57 Warner, ed., introduction to *Fear of a Queer Planet*, xviii. See also vii–xxviii.

58 See Rubin, "Thinking Sex."

59 Saghir and Robins, *Male and Female Homosexuality*, 92.

60 Althusser, *Lenin and Philosophy* (London: New Left Books, 1977), 1.

61 On Friday, July 27, 1990, at approximately 5:30 p.m., a group of black Muslims, members of the Jamaat Al Muslimeen, took over the nation's parliament at the Red House in the capital city of Port of Spain. Nineteen hostages were captured; among them were the prime minister, members of Parliament and other civil servants. For more on this, see Ramesh Deosaran, *A Society under Siege: A Study of Political Confusion and Legal Mysticism* (St. Augustine, Trinidad: McAl Psychological Research Centre, University of the West Indies, 1993).

62 On June 5, 2002, the Jamaica Forum for Lesbians, All-Sexuals and Gays (J-FLAG) made a historic presentation to the Jamaican parliament's Joint Committee on the Charter of Rights to make the case for protecting Jamaicans from discrimination on the grounds of sexual orientation. J-FLAG, *J-FLAG Newsletter*, June 2002.

63 Riggs, *Black Is . . . Black Ain't*.

64 Hall, "What Is This 'Black' in Black Popular Culture?" 31.

65 It might be presumptuous of me to assume that the women's struggle in the Caribbean will bring the debate for same-sex recognition closer to the local human rights agenda. But I make this statement as an observer of the feminist struggles in North America, which also created an opening for debates about redefinitions of the family, which in turn led to legal discussions about same-sex rights, which eventually became law.

66 Anzaldúa, *Borderlands/La Frontera: The New Mestiza* (San Francisco: Aunt Lute Press, 1987), 3.

MABEL CUESTA

Other Islanders on Lesbos:
A Retrospective Look at the History of
Lesbians in Cuba (2004)

MATANZAS, CUBA, TWENTY-FIRST CENTURY

In a Cuban city in the winter of the third year of the twenty-first century, fed up with sleeping in rooms borrowed from generous friends, in hotels, or in our own houses subject to our mothers' changing moods, Clara and I decided to build a room of our own. To demonstrate our concordance with the thesis of Virginia Woolf: Clara and I are both writers. Our annual income in pesos is scarce. Building a room with the same hands with which we make love to each other would be difficult and the results rude at best. We're weak, fragile of body and *ánimo,* we lack brothers or fathers, and we have few friends strong in ánimo and body. But we decided to put the dream in motion nonetheless. And so trucks appeared in the street where we planned to raise the walls. Trucks loaded with bags of cement, stones, artificial sand, sheets of steel. Clara and I set ourselves to the task of carrying them, getting them safely under a borrowed roof until construction day should arrive.

We took up shovel and wheelbarrow, but our effort lasted only a second. As in some fantasy movie, young men blossomed from every corner. Handsome, very strong, from the neighborhood. Macho, probably promiscuous, probably abusers too. They know who we are and why we want to build our own room. Nonetheless, glowing, cheerful, cooperative, and anxious to compete among themselves to see who was strongest, they carried our construction materials for us.

This event, of course, can be read in various ways. Implicit in the story is the survival of a style of upbringing based on a strict distribution of roles, walled compartments which a man cannot permit that women should transgress in his presence. There is also the old competitive instinct which lays siege to men. The presence of three or four piles of material needing to be shoveled is a magnificent opportunity to create a small championship competition, to test who is the best. The values in this competition are strength and agility, which redound to the *areté* of the hero. And the hero is always the best man.

But if the center of the spectacle is a dissonant element, then all the foregoing is destabilized. The dissonant element is a lesbian couple. These men don't need to prove — to us — anything about their areté, their manliness, their capacity for seduction by way of strength. They know beforehand that there is no point.

In the world view of orthodox masculinity, two women who have chosen a sexual variant that excludes men are empty of all value not only as social subjects, but also as actors within a reality in which we supposedly don't exist, because our world is walled off by silence. Of course, there may remain another possibility: the typical male fantasy in which two females make love to each other only so that men can watch them, later to skewer both women with their members, demonstrating that every woman's true pleasure is crowned by heterosexual intercourse. Probably in helping us to move the material, those young men hoped to ensure their nocturnal entrance to the room Clara and I would build. Helping us helped them to consolidate their fantasies.

There remains, though, yet another possible thesis to explore: that of authentic and disinterested aid. That thesis would demonstrate an emerging possibility: perhaps in Cuba in the twenty-first century, the only participants in reality who continue to marginalize minorities are those in power. This might be bad news, given that power generates 100 percent of the visible discourses. But I have always had faith in the interstices, in that which slips secretly through the cracks. In the Cuban case this becomes one more form of response to a political discourse that has always tended toward the masculinization of the nation. Such masculinization is reinforced by the image of a bearded and booted leader, the size of whose reproductive organs is always emphasized through slogans and symbolic images, to reinforce the value of his invariably positive feats.

In a country where children, every morning for the first ten years of their schooling, chant their aspiration to be like another great leader praised for his masculine attributes, his power of seduction, his daring and his beauty (Ché Guevera), we have to understand that the hour of over-saturation of these manly fetishes has arrived. Along with the crisis of power, a crisis of masculinity is slowly developing. This of course has its echoes in the Cuban lesbian community.

For a good portion of the male heterosexual population, women who have excluded them from their sexual preferences are no longer sick and obscene aberrations. Of course, this change is not quantifiable. Nothing in Cuba is. The statistics on violence, homosexuality, transvestism, transsexuality, workplace discrimination against women, racism, and many other symptoms that the "revolutionary" society finds unpleasant have been placed firmly out of sight. All Cuban and foreign researchers who have taken on the task of examining such data have met with prohibitions and the consequent frustration of their projects. Nonetheless, the simple and localized gesture of a group of young men uninhibitedly collaborating with the building project of a pair of provincial lesbians speaks, at least, of a positive displacement that has taken place in the world view of Cuban heteronormality.

THE '80S AND THE "DANGEROUSNESS DOSSIER"

For those with some knowledge of the history of the last twenty-five years on the island, it is no secret that in the '80s, when socialism supposedly brought its first real dose of security to the island's economy, the first signs of disillusionment and crisis paradoxically appeared within several generational groups. The explanation for this paradox lies in the fact that the security was more apparent than real. Any growth in the economy did not stem from internal development of the country's industrial capacity, but rather from strong injections of capital by the Council on Mutual Economic Aid (CMEA), made up of the countries of eastern Europe. A new generation, a new group that advanced silently — young people, who had been completely educated in the "revolutionary ideology" — observed this cosmetic growth skeptically. They also observed, with fascination, the North American model of progress that arrived secretly in the photos of family members exiled on the other shore of the Cuban island: the city of Miami and other small emigrant enclaves like Madrid, Mexico City, New York, Orlando, Lima, or San Juan.

Those in power took note of this double stance of incredulity and fascination. As is the custom in such situations, the habitual policy of taking a hard line intensified. So began the so-called and much-feared *expedientes de peligrosidad* (files or dossiers of "dangerousness"). Police offices across the country opened such files on young people of both sexes who committed crimes such as: wearing T-shirts that bore messages in foreign languages other than the Slavic ones (English was, logically, the most demonized); meeting repeatedly in streets and other public places with groups of young people of dubious political conduct; failing to study or work within state institutions; appearing or being homosexual; having very close relations with others who were members of such suspicious sectors; engaging in prostitution either openly or secretly. In sum: being *suspicious*.

The policy of maintaining such files was aided by two indispensable bodies: the CDRs (Committees for the Defense of the Revolution), long organized in every street and neighborhood of the country, composed of neighbors themselves and directed by the leaders of each block; and the secret police, or G-2, whose agents in many cases sprang from those same supposedly marginal groups.

Daysi Gómez is a lesbian who was born in 1966. At twelve years of age she discovered her sexual identity and began to manifest it — not without some fear or distress. At sixteen, tired of her schoolmates' teasing about her androgynous physique and steadfast silence, she decided to drop out of school. She shut herself inside her house, where she tried to survive with minor black market businesses and minimal family aid. When she turned eighteen, she needed a real love. By then she was sick of being confined like a convalescent within the walls of her room, of the inquisitive looks of her neighbors, and especially of her mother's insistence that she find a husband or go to work. Daysi decided to go every night, in the darkness, to the main plaza of the city. There she met Ana, a woman of thirty-five who jumped out the window of her bedroom when her husband began to snore and went with her young female lover to the banks of one of the rivers that passed through the center of the small city, to release her secret passion. Daysi was able to love Ana for no more than three months. By the fourth she was in jail, and her lover too. They were accused of being "women dangerous to the citizens' welfare, to civic decency, and to the values of the revolutionary new man." The sentences handed down to these women were ten years' privation of liberty. Their crime: to meet and kiss in the darkness on a riverbank.

THE '70S: THE UMAP, "PARAMETERIZATION," OR MARRIAGE AND FORGETTING

When the writers Heberto Padilla, Lina de Feria, Antón Arrufat and others were publicly accused of creating works that did not respond to the interests and ideologies of the revolution, the witch hunt caught up many more intellectuals and artists as well. These others were not witches by virtue of their political stances or their ideas, but rather because of their intimate lives. For, by definition, artists and intellectuals had to be consenting and forgiving actors in the construction of the new society.

In a sadly celebrated speech given by the commander in chief in 1962, the positions which a thinker or simple Cuban citizen could assume were reduced to one. The order was clear: "Inside the revolution, everything; against the revolution, nothing." Those singulars — inside or against — clearly marked the frontiers of what might be imagined, and they were consistently dictated by those in power.

From that order stemmed a vehement and meticulous hunt for homosexuals, both intellectual and otherwise. To that end were created first the Unidades Militares para la Ayuda de Producción (UMAP; Military Units in Support of Production) and later the process of "parameterization." Both had the same goal: to remove the intellectuals and artists from their workplaces (usually in cultural institutions) and send them to camps or factories to work in jobs ranging from agriculture to construction.

There was, however, one avenue of escape from such punishment: to lie. In 1973, Onélida Rodríguez was studying humanities at the University of Havana. She was in love, and the person with whom she shared this love was a female classmate. After a year of maintaining an intense and half-visible passion, both were called into the office of their dean. In a friendly manner, and completely ashamed, he asked them to request withdrawals from the institution. That was the best option they had. If they didn't take it, he would be obliged to fill in their dossiers, declare them lesbians, and send them to the UMAP or "parameterize" them to some factory in the provinces. They were high-achieving students, and he did not desire such ostracism for them. Better they should go home, wait for the bad times to blow over, and then re-register in a new major, maybe in another city where nobody knew them. Maybe get married, perhaps to friends under some mutual accord. . . . They should do something, but they should get out of his institution, and soon.

Onélida went to the city of Matanzas where she met Juan, a gay man who had been expelled from the concert choir of the Ministry of Culture for his uninhibited projection as a man who loved other men. They agreed to get married, and did. They had a daughter, and have passed the last thirty years of their life writing horrible radio musical shows. They have each had an endless number of homoerotic relationships, but always past midnight in places where they think no one can see them, or in a household they put together with friends of both sexes under the pretext of a work collaboration, where they lived for a certain time so that "the project they were carrying out could yield the best results."

A VERY ELOQUENT FLASHBACK

In the 1920s, the outstanding feminist journalist Mariblanca Sabás Alomá tried to establish all possible distance between feminists and lesbians. To this end she publicly declared that lesbianism or *garzonismo*[1] was "a disgusting worm that is eating away at a generation of women." Thus one of the pioneers of the women's suffrage movement (which became the feminist movement) in the Cuban republic was also a pioneer of one of the oldest unresolved debates within traditional feminism: that over the exclusion of lesbians from the most orthodox and militant body of feminism. That separation, and the resultant exclusion from future feminist discussion, inaugurated the sustained silence within which lesbian women on the island have lived. As a result they have not participated in the emancipatory projects or the demands for basic women's rights which have taken place in both pre- and postrevolutionary Cuba.

For the forty-five years since 1959, the organization which has concerned itself with problems that affect all women, the Cuban Women's Federation, has not carried out any project that recognizes or evaluates the rights, visibility, and representation of lesbian women. With respect to lesbians, the government of the revolution has retained the same mechanism for minimizing their concerns that it also applies to blacks, mulattos, heterosexual women, homosexual men, transvestites, transsexuals, and peasants. This is none other than the democratizing maxim that declares an equality of duties and rights for all subjects living in the nation, independently of their conditions of race, class, or sex. Underneath this tabula rasa that equalizes all subjects, all the interests dissonant to the project of creating the "new man," which the revolution defined very early, have remained buried. The definition of the "new man" logically empathized most with the modern occidental subject: male, white, heterosexual. This subject has been enthroned in the center of the imagery despite the country's leadership's many verbal struggles to dislodge it.

Similarly, the Cuban Women's Federation has always carried out its dialogue with an archetype of the Cuban woman as "the socialist and federated worker": mother, wife, and worker, too. That is the woman to whom songs are dedicated and for whom an entire iconography has been designed in which she tends to appear with a child in one hand and a rifle or tool in the other. She may be seen in the factories, or working abroad as a doctor in some fraternal country. Stoic and happy.

Over the past decade, both Cuban reality and a good part of the traditional iconography have changed drastically, in parallel ways. A new type of woman has appeared, one to whom the Cuban Women's Federation attends directly and with priority. These women are none other than the prostitutes (also silenced until their explosive entrance into the tolerance zones for tourists). Women who engage in prostitution have recently been portrayed in television soap operas — always as negative characters, yet near at hand and humanized in their conflicts. In spite of appearing in the context of a conventional morality that teaches what one should or should not do, they are there, on the screen, an image and a possibility. Lesbians, meanwhile, though they have also grown in numbers in recent times, are still a pending future episode for a federation which in principle should include us, since we are Cuban women too.

SEEING IS BELIEVING

To continue with the theme of visibility, there are two very illustrative examples that speak to what occurs in the local mass media, especially television. In 1998 Cuban television produced a *telenovela* called *La otra cara de la moneda* (The other side of the coin; TVC 1998). It showed controversial subjects which up until then had remained invisible in Cuban media: alcoholism, prostitution, domestic violence, homicide, use of drugs among young people, and finally, a story of love between women. The appearance of this last subplot was surprising — as surprising as it was brief. This quick love story lasted only three episodes. In the first, the two young women met and fell in love. In the second, one of them left her alcoholic and abusive husband and revealed the love she felt for her new friend. In the third, one of them died in a train wreck.

After a lapse of five years in which no other male or female director of either TV or film was moved to kill off any more lesbian lovers, a new lesbian love story appeared in a telenovela called *El balcón de los helechos* (The fern balcony; TVC 2004). This time nobody died. The two women lived together, they were happy, they took on the raising of a small boy, and acted like any other family, except that their relationship as a sexual couple had to be guessed by sharp-eyed viewers. In none of the fifty episodes of the series did any character allude to their status or functioning as a couple. There was no touching or other visible detail to represent them as such. They lived together and were not blood relatives. They were equally devoted to bringing up the child and offered him equal caresses and pampering. Through the figure of this little boy, the anxious scriptwriter exhausted all the possibilities of legitimizing the young women's relationship. The required verbal and gestural omissions could be concretely expressed only in the affection the two women showed toward their son.

A DOOR, A LITTLE DOOR

One year ago, under the auspices of the Centro Nacional de Educación Sexual (CENESEX; National Center for the Study of Sexuality), the Sociedad Cubana Multidisciplinaria de Estudios para la Diversidad Sexual (SOCUMED; Cuban Multidisciplinary Society for the Study of Sexual Diversity) emerged. Its objectives, among many others, include the elimination of a series of ambiguous statements with homophobic edges in the Cuban penal code. Both in its headquarters and in other sites, the society has offered space for the exhibition and promotion of art works, documentaries, concerts, and theater pieces which directly address the theme of homosexuality in general and lesbianism in particular. This news is encouraging, more for the hope of long-term projects that it raises than for what has been achieved so far.

In Cuba, with the creation of SOCUMED within CENESEX, the usual gap (unquestionable and often unbreachable) between theory and practice has been reversed. In this case, it's theory and official support that are catching up. For once the signs of reality in daily life have come first. These signs are making the displacement of the heteronormative world view visible, as I illustrated by beginning with the story of young men who collaborated in the building of our room and those of many other couples who manage, with increasing ease, to live together.

Our room in itself, besides being symbolic, is also symptomatic of a change in the degree to which Clara and I respond to certain oppressive class-based conditioning and is indicative of our new role in raising an adolescent girl for whom we feel profoundly responsible. We have to admit that twenty or thirty years ago, probably neither of us would have risked our professional jobs or the girl's "healthy" membership in the non-marginal circles where the children of heterosexual fathers and mothers reside.

We are making ourselves visible by way of a highly significant space: a room in which to live together, in a country where it is almost impossible not to share intimate space with family members, neighbors, and workmates because the classic borderlines between private space and public space have been dynamited.[2] This is an event that speaks to the relaxation of both official and popular repression on the island.

Logically, no one at any level of the power structure has begun to speak of rights for female couples or homosexual men. Marriage, adoption, recognition as de facto couples, pensions, or other elemental recognitions granted heterosexual families are another still pending episode in Cuba. There is no indicator to verify the existence of a social movement, and the Cuban homosexual community remains, as in the rest of the world, closed in on itself. This may be seen particularly at the time of popular festivals, when gays and lesbians tend to go to very localized meeting places, always semi-removed from the rest of the participants.

In a city in the center of the island, Santa Clara, there is a night club which, since the end of the '80s, has challenged all levels of power and all the boycotts that have attempted to erase it. This club, El Mejunje, has officially presented transvestite shows. Gays and lesbians from all over the country have visited El Mejunje, and only there have expressed their love in an uninhibited and legitimized way. In the rest of the country, they have secret, illegal parties in private houses whose owners charge admission to homosexuals who decide to attend, dance, embrace, kiss, or — as García Lorca says — *draw a map of their desire so they can live in it.*

STILL SIMMERING BEANS

As this brief and fragmented panorama shows, Cuban society is one more arena in which, as we say in Spanish to indicate that a given phenomenon exists in all parts, the beans have simmered and are simmering still. And this means beans of all kinds. But the beans of which I am now speaking, our own, have simmered very slowly and under cover, and their progress has always depended on the cook. The cook has always been in charge of the regulation and consumption of the beans. Sometimes the decision has been to ration them, and sometimes to hide them away because they stink. Sometimes the cook has pretended not to see them, and has served a spread to suit any and all tastes. What the cook has never done is to post the whole menu outside the door. Potential diners have always had to guess what dishes are being served — to take a risk.

For now, what the cook has not been able to control is the aroma of the beans, which floats out the windows of the closed kitchen. The aromas, all of them, ensure that now — after so many years of resistance, of imprisoned lesbians still unknown, of suicide victims who seem never to have existed, of families separated by shame and resentment — the young men of our *barrio,* as I write, are keeping tabs on our construction, asking when we'll be living in this room of our own, and our daughter dreams of throwing a party there for her friends.

If I sound hopeful, it's because I am.

Matanzas, November 2004, while the masons spread a mixture of sand and cement on the roof.

Translated by Dick Cluster

NOTES

1 Term derived from the French *garçonne*, used to designate lesbian women in the first decades of the twentieth century.

2 The long economic crisis which has beset Cuba almost since its discovery has resulted in relatively frequent invasions of private space. To begin with, very few couples can live alone because of the difficulty of renting, buying, or building a house. Also, neighbors and relatives may appear unannounced at any moment. There are few telephones with which to make plans in advance. The heat and the high indices of unemployment lead people to spend a lot of their time outside, on the street. But all this is fodder for a different, anthropological article on Cuban reality and the generation of world views from a situation of scarcity.

OCHY CURIEL

Autonomy in Lesbian-Feminist Politics (2004)

1 MY POLITICAL STANCE

I'm a feminist. I see feminism as a political and theoretical construction, a form of seeing and constructing the world so as to destroy a patriarchy based on sexism, economic exploitation, obligatory heterosexuality, classism, and racism — linked systems that fundamentally affect women.

As a result, my lesbianism is also feminist. To me, this is not a sexual identity that implies an essentialism by which we must define ourselves. Rather, it is a strategic position which deeply questions one of the institutions on which patriarchy is based: heterosexuality as a norm that defines women's fundamental function as reproductive within the space of a heterosexual family where they are economically exploited by their husbands. In that sense, lesbianism is for me a way to subvert the heterosexual institution and its functions, as well as its legitimacy and its compulsory status.

I also see lesbianism as a questioning of roles and identities defined as "feminine" or "masculine," so as to create other logics, neither stereotyped nor dichotomous, and other social relations.

I further believe that lesbianism allows the creation of solidarity among women. It has the potential to turn complicity into political and personal ties and eventually create strong collective movements to transform the subordinated position in which women, especially lesbians, find themselves. As Adrienne Rich says, "It is crucial that we understand lesbianism in the deepest, most radical sense: as that love for ourselves and other women, that commitment to the freedom of all of us."[1]

My political position also springs from my African descent, which makes me consider the historical conditions that have generated racism, xenophobia, and economic, social, and cultural exclusion. These fruits of colonization and neocolonization affect a large portion of the world's population, especially women and many lesbians.

This clarification is important because it explains the stance from which I carry out lesbian politics (fundamentally with lesbians, but not exclusively so) and create alliances with particular groups of women.

My feminist political work, too, is autonomous — both in the personal sphere and in the collective one.

2 THE MEANING AND CONTEXT OF AUTONOMY

DEFENDING AUTONOMY

One of the strategies of patriarchy is to create dependence on its own institutions and norms: the state, churches, political parties, the heterosexual family, couples, money, compulsory motherhood. With this in mind, I see autonomy as ideological, material, and normative independence from those institutions and mechanisms, which otherwise defeat or distort the political struggle of any collective social movement or individual social subjects, depriving them of their radicalism and their goals. The effects of such conditioning on political struggles can appear in their visions, their political positions, the issues they address, their strategies, and their actions.

BUILDING AUTONOMY IN WOMEN'S HISTORY

Throughout history, many feminists have put forth autonomy as a goal. They have opted for autonomy in the face of differing systems and institutions, permitting many women to throw off a large part of the logic of patriarchy. The type of autonomy has been neither homogeneous nor unchanging. It has varied according to historical contexts and social conflicts.

The first underpinnings of the feminist movement appeared in the context of the French Revolution and the Enlightenment, which transformed the world according to principles of equality, fraternity, and liberty. However, they did so by universalizing a subject that excluded a great part of the population: women. Many women questioned the male-centered vision of humanity that was woven into universal declarations of the rights of "man," and they began to create autonomy in their political world. As they demanded rights of citizenship, equality in working conditions, suffrage, and educational opportunity, they formed women-only associations, organizations, and clubs.

In the years after World War II, the women's liberation movement emerged. Feminists no longer paraded under the banner of equality as members of a universal humanity, but rather began to redefine themselves as autonomous political subjects. Groups of women began to organize in the countryside, in neighborhoods, and within unions. Inside the parties of the Left, feminine groupings formed, made up of feminists and other women striving to shape a revolutionary project that would include their agenda. However, the entrenched power and machismo of the male "revolutionaries" of the era did not make room for the promotion within those parties of the feminist vision which many women had begun to adopt. Later, many feminists broke with the parties of the Left, thus increasing the number of women-only collectives and associations. Once again women, feminists, created their own autonomy in the face of political institutions that would not include their goals.

The 1970s saw the emergence and growth of consciousness-raising groups, important autonomous spaces for the feminist politics of the era, in which the personal became political.

The fall of the Berlin Wall in 1989 and the end of the USSR in 1991 provoked a profound change through which the world became unipolar, under the domination of the United States and western Europe. This change brought with it what many have called the "loss of utopias," as well as an absence of clear structural alternatives, which affected all social movements. At the same time, we can see a change in much of feminist politics. Starting with the first World Conference on Women in 1975 — followed by one in Nairobi in 1985, one in Vienna on human rights in 1993, one in Cairo in 1994, and finally the World Conference on Women in Beijing in 1995 — we entered the era of the "politics of the possible." NGO-ization, bureaucratization, and experts on gender all institutionalized feminism to the point where it lost its radicalism, its subversive project of transformation. Dialoguing with governments, lobbying at world conferences, and following up on the accords reached at those conferences were and still are the most common forms of feminist politics. Much of feminism did and does follow the agenda of the United Nations. Some lesbian feminists have become enmeshed in this logic as well.

International cooperation played a basic role in this change. The financing of feminist politics shaped and conditioned it in terms of what issues it confronted and how it functioned internally (more efficiency, less politics). Autonomy was no longer the vision to support. On the contrary, the agenda of the UN and international cooperation agencies (especially the United States Agency for International Development [USAID], the World Bank, the Inter-American Development Bank [IDB], and many European agencies) was creating units of production, micro credit for women, participation in national dialogues, the inclusion of feminist leaders within government bodies, a "gender" perspective that replaced and depoliticized the concept of "feminism," the rise of male studies, the change from "abortion" to "reproductive and sexual rights," and conflict resolution. That is, more economic dependency for women, more debt, more promotion into male spheres, less confrontation. The feminist movement was co-opted. This co-optation has had dismal consequences: the depoliticization and division of the feminist movement and of the lesbian feminists within it.

Some feminists, among them many lesbians in the Americas, began to question this phenomenon. The late Miriam Botassi from Brazil was the first in South America to denounce the role of USAID in planning the Beijing World Conference on Women, as well as the great quantities of money that agency invested in the forced sterilization of women, especially the black and the poor. In the Sixth Latin American and Caribbean Encuentro Feminista (feminist conference) held in El Salvador and the seventh held in Chile in 1996, the tensions between different currents became visible and palpable. On the one hand, the so-called institutionalists (based in spaces like NGOs or government and international organizations) were the experts in gender, the representatives of the movement, the ones who negotiated with governments and the UN while being subordinated to the interests of those organizations. On the other hand, autonomists questioned the dependence on international cooperation and funding in feminist political work, and denounced the interference of USAID, the World Bank, and the IDB as institutions devoted to promoting neoliberal politics and the role of the UN in the depoliticization of the movement.

The Fifth Encuentro of Lesbian Feminists, held in Brazil, did not discuss this issue very much. Later, the First Encuentro of Autonomous Feminists, held in Bolivia, weakened the autonomist current rather than strengthening it, because of conflicts and differences about autonomy among the autonomists themselves. Two further feminist encounters in the Dominican Republic and Costa Rica also revealed the crisis of feminism as a social movement, and of the lesbian movement too. The fact that the Sixth Encuentro of Lesbian Feminists was held only in 2004, so many years after the lesbian meeting in Brazil in 1998, might serve as a significant indication of the movement's weakness.

Today, although some collectives of autonomous feminists and lesbian feminists do exist, this outlook has not had much impact in Latin America.

In short, the autonomous project within the feminist and lesbian feminist movement has passed though many eras: from autonomy with respect to the state, to political parties, to mixed organizations, to international cooperation, and to international organizations like the UN.

3 TWO DISPUTED ISSUES: THE STATE AND FINANCING

Our context right now is difficult and disastrous: more wars, more racism, more xenophobia; more murders of women, gays, and lesbians; alarming levels of poverty; consumerism; fundamentalism; the great rise of the extreme Right; and "take care of number one" as the order the day. The social movements need to rethink their utopias. Otherwise, confusion and impotence often take over, at both the individual level and the collective one.

When feminists talk about autonomy today, two issues stand out as points of conflict: the state and financing. I would like to speak about both.

In the new context of economic globalization, the globalized state, particularly in the West, has a new role. No longer a beneficent-protective state (one that invests in social goods such as social security, health care, and public education), it is a state that administers the policies of neoliberalism. It is more repressive of individual and collective rights through the application of security measures and the control of individuals. Its fundamental power is based on the military machine. The formation of economic blocs, like the European Economic Community and the North American Free Trade Agreement, and the power of the International Monetary Fund and the World Bank are the most evident examples of how the interests of Western states are joined to defend big capital at all costs. All of this creates more poverty and more economic and social exclusion in our countries. Neoliberalism seeks the disappearance of the state as administrator and coordinator of public policies. Today the state is a counterweight to transnational companies and, at the same time, an ally.

Faced with this situation, what is our goal as autonomous feminists? To make the state disappear or to transform it?

Either of those two goals requires concrete and clear actions that I think we need to debate. How do we stimulate the creation of a society around a different logic, growing out of more collective participation, with less control, less power, less hierarchy? This is a subject we need to think through, and think through again. At this time I don't have a clear proposal, but I would like us to give it deep consideration.

What does autonomy with relation to the state mean today?

In my view, it means not entering into the logic of the political parties, the organizations that constitute the government, the structure that sustains the state. The political parties have revealed themselves to be ladders providing access to power and money, access to spaces of political corruption; they don't at all represent the interests of the majority. In this sense, one autonomist strategy is to make the parties disappear as expressions of public politics, and to create politics out of the social movements instead.

Autonomy also means — above all for lesbians — not helping the state to gain power over our bodies and our sexuality. Demanding lesbian marriage, for example, would be legitimizing that power. It would also be demanding one of the most patriarchal institutions, which is what marriage is.

It's a fact that patriarchy avails itself of our strategies, making us enter its logic to counter our lack of rights. As lesbians, for instance, we lack access to adoption, health systems, employment, and visibility in the educational system, we can't emigrate and establish ourselves in other countries with our partners, and so on — all things which a heterosexual relationship often guarantees.

So, the question is (and it's a question that often scares us): should we enter into dialogue with a patriarchal, sexist, racist, and lesbophobic state?

Not necessarily. Instead we should be generating other logics of social organizations — based on the personal, on the communitarian — until we can arrive at social transformation in the most general sense. And transformation means renouncing the handouts that the system offers at its own convenience. Surely we have to think carefully about how to do this, how to organize, and how to avoid falling into the logic of "replacement of representation" (since the government doesn't represent us, then instead we'll be represented by the leader of such-and-such a social movement). That doesn't change the logic unless we guarantee ourselves participation as subjects, unless we can guarantee that economic inequalities, discrimination, and subordination of groups of people will end.

The other point of conflict among autonomous feminists is money: money necessary to survive and do politics outside of the state and the political parties.

In the '90s radical autonomists went so far as to question whether to participate in spaces such as the Academy or the NGOs, because those were the spaces that were depoliticizing feminism. We still believe that was true — and is true — but the question does not have to be whether or not to participate in those locations as places of employment, but rather whether to make them *the* spaces of feminist and lesbian politics. (Also, it depends on which Academy and which NGOs we're talking about and, faced with lack of employment, we don't have many alternatives.) From inside the Academy and the NGOs we can do some feminist and lesbian politics, but only within an institutional system that exercises a certain control and imposes many limitations—and, particularly, that only allows us to act as individuals. Those spaces often don't permit us the ideological autonomy we need to confront patriarchy and its expressions. Therefore, feminist and lesbian politics have to be carried out from other spaces—not our workplaces and not so conditioned—such as collectives, groups, and associations not linked with any institution.

TAKE THE MONEY OR NOT?

Another concern is whether collectives should accept money for their activities.

To create autonomous spaces means to generate the creativity to carry out activities that don't necessarily require funds. It requires putting together our varied potentials, our human and material resources, our feminist and lesbian willpower to do politics. That is how feminism as a movement began —with consciousness and conviction and a will to act—and the actions followed from there. That was feminism's most radical and transformative era, and the time of its greatest splendor.

Of course there are obviously activities that require money. The problem is that often we don't even ask ourselves where this money came from, and what the political positions of the financial sources are. We come up with justifications like "It doesn't matter where the money comes from, because we'll do what we want with it." And that's the trap. The system is not so dumb or so foolish as to offer money without knowing why it does so. I'll give you an example: the World Bank is going all-out among African-descended communities in the Caribbean. It has undertaken dozens of research projects about these communities, gathering information for supposed use in social projects to benefit them. These are actions of *mea culpa* for neoliberal politics, because it is the very same World Bank and USAID, along with the International Monetary Fund and the IDB, that are pushing the neoliberal policies that generate more poverty, raise more barriers, and cause racism to be on the rise. Those most affected are the African-descended communities and the women within them.

Another example is that many homosexual and lesbian groups rely on external financing for a large number of projects dealing with HIV/AIDS, the issue that attracts the most funding. (Brazilian groups are some of the most pathetic cases in this regard.) What does this type of funding imply? First of all, it continues to stigmatize gays and lesbians as the main carriers of the disease; secondly, it directs homosexual and lesbian politics toward the less radical, less confrontational. At the same time, it relieves the state of its responsibility for health care, employing the NGOs as a sort of substitute.

I believe in material solidarity between North and South, and often in what the mixed movement and the movement of black women demand: reparations for the inequalities generated by centuries of colonialism. But to pursue this goal, we need to know the sources of these funds, and what their political interests are.

Above all, though, the most important thing is to avoid making feminist and lesbian feminist political struggle dependent. We should not depend on money in order to act.

4   AUTONOMY WITH RESPECT TO
THE LGTTB MOVEMENT

Another important point to discuss is autonomy with respect to other social movements. Specifically, let me refer to the Lesbian, Gay, Transgender, Transsexual, and Bisexual movement.

Certainly my goal as a lesbian is to challenge heterosexuality as a norm. Logically, my best political allies ought to be gays, bisexuals, transsexuals, and transgendered people, because all of them represent a questioning of genders stereotyped according to sex. Though this is true in part, the problem is that the symbolic and real images of the great majority of gays also embody features of patriarchy: androcentrism, machismo, consumerism, authoritarianism, phallocentrism, but above all misogyny. Transgendered people are often returning to gender more than destroying it, while transsexuals center their demands on the biological (sex change), losing sight of the cultural construction of sex, and thus paradoxically fall into essentialism. As a lesbian feminist, these are not my political objectives.

In recent years, queer politics (including those put forward by feminist post-structuralists like Teresa de Lauretis and Judith Butler) have had a significant impact on the LGTTB movement. Queer politics challenge the notion of sexual identities as essences, and they question the category of gender because of its origins in a dichotomous and heterosexual paradigm. I agree with this part of queer theory and its goals. Its weakness, however, is that by proposing performance (outfits, clothing, repetition of acts) as a form of questioning institutionalized heterosexuality, it decontextualizes subordinations according to categories of race and class. The problem, as Sheila Jeffreys says in her book *Lesbian Heresy,* is that "the image of a man in a skirt or a woman wearing a tie is not enough to liberate a woman from her heterosexual relationship, while abandoning her oppression can bring her social, economic and probably even physical suffering, and sometimes the loss of her life."[2]

It is not the same to be a white middle class or bourgeois lesbian as to be an African-descended lesbian in any Latin American or Caribbean country. Queer theory limits itself to the discourse of language and meaning, and doesn't touch the fundamental social relations (the contexts of race, class, etc.) of lesbians. So, to my way of thinking, it's a kind of "light" politics. The LGTTB movement, especially now with the queer perspective, is led more and more by gays and transvestites, with the lesbians once again left behind.

Thus, though certainly heterosexism has to be fought, I'm not interested in doing politics with those who, although they may have non-normative sexuality, continue to reproduce the patriarchal norm or to invert rather than destroy it. Moreover, the lifeblood of much of this movement is the demand for sexual rights, recognition, and visibility — a strategy that, from my point of view, is limited with regard to the other world I want to build. I don't want to be recognized by patriarchal institutions. I want to create new logics of human survival with other lesbians and other women.

So I believe in some conjunctural and strategic alliances with the LGTTB movement, but I think that above all we must continue building our autonomy as lesbian feminists.

5   SEPARATISM VS. AUTONOMY

Before I end, I'd like to refer to an issue that creates some confusion: separatism within the feminist movement — which I think we shouldn't confuse with autonomy.

Feminism, being a theory and a political project born in Europe in the context of the Enlightenment, on the one hand questioned the universality of the *male subject* in the principles of the French Revolution, while on the other hand it reproduced this same universalization when dealing with the oppression of women. The category "woman," even if recognized as a social construction, was a myth because it emerged from a white, middle class, heterosexual outlook, and did not represent all women. Groups within feminism questioned such elitist, classist, and heterosexist universalization. From this questioning emerged, inside feminism, groupings according to different categories of oppression or specific political identities: lesbians separating from feminist heterosexism, African-descended women separating from feminist racism, and so on. In spite of carrying out their politics relatively separately from other feminist groups, these groupings never rejected feminism as a political project. On the contrary, they challenged the theoretical and political bases that discriminated against other women, while broadening the spectrum of possibilities in the political struggle against patriarchy and sexism on the basis of their own contexts and projects. Thus separatism emerged within feminism.

I believe, therefore, in separatism as a political strategy among feminists. It is a way of building politics out of historical reality, because patriarchy does not affect all women the same way. Class, race, and geography locate us in the world in different manners. So I think it's important and necessary to create those separate spaces for lesbians, for African-descended women, for young women, for indigenous women, for differently-abled women, and others, because that lets us define more specific politics with respect to the different forms of oppression such as racism, heterosexuality, classism, and so on. Nonetheless, we have to be clear about the limits of such separation, so we don't atomize ourselves as feminists organized into a social movement. We must not lose the vision that sees patriarchy linking systems of exploitation and discrimination such as racism, heterosexism, classism, and sexism. I think that all feminists should adopt a politics that has an integrated vision of those systems of oppression, because that is the only way to make feminism a project of real transformation.

Within a globalized and neoliberal world, we have to begin with our differences, but we also must re-articulate feminism as a utopian project that fights all types of oppression. There is a pressing need for alliances and solidarity among women locally, regionally, and internationally.

As an African-descended feminist and lesbian I want to create a lesbian politics that puts together an integrated vision of reality: one that includes the economic and cultural situations of many lesbians and women in the world. This might require giving up a lesbian politics that is limited solely to demanding lesbian visibility and recognition of lesbians and lesbian identity. This new politics, instead, would conceive of a world that includes not only parts of women's sexuality, but all of it — a sexuality embedded in historical, political, and cultural contexts, which require us to do lesbian politics in a way that takes racism, sexism, and classism into account. That is the lesbian politics I think is needed in this historical moment to achieve social transformation.

Translated by Dick Cluster

NOTES

1 Adrienne Rich, "La heterosexualidad obligatoria y la existencia lesbiana," in *Sexualidad, género y roles sexuales*, ed. Marysa Navarro and Catherine R. Stimpson (Buenos Aires: Fondo de Cultura Económica de Argentina, 1999), 188.

2 Sheila Jeffreys, *La herejía lesbiana: Una perspectiva feminista de la revolución sexual lesbiana* (Valencia: Editorial Catedra, 1996), 156.

FAIZAL DEEN

Three Poems

YOUNG FAGGOT (2003)

The discos
Will take you, spilling out
Of your jeans
Into the coming freedom.

You will see
That first display
Of bodies. The grind of them
Against the coffins of ocean. This will be
Your last memory of Trinidad. This steel pan
Jump up 1976. Sounded out from memory.
You will grow bacchic. With this crop-over,
You will learn that joy is something
Earned. Though your freedom
Will be different, you will carry
That history of dance with you
To the whiteness of him who will spill you
Out of your jeans into those spinning
Discos of riotous night.

You will carry him
Through the night. But the mornings
Will also be yours. In parks and beaches,
The asses will be on parade. Some from
The jump up night. Others on the sly.
Like Proust's innocent Spring. The fit
Of bee in flower. The monster always searches
The plug in desire. In any season. No matter the habitat.
Faggotry scatters the love wherever it dances. The men

Of the mountain. Of the forest. Of the sea. The pick ups.
In parks, latrines, alleyways, baths. When we fit. When we swell.
When the throne is red.

Young faggot,
You will wear
The red eyes
Of pleasure.
6 a.m. eternal.
The trains
Zoom zoom
In the Glenfidditch
Eyes. Young faggot,
Do you catch
Yourself in the eyes
Of the aunties going
To work?

Do you spit at all this civilized
Love? Of family and work. The old
Queens will tell you there was that time
For us too. We had garages of paradise. The phantasmagoric
Saint. We were born of the hustle. Concrete. The lure
Of the big lights. The fast modern. Where the faggots
Could scatter. Appear and reappear. With flicks of the wand.
The prick could find it all. Yes, there was that time.
I too refused my father's nation. I took to the sky after
Each and every seduction. Stayed in the song and dance
For as long as my muscles held up. In the machine. Of fucking
And her scorecards.

Young faggot,
Soon you will be an old regular.
Like all the rest. If you're like me, after
You've lured your impossible men away
From their Mas. You will still want. The sagging
Geometry of your age. To watch it stand up
At 20 or 60. To watch it tug. Tug the mouth. Warm.
Worthy. The hungry milky way. The hand that shook it off
All the while.

THE MAGICAL REAL (2003)

TOBAGO, 1999

Fool,
With your magical real.

Yes, once in Tobago
A horsewhip snaked
Past me. I heard the rustle
Of grass. There was no singing,
Just that warning:

Sometimes, the reptile
Returns,
Curious
In its horror.
It will whip you
Like a horsewhip.

You grew foolish
In your fear. He smiled,
Slid away proud
Of that stinging lash.

Sometimes, Fool, when you think
You are here to learn the geography
Of your father. All bookish. Inheritance
Already that essay that will pay the bills.
Inheritance, just this rum bar and that, this roti shop,
That roti shop. He ate there.
He drank here.

And bored with all that history
Of fathers, Tunapuna, India and this shore
Of color and arrival, this new theatre of brown bones
And blood, I lay my love down.

I go out
Into the night
And search for that
Horsewhip that bruised me once

When I got tired of you, Fool,
And went out to see the Magical
London Tower and her parade of parrot
Fish. High as a kite, I snorkeled all day.
There was no English in me. There was no outside tongue.

No coolieman split up split up in the Di, you know, that great
Spread of brown bones and blood aspora.

Just this love
That once turned the fallen
Into the back of an anaconda. Just this love
That once brought Paul Coffey back on the back
Of anaconda. Just this love that once brought Paul Coffey
Back on the back of an anaconda bringing you back to the land of rivers
Where the surprise of history lies buried and you pray for flight and you pray
For that child of islands you are not and never will be.

SURRENDER (2003)

Let's talk about the men.
The green ones. They've taken
The fire. Stole away from Dad's
Mountain to the unspeakable mystery
Of the Disco. The mystery of man on the
Beast. And if this is Babylon and the fire awaits
Then trap it. The heat of their flaming souls
In Revelations. Green now. Different now. Abomination
That thing of beauty. Where climax feeds on the riddles
Of Disco's lusty lyric. Trap
Them.

The men.
They are the speaky spoke
Of all my pages. I've tried to yank
Them out of the crooked arm
Of Dad's history. But they like the queer.

The bent bend of it. They like the waters
They see. The multitudes of pleasure. Their bath
In the waters of the Fallen. They give the beast
The power to roar. Midnight calls. Over the howling
City. Everything's gone green with them. With them
The city is never woeful. The soul, too. The searcher bright
In the multitudes. The light of them aflame. Alive.
In the same fire sent to destroy them. The blazing
Disco. The solemn mountain.

The green ones.
I surrender to them. I suffer
The applause of their teeth.
My beast. My rectum. My torture.
My grief. My filth. My tomb. My faithless
Luxury. I surrender to them. They are
That body I need before night's through.
Another book opened where the hero dreams
The King of Kings. The 3 a.m. disco. High
On his throne of hips. No costume. Just the ripple
Of his raw work. I surrender to him. My mother's
Calypsos. My father's librettos. All the paradise
Of the child's first music. The pull of hearts. Sugar
Coated hips.

Let's talk about the men.
The green ones. I became one
Of them. I took to the sky and found
Their islands of sprinting Porno. The ten
Horns of all the beasts. The faggot kings
Luxuriant in their grand refusal.

The Portrait (1998)

1

Her name will be Ana. She'll be a painter.

His name was Jorge. He was the owner of a '57 Chevy, and a taxi driver.

Their names are Gabriel and Héctor. The former is beautiful. The latter possesses the former.

2

Ana will meet Jorge on the sidewalk in front of the Hotel Presidente one day when she's trying to get two North American art dealers to her room at Animas 112. They'll pay the five dollars Jorge charged for the trip in his Chevy, and Ana will, provocatively, invite the driver to visit her when he found himself in Habana Vieja again.

He went the next week, without pretexts, imaginary trips, or last-minute coincidences. She'll have liked his solid, rather hairy body, his manner of speaking which was free and slangy almost to the point of vulgarity, the well-defined hips, the thickness of his hands, his dark hair cut very short, his incipient beard, his long and abundant sideburns, his ears unpierced and ringless despite the current fashion, his torso muscular. She'll baptize him Toulouse-Lautrec but keep this to herself. She'll have liked his sweaty olive skin and the unconcern with which he let the small drops gather on his forehead and the large ones drip from his abdomen and chest. At most, he unbuttoned his shirt and tried to fan himself by flapping the cloth against his flesh. She'll have liked both his primitivism and the assurance with which he exhibited it. She'll like the sort of men considered attractive before the sexual revolutions and feminist movements. She'll adore the feeling of being penetrated, subjugated by a weighty body that covers her completely and takes her to the portals of asphyxiation. Only this will infuse her with the strength to paint, and then drain it out again: a vicious cycle that will ruin her as an artist. "I'm not a painter; I'm one of Toulouse-Lautrec's whores," she'll write in a diary that no one will care to read: it will never appear: it won't exist.

She'll open the door, be truly surprised, and, surprised, will prepare cinnamon and ginger tea because she won't have any coffee. It will be nighttime. They'll be alone. While the water boils she'll rush to examine herself obsessively in the bathroom mirror, the ugliness of her long and skinny face, her misshapen nose, forehead too wide, hair lank and dry, inadequate scrawny neck. She won't resort to makeup. She'll tell herself the liveliness of her expression will make her pretty, and with that conviction she'll return.

He asked about the North Americans, and she'll reply that she won't have had any luck, that her paintings won't have interested them. That was when he knew she'll be a painter. A painter. The word didn't suggest much in particular, just a strange image that alighted in his mind: Ana's fingers squeezing a brush, possibly one of those narrow ones that artists used. Ana will trump this image with photographic speed: Ana's hand grazing his member through his pants. She'll ask him to undress right away, explaining that she can't have a relationship with any man without first having seen his cock.

He undressed, but with a deliberate slowness which will only increase her desire; from so much desire, her knees will shake. Her throat will tighten. She'll think she's forever lost her voice. But not her gaze: the intentness of her gaze will tug at Jorge's clothes like mute but constant scratches. The liveliness of his penis during the ceremony of undressing will serve to corroborate the correctness of her choice. A man who did not wonder or doubt. A man who knew how to recognize the fury of her gaze and not reproach her for a coldness that won't exist. Several times she'll write this idea in her diary; she'll be tempted to term her behavior as that of a post-sexual revolutions woman. But she won't write it, nor even think it. She will merely affirm: "Contradictions are what I detest."

Jorge naked was Ana's destruction. Still clothed herself, she'll crawl on her knees toward that destruction, a few centimeters from her mouth. She'll use cushions to put it within reach. She'll moisten it with the tip of her tongue, nibble it with her lips, chew it very softly, suck it, hide it inside herself with the false security that assumes things submerged will disappear. She'll play with this destruction, she'll want to have it and leave it, she'll take it out and discover it again, huge — why will she always have to suppose that destruction is something huge? — and won't dare to touch it for fear of losing the chance to destroy herself. She'll cry.

Jorge tried to lift her up by her elbows, but Ana, reluctant, will resist. She'll go limp. He gathered his strength and tried again. Ana will have to accede, standing up until his penis brushes her navel. She'll feel cool saliva on her belly. She'll beg him to walk around the room.

He moved with astonished awkwardness. (He was a taxi driver acting as a model.) But his penis remained vibrant, bobbing precariously in the air. Ana will dry her tears and, ecstatic, begin to suggest daring positions. At last, twenty poses later, he was required to mount her on the floor in a corner of the room with her head bumping against the leg of an old cane chair.

When Gabriel and Héctor knock on the door, Jorge had come three times and Ana will be anxious to take up the brushes abandoned since her last erotic adventure, weeks ago. She'll have just a vague idea. She'll want to paint her own gaze.

Jorge got dressed in a hurry. Ana will do so slowly. Gabriel and Héctor make their ill-timed entrance without paying any attention to the stranger, as if he did not exist. Jorge left as soon as he was introduced: Ana won't be able to handle the mishmash of lovers and gay friends. After greeting Ana with a theatricality typical of those who haven't seen each other for a year, Héctor comments in a jocular tone on Jorge's flight. Ana will once again defend her separatist conception of the world, and Héctor crafts a riposte:

"That's not a stitch in time saving nine, that's sewing in a new seam every day just in case. That's cheating, is what."

Maybe she'll record this quip in her diary, as a proof of the cleverness of her friend.

To divert the course of the conversation, Ana will ask Héctor about his travels in Spain. He'll answer at length but with the same neutral tone he always uses in front of Gabriel. All that stands out is the Humboldt complex in the Canary Islands: "A place of ours, but without transvestites or transsexuals or effeminate gays; no lesbians either, of course. Four stories around a park that has a neon sign with the emblem of the place: a dinosaur. All four floors are full of discos, bars, porno films, saunas, darkened rooms . . . It's immense, five or six times as big as the Manzana de Gómez."

She won't open her mouth to express amazement. Gabriel remains silent. Taking her hostess role too seriously, she'll want to bring him into the conversation:

"And you, Gabriel, did you miss Héctor very much?"

"Stupid question," she will note. Gabriel misses him very much, he's been missing him since the beginning of their relationship, as if Héctor had been far away the entire time. But that kind of distance cannot be touched, it's more of something you begin to breathe: it's like a dense air that accumulates around Gabriel — until it gets in the way of his breathing, so he grows blind and deaf and loses his capacity to feel distance at all. He grows separate. Living is knowing how distant others are from oneself. The voyage of the one Gabriel loves awards him this privilege of lucidity. It is a relief to know that a real ocean separates him from Héctor, and not that bottomless daily asphyxiation.

"Yes, so much."

Ana will act agitated and vague, and then will tell them that it's time for them to go. As an excuse, she'll cite her muse. Before leaving, Héctor takes from his backpack a box containing tubes of paint. Ana will nearly faint from happiness over such an opportune gift. She'll plant a thousand kisses on her friend's cheek and mouth. Finally, when the couple is already on the street, she'll praise Gabriel from the stoop:

"You're as beautiful as ever."

Really this phrase will be addressed to Héctor, and only he enjoys it. He hugs Gabriel tightly around the shoulders as if to say, "You're beautiful, you belong to me." Aloud, he asks, "Did you really miss me so much?"

Silence. The most absolute manner in which we may be dispossessed.

"Really?"

Insistence. The attempt to exorcise silence, that fissure through which we glimpse that the other is escaping us.

"I almost died."

Héctor kisses him on the mouth. He shows signs of wanting to make love.

Making love. Making love is getting naked and asking the master, "Please master . . . lift my ass to your waist / . . . please master make me say, please master fuck me now please / . . . please master stroke your shaft with white creams / . . . please touch your cock head to my wrinkled self-hole / please master push it in gently . . . / please master shove it in me a little, a little, a little / please master sink your enormous thing down my behind / & please master make me wiggle my rear to eat up the prick trunk / please please master fuck me again with your self please fuck me please / master drive down till it hurts me the softness the / softness please master make love to my ass . . . & fuck me for good like a girl / . . . please master make me go moan on the table / go moan O please master do fuck me like that / . . . please master call me a dog, an ass beast, a wet asshole / & fuck me more violent . . . / & throb thru five seconds to spurt out your semen heat / over & over, bamming it in while I cry out your name I do love you / please master."

In Spain, Héctor has read a long poem by Allen Ginsberg; he has recognized himself in a few lines, he has copied them, he remembers them as if those fragments were really the whole poem. But he doesn't bring them to Gabriel. In Angola his chief, also his lover, has possessed him like this, brutally, on top of the desk where Héctor has typed so many company reports. The shoving has broken the glass and wounded one of Héctor's thighs. But Gabriel must not read these things, must not know anything about this captain, this master. The first time Héctor and Gabriel go to bed, Gabriel wants to know about the scar. "I fell on a broken bottle when I was a kid." The first time Gabriel goes to bed with a man, that man has a scar. Gabriel asks about it and is deceived.

Making love is, for Gabriel, that Héctor moves in close to him, kisses him, touches him, licks him, goes on kissing him, touching him, sucks him, kisses him, kisses him, oh, and masturbates him. Gabriel is Héctor's mirror. Making love is, for Gabriel, living the experience of this symmetry. How many times has he wanted to break up that image, those reflections? That would be unmaking love.

There must be something that makes homosexual eroticism different, Héctor explains without Gabriel ever having asked. Gabriel's kingdom is silence. The superiority of homosexuals over heterosexuals lies in the fact that the former can do without penetration, transmute surrender into tenderness, spirituality, Héctor goes on arguing. Héctor's kingdom is insistence.

Héctor is an artisan. He's thirty-two years old. Gabriel studies philosophy at the university. He's twenty. Tonight they make love. What is making love?

"Making love with a man who doesn't think he's making love, inspires me," Ana will write in her diary. After Héctor and Gabriel leave, Jorge came back. She'll embrace him, beg forgiveness for the delay caused by this visit, say that she won't have been able to cut it any shorter than that. She'll show him the gift, she'll caress his cock, she'll divest him of his clothes and ask him to lie down motionless on the couch.

Ana will have a canvas ready, beforehand. She'll dab at it timidly. She'll want to capture the devastating force of her gaze acting upon Jorge's body, not the characteristics of the eyes that produce it. "The drawing has no force, it doesn't work. What I want is not a portrait, not a face, nothing that can be defined. Force has no shape." Will she write that, knowing it is neither original nor completely true? So what? She'll be a whore, not a painter, after all. She'll allow herself any impropriety, any madness: to hurl euphoric brush strokes upon the oh-so-passive cloth.

Jorge slept without uttering a word. Thus asleep, he could be more easily profaned. She'll revel in this defenselessness, examining him will bring her to a fever pitch. Her eyes red. Crying once again. But it will occur to her that it

would be more exciting to have him lie in a room with a hole through which
she'll be able to watch him without his posing for her. Ana will require the
presence of a limit, a barrier; simply knowing that this body does not belong
to her will impel her to conquer it. She'll need the thrill of transgression, the
pleasure of theft. "Héctor always tells me I'm a fag with tits. I think it must
be true." She won't be able to paint any more, she'll cover Jorge with a sheet.
Will she be a post-sexual revolutions woman? What should a woman be,
after the sexual revolutions? Those thoughts will infect her, fleetingly, but
she won't write them down. She won't even have thought them. "I detest
contradictions" will be the most oft-repeated phrase in her diary, but she will
never explain.

"Were you unfaithful?" Héctor persists with the same question, taking
advantage of the moment to lift the sheet from Gabriel and make him display
the beauty of his nakedness. Modestly, Gabriel covers himself again. Finally
he decides to break the silence.

"Never."

"I don't know whether I believe you," and he lasciviously uncovers him
again.

"What is belief? That which does not exist. What exists is the need to
believe" (Gabriel's manuscript, *Philosophical Notes*, page 34).

"I want to make love again," Héctor insists, in reaction to Gabriel's mute-
ness.

Neither one desires the other. "What is desire? A belief. Something which
does not exist. What exists is the need for desire" (ibid., p. 78).

Gabriel doesn't answer, he surrenders: he goes looking for desire.

3

Ana will tell Héctor every detail of her relationship with Jorge and the need
to find the right place to steal views of her lover. In return, Héctor tells her of
his affairs with Spanish men, necessarily omitted during his previous visit.

Ana will adore this confessional and enthusiastic Héctor who reveals
himself when alone. Nonetheless, she'll ask about the other. Ana will not
understand how such a beautiful boy can live as cloistered as women of a
century past. Héctor disagrees, argues that Gabriel goes out for what is
indispensable, for school. He doesn't even need to go to libraries, because
Héctor has brought him books from Spain. Things are bad on the street,
Ana; Gabriel doesn't lack for anything, he gives him everything: money,
clothes, food.

Ana will be tempted to reproach her friend for his selfishness, but good sense will restrain her. Héctor remarks that the two small rooms of his duplex apartment, which he usually rents out, are unoccupied now. They are adjoining rooms and spying on one from the other could be arranged. She'll make it clear that she won't have any money, and he offers her the rooms rent-free until the painting is done. Ana will be skeptical of such kindness, will think that Jorge could have felt uncomfortable in the home of two gays, she too will be bothered by having them so close by. Will it be worth risking her relationship with Toulouse-Lautrec for this idea?

Ana will accept, and she'll invent some way to explain the change to Jorge. He believed her.

Gabriel doesn't understand Héctor's sudden altruism, Héctor who is so reluctant to share his space with friends whose need is much more pressing. But he keeps quiet and welcomes the refugees with his usual beautiful and inexpressive face. He can't stand the taxi driver's vulgarity, doesn't understand this mixture of art with street talk, but he keeps quiet. His silence is complete.

Ana will praise the intricate carving on the wall that will separate her from Jorge. He was surprised on first seeing this large room divided in half, and when they were alone he let his bewilderment out. Didn't they come here to be alone, he asked. Yes, but when he was dead from so much fucking, she will stay by herself and paint, in spite of physical exhaustion that way. He accepted all this, still without understanding it. He didn't need to understand.

Through tiny spaces between the geometric figures that will make up this wall, Ana will scrutinize Jorge's body. She'll ask him to sleep naked. He didn't investigate her reasons. The almost ethereal massage she will award his genitals was enough for him to sense that obedience was indicated. Only later, when he was alone, did it begin to feel strange. He looked at the ceiling, the images in the wood, the lamp. What was he doing here? There was something incomprehensible about it all. He had never before been with a woman this weird.

When the word "weird" appeared in Jorge's mind, Ana will inundate the canvas with an intense ochre that will transfigure the tiny splashes of yellow from the first day. Frenetically, she'll advance. She'll uncap another tube of paint: green. She'll hesitate. She'll feel that *something* will be observing her lasciviously from the painting-in-progress. She'll want to free herself from all her clothing, shamelessly, impelled to do so by *that* force. Might it be her own gaze, which will have begun to present itself? Might her own gaze really exist outside herself?

When the word "weird" appeared in Jorge's mind, he got up, felt the dozens of triangles, ovals, and pyramids that will stand between the weirdness and himself. Almost by instinct, he pressed his eyelash to the varnish. He looked. He saw the painter naked, upright over her easel, her back to him, rocking like a schizophrenic in crisis, throwing paint this way and that. He suddenly felt himself discovered, was afraid, and for an instant he pulled away from the crack in the wall. But the attraction was greater.

It won't be Ana's slender body that will seduce him, but a warm and indecipherable emanation. He began to masturbate while watching Ana because she will be the only concrete available thing. He felt that he too was becoming weird. He imagined other bodies, superimposed them over Ana's. None of them was motivating him. The cause of his arousal was *something else.*

Ana will be hieratic, leaning forward over the easel, her clitoris brushing its leather leg. She won't know what could be exciting her to the point where she'll have to wrap her fingers around the seat. Will she want to make love with Jorge? Will she want to make love? She'll have to seek out Toulouse-Lautrec in order to know. She'll have to seek out someone.

Ana will rise and go slowly, tense and hunched.

Jorge lay down again, with his eyes open and his cock hard and breakable. She won't look at him.

He didn't look at her either.

She'll feel those repeated tremors. He spurted epileptic brush strokes.

She and he, for the first time separate, mutually unrecognizable.

Héctor can't get to sleep, sweats, turns on the desk lamp, paces around the room. Gabriel follows him with half-closed eyes, the sheet pulled taut, trapped under his heels and in his fingers. Héctor leaves the bedroom, walks into the hall, stops before the door to the other room. He is aroused. He thinks of Gabriel but in fact he's not thinking of Gabriel. He is aroused. He can't go out on the street, walk, seek amid the darkness. He thinks of Gabriel, he says so many times to convince himself. He goes back, opens the door, approaches him with fury, tears off the sheet, lowers his shorts, tries to suck him. Gabriel is frozen, terrified. His eyes have become two enormous globes, his penis is a fat wrinkle that cannot be grasped. Héctor sits upon him, rubs his anus against the wrinkle which is ceasing to exist. He squeezes against that which no longer exists. He attempts Gabriel's lips, which hardly open at all. He licks them, sloppily. Gabriel shivers. The air conditioning is very cold. Gabriel doesn't speak, Héctor recovers his wits, he dismounts, shuts off the air conditioner, turns out the light, lies down. Gabriel covers himself. Héctor says he had a nightmare.

Ana will separate from the anonymous body which went through her, and will walk, intense and unconsummated, about the room. She'll feel as if *something* is impelling her toward frenzy and exhaustion. If she can't control *that,* she'll end up turning on herself, lacerating her own body. Nevertheless, she'll be helpless. She'll pick up the objects in her path and squeeze them until they threaten to break. The pressure will drive her to stand before the canvas; the idea of destroying it will make her bunch her fingers. "That's a grimace, my hands grimacing," she'll think. No, she must not unleash *that* against her own work. She'll try to preserve the painting by turning it to the wall.

There will be slow relief, and then a sleep-inducing calm. Ana will recognize Jorge, and embrace him. He kissed her, peaceably, like someone who has brushed against a memory.

4

The next morning, when Ana will turn the frame around to resume working, she will experience the same unease. Finding no plausible explanations, she'll wind up accepting the only one in which she's never previously believed: genius. A sensation as strange as *that* could come only from a deep and essential spiritual connection between the artist and her work, and between mysterious cosmic rhythms and both.

"During those days I did not feel like a whore but like a painter; all my sexual energies went into the canvas. My dedication was so complete that I forgot about Toulouse-Lautrec. He was just Jorge. He wasn't even that," she'll be able to write.

Jorge too awoke with unusual appetites. This time, far from feeling worried, he accepted them with pride, as instincts of his own. Their exaggerated shape testified to his virility.

Héctor opens his eyes, having had a fabulous dream about the captain, a dream that might be memory or premonition or fantasy, he doesn't know. Whatever it is, it's good: Héctor doesn't want to let such a lifeline go.

Gabriel remains tense, stretched and stiff like the night before, suffering from a withdrawal which doesn't yet express itself physically. The slightest touch would curl him into a ball.

Jorge, naked, walked toward Ana, endlessly at her easel. He laid his stiffened cock upon her back, along her backbone, and then pressed his body to hers and hugged her from behind, his hands cupping her breasts. Ana will grow goose bumps, but she won't stop handling the brush. She won't turn to kiss him, or look at him, or speak. He exhaled his own hot breath in her ear. Her body will be a string of endless spasms, as she treads the insistent call of the edge. He redoubled his efforts. She'll make the slightest gesture of separation. Without understanding, he obeyed her sudden distancing.

He stepped back, off balance, and right away closed in again, trying to get between her and the painting, but Ana's arm will fend him off. With his meaty hand, Jorge kept that arm frozen in place. At last she'll react, she'll know he's there, know that destruction waited a few centimeters from her mouth. She'll close her eyes in annoyance and open them, almost violently, when she feels this enormous thing beating against her lips. She'll push away with her feet and the easel will fall down. He tightened his hold on her arm still more, and made her straighten up. Ana's fingers will have let go of the brush, which will leave a blue mark on the floor.

She'll argue, speak of mutual respect, of artistic necessity, of insult. He accused her in return of coldness toward him. She'll repeat the same arguments. He stopped, alarmed by Ana's unusual flood of words, and let her go.

Ana will pick up the easel, set it in its place, and sit down before it once more. She'll need a few minutes to recover from the trembling that will render her hand useless. Jorge left the room and stormed down the stairs in a fury. Héctor, dazzled, goes down as well.

Through the living room window, Jorge, seated, tried to lose himself in the ungraspable flatness of the horizon. His eyes and his mind longed for a constancy that could mean whiteness, nullity, stripping away. Impossible.

On his feet, Héctor observes the multiple lines of Jorge's body. Sinuous, precise, and attainable. Héctor ponders the magnificent cloud that emerged from Jorge's waist and keeps him from concentrating on the integrity of the landscape.

Jorge no longer existed. There's just this cloud, no horizon, no real or imaginary space on which to rest or float. There is just this impulse, this faith, these knees on the floor, this famished mouth swallowing the cloud, this lightning tongue, this rain, the triumphal acidity that reaches his stomach.

Whiteness. Stripping away. Nullity. Jorge counted, stubbornly, on the line of the horizon, which little by little was turning blurry and absurd; then he latched onto the windows, which were too clean to deny the image of Héctor kneeling and all-inclusive; then he shut his eyelids; then he didn't know.

"Excessively abstract," Ana will judge her painting in a moment of detachment. Could those shapes without harmony, those live colors diluted by whim to a deathly pallor, translate her gaze? The fear of being wrong will oblige her to continue, because she will find the answer only in her hand, only in its advance.

"Perseverance is fear. Every repeated question, every obsessive pursuit, is guided by the same essential timidity. We are not daring when we interrogate. To ask something is to be trapped in doubt itself; every movement it creates is false, covers an inertia which we are forever incapable of overpowering. And what is life: an affirmative, arbitrary act, or a paralyzing question mark?" (ibid., p. 99).

Gabriel dares to sit up in bed. He crosses his legs until his feet touch the cheeks of his behind. The sheet is a very intimate shawl that falls softly on his solid shoulders. Gabriel is free. He *knows* all this: Héctor and Jorge have gone downstairs, Ana is painting, nobody will be sniffing after his beauty. Gabriel enjoys the privilege of being absolutely forgotten. He does not exist. He'd like to run around the room, dance, hum a tune, perhaps a children's song, ta-da. He has read, or someone has told him, that freedom is that ephemeral joy that comes with oblivion. The word ephemeral stops him— or is it that his desires have suddenly slipped away and made him think of the word?

He flexes his chest, reaches his hand toward the drawer built into the bed, rummages inside it and finds the stick of incense, the lighter, and the Tarot pack. Gabriel *knows* that downstairs, after sucking Jorge, Héctor has stood up and begun to masturbate in front of him. The taxi driver was surprised by the grandiosity of that penis. Outsized and robust. Smooth and uniform. Imperious. Haughty. Gabriel *knows* that Héctor is not purposely posing for the other, in fact a suspicion that Jorge's close examination of his genitals is a reproach, a blasphemy, or a hidden blame makes him turn around. The lobes of his ass are round.

Gabriel *knows* that through the window Héctor fixes his eyes on the exquisitely languid body of Jorge upon the couch, as if it were a horizon that once, in a dream, became tactile and now is just that: memory, sadness, dying captain, horizon stretching toward blindness.

But Gabriel *knows* that Jorge demolished all the landscapes. A storm in motion. Impetuously he advanced, upright and towering, disposed to blot everything out. And he *knows* as well that Héctor, valiant and courteous, bends forward in secular reverence, separates his cheeks with his two hands, and is on the verge of saying "Master" to him.

"Too academic," Ana will judge. Gabriel *knows* that she, against her own intentions, will have outlined an almost perfect cloud on the canvas. "And to think that I've given and risked everything for an image that wasn't my gaze after all!" But Gabriel *knows* that is not the end. Ana will persist. She will commit herself to erasing or perpetuating the image — after asking herself whether in reality her gaze might not be that cloud, and not being able to respond.

"The end is always an affirmative and arbitrary act, the sworn enemy of the question mark" (ibid., p. 112).

Gabriel *knows* that Jorge was sticking it into Héctor, gently, a little, a little, a little, finally sinking it completely into his bottom. Without lubricants, without table, without benefit of supplication or instruction — without Jorge calling him dog, anal beast, wet asshole, or anything of the kind. What is making love? What should it be? What can it?

Gabriel *knows* that when Héctor begins to rub his penis Jorge covered Héctor's hand with his own. Jorge moved from the waist and pushed, aggressively, against the cloud; he passed through it, converted it into a transparent film — a pane of glass in the middle of the room — so thin that he could touch Héctor's convulsive hand that sketched a horizon on the other side.

Gabriel *knows* that the assault of Toulouse-Lautrec's broad and rapid brush strokes pressed violently against that hand, to eliminate it from the landscape and consummate the creation of the horizon — flat, white, possible — with just his own, the only hand. The worst.

"Poetic. Very poetic. False," Ana will judge. Standing back from the canvas, she'll evaluate the cloud, which will be there still, protuberant, permanently attached like a challenge or maybe a truth. Mistreated by the dabs of paint, cracked and dripping, nearly a total loss, but never a loss: always there.

"Primitive. Common. Kitsch," Ana will prolong her suffering.

Gabriel *knows* that Jorge regretted nothing, did not even reflect on the event, but rather turned to imagining with infinite morbid pleasure what had to happen between Héctor and himself later, soon, because Jorge's intensity was great and did not accept delay. He declared: "If I had a cock like yours, I'd be the happiest man in Cuba. I'd have thousands of women. It's really too bad."

Gabriel *knows* that Jorge's envy seems abominable to Héctor. He *knows* that Héctor has sheltered the couple so as to seduce the taxi driver in a preconceived and unalterable fashion: inaugurating him as Master, investing him with the rank of Captain, like one who grants and places a crown of laurel, a toga, or a diadem on the head, body, or brow of a chosen one. (How long has Gabriel *known* this?) And Héctor does not pardon Jorge's assuming the authority to modify and destroy the best and most important acts of the rite. Gabriel *knows* this: Jorge's spontaneity, his absence of guilt and his compulsive bedazzlement by Héctor's penis are all major crimes.

"Fantasy is the opposite of freedom, its irreconcilable antagonist. Fantasy is dogmatic and authoritarian; it admits neither rebuttal nor exception. In its renunciation of questions it appears to be an end, something that brings closure. But it is always a goal, something which must and can reopen. Hence its paradox and pathos" (ibid., p.127).

Héctor's response is a quip, another riposte that might become famous if Ana were to include it in the diary that won't exist: "And if I had yours I'd be the happiest gay in the world. I'd have nobody but you. It'd be something to be proud of. Isn't it too bad?"

Gabriel *knows* that Jorge didn't utter another word. It was much simpler to pounce on Héctor and possess him, a thousand times. Now, when Jorge embarked on the nth one, Héctor, his back to Jorge upon the granite table, feels he has to stop everything, turn around — inventing his own pane of glass beneath him — and propose to the driver: "I'll pay whatever you ask, even the horizon. Be Master. Be Captain. I'll be Dog. Anal Beast. Wet Asshole. Wounded Thigh."

But giving it for free, and the resulting naked proofs, would go on tormenting Héctor. To give oneself is to expose oneself. Payment is impossible after that — even more so if Jorge was bestowing on him, just then, the deepest kiss, and the first: atrocious, unlawful, defining. That kiss was destroying everything.

Gabriel *knows* that Héctor enters his destruction, stoic and rebellious at the same time, as if the novelty of saliva, of the eyes that disappear and resurge and are lost, of panting that pauses into inexistence, of a caress ever more caring and melancholic, were a density ever denser from which he had to protect himself even though all prevention was useless, because that density was reality, claw-stroke, and death.

"To live out a fantasy is to risk convoking the vacuum: to close a door and open it simultaneously. Madness. One would have to be the door, not the hand. One would have to not be" (ibid., p. 141).

Gabriel *knows* he has not written anything original, not because he has read or heard words similar to his, but because they are so obvious that they mimic the echo of an unknown yet familiar voice, of an unobjectionable presence. That does not deflate or distress him. He *knows* he is a beautiful youth, not a philosopher. His manuscript does not exist, only his beauty and his youth. Can there be anything more?

He *knows* too that this gesture, the three cards picked out at random and tossed upon the bed, the so-personal reading he makes of them while the incense burns, are redundant, dispensable. The Empress and the Tower, and the Devil in between. Art, nihilism, temptation. Trap, desire, descent. Dark knowledge, danger, pain. Without shading or elliptical language: incisive, necklace of few but very heavy pearls that forces us to bow the head and fall prostrate upon the ground: golden chain.

Ana paints a disturbing canvas and, under its mysterious influence, peace and order crumble. In the center is the Devil. Gabriel *knows* that someone has written this story, that it's all a mixed-up vaporous repetition of that other story: the portrait of an old man whose eyes were drawn with such excellence that they didn't seem to be a copy; they looked out so humanly from the canvas, they destroyed its harmony. The old man was the Devil. The portrait passed from hand to hand, sowing anxious, sordid sensations in its owners. At last, someone stole it during an auction.

"Brilliant. It was a masterwork. Losing it meant ceasing to be a painter, meant never coming to exist. From then on I was just one more indistinguishable whore," Ana will affirm a few months before dying, in a diary that will never appear.

"Brilliant. It's a masterwork. I'm a painter," Ana will think as she stands before that disseminated cloud, that grayish unformed whirlwind laced with the thinnest black inlays and mottled with rough splotches of many hues. She will repeat — a psalm, a chorus — that it is brilliant. Three, five, twenty times. She'll masturbate, babbling this, and fall asleep hoarse.

Gabriel *knows* that he, with the shawl over his shoulders, goes into the room where Ana will be lying. Above the easel the painter will have left her palette and brushes. The youth, more beautiful than ever, wraps his fist around the head of a brush and, while rhythmically piercing the canvas with the point of this improvised weapon, feels the humid paint on the bristles sniffing the palm of his hand. His breathing dictates the frequency of the blows. Gabriel *knows* this: the sheet slips off and falls onto the paint-stained floor. He does not retrieve it until the gaze has become extinct, until Héctor and Jorge are paralyzed, one of them facedown on the granite table; the other, Master for only a few seconds, his chest upon Héctor's back.

Gabriel *knows* that Jorge, astonished and alarmed, pulled away from Héctor and ran up the stairs, pounding the cement with a speed that Héctor hears as punches, doors, and endings.

Gabriel *knows* that a long time goes by before Héctor decides to come upstairs too. He trudges up tiredly; the sweat of his bare feet marks the trajectory of this slowness.

Gabriel *knows* that he washes the paint-smeared hand and then drops the sheet into a bucket of soapy water to let it soak until he and Héctor are alone.

At dawn Ana will awake, startled, before the shreds of canvas and the empty frame, and she'll throw herself upon Jorge shaking him by the shoulders and berating him for having given in to such base impulses, having betrayed her so treasonously. Jorge thought Ana had discovered about him and Héctor. It was not worth rebutting anything, or even justifying it; it was better to leave it all behind, to get dressed without looking at her and leave without saying goodbye to anyone.

Gabriel *knows* that Héctor is consoling his sobbing friend, that he helps her to gather her belongings in a backpack, accompanies her to the apartment door, and almost pushes her into the elevator. Sheet of metal. Amputated image. Inexpressive goodbye.

Gabriel *knows* that Héctor returns and that another man, without face or defining characteristics, anonymous, seeks Gabriel somewhere, and stops now, overcome by the rash absence of the youth. That man desires him. There is no silence to immunize them or make them healthy and false. Only the night, Gabriel's tremulous and passionate words, uncoercible like the first babblings of a child; only that truly warm kiss after the words, only their naked bodies, weightless, almost unreal. Only desire, simple and atavistic. That man is the only one who exists.

Who is the other who now comes toward Gabriel? He *knows*: it's Héctor, who comes and sits on the edge of the bed, looks at Gabriel lying there, and cries mutely in front of him. Then he lies at his side and hugs him and still does not speak. Atavistic and simple as desire. Gabriel allows himself to be embraced, and *knows* that the unknown man begins to move, moves away while Gabriel lets himself be embraced, and disappears around a corner. Only the two of them exist, Héctor and Gabriel. Ana will never meet Jorge; Jorge never met Héctor. It's all the work of the Devil. Gabriel *knows* that, he gets up and goes into the bathroom, sinks his hands into the bucket, and scrubs the sheet devotedly.

5

Her name is Ana. She's a painter.

His name is Jorge. He's the owner of a '57 Chevrolet, and a taxi driver.

Their names are Gabriel and Héctor. The former is beautiful. The latter possesses the former.

Translated by Dick Cluster

R. ERICA DOYLE

Tante Merle (1999)

Tante Merle did use to promenade through Brooklyn, striding down Nostrand Avenue, Atlantic Avenue, out of Bedford-Stuyvesant, through Crown Heights, Park Slope, give a nod to Fort Greene-Clinton Hill, until she finally turn around when she reach the river. Then she coming back around— Atlantic Avenue, Nostrand Avenue, until she finally reach Macon Street, where she did live.

All of we did use to ask she, "Tante Merle! You come to United State since nineteen fifty-six, own five apartment building, manage six. Why you did never buy yourself a car?"

And Tante Merle just puff she big breast so, like fighting cock, swing she hips round, hand on hip, arms akimbo, looking at you in the eye.

"Well, my dear," she say. "I ain't have a car like I ain't have a man. If is ain't me own wheels I turning, I ain't interested!"

And she walk off again.

Now Tante Merle is one of them aunties you ain't seeing too often.

You use to see she at holidays and holy days.

Use to see she at big family fete like when Boboy get christen. Use to see she at Trinidad and Tobago Benevolent Association Annual Dinner and Dance, but it seem somehow that since she have them eleven building to be taking care of, you ain't seeing she so much.

Now you know since Trinidadian can't call before they does drop by somebody house like American do to warn you they is coming by, every Sunday when my parents take us on family rounds, we can't find Tante Merle when we reach. When I ask my mother why it is we can't call Tante Merle, must instead brave five hours Sunday afternoon New York traffic in vain, she only stchupsing, saying, "Why you must call if is you family?"

Now I was a miserable child, yes? Always wanting to know somebody business. So next I see Tante Merle at Carnival on Eastern Parkway, I only asking she: why she never home when we reach?

Tante Merle only smile small small smile, saying, "Child, I have business to take care of. Can't be sitting round the house all day drinking rum like you Auntie Marjorie, you know!"

Tante Merle was at that ripe old age when the women in my family does start to blossom, seem round sixty-two, when the men does start to drop off. Tante Merle always dress fine, fine, fine. Auntie Marjorie say she think she fancy, she dress like parrot. She did have a set of jewelry, red, orange, and purple she find at corner pharmacy, and full dresses my father said made by Omar the Tentmaker. So she looking full and bright like flamboyan.

One summer, I come home from temporary job, and my mother say, "Child, Tante Merle catch sick, girl. Tante Merle have walking pneumonia. Tante Merle can't leave the house for six weeks. She have she home health aide name Hazelle. If you please, go look for she. I make up some stew chicken and rice, some dahl and salt fish, for you know home health aide can't make food proper."

So I heave a inner sigh (kept it in my belly for I know I ain't too old to have ears box), and my mother pack up a box with cast iron pot and Tupperware she buy from Auntie Kathy. I catch the bus to the subway. I catch the train to a next train, and a next train to a next train, and a next train to a next train and a next train to a next train, until finally I heave up the step smelling like piss bound for Macon Street. Walking up the road to Tante Merle house with this big set a food in my hand — sweating, boy, sweating, cause it hot, yes?

So when I reach Tante Merle house, you know I vex.

I stand in front a big brownstone where Tante Merle living, go to parlor gate, ring the bell. The bell ring through the foyer like a dark voice. I wait, for it always take fifteen — twenty minutes for someone at Tante Merle house to open the door.

A little rumfle-up brown face woman hobble out and open the gate.

I say, "I Tante Merle grand-niece, Errol daughter, come to look for she." Woman nod silent-like and let me in.

In the house now, Tante Merle have bottom floor parlor fix up like a bedroom. Tante Merle have dark red cloth like blood across the window. Tante Merle have Seven Powers candle burning on the dresser, echoing light onto mirror. Tante Merle ain't have one window open, boy, so you know it hot!

Tante Merle looking shrivel up on the bed.

I clear my throat, say, "Tante Merle, is I, Errol daughter."

Tante Merle face crack open.

"Oh, yes, my dear, come here let these old eyes have a look at you! You look pretty, pretty! Your hair grown out nice, nice, it so fine! You know you great-grandmother was a coolie? Pull up a chair, let me talk to you a minute, nuh?"

I pull up a old chair, upholstered, green. It does have the sunken space of Tante Merle backside groove into it, so the spring jooking me in my backside. I wiggling in the chair.

Tante Merle looking at me, she eyes laughing, laughing.

"Tante Merle," I say. "I bring you a set of food. My mother send it."

"Thank you, my dear," she say, extending she hand. I take it. It wrinkle like parchment, delicate like butterfly wing.

"So," she say. "How is you *friend*?"

Is now I a little unsettle.

You see, my father pass not so long ago, and my head so wrap up and knock up at the time, I feeling so low, I bring my lady friend with me to the funeral not caring what anyone would think, for my heart felt like it was like to fall apart. And I know the way she say *friend*, that is *this* friend about whom she did inquire.

So I say, *"Fine."*

Tante Merle laugh. The laugh start not from she mouth, not from she throat, not from she extra large chest, but the laugh start from she toes — I swear the bottom of the bed begin to shake and rattle. The laugh pass through she legs, through she hips, it start to roll, I feeling it, she lungs rattling bad, man, bad, but Tante Merle laughing, until she start to cough.

"Girl, you know, let me tell you something, eh? Not so long ago, before your time, when I was living in Arima, was a fruit vendor used to sell coconut, mango, and fig by the savannah. I used to pass she everyday in jitney bus on my way downtown to work in the office where I was a bookkeeper. Every morning I buy a fresh sweet julienne mango from the fruit vendor.

"Fruit vendor was like coconut milk and cinnamon. Was like sage on she breath. Fruit vendor look at me everyday, look at me like she seeing me, like no one ever see me before. Is the first time I feel like jumbie watching at me. Strong jumbie. I see a bundle a herb tie hanging above the bit of stick she had tie together to make a shelter and is then I knew the fruit vendor was powerful obeah woman, to have she bundle tie up in the air like that for all to see.

"Each time I pass, she ain't never say a word. I ask for two fresh julienne mango and she take a machete and slice the stem, cut round the center, open, expose seed, slice back and forth, till she make a patchwork quilt of mango cube.

"Each morning I pass, begin to leave early, so as to savor julienne mango standing by the savannah in front of fruit vendor.

"I come home, ask my sister what she know about fruit vendor.

"Sister say, 'Fruit vendor man leave.' Sister say, 'Fruit vendor man make revolution camp in the bush. But everyone does know that fruit vendor woman does only take up with woman.'

"Is then I interested!

"One day I come by fruit vendor woman. My paper just come through immigration, my sister sponsor me come live in United State take care of she miserable Yankee children.

"'Well,' I say. 'This the last morning I coming here, for tomorrow I leaving on big ship to New York City, go live with my sister.'

"Fruit vendor woman look up at me, she eyes burning. She take me in. She breathe me out. She drink me like coconut water. She speak, first time.

"'You know,' she say, 'it hard to be fruit vendor these days. They does have all kind of new shop downtown; and each shop does have it own particular fruit; and each fruit does have it own particular seed; and each seed does have it own particular need; and each need does find it own particular root. Each soil, rootless, does have it own particular sorrow. It hard to be fruit vendor on the savannah.'

"She take me mango, slice it ever, still wind blowing, slow, slow, slow. Sweat starting to crowd my brow. She bangles tinkle in the wind as she cut with machete, slicing through to the seed.

"How I savor that mango that day, yes."

Tante Merle stop. Tante Merle eyes looking past me, past me. Looking far into the past and the distance. Tante Merle feeling hummingbird beat on she face. Smelling orchid growing in front yard. Not hearing rain pounding down on Brooklyn street.

"Is good, girl, you," she say. "It hard to be fruit vendor."

She eyes drop off, close. She snort. She start to snore back in she throat like she always do, for Tante Merle one of them aunties that does fall asleep anywhere, anyhow, anytime.

But you know? I feeling all right. Butterflies gone. Iron pit in stomach like it melt. Knowing Tante Merle, who did like to promenade down Nostrand Avenue, two shopping bag hung in the crook of she elbow, proud and round and brown eyes, settle somewhere on a savannah, all the way through Brooklyn, through Bed-Stuy, Clinton Hill, Fort Greene, Park Slope, Brooklyn Heights, all the way back to she place on Macon Street. Managing she eleven building. Never buy car. Never want car. But did savor sweet mango from coconut cinnamon fruit vendor woman, she breath like sage.

Whose Caribbean? An Allegory, in Part (2005)

And so it came to pass that upon that time, not so long ago, in that part of the world, there lived a child who dreamed. I am not so sure even now as to the definitive facial features of that child, but I am fairly certain, having myself wandered through various dreams that became stories that were told and did not fade over time, that the child was both female and male—a common enough occurrence in that place of the child's origin at that time, as, contrary to numerous prevailing opinions, happens frequently today. The child—let us know him/her as "s/he"—possessed a slender penis of startlingly delicate green, the truest color of the sea that s/he had always loved— that sea which licked and foamed out and back, out and in again, all about the shores of that place; as s/he also possessed a pair of luminous blue breasts the tone of the purest skies, which, on the gentlest days, nuzzled their broad, soft chins against the sea. Nipples did not grow at the end of the child's breasts, but rather berries the inflamed color of hibiscus in its most passionate surrender to the sunsets and dawns that for millennia had washed over that place. The child also possessed a vagina and uterus, which, as was common knowledge among all who knew him/her, produced at least two or three times per year, without assistance from anyone, a race of brazen dolphins—creatures the fierce color of the sun, silver-speckled and gray-bottlenosed; creatures which, despite the rude raucousness of their cries upon emerging from between his/her thighs into the light, leaped without fail with the gravest of countenances into those waiting waves.

The child dreamed; again, nothing unusual in what would come to be known by some as a region of dreamers. S/he dreamed of tamarinds, of course, and of star-apples and green mangoes that, eventually rendered senseless by the days' stunning heat, plunged from their trees to ooze their fragrant juices along the largely still unexplored inner paths of her/his thighs. S/he dreamed of plummeting stars providing a last flash of hope (or, in other instances, a vision of death) to condemned slaves, their wrists bound with heavy chains and thick cords on so many mornings and late afternoons on a public square's auction block; s/he dreamed of tormented hands outstretched, at last vanished forever beneath the night-blackened waves of that eternal sea, as dawn brought her/him dreams of violet hummingbirds intent on sweetness and color, and dreams of shrugging mountains, and cane. Always cane. Field upon field of it, whispering. Muttering. Cane thick with secrets but also with the day's tragedies and joys—the few joys there were, could have been, in those times—and, on nights of the fullest moons, the calls of three-hundred-year-dead jumbies, or duppies, or soucouyants rising so slowly from the vast water, green-dreadlocked and sober-eyed, intent on possessing her/his soul, and yours, and mine.

During my many travels to that place and by way of my own history there—that place which, through the wills and workings of Osun and Oya, stealthy buccaneers or cruise ship companies, slave traders or airline advertisements, or a combination of any and all, became what we call today the Caribbean—I have thought often of that child and her/his dreams. In the dreary halls of immigration, while wondering which passport to use on this trip or that one, Jamaican or U.S.—which citizen will I be this time, (re)entering "my" country?—I have conjured her/him: the (surely) skinny legs; the (perhaps) slightly mottled skin; the all-too-wide eyes and sun-bleached hair which, even this late in human time, yet bears evidence of ringworm, just there, on the scalp; and the gleaming blue breasts ending in those bright red berry-nipples. I conjure him/her, wondering as I conjure if, during this tourist season or the last one, anyone has propositioned him/her for a quick suck of that lovely green child-cock. A few pennies, little one, to touch . . . or no, to *caress* your body, all its secret parts, and most especially that tender place from which, each spring and autumn, braying dolphins emerge into light amid the noise of their own frenzy. A few pennies, relatively speaking, to trail my fingers along those pathways where star-apples and green mangoes, finally bored with an entire lifetime of murmuring hours passed among the smaller secrets of leaves, consent to drop and ooze their most precious parts over your lap. A few pennies, a dollar here or there, and then I, whomever "I" was or will be this year or last, will return to my distant capital, to my own dreams of vengeance against the swarthy and those who, like you, child, threaten through wild breeding and proven savagery to overrun my peaceful pastures and geometrically ordained, mercilessly swept cities. I will think no more of you until the next time and the next, even though, in truth, I might live quite nearby you; but you will of course understand that you mean nothing to me, absolutely nothing at all; not even your shimmering blue breasts and magnificently green penis finally mean much to me, except during those passing moments in the darkness of unspoken illicit dreams and echoing silence that we share, have always shared—that darkness that is yours, yes, and mine. Darkness and silence shared for all time. For all time, I say, and I am gone, leaving you touched, possessed, not only by me.

When I conjure this child—when s/he speaks to me on dim nights out of waves and centuries of un-voicedness, complete despair—I imagine that s/he yearns for two things only: to be loved, of course, and to be safe. To be able to walk past the mountains that slouch over her/his town, along the glistening shores that stretch just beyond, secure in the knowledge that s/he has never had, could never have: that no one, not anyone at all, will come crooning at her/him with a few pennies, lately grown to dollars, for a prolonged taste of his/her various parts; that no one will run shouting at him/her, wielding a machete, because s/he possesses not only breasts, but blue ones; not only a penis, but a green one. S/he prays, I know, that in his/her town and time, s/he will not be perceived, for whatever reason, as disposable (because s/he is poor, perhaps) and thus worthy of erasure or, worse, annihilation. S/he prays not to be perceived as "other," perhaps, by those among whom s/he has long dwelt, occasionally in the realm of history-tinged dreams, while received as an exotic morsel by many of those in pursuit of sun, sex, and the two-bit, so-called third world trade long ago made a reality by marauders, and held tightly in place by those of today: the International Monetary Fund, the World Bank, the transnational corporate behemoths, and, first and foremost as nexus of all three, the United (severely capitalist, fiercely indifferent to human and most life) States. In his/her wandering, s/he continues to dream of a stable economy for her/his region, not disastrous exchange rates; of adequate housing and health care, not shanty slums and intolerable taxes; of the freedom of *not* having to migrate to a so-called first world country in search of work and a life-sustaining wage where, because of her/his color and/or class, s/he will often be even more despised, or despised in a new and different way. He/She imagines what it would be like to be able to remain in his/her country as a citizen with complete rights and privileges, in a nation in which the idea and practice of actual sovereignty are more than measly yearnings scoffed at by presiding (corrupt) officials. No more for him/her, s/he imagines, the long queues in front of embassies where people wait for visa applications to nations interested only in their cheap labor; no more for her/him the insulting empty promises of parliaments and congresses and long-winded, ineffectual inter-

Caribbean councils, but *some*thing, something for once, s/he imagines, akin to a place in the shade: beneath the ample spread of a lignum vitae tree or a guango, maybe; somewhere far from the soul- and body-killing work of hacking cane for next to nothing, of hauling fish out of the sea for scraps, of caring for other people's homes and children for much belligerence and scant gratitude. Somewhere well in the shade for the first time in his/her life, where those hands and they alone can at last, in the peace and solitude that are the nurturing grounds for the soul and its companion the imagination, stroke and take pleasure in those berry-tips at the end of his/her breasts, as the ears of the stroker delight in the bawdy commentary of randy humming-birds agog at the green fullness of her/his penis finally granted leave to stretch out completely to the shading leaves above, and to the sky.

I am certain that this child's whispers rustled through our individual and collective spirits six years ago when, in Kingston, Jamaica, a small group of us, against all odds and good sense but profoundly possessed of hope and faith, decided to form the Jamaica Forum for Lesbians, All-Sexuals and Gays, or J-FLAG as we came to be and still are known.[1] Like that child and others, we had obviously begun to believe, even if we hadn't completely acknowl-edged, that dreams of one kind or another invariably bespeak both hope and faith — the roots of all political civic action. Hope that we could engender social and political change in a nation that, broadened through our efforts, would ultimately be worthy of all Jamaicans: a nation welcoming to all, irrespective of sexuality and perceived gender transgressions. Faith that our fellow Jamaicans would civilly receive us, extend, and, in so extending, grow. Grow into the nation we had and have yet to achieve: the island of matchless mountains that has produced the likes of Paul Bogle and Marcus Garvey yet continues to wage vicious war on itself through the very violence their visions deplored; grow into the nation that could produce lights like Nanny and Claude McKay, Bob Marley and the Manleys — Edna, Norman, and Michael — and Miss Lou Bennett, and Rex Nettleford (this being, of course, a highly incomplete list), as well as redoubtable, though unfortunately homophobic and sexist, talents like Shabba Ranks and Buju Banton, to name only two. There, in that part of Jamaica, in strictest secrecy and with the widest how-the-backside-can-we-be-doing-*this* expressions on our faces, we seriously attended the child's echoing whispers — that child whom I now believe must have been some sort of god/dess. Because yes, man, all right, now, the whispers said. Time fi stop de foolishness and get past de fear and get on wid making a place fi weself inna dis ya country. A fi we time — this time is ours — and no matter wha de people dem a seh, oonu haffi *work* fi mek de people dem understand dat we nah go tek de burning and de fireburning and de acid dash pon we face and de screams pon de road of "Batty bwoy!" and "Battyman fi dead! Battyman fi bu'n!" and "Sodomite bu'n inna holy fire!"[2] Mek *one* a dem touch oonu, the whispers said, and see what rass-backside tings happen nex inna dis ya country—and mek sure to know seh dem might touch oonu and bawl out oonu name pon de road and shout dat oonu is a batty bwoy or a sodomite. Dem might go do it, because dis is Jamaica. Still. The Jamaica of "boom-bye-bye in a battybwoy head, rudeb-woy nah promote de nasty man [or sodomite], dem haffi dead."[3] Mek sure seh oonu tek care wi wha yu a do, but oonu *do* it. Inna Jamaica. Now.

Now, I say, which was then, which remains and always will be now. Now, when, if your breasts end in red berries and your penis is green and attractive to hummingbirds and your uterus delivers raucous dolphins unto the world twice or even three times per year, or even if you merely wish to hold the hand of the person, a person, whom you love or desire and that person is the same gender as oonu, oonu had best watch yu backside inna Jamaica (and other parts of the Caribbean, and, in truth, the world at large), and tek care dat de people dem nah chop yu wid machete. Except that now oonu have a choice: to join the company of dreamers who have survived and, for all I know just might, beneath their sensible tropical clothes, sport blue breasts and green penises and uteruses filled beyond capacity with cavorting baby dolphins. They survived. We did. Survived years of bellicose, religiously fundamentalist radio announcers who denounced us, froth-mouthed cit-izens who threatened to murder us if they ever discovered who we actually were as people living among them, and a repressive government that to this very day refuses to take seriously or effectively consider in Jamaica's parlia-ment any initiatives that would begin—merely *begin*—earnest movements toward ensuring the lives, safety, and ultimate human fulfillment of its non-heterosexual citizens. And I say "merely," but that "merely" would in this instance be a hugely significant one, and one not at all lost on a government consistently more interested in maintaining the politically expedient status quo and its legacy of corruption than in developing true democracy—the ideal and aim of all humankind. True democracy itself, however, knows that it cannot flourish—indeed, it can barely breathe—in an environment of sustained and enforced ignorance. True democracy delights in having its belly rubbed by lively congress through which wide room for all voices is made. It can no more thrive beneath Jamaican Prime Minister P. J. Patter-son's savage disregard for the lives of gay, lesbian, bisexual, and transgen-dered people[4] (as evidenced, in part, by his administration's steadfast refusal to consider doing away with the Offences against the Person Act and its "buggery law," both of which criminalize male homosexuality)[5] than it can survive — if it ever existed — beneath the vicious neoimperialistic militarism of "President" George W. Bush, a successful election thief and warmongering, would-be despot. It remains to be seen if Patterson's successors willl show any more compassion in this regard. The actions and intentions of these "leaders" and their kin will always be enabled by a politically apathetic citizenry — by a populace that is perhaps complacent, beguiled, and intellectually dulled by the allurements of consumerism, but that in any event is comfortably, if dangerously, mired in ahistoricism and the indifference to and ignorance of human suffering that an ahistorical intellect bolsters, such ignorance and indifference numbering among the most tragic, yet avoidable, human states.

It is a known fact, of course, that for any form of actual, truly practicable democracy to succeed, its citizens will be required — demanded — to maintain a constant, energetic, interrogating engagement with history. The past — "the good old days" for some, depending on one's point of view — is always present; even the most hell-bent demagogue understands this truth. The demagogue or the truly principled head of state also understands (and risks not understanding at our peril) that true democracy, as fragile as the most endangered of ecosystems, requires respect for and attendance to not only its ideals and aims, but also its scrupulous, honorable practice. Actual, practicable democracy quickly fades in the face of hypocrisy and corruption — political chicanery. The harsh irony is not lost on us, of course, and it should never be lost on us or forgotten, that in so many modern Caribbean nations developed out of the atrocities of slavery, genocide, and a racism that continues to snarl and lick its chops, what we are unfortunately charged to term, correctly, "almost-democracy" stumbles along as a bandy-legged specter, crippled in its posture and regularly short of breath. "Almost-democracy" in that still too many Caribbean citizens in the *twenty-first* century (for all that is worth) do not have access to adequate healthcare, housing, and education; endure poverty's systematized depredations; and, in the case of those of Jamaica and other locales, if they do not meet the requirements of gender role norms and other demands of expected and imposed heterosexuality, are forced to contend with the continued assaults of heterosexist, homophobic tyranny — literal assaults, murder and other violence included, all of which rear vicious heads in the context of global human rights struggles.

These problems — those of simple, but fierce, inequalities between human beings — are by no means unique to the Caribbean. In regarding most, if not all, present-day nations, we can easily enough recall and paraphrase George Orwell's apt words from *Animal Farm* (Orwell's admonishments unfortunately increasingly apropos in the post-September 11 world): all animals are equal, but some animals are and always have been — yes, of course! — far more equal than others.[6] As citizens of the so-termed modern world, we understand that, notwithstanding Caribbean and other anticolonial movements for independence and their subsequent postcolonial struggles (resistance to, among other scourges, transnational corporate encroachments, IMF and World Bank machinations, and latter-day dependencies of developing-world economies bound to tourist dollars and enduring "banana republic" oppressions), "democracy," so loosely imagined, is invariably practiced selectively. Thus in 1980, Cuba — a revolutionary, presumably anticapitalist, and allegedly democratic society — could expel from its shores by way of the Mariel boatlift thousands of its citizens alleged or known to be, á la state rhetoric, degenerates: homosexuals, sex workers, the mentally troubled, drug users, and HIV-positive and AIDS-afflicted people among them. In our time, Jamaica may still turn a coldly indifferent cheek to the plight of its poor, to many of its children and women, and to all of its (identifiably and not) non-heterosexual people — at least those not among the wealthy — as indicated by reports, those which are actually taken seriously and documented by the police and government officials, which seep through to anyone who cares about another homosexual murdered in Kingston, another stoned in Spanish Town, another burned to death in St. Elizabeth, or Trelawny, or St. James, or. . . .[7] It is impossible to know at this time how many more of these people have been driven over the years into the trauma of exile or the even greater trauma of applying, as gay refugees, for political asylum in a foreign country.[8] It is also not lost on us that these realities proceed in a country already beset and factionalized by widespread violence; daily, often grisly murders; all forms of sexual abuse, extortions, thievery; and — the cake's proverbial icing — untenable inflation and taxation. And so in a similar but distinct context, in the late 1990s the Cayman Islands refused entry to a cruise ship loaded with gay and lesbian tourists, many locals greeting the docking ship with hateful jeers and thrown objects, as, at about the same time and afterward, people in the Bahamas did the same. All animals are equal, our various constitutions have extended so nobly on paper, but please do excise from that list all faggots and sodomites, most of the poor, a good number of women, and certainly all ambiguously gendered children with blue breasts and green penises.

And make trial to remember what is true: that some Jamaicans — elected officials and citizens alike — have already made it clear to you how they would prefer that your son become a thief rather than a faggot. Do not forget how, in so many ways, they let you know that, yes, they most certainly would prefer that your daughter grow up to be a (perhaps casual) whore instead of a sodomite. And while, even after all these centuries, too many in so many cases would still prefer that the majority of their citizens, neighbors, children, and fellows turn out to be light-brown-skinned and at least middle class, educated, and possessed of sufficient coin to purchase deodorant soap, always remember that, under certain conditions, they will be willing to tolerate even the darkest ones and the poor — the missing-teeth ones, the one-legged ones, the ones who stink (those underarms, the need for deodorant soap) and spit in the street, the ones who carry on in public places like wild dogs. They will tolerate even *them*, provided they are not one of those people who are not even really people, are they? The despicable ones. The ones who would, just that quickly, become pedophiles. Those who would, without doubt, perpetrate carnal abuse. Need we say which?

With the education and amplitude that time and experience have permitted us, we have learned at least one thing: political activism is not, nor should it be, a romantic or, God forbid, sentimental pursuit. It will always require a nuanced, astute, and sometimes even painful historical and social analysis of the society in which it functions and, toward the greater truth and clarity that are always attainable, a willingness to investigate, dismantle, and move through the fraudulent, truth-debasing and -obscuring statist languages that affirm and maintain the abuses so beloved by dictators, parliamentary and congressional pretenders, would-be thespian pundits, and plain old charlatans. Among the beleaguered, hostile political climates of today's narrowing world — be they Jamaica, Zimbabwe, the West Bank, the right-wing landscapes of a still-fissured German union, or the more than ever police-stated United States — the most generous, sophisticated political activism will increasingly *and justifiably* expect of its practitioners nonreductionist, nonpartisan thinking, a widening of ideological and philosophical boundaries, and a disavowal of the single issue, myopic political imagination. This last looms as particularly critical given the abiding complexities of lives weighted by poverty and globalization, and further complicated by the prejudices visited on those with genders and sexualities viewed as non-normative. It is entirely likely that the (brown, black, yellow, white) woman who cuts cane and is poor and functionally illiterate might also have a female lover in similar circumstances — a woman who herself might have (two, three, four, more) children and a memory of abusive treatment at the hands of the man who owns the house from which he evicted both her and her

children. Undeniably, the minimally paid and uninsured, uneducated fisherman whose skin spans any range of colors remains, irrespective of his yearnings, a (post-) colonial subject vulnerable to the caprices of the presiding
powers' geopolitical chess games — powers both at "home" and abroad —
whether he sees himself as such or not, whether he views himself as head of
his household or not, whether he finally obtains a visa to the United States/
Canada/the United Kingdom or not, and certainly whether he erotically
desires and has sex with men or women, or both, or not.

Regarding the relevance of dreams, we can allow that activism will occasionally begin in dreams, provided that it moves onward from them into
definite action. And so the child longs to move unscathed through open
public space with his/her red-berried blue breasts but must eventually do
battle to be permitted full and unmolested possession of them, at least in this
world in which we live — this world which, from its very beginnings, has
been a realm both centered on struggles for power and dominion and one
which, to the best of its ability, has consistently obliterated all traces of the
"other" and "otherness." And so the person focused on erotic/romantic
interactions with another person of the same gender fantasizes of being able
to meander a country Caribbean road while holding the hand of a partner
without fear of a machete's sudden slice across the neck, but must sooner or
later be prepared to challenge the constricting, policing forces — local, national, global — that impede his or her ultimate human freedom. The woman
who lives in fear for her body, if she is ever to become more than fear's
afterwipe, will eventually have to work with other women, and hopefully
with progressive men, toward securing the unquestionable right to occupy,
in absolute safety, her body. And whether one marches in Washington
against a so-called president's genocidal intentions in the name of making
the world "safe" for "democracy," or against military dictatorships in Nicaragua, Panama, El Salvador, Guatemala, or Chile (to name only a few of the
nations in which dictatorships were financed and otherwise supported, often
covertly, by the United States), or whether one meets with grassroots gay/
lesbian/queer groups in so many small rooms in Kingston, Havana, Port-
au-Prince, or Willemstad, the aims are consistently the same: to secure true
freedom for all human beings, toward the realization of a world in which the
word *freedom* will come to signify more than a mere two-syllable noun that
was once a lovely idea that somehow, somewhere along the path of human
progress, failed; more than a pithy word of little use or meaning in these,
our increasingly *de*freedomized (if we are not constantly vigilant) twenty-
first century lives; more than a silly little word, sadly obsolete, but still to be

found, never fear, in our dust-covered dictionaries, on that page, right there, still somehow arresting our eyes among the many F's.

I titled this essay "Whose Caribbean?"—wanting to explore, among other questions, the idea of whose Caribbean for the living? Whose for the being, in an ultimately more dignified, more equitable daily life? Whose for the dreaming and the imagining, as well as the fulfilling? For the walking on country roads or city streets while holding, without fear, the hand of a same-gender partner? For the walking, unaccompanied, in a female body? In an ambiguously gendered body? For the lyming and the laughter, and the participating without hesitation or shame in every social ritual, including those of family, to which we have and have always had a right? For even, if we are so fortunate, the baring of our shining blue breasts to the vaulting sky, as our penises scorn, if they choose, the ill-mannered behavior of those dolphins still leaping forth from our uteruses?

Whose Caribbean, and whose freedom? But ours, of course. Our very own. Our own, though as we know, or ought to know, such freedom will rarely, if ever, be achieved easily. Our struggles for true democracy just might end in our lives' termination following the swift hiss of a machete's stroke. It is irrevocably true that, in our lifetimes, we will not see all of our ideals achieved, pulled from dreams into actual life. These incontrovertibles aside, however, *that* Caribbean, the one of today and always, remains ours and is (if we never knew it before) us. Alive to these truths, we must never forget that the Caribbean needs us far more than it needs its disdain for and even occasional hatred of some of us. We must remember that we—*all* of us—are indispensable to its future, even as it growls at the complexities our sexualities and political practice bring to its here-and-there intransigence. In an increasingly desperate, increasingly Balkanized post-September 11 world, that Caribbean needs our energies, against corporate and global hegemonies; our talents, against (neo)imperialisms; our wills and intelligent resistance, against the destructions and self-destructiveness of inhumane rhetoric, legislations, and ultimately spurious democracies. Whose Caribbean? I ask once more, awaiting a response.

Yes, a response, as—for this brief while, toward the closing of these reflections that will hopefully open to another kind of beginning—we return to the realm of dreams: to the scents of tamarinds and green mangoes and the redolent nostalgia of freshly sliced star-apples. We return to the sea and the shores and once upon a time, which transposes suddenly to this time, which it always was and which it must, in the so-called natural order of things, steadfastly remain; the present ever inescapably itself, never past or future and invariably the most difficult period of "time" for human beings to live in, simply live in peacefully and without rancor, as suggested by words like *live in the present, live only for today*—desirable, yes, even the ideal, but how many succeed at it, how many of us ever seriously consider it?—the past forever embedded in the present, in the pain and inevitable horrors confronted by conscientious unblinking memory, in the tragedies and occasional triumphs of history always ravelled by so much needless suffering, by the unbearable human misery and degradation that must not, for our collective sakes and the continued growth of this body we call "humanity," ever be denied. We dream, fully aware that we are and always have been much more than dreamers; we engage with sundry phantasms of the past, astonished at how, in that muting light, their faces and hands bear such unmistakable resemblance to our own. Gradually, over the years that slowly lose measure, we learn that things, all things about us, have begun to change: great lavender-furred lions have begun to crawl up out of the sea in search of the coconuts that alone will slake their yawning thirst, as more than a few mountains simply shrug their shoulders and get up and leave, longing all at once for cooler climates in which they may copulate for all eternity with the low-lying hills they had in fact, from their very birth, always wished to be. We dream that, over the centuries, through the millennia, we have done much work; that we are tired, well exhausted; that, in spite of that great fatigue, we have, we know, gradually achieved something of high value. We are confident in the assurance, even as we feel ourselves so weary, that much remains for us to do: work having much to do with the words *necessary*, *vital*, and even *gallant*.

Lying there on the sand as we now do before the late-in-the-day's bronze receding waves, we are not at all surprised to note the deepening blue of our breasts, and the yammering flock of hummingbirds, a good three hundred of them or more, that, smirking as only they can, come to light and gossip away the evening on the emerald rod between our legs, now a deeper green than ever—the most secret tone of the sky. Should we gasp and rise to attention, then, when all those children, bearing similar colors to our own over their various parts but brighter, come walking across the waves toward us, followed by all those women, and men, and the additional million-or-so-fold in between? We should not, of course, and we do not, knowing as we do upon those sands, before that sea, that, like ourselves, they have always been there. "Safety," their faces seem to say, with a hint of "and now in search of . . ." but whether the words are questions or simply quiet statements we cannot—not in that moment that is also this one, anyway—yet tell. But then look at some of them now, we think, as they move back out across the waves. As they fall into those waters, and rise. Rise and fall, to gaze back at us now and again, pondering our watching eyes as, with certainty of the work that we know is and always will be ever so much more than a dream, we stir, aware of hummingbirds busy between our thighs; aware of our hands reaching just there, in that way, as, this time, we sense the deepening red of those lively berries at the ends of our breasts. It is then we know for sure that, in this dream that will shortly transform to waking, we will at last throw back our faces to the sky and hear, not for the first time, the word—*that* word that makes possible all things beginning with the deed; that word, passing upward from our recently opened mouths: the finally untethered, always respectful, ever necessary human Yes.

NOTES

This essay originated as a keynote address ("Whose Caribbean?" presented at Caribbean Heritage Week, Brown University, Providence, March 10, 2003). A later version was published in *Callaloo* 27, no. 3 (2004): 671–81.

1 See http://www.jflag.org.

2 *Batty bwoy* is a profane Jamaican Creole word for gay man or homosexual, literally "ass man" or "ass boy"; *sodomite* in Jamaican usage is a condemnatory word for lesbian, occasionally also used in reference to males. The phrase "battyman fi dead" translates as "faggots should be killed"; "battyman fi bu'n" translates as "faggots should be incinerated."

3 This quotation is from Buju Banton's notoriously homophobic dancehall song, "Boom Bye Bye," written by Mark Myrie, *Buju Banton: The Early Years 90–95* (Kingston, Jamaica: Penthouse Record Distributors, 1992).

4 While I use the words *gay*, *lesbian*, *bisexual*, and *transgender* here, I sometimes— though not always—prefer the all-encompassing term *queer*, which includes all the aforementioned not only as sexual identities that are often, though not always, self-selected, but also as sexual behaviors, as in "gay" (male-male) sex. *Queer* also makes room for various political/ideological practices, such as lesbian and transgender feminism. It is critical to remember, however, that much of what some Western quarters term gay, lesbian, bisexual, or transgender is not necessarily so viewed or named by those who practice the behavior. Thus "men who have sex with men," a term seen frequently in some North American and European (and increasingly Latin American and Caribbean) AIDS/HIV education contexts, accurately describes the *behavior* of individuals who participate in same-gender sexual and romantic unions but do not particularly, if at all, view themselves as gay, homosexual, or even bisexual.

While the word *queer* also makes room for various behaviors and identities that would be viewed by many as unquestionably "non-heterosexual," it also includes behaviors often viewed as "subversive" by many, such as that of "straight" men

who enjoy cross-dressing in their female partner's undergarments, straight people's use of body piercings, hair dyes, and tattoos (some of which presentation has
come to be seen as "queer," but not necessarily a definitive statement of gay,
lesbian, or bisexual sexuality), various or all sadomasochistic practices, same-
gender participation in sexual fetishes by people whose sexual or romantic lives are
otherwise "heterosexual," and so on.

The word *queer* has also been much used in recent years as both verb and
adjective by many scholars (principally those from or working in North America
and Europe, although use of the word has extended beyond these regions), as
seen in the uses of "queer" theory/theoretical discourse and the possibilities of
"queering" or "queerying" a text (providing a "queer" reading of or "queer"-ed
investigation of a text). With such linguistic and intellectual fluidity and expan-
siveness, almost anything can be "queer"-ed or "queer*y*"-ed: texts (queer theory
applied to the works of Derek Walcott or C. L. R. James, for example); philoso-
phies; scholarship (the "queering" of a historian's scholarly gaze); public and
private spaces (the "queering" of Buckingham Palace, however this might be
imagined, or a "queer"-ing study of the cricket match as a homosocial, homoerotic bonding ritual); ideological, cultural, historical, and national narratives
(the still largely unexplored reality of queer/same-gender sexual/romantic desire between slaves and between masters and slaves, for example); metaphors,
and allegories, and so on. While I believe in and support the inclusive, imagina-
tive, and political possibilities of the word *queer*, I chose not to use it in this essay
principally because it is not yet in the Caribbean at large a word that has either
been used much or considered for its potential in application to non-heterosexual
sexualities, practices, and identities. By way of amplification with regard to *queer*,
a similar, but somewhat differently employed term has recently emerged in some
African American lesbian and gay circles: "same-gender-loving."

5 As cited in the "Parliamentary Submission" section of J-FLAG's web page, "The
Offences against the Person Act prohibits 'acts of gross indecency' (generally
interpreted as referring to any kind of physical intimacy) between men, in public
or in private. The offence of buggery is created by [the Act's Article] 76, and is
defined as anal intercourse between a man and a woman, or between two men [or
between a human and an animal]. No force is required for the commission of the
offence of buggery. Most of the prosecutions in fact, involve consenting adult
men suspected of indulging in anal sex." Article 76, "Unnatural Crime," states
that "whosoever shall be convicted of the abominable crime of buggery [anal
intercourse] committed either with mankind or with any animal, shall be liable
to be imprisoned and kept to hard labour for a term not exceeding ten years."
Article 77, "Attempt," states that "whosoever shall attempt to commit the said
abominable crime, or shall be guilty of any assault with intent to commit the
same, or of any indecent assault upon any male person, shall be guilty of a
misdemeanour, and being convicted thereof shall be liable to be imprisoned for a
term not exceeding seven years, with or without hard labour." See http://www
.jflag.org/programmes/parliamentary__sub.htm.

6 Orwell, *Animal Farm* (New York: Harcourt, Brace, 1946), 112.

7 Interestingly — and sadly — toward the end of 2004, roughly a year and a half after

this essay was written, Human Rights Watch issued a report entitled *Hated to Death: Homophobia, Violence, and Jamaica's* HIV/AIDS *Epidemic* (New York: Human Rights Watch, 2004). The report featured harrowing (to say the least) documentation of antigay, anti-lesbian human rights violations in Jamaica. Within days, the report and its recommendations for future progressive action were brusquely dismissed by members of the Jamaican government, including the prime minister and members of Parliament. Reactions to the report in the Jamaican press and on local radio stations ranged from occasional grave consideration of the report's findings to outright contempt for its subjects.

8   I use only the term *gay* here, meaning self-identified gay or homosexual men, and do not include lesbians because, to date, the significant majority of political asylum cases involving Jamaican refugees fleeing homophobic persecution have been those of men. This reality comes as no surprise, given the ways in which homophobia and homophobic violence are leveled in such radically different measures toward men, women, and transgendered people in Jamaica. (In this regard, one might rightly assume that transgendered people, unless they are able to "pass" visibly as a person of one gender or another, bear the discriminations visited on people who, in a strictly gender-demarcated society, possess the physical and visual attributes of both genders. Even if they are able to "pass" completely as women, they must still contend with the hostility and sexism regularly visited on women.) It is also important to remember that the oppression of women who are perceived to be lesbians in Jamaica (and in many, if not most, societies) occurs within and beneath the prevailing oppressions of sexism and misogyny, which, in their stern ideological insistence on adherence to rigidly imagined and constructed gender roles, impact women's lives differently from, but similarly to, the ways in which they bear on the lives of men who stray from the gender role of "normative" male behavior expected of all men. Men of whichever sexuality, of course, always possess some measure of male, patriarchal privilege, which is especially, though not only, granted to the male perceived as "masculine" within a given society's specific definitions of masculinity.

ROSAMOND S. KING

More Notes on the Invisibility of Caribbean Lesbians (2005)

CARIBBEAN LESBIANS DO NOT EXIST.

So we are told by our own people, by our journalists and elected officials, by our religious leaders, by our own families.

Caribbean lesbians do not exist — so we are told in newspaper articles, on radio shows, and to our faces.

Caribbean lesbians do not exist: so it is implied by historians, sociologists, and other scholars, and by our singers and writers who overwhelmingly choose to portray the lives of "straight" men and women, and occasionally gay men's lives and realities, leaving the rest of us out.[1]

Of course, Caribbean lesbians do exist. As soon as I write this — as soon as I say it — I am attacked and dismissed: not my existence, but my authenticity as a Caribbean person and whether or not I have a legitimate claim on that identity. For instance, people might insist that I must not have been raised with "Caribbean values," must not have spent enough time in the region, or must have been "contaminated" by the U.S.A. And if the speakers do not convince themselves, they will move to attack my lesbianness, insist that I am "confused" or "scorned," that I was "interfered with" at some point, or that I "just need a good man."

How does a living, breathing, loving person prove her existence? And why should she have to? The effort is itself a kind of trap; those whose existence society acknowledges and affirms do not need to prove themselves. More than fifteen years ago Makeda Silvera published the essay "Man Royals and Sodomites: Some Thoughts on the Invisibility of Afro-Caribbean Lesbians."[2] I have, since then, often been struck by how much this essay's title and content still ring true. We are still invisible *as* lesbians in our cultures because of the silence around lesbians in Caribbean communities and to some degree even in the growing gay, lesbian, and all-sexual movements in the Caribbean region. When our sexuality is revealed or discovered, our families still fear for us and our female friends still fear for themselves (fearing "guilt" by association). And years after Silvera's essay, many Caribbean people can also recall women in their communities who were "that way" and who went either unmolested or were physically attacked for their difference.

We are still here. In fact, I think that between the moment of Silvera's essay and today it is possible that we have become *more* invisible in the Caribbean, gone more underground because of the increasingly vocal homophobia of our cultures (as exemplified through the public words and actions of politicians, musicians, journalists, and religious leaders, among others) and through the growing conviction that to live *openly* as a Caribbean lesbian, one must, or should, emigrate.

CARIBBEAN LESBIANS *DID* EXIST.

Silvera's important oral history of Afro-Jamaican lesbians (told, ironically, by heterosexual women who scorned Silvera's own lesbianism) is far from the first evidence of Caribbean women who romantically, erotically, and sexually loved other women. While researching nineteenth-century Trinidadian carnival, I came across the original meaning of *jamette*, a term that now means "slut." It derives from the French word *diametre*, which in the 1880s in Trinidad referred to men and women who lived below the "diameter" of "respectable" society—the madams, prostitutes, gamblers, stick-fighters, and others. As many have noted, poor black women during this time were "catchin dey tail"[3] in several ways: they were often unemployed, and laws and public scorn were overwhelmingly focused on criticizing and policing their bodies and sexualities.[4] So perhaps it is not surprising that *jamette*, once a word for a member of a social and economic class, came to refer to women with unacceptable sexualities.

Not much information has been unearthed on which to base conclusions regarding jamettes's and other nineteenth-century Caribbean women's sexual behaviors, especially since what remains from that time are records written by Europeans and white Creoles, from their point of view. Nevertheless, what information is available does point to the existence of Caribbean lesbians, even more than one hundred years ago.

Some nineteenth-century colonial records hint at non-heterosexual sex and pleasure among Creole working class women. Two all-women carnival bands in Martinique's 1888 carnival, for instance, were described as "feminine associations . . . established with a view to pleasure."[5] Unspoken here is *what kind* of pleasure these exclusive women's groups congregated to fulfill. This very silence, this invisibility, implies a pleasure considered unspeakable. Similarly, an account of Trinidadian carnival published in 1884 states:

> It is really painful to hear them — the female singers especially — singing at the top of their voices, as if in defiance of the law and of all decency. It cannot be surprising that the conduct, in prison, of creatures so callous to any feeling of shame is extremely bad, and that *'a fearful amount of depravity is practised between them when in an unwatched association.'* Are they not, in the majority of cases, members of *bands* notoriously formed for immoral purposes, and there practically taught to scorn all that society respects and appreciates, and to indulge in unbridled licentiousness?[6]

Since men and women were not imprisoned together, the "depravity" described here is probably a reference to sexuality among women. The author accurately refers to the fear such sexuality inspired. Concerning contemporary Trinidad, M. Jacqui Alexander writes that "heterosexuality promotes order while homosexuality, its antithesis, promotes chaos" in patriarchal, heterosexual Caribbean societies.[7] The possible unleashing of this chaos was and continues to be *embodied* in women who dare to be true to their same-sex desires.

Black and brown Caribbean women's sexualities have always been considered "queer," odd, and less moral by European (and often by "colored") elites. Women who choose extramarital sex and childbearing, non-monogamous relationships, non-nuclear family structures, or lesbianism have always been maligned by those in power. In earlier centuries this persecution was by European colonizers; now it is perpetrated by black and brown Caribbeans who often aspire to Western middle class values with roots in Victorianism. But in committing this oppression we deny ourselves. We have a long history of creating our own families; everyone in the Caribbean has "pumpkin vine family": people related to us out of love and history, not blood. And in most of our families there are women who stepped outside of the strict sexual morality some of us hold dear.

We, black and brown Caribbean people, have a history of not having been seen at all, or having been seen, but not as people — not as ourselves. We have a history of being misrecognized and maligned; of having our bodies and what we do with them labeled "deviant," "vulgar," and "disgusting" — and we have a history of having these labels, which we did not choose or create, then thrown at us to *prove* our deviance and vulgarity. We have a history in which the economy and politics of the world have depended on us, and yet there have been those who wished that we did not exist, who wanted us to be invisible.

We have learned those dehumanizing tricks so well that we now use them against each other.

CARIBBEAN LESBIANS DO EXIST.

You pass laws against us.[8] And yet, you "love" us. You eat our food, laugh with us, sing with us, fete with us. You see us but do not recognize us. You do not see, or choose not to see, those of us who really enjoy winding on and dancing with each other, those of us who have "roommates" or "best friends" (*buenas amigas*) for ten, twenty years. Yes, you love us, openly and privately, as long as we don't use the word *lesbian*, and as long as we don't link it to the word — the identity — Caribbean. Then, all too often, we are on our own.

You have names for us: sodomite, *tortillera*, antiman, *zami, mati, macomère*. And auntie, *mami*, best friend, neighbor, cousin, *grand-mère*. And Natalie, Patricia, Wardie, Consuela, Suzanne, Gigi. And, yes, Trini, Yardie, Bajan, Vincie, Plátano . . . You spit, or sing, or call out our existence, depending on which name you use. But our existence does not depend on any of these names.

Ironically, your denial, your scorn, your disgust, hate, and violence prove our existence and your fear of difference. You use us to confirm your own "normality," even while — and partly because — those with more money and power spit in all of our dark faces, our "small island" faces. You deny us and yet we are still here, screaming in our silence, ever present in our invisibility.

We are. We exist. We love other women as lovers. We love our children as parents and our parents as children. We are aunties and sisters and friends, and some of us love God in various forms. Despite social stigma, threats, fear, and internalized hate, Caribbean lesbians are not always invisible, especially to each other.

So why do we need to speak our existence? Not all of us do, and not all of us can. But some of us must speak, because we believe that silence will not protect us. We speak not to convince anyone of our existence, but to sing ourselves to ourselves and to remind those who despise us of our humanity — of our living, loving presence in the midst of their loathing.

We are seen every day, but we are still invisible *as Caribbean lesbians*. The dream still to be acted on and realized is not only to stand with gay, bisexual, transgender, and all-sexual brothers and sisters, but also with heterosexual sisters and brothers.[9] The dream is to pursue genuine change and acceptance for all Caribbean people, so that we can live and love and work together while acknowledging each others' existence in difference.[10] We have a lot of work to do.

NOTES

1 There are, of course, several Caribbean authors of various sexualities who have portrayed Caribbean LGBTQ (lesbian, gay, bisexual, transgender, "queer" and "questioning") lives beyond those of gay men, including Dionne Brand, Mayra Santos-Febres, Shani Mootoo, and Achy Obejas, in addition to authors quoted in this essay—and this very volume goes a long way toward bridging the gap. Still, although they are easier to find than before, the stories of Caribbean lesbians and transgender people remain relatively few, and relatively difficult to locate.

2 Silvera, "Man Royals and Sodomites: Some Thoughts on the Invisibility of Afro-Caribbean Lesbians," in *Piece of My Heart: A Lesbian of Colour Anthology*, ed. Makeda Silvera (Toronto: Sister Vision Press, 1991), 14–26.

3 "Catchin dey tail": in local usage, to have a very difficult time.

4 See David V. Trotman, "Women and Crime in Late Nineteenth Century Trinidad," *Caribbean Quarterly* 30, no. 3–4 (1984): 60–72; and Rhoda Reddock, *Women, Labour and Politics in Trinidad and Tobago: A History* (London: Zed Books, 1994).

5 Lafcadio Hearn, "La Vernette and the Carnival in St. Pierre, Martinique," *Harper's Monthly Magazine* 77, no. 461 (1888): 771; qtd. in John Cowley, *Carnival, Canboulay and Calypso: Traditions in the Making* (New York: Cambridge University Press, 1996), 110–11.

6 Emphasis added. L. A. A. de Verteuil, *Trinidad: Its Geography, Natural Resources, Administration, Present Condition, and Prospects* (London: Cassell & Company, 1884), 182–85; qtd. in Cowley, *Carnival, Canboulay and Calypso*, 75.

7 M. Jacqui Alexander, "Redrafting Morality: The Postcolonial State and the Sexual Offences Bill of Trinidad and Tobago," in *Third World Women and the Politics of Feminism*, ed. Chandra Talpade Mohanty, Ann Russo, and Lourdes Torres (Bloomington: Indiana University Press, 1991), 141.

8 As is so eloquently documented and examined in M. Jacqui Alexander's article, "Not Just (Any) *Body* Can Be a Citizen: The Politics of Law, Sexuality, and Postcoloniality in Trinidad and Tobago and the Bahamas." *Feminist Review*, no. 48 (1994): 5–23.

9 I build here on the representations of dream in Silvera's "Man Royals" essay: "We will create a rhythm that is uniquely ours—proud, powerful, and gay. Being invisible no longer. Naming ourselves, and taking our space within the larger history of Afro-Caribbean peoples. *A dream to be realized, a dream to act upon*" (emphasis added; Silvera, 26).

10 I build here on similar ideas in Audre Lorde's essay, "Uses of the Erotic: the

Erotic as Power" in *Sister Outsider: Essays and Speeches* (Trumansburg, N.Y.: Crossing Press, 1984), 53–59. I also draw on other essays from that collection and from *Zami: A New Spelling of My Name* (Trumansburg, N.Y: Crossing Press, 1982). In "Uses of the Erotic," Lorde writes that "Recognizing the power of the erotic within our lives can give us the energy *to pursue genuine change within our world*, rather than merely settling for a shift of characters in the same weary drama" (emphasis added; 59).

HELEN KLONARIS

Independence Day Letter (2004)

Dear Beloved Community,

It is the night of Independence Day. This country has turned thirty-one years old. I am only four years older. This is my home. This country, where my grandparents came looking for new life, opportunities, a new way. Hope. But I don't feel up to celebrating. Tomorrow, I have been told, at five o'clock p.m., there will be a protest in Rawson Square to show us gays and lesbians, bisexuals, and trannie folk how much we are not wanted in our own country; to show us just how much we are not cared for, not valued by our brothers and sisters, who believe they know what is good, and righteous, and godly.

I live in a country that doesn't think I should exist. I live in a country where not one church leader has come to our defense publicly; where not one church leader has risen to the call of Spirit, to say loudly that this is a time for understanding, not hate. Instead, the church has — almost of one accord, it would seem — turned its collective back on the gay and lesbian community, condemning us all as sinners, or, worse still, knowing that we are not sinners, keeping quiet anyhow, because it is too afraid to show authentic compassion. Such compassion might be dangerous; it might expose a sympathy not permitted. Such compassion might create affiliations that could put jobs and reputations on the proverbial line.

It is a Saturday night, Independence weekend, and there is not one church on this island that would welcome me and my kind publicly, speak our names openly, with respect, and honor us for who we are. I don't want to be accommodated. I want to be embraced. I need witnesses who are not afraid of what I am. If I'm going to be born again, I want to get born with greater love for and pride in who I already am. I need a minister who sees the sacred in me and won't turn his back on that sacredness because he doesn't know how to explain this kind of sacredness to his neighbors. I need a church, and there isn't one.

I am angry at the church. Angry at the Catholics (our local Bishop Burke recently likened gay unions to unions between human and animal), at the Anglicans (Bishop Gomez warned that if he finds out you're gay and an Anglican priest, you'll be out of a job), at the Baptists (Bishop Ellis cast a spell to send metaphysical missiles into our front rooms). I'm especially angry at the gay priests in this country who won't stand on the ground of their own truth and create a ministry for their own community—for the walking wounded who are told over and over that we are not right, we are not good, we are not welcome. But this is our home too. I am angry at these priests because they enjoy the privileges of priesthood: a priesthood built on secrets, half-truths, and lies, in which they remain too invested in that privilege to confront the church's and their own hypocrisies and injustices. I am angry at suppressed truths, at pedophiles fired from church-run schools but never brought to justice, at violations suppressed.

I am angry because I live in exile in this, my own country. I am angry because I hear the same tired (and misconceived) arguments over and over —and they're wearing me out. Down. Missiles in the spirit are setting down in my front room every day, and every day I do the work of cleaning up the mess, the debris, shaken and outraged. And grieved. Every day I pray for protection from the church—the church itself perpetrating a war on lesbians and gay men in this country, my home. Every day I hear apostles and pastors and bishops ranting and raving about how we are unnatural and deviant and dangerous. There is no love in their voices. No compassion in their words, "Love the sinner, hate the sin."

I talked with Pastor Mario Moxey[1] just the other day. He introduced himself to me after a press conference, and I spoke with him, wanting to be real. I told him that I respected his right to believe what he does. I told him that I would be one of the first to defend his right to speak freely and to act as his conscience bids him to. I told him that I hoped one day for us to stop this fighting across this imaginary line that divides us, and begin telling the true-true stories that make us the people we are, acting and speaking out here in the world, because it's these stories that tell the truth about us and can speak to the heart of each of us. I told him that gay people aren't all about doing whatever pleases us and caring less about anyone else. That is a misrepresentation. I told him that gay people's lives are often full of pain. He looked at me with what seemed like sincerity, and said, simply, "I know."

Throughout this exchange, Pastor Moxey seemed to be listening. He seemed to want to hear what I had to say, human being to human being. It felt good to be that real with this man whom I had thought was my enemy. Perhaps I had misjudged him. We bade each other farewell, and then, as I turned to go, I heard a laugh. It was a laugh that belonged to a woman, a Reverend Lenora Sands, Pastor Moxey's friend and colleague, come to stand beside him. She laughed smugly and I thought I heard the words, "Well, if they in so much pain, they should come back to God!" And then I heard Pastor Moxey's laugh too.

Now, if I were a more bigetty woman, I would have turned back and asked Rev. Sands why she was laughing. I would have asked Pastor Moxey if he thought what I had revealed to him in earnest and in sincerity was funny. I would have told them how self-righteous and arrogant and wrong they were to presume that I had ever left God, or that God had ever left me to stand with them alone.

But, alas, I did not. I can only say that I left feeling that all too familiar outrage that comes with just being alive.

In the distance I hear the staccato of fireworks, Independence celebrations underway, but I do not feel part of them. Tomorrow afternoon, in the middle of downtown Nassau, Bahamians, my sisters and brothers, will gather to make certain I am aware of how I am not welcome here—of how much I am not cared for, nor valued, as I am; of how much better it would be if I did not exist. It is that personal. It is that real. The truth is, gay men and lesbians do exist. Bisexual and transgender women and men do exist. We are real. We are not deviant. We are a sacred part of the natural diversity of this planet. We are part of the multi-colored, multi-textured, multi-faceted image of God/dess. We are your daughters, your sons, your brothers, your sisters, your grandchildren, your cousins, your mothers, your fathers, your aunts and uncles. We are your great-grandmothers. We are the children not born yet. We have important roles to play in the shaping of our society, the one we share with you. We are your family. Cut any one of us away from you, and we both will bleed. We both will hurt. We will miss each other profoundly.

This is not the letter I had hoped to write in honor of this day. I had hoped to tell you how hopeful I am: how much I love us, this culture, this society of ours, which is strongly rooted though we still are struggling to find our way forward, upward and onward, together. I had hoped to tell you that I love how passionate we are about our everyday culture, Saturday morning souse and the beat of a goat skin drum that has the power to make you and your spirit get up, stand up, and go find out what it is you been missing. I love the everyday spirituality that calls acquaintances "cousin," neighbors "beloved," and children "baby doll" and "sweetness." I love that there is still a spiritual wisdom that endures, outside the walls of prestigious churches, on the streets — the kind of wisdom that doesn't just believe, but *knows*, without need of political slogans, that we are all family, regardless of skin color or what side of the wall or fence we live on. And, too, there is the righteous anger that comes with that same knowing, when people forget. Forget where they came from. Forget that we all were birthed from the same Divine Mother, like it or not.

And this too is truth: that I do love us. And it is also true that I am angry at us and grieved by us.

Steve McKinney[2] asked me some weeks ago, "What is it that you all really want?" I want to answer that for you now, Steve, and anyone else who may be listening. I want to answer that now, again, and again. What I want, on this night of Independence, is this: a Bahamas that is committed to becoming honest enough and brave enough and, in the words of Chicana lesbian writer Cherríe Moraga, "strong enough to embrace a full range of racial diversities, human sexualities, and expressions of gender," as well as a diversity of spiritual traditions and philosophical and ideological opinions.[3] I want a Bahamas that is committed to re-structuring its internal foundations — the patterns of our hearts and minds — so that it can better respond to issues of difference, not with the fear and anger that are now plaguing us, but with openness and genuine desire for understanding and communication and relationship. I still want a Bahamas in which women's lives are as important as the lives of men, and where children are seen and heard and listened to for their advice as to how we can be better parents and teachers and friends to them. I still want a Bahamas committed to decolonization — the taking down and the taking apart of old colonial ways of seeing, working, teaching, learning, being. I want a Bahamas wise enough and courageous enough to support progressive vision and to empower those with the emotional, spiritual, and intellectual creativity to put that vision into action.

"Without the dream of a free world," wrote Moraga, "a free world will never be realized."[4] I want a Bahamas where we aren't afraid to keep on dreaming, no matter how heretical our dreams may at first appear.

Keeping the Faith,
HELEN KLONARIS
July 10, 2004

NOTES

This letter first appeared in slightly different form in the *Nassau Daily Tribune* as an open letter to the community ("Living in Exile in My Own Country," August 6, 2004). It is part of a larger work entitled *Letters from a Heretic at Home: An Island Woman Speaks Out on Sexuality, Spirituality, and Community.*

1 Mario Moxey is the pastor of Bahamas Harvest Church and has led three separate anti-gay demonstrations in Rawson Square in downtown Nassau.

2 Steve McKinney is a well-known Bahamian talk show host who has interviewed several members of the local GLBT (gay, lesbian, bisexual, transgender) community.

3 Moraga, "Queer Aztlán: The Re-formation of Chicano Tribe," in *The Last Generation: Prose and Poetry* (Boston: South End Press, 1993), 164.

4 Ibid.

De un pájaro las dos alas: Travel Notes of a Queer Puerto Rican in Havana (2002)

Cuba y Puerto Rico son
las dos efímeras alas del angel del amor.
Cuba y Puerto Rico son
dos hombres sudorosos exilados al sol.
— MANUEL RAMOS OTERO,
from *Invitación al polvo*

Fireflies. By the shadow of the National Theater, under the loving gaze of El Ché, in front of an ivory tower as tall as the horizon. Galloping, heroic, traversing the eye with sharp quills that flow from a majestic, translucent parchment. That will be Josué, fearful leader of failed rebellions on Línea, near the Almendares River. Lighted by the incandescent bulbs of the Yara Theater, across the street from Coppelia, even if the recent construction has left you without customers for strawberry — much less chocolate — melting in these too-warm tropics. You foresee the fall of a great wall of noise, of the *son de la vega* that does not wander down your streets, Old Havana, of walls consumed by termites that no poison will kill. You've always liked frozen treats, even if they lacked milk, but nobody believes you.

What if a car wandered down Calle Veintitrés and careened into the sea, guided by a lighthouse, an unmarked taxi chauffeured by a certain chemical engineer who had abandoned his profession, who told stories about the virtue of American dollars to anyone who had the patience to listen? The car could become a submarine, or a boat, or something else — a magical 1950s contraption redesigned for flight. But it's just a fantasy that reminds you of Abraham, your other friend, who is also an engineer, but mechanical.

Truth is, the Cubana de Aviación plane arrives from Santo Domingo — your circuitous route to avoid the embargo — and the suitcase takes ages to appear, lest you were bringing along a mortal plague. You've been traveling for nearly a day in this roundabout way and are exhausted, although the adrenaline and excitement keep you going. And all of your companions on this pilgrimage leave, and the X-rays and dogs with drug-sniffing powers forgive you and let you depart shortly past midnight from José Martí International Airport's Terminal 3, so beautiful with its spanking-new, Spanish-paid red-and-white metal structures and walls. But then, traveling down the road, two very young-looking *guajiro* officers with state-issued guns stop your taxi for speeding; the driver insults them, and, while you curse under your breath, the adolescents finally tire, leaving you free to continue your ordeal. You are the two wings of a dove — *de un pájaro las dos alas* — but you cannot fly; the celestial clockwork does not allow it.

On another day a street full of columns in Centro Habana rises to your right, and Abraham warns you about the possibilities of crime. You immediately look around, and the first person you see seems menacing; fear and paranoia assail you. Vertical wing sends Josué off, and you follow the first down a street pockmarked with holes that looks more like Beirut than *Nuestra América;* my America of José Martí's dreams slides down a path that you didn't realize existed in these tropics. Abraham shows you the way, and when you arrive you have to go up hundreds of steps without light, wander through the darkness of a wolf's mouth to reach the small apartment where the black-and-white television proclaims the wonders of the revolution right after the Brazilian soap opera and the Canadian cartoon show — an inter-American celebration! You greet his family and burst into sweat, while they bring you a glass of water that might not have been boiled.

"Do you want to drink tea in my house?" Josué asks after the performance of *La zapatera prodigiosa,* and it makes you laugh; it's just like the movie! It's the centennial of Federico García Lorca's birth, and this afternoon you cried when you ate strawberry ice cream on Presidente, several blocks from Casa de las Américas. Kitsch attracts you, my love, and go figure, to arrive in such a dignified and pearly-faced city after so many years, where he who does not carry the blood of the Congo has that of the Carabalí, even when there are so many redheads and blondes and even Chinese. You explain that tonight you can't go because Abraham is coming to fetch you — a friend of a friend, you know — but he comes along anyway, and you all end up by the Hotel Habana Libre, and before you even know it you're seated at La Rampa, eating a sorry-looking salad for five dollars and inviting the two of them to join in. Vertical wing only drinks a mojito, but lateral eats just like you. He suddenly takes García Márquez's *Love in the Time of Cholera* out of his bag, asks you if you've read it, and you laugh. Which came first, the chicken or the egg?

Josué is a stage designer and light technician, and Abraham is now a professor of electronics, although he also trained at the Instituto Superior de Arte as a singer of zarzuelas and opera. You are a cultural journalist of sorts;

you've come to Cuba to attend a weeklong conference, see theater as part of Mayo Teatral, and meet people, led by a longtime curiosity to visit *la perla de las Antillas,* the site of such renowned controversies and social utopias. Just in case, you walk, and all is splendid. There are almost no *jineteros* out tonight because it is Monday, but you will soon meet them. You run into lateral's brother on the street; you've already seen his photographs at the dinner table—his many transformations, including mustaches and long and short hair—and now he's wearing a brand-new long-sleeved shirt, something akin to Ralph Lauren Polo Sport. He almost seemed like a prep-school boy, adored by his older brother, bronzed by our scorching sun, solar fingers over gold skin turning everything into darker caramel. Josué asks you if you like his sibling and tells you about a stud near his house with a prick a foot long. "I've already sucked him, but he came in my mouth and I don't like that," he says.

Lateral and vertical know each other only through you; the Puerto Rican theater critic serves as a melting pot for two Havanas that march full steam ahead down different paths, in spite of the common link of the arts. And under the shade of some giant trees—pines, perhaps?—on Twenty-third Street in El Vedado (but in the opposite direction) you hear a *danza* and see the brown bodies that move mechanically as they partake of a seductive dance, a transaction between Cubans and damned Spanish and other European tourists who arrive with their tainted money, and you looking at it all.

A friend of Josué tries to go into a dollar-only cafeteria full of foreign johns, only to be stopped at the door. The adolescent diva with translucent mother-of-pearl skin curses loudly the whore mothers of a country where *mambises* aren't allowed inside. Deep eyes. "He's a *pajarito,* do you understand?" lateral asks, and vertical looks. This is not his world, but it still fascinates him. "There are *activos* and *pasivos*"—but Abraham interrupts: "He understands all that, you don't have to explain," and you try to remember the word *bugarrón,* but it does not come to your mind until several days later. You will remember the words *joseador* and *vividor* only when you leave the country.

The lateral children live with their grandmother, who cooks for them; their mother comes by on occasion to scream at her delinquent progeny, who spend their time with foreigners in countless businesses. "The Spaniard brought a bottle of olive oil today. Did he give you the twenty dollars he had promised?" But he only has half, caught with excuses once again and false hopes, or perhaps lying to his mother. . . . The laterals have a color television and eat *congrí* with picadillo and spaghetti with hot dogs from the government dollar store, hot dogs that you bought with Josué when you went for something to drink, after getting ten pounds of tomatoes from a street vendor. "In my house you can't drink the water, it's from the tap." Ten pounds! Isn't that too much? The food in the cheap hotels and state restaurants is horrible, and you're about to give up on eating; you haven't been to the *paladares* because they are far away or you don't know where they are; the Cubans don't take you, and you don't want to pay for a taxi to eat by yourself. The stress has taken away your appetite, until you discover sweet rolls sold in the street for a Cuban peso and pizza made with soy-based cheese. It suits you to lose some weight. The only two decent meals you have that week are at the laterals' house, and for once you're glad you met them.

The color television broke at the verticals' house, and now it's like it used to be, black and white; they serve you coffee. "It's all we have, I'm afraid, *pero es café batido al estilo cubano,*" the father says, while they make fun of the dark-skinned neighbors from Oriente, even though the mother is an economist and the stepfather a high minister of the postal system. Abraham's parents are professors of physical chemistry and biology. "No one can take it anymore, but if you say anything you lose your job, and at our ages, where are we going to go?" They speak of *balsas* and sharks and *ese hombre,* the bearded one, a phrase always accompanied by a downward hand motion near the chin; they tell stories of ferries to Regla that put out to sea with meringue-covered cakes that hid gasoline tanks. Mother's Day is quickly approaching, and they have all received their poorly made state-issued cakes. Abraham earns scale three or something like that, three hundred pesos or fifteen dollars a month: a two-liter bottle of Najita orange soda to quench your thirst costs a dollar seventy; mayonnaise — forget about it. If they like Cuba so much, why don't they come live here and receive a *libreta,* seven eggs, powdered milk only up to six years of age, five pounds of rice and beans a month, no meat, and the toothbrush and toothpaste of a foreign friend who came for a visit were stolen by a neighborhood boy who crawled in through the window. All so you can live in a one-bedroom apartment with four adults — Grandma sleeps in the kitchen, you know — and you remember to send her calcium pills when you get back home, to fight osteoporosis and to overcome your overwhelming sense of guilt.

The saintly tourist takes off around Havana at night, accompanied by his lateral and vertical wings, thinking sardonically that Cuba and Puerto Rico are the sad flip-flop sandals of a myth that rots between the fungus-infected toes of a sickly, tired foot. Forget about medicine — nothing without dollars. The secret here is to never get sick. Gossips repeat it while they take advantage of you left and right. He who gives a finger loses a hand, and if they don't offer a taxi, tobacco, or a body for sale, they find a way to enjoy themselves at the expense of your hard labor and the many sacrifices your family made so you could come here and see, with your own eyes, before it all vanished into thin air. All foreigners are perceived as rich, from lands where money grows on trees, but the fact is that, fortunately, your parents paid your airfare, for you've run up twelve thousand dollars on your credit cards, and you can't wait for the day that you complete your studies and lift yourself out of this hole. That's why you cry — because you live off capitalist illusions and balance transfers and shifting interest rates, and your debts multiply without stopping, and coming to Cuba was pure idiocy for your pocket, and now even more. Seven hundred dollars from your parents, and you paid two hundred for the hotel, one hundred for the cultural event, fifty to enter and depart from this lovely country, twenty multiplied by two to cavort through the Dominican Republic, thirteen for the taxi, et cetera. And don't mention God, for everyone here is a materialist and will laugh in your face, even if you've never been much of a believer — and even though the pope was just here in February!

Abraham accompanies you on a tiny pilgrimage to Regla to visit a church — blue and white, *azul y blanco, los colores de la reina del mar.* Your orisha Yemayá lives in the guise of the Catholic Redeeming Mother, and you light a candle and place two thin stalks of tuberose at her altar, praying for spiritual peace and clarity, but it seems to have done little good, although who knows? Was it she who protected you when the swarms of children grabbed you on the Malecón, or later in Old Havana? Wherever you go, you attract multitudes as if you were the Pied Piper of Hamelin, but you don't let go of a penny. You send them off, leaving nothing in their wake but the memory of a brief scare. The Lonely Planet guidebook says that Cuba is the safest country in the hemisphere, but you are hard-pressed to believe it; you've never had such bad luck, and have you ever traveled through this open-veined, long-suffering continent of rich and poor, of stark contrasts (and is Cuba so different?) with Visa, MasterCard, Discover, and American Express? Better alone than poorly accompanied, but plastic is so compact! Oh, and the bother of having to bring it all in cash, so it can be stolen all the more easily, Grandma repeats, all the while masked as Little Red Riding Hood. Perhaps it is that the expectations have never been so high, or the fall so precipitous.

No one is starving, to your knowledge, but there are plenty who don't have a thing to their name. Blessed be he who wanders aimlessly through Centro Habana possessing the face of a gringo like yours, even if you are from the oh-so-esteemed other wing. Blessed be the ride you go for with Abraham on a pedicab, your divine chauffeur Roberto a master of gorgeous bicycle pedals, but vertical spends the whole trip interrogating him about businesses and budgets and suntan lotions, and you get a splitting headache. "Why can't we just calmly ride by the Capitolio?" you wonder, and they show you the house of Martí, the great national martyr. "Why didn't you speak with him? Why didn't you give him your phone number? Why didn't you say anything? I had to"—thought interrupted, vertical and lateral, sex pursues you, and you sweat horizontally, wiping off your brow with a handkerchief that by now smells strongly of some foul chemical that you seem to perspire in this intense heat.

Did you come to fuck? Perhaps, but that was never at the top of the list. In fact, when they told you about sexual tourism, you felt sick, not because of the jineteros but because of the power of dollars, and perhaps because you envy them and it bothers you that you are too shy or scared to try it. But it's better to think of other things and displace these lingering concerns . . .

The water of your filthy bay contaminated by the petroleum waste and debris from a thousand ships, the suffocating heat in a raft full of bicycles, there is almost nothing in Regla except for the church, so you return quickly, but on the way back Abraham runs into a quite pregnant friend, an old schoolmate who abandoned their profession and now works as a tour guide. Engineering is worthless when the only dollar around stays in a hotel; she who doesn't hustle with her body, if she wishes to survive, hustles with her soul. In this life, let me clarify, for I prefer not to speak of the one to come.

At Casa de las Américas you meet the heir of Electra Garrigó, with his shaved head, and he talks about dance theater and songs about fallen boobs and fake dentures from Virgilio Piñera's wedding, and you are speechless; his partner is cute as can be, and when you visit their home, they give you coffee and sweets and you fall in love with both. Josué tries to get you to pay his neighbor, the one with the ungodly dick, but you resist, and Abraham introduces you to his boyfriend, a student translator and interpreter of German and Russian—that is, before that career path was closed at the University of Havana, just like sociology, which ended long ago, when all the problems of revolutionary society were solved.

Vertical plus one form a funny couple—explain the difficulties of your field to him and they start a fight, which would be unbearable if lateral were not right next to you. They seem like a married couple quickly approaching their thirtieth anniversary, but neither one of them even reaches that age! "NO, NO, NO," he repeats, and you laugh and ask him if they always argue like that, always bicker, but you suspect that they understand each other in their constant, brutal exchange.

At Clitemnestra Pla and Electra's house you become Antígona Pérez, so *criolla,* the poor thing, swinging in a hammock under a poster of Marilyn Monroe, and you speak with the mother-in-law who got them the apartment through a *permuta* so the boys could live together in El Vedado, near their jobs. Right there, around the corner, are the university steps of the famous Machado protests, or was it Batista? So many dictators, you get confused, the one you saw in *I Am Cuba,* with a script by Yevgeny Yevtushenko — transportation around here is so bad because of the "Special Period," you know, that if you don't live near your job you never get there. The motorized *camellos* or buses the people travel in seem more like trains for livestock, and you don't dare ride for fear of having your pockets emptied, looking like the foreigner you are — or at least that's what everyone says. It's better to ride in the ten-peso taxis that Josué fetches for you, or to take advantage of the generous rides offered by ladies who explain that they often help out those in need of a lift, all the while pretending that you are a Cuban.

Poor Mrs. Pla has just lost a son, and she is in Havana to visit his tomb in the necropolis; it has been a month since the burial, and the remaining daughters gather in the kitchen of their apartment. Each act of generosity in this city of ghosts amazes you, and when Electra gives you a theater magazine with her photo on the cover, your jaw drops; this simplest of forgotten gestures moves you to tears. The Garrigós' dachshund is in heat, and you are witness to her courting dance in that third-floor interior apartment, with clothes drying in the wind. "I hope she gets pregnant," you think, for the miracle of life never ceases to amaze you, even here.

You explain to lateral a thousand times that you don't want to bed anyone, that that is not why you came, and finally the concept bores a hole in his Celestina-like head, although he will never cease to repeat *"¡Qué buena es la carne cubana!"* And you know that Cuban flesh is good, because you have tasted it in other parts — one of your former boyfriends in New York, for heaven's sake! — but here you have neither the money nor the condoms nor the place, much less the desire, although that may be only because of the other inconveniences, like the fact that vigilante hotel doormen keep all Cubans strictly out of guests' rooms. Like a penniless child in an ice cream shop, and the treats are sharks on the prowl. Josué starts to tell you of the guys who have made him a woman and complains in a sad tone how expensive they've become. "I met him when he was nobody; he didn't have those clothes or gold chains, and he slept with me for ten dollars that I had gotten from a Spaniard. Now they all ask you for something, a shirt, a pair of trousers." And when you greet the gorgeous perpetrator, he shakes your hand very firmly, with strong, large fingers, and you feel your knees buckle, and when you joke about your colleague's deflowering—*lo hiciste mujer*—the stallion acknowledges his paternity. "How's the pregnancy going, *mi amor?*" he says, with a smirk. No wonder lateral and you seem like lifelong friends. And Josué complains that there are no real men left in Havana, but it's a lie.

You are standing on the other side of L Street, and all of a sudden Ochín arrives, the most fabulous one of all in her black dress and Chanel handbag, and you are fascinated by her eyebrows and sunglasses and almond eyes. Lateral and vertical are pale reflections of Auxilio and Socorro rushing through Cuba on their way westward, back here, like Fidel, but they are yours, all yours, even if you hallucinate that they suck your blood like Mafia cartoon vampires in Havana. Ochín and Madonna will be your wings, Madonna with her hormones brought to her by a nice punk-style Spaniard (who else?) full of tattoos and piercings—perhaps a little like you—like Almodóvar, who loves to come here, after all, and goes to all the clandestine parties and hides from the police. Then they ask you if the eyebrow ring hurts, and you say no.

Josué explains that you can go to a park where people masturbate, married bugarrones in search of occasional sex, and it tempts you, but Havana has left you adrift between sexlessness and the fear of robbery. Abraham walks with the two of you for a while and sits on the side ledges of a building but says good-bye when two guards appear down the street. "They don't arrest us anymore," Josué confesses, and you are glad that you are not a native product. You've heard enough stories about UMAP and Mariel boat lifts not to feel nostalgic for something that has always held you in contempt. A marvelous Cuban arrives, and everyone wants to hustle him, but he is a self-identified *putita* who left for Scandinavia and is now back for a visit. A boy asks him if his parents are still in the same place, and he responds, without batting an eyelash, "The little whore got them a better apartment, in the same building, but bigger." You meet another one who lives in Bologna and works as a dancer, and he is so handsome that it pains you to look, but later in the evening you end up talking a little bit. He is nice, even if he does look like a brunette, blue-eyed Fabio.

You were going to meet Abraham and his boyfriend to go to the movies, but there has been a change of plans: you end up on the corner with Ochín and Madonna, and lateral asks around for several hours until you find out where there is a private house party; he then fights with a taxi driver to fill up his car and charge only a dollar a head. You ride squashed through several neighborhoods unknown to you, and you are glad that you could go out your final evening, especially since you'd spent the whole afternoon crying in your windowless (but air-conditioned) hotel room, in the dark. You had made plans to go to the beach, but you couldn't stand the thievery any longer, the constant grubbing for money. They wanted fifteen dollars for gasoline, and the night before you'd unexpectedly spent ten for a bottle of rum at El Morro and five more for Cokes before running out of American cash. It had been an embarrassment to have to pay the waiter at the National Theater's piano bar with Cuban pesos — Cuban pesos! "It's all I have, I'm sorry, there's nothing I can do," you said, as he stared at you with a mixture of disdain and hatred. "This is a dollars-only establishment!" Los Tres de la Habana don't sing anymore, and you start to realize that it was all for money, the blue madness of Zafiro Azul echoes everywhere, all just for a ride and a good time, while they made fun of your accent and didn't even look you in the face.

"Give me a dollar, let me pay your cover charge, they don't have to know you're a foreigner," Josué tells you, and you reply that you don't mind paying more to get into this house in Diez de Octubre, bursting with sounds and disco lights that can be felt from afar, but you well know that the more you save, the more you can spend on him; or perhaps it is yet another ruse. You even start to suspect that there is a certain tenderness, even while everything is so marked by the commercial exchange. You meet another friend, Chino, who asks you to buy him a drink, and you offer him a beer, but he wants a bottle of rum — it'll last longer, and it's only two dollars more — but you say no, out of principle, although you actually don't have that much money left anyway. "Why did you go out with so little money?" Chino asks, and you tell him your trip's over and you'll be leaving tomorrow, and you have to give twenty to Fidel if you want to get out. So he half-heartedly dances with you, in a sexy but distant way. It's pretty late, and the chances of netting bigger fish are slim.

"Can I have that shirt you wore yesterday?" lateral says, referring to a light olive-green Esprit one, and it makes you laugh, you got it as a hand-me-down from your American ex-boyfriend, *putita tú al fin,* and you say yes without mentioning its origin. You have always known how to surround yourself with wealthy people and let something nice fall on your plate. "Is it brand-name?" he asks, and you are struck by the insolence, but who cares; let him enjoy it. When you return at four in the morning to the shithole El

Morro, where peeling paint falls from the walls onto the beds, you run to the room to fetch it while he waits with the taxi driver whom you *personally* chose from among several others because of his white clothes and gold chains that reminded you of Obatalá. And you leave the next day, and he doesn't come to say good-bye, but he calls when you are about to step out the door. He'll even write in a couple of weeks, and you'll send him vitamins and film magazines and new socks and T-shirts with a traveling acquaintance. Vertical has breakfast with you, gives you a miniature glazed porcelain bowl, and you speak of a thousand things, but Cuba has exhausted you; you start to understand, but fatigue has left you without any enthusiasm, and while you start to get a little sad, you want to leave.

POSTDATA: METATEXTUAL WINGS OF A DOVE

I wrote "De un pájaro las dos alas" in Spanish in May 1998, shortly after returning to New York from my noticeably difficult first (and, so far, only) trip to Cuba, where I attended a yearly Latin American theater conference at Casa de las Américas, a renowned cultural institution that has done a great deal to advance Latin American arts and knowledge. At the conference I presented a paper on the gay Nuyorican performers Arthur Avilés and Elizabeth Marrero and screened a video in which Arthur dances naked.[1] It is fair to say that, in the restricted institutional space of the conference, I was well received, and the topic of my presentation generated much interest and curiosity, as well as amazement and disbelief that nudity was such a contentious issue in the United States. While *Conjunto,* Casa de las Américas's quarterly theater journal, declined to publish my paper along with those of other conference participants, it has published my review of a queer Puerto Rican performance by Jorge Merced of Teatro Pregones, based on a story by Manuel Ramos Otero, as well as an article on queer Puerto Rican theater by José O. Rosado.[2]

The abridged text presented above is a fictionalized, experimental narrative or autoethnography based on my travel experiences as a gay Puerto Rican theater critic and former graduate student and is structured principally around my interactions with two very different "gay" Cubans, identified as Abraham and Josué (Joshua), the vertical and lateral wings of an imaginary bird that Cuba and Puerto Rico have symbolically (and historically, since the nineteenth century) come to represent.[3] The text also presents a cast that includes other gay men (Clitemnestra, Electra, and Chino), drag queens or male-to-female transgendered individuals (Ochín and Madonna), and numerous family members of some of these people. Names were changed partly for discretion's sake but also because of the possibility (seldom realized at present) of political persecution of homosexuals in Cuba, particularly of those interacting with foreigners.[4]

"De un pájaro las dos alas" does not limit itself to issues of homosexuality, such as gay identity, sexual tourism, *jineterismo* (the myriad commercial transactions with foreigners, including prostitution, at all levels), and the gay public sphere, because to do so would be to deny the complexity of the Cuban situation and of my experience in Cuba. In this sense, I feel a close affinity to Carmelita Tropicana's (Alina Troyano's) expansive, deeply political gaze as presented in her performance piece *Milk of Amnesia/Leche de amnesia*, which recounts the return trip of a lesbian Cuban American to her native island and which, in fact, does not privilege issues of sexual orientation above other questions at all.[5] It would go profoundly against the notions of intersectionality defended so eloquently by Chicana third world feminists such as Gloria Anzaldúa, Cherríe Moraga, and Chela Sandoval, which I embrace as methodological tools, to brush aside the impoverishment of the professional (middle class) and working class sectors, deteriorating healthcare, widespread hunger, political censorship, increasing criminality, and transportation difficulties, and instead focus on only one issue.[6] In this "postdata" I attempt to contextualize "De un pájaro las dos alas" and present wider considerations pertinent to an understanding of queer travel in Cuba, particularly the understanding of a self-identified leftist queer Puerto Rican.

That this is not the only type of gay (or even gay Latino) tourist experience or travel narrative is evident from other published accounts, some of which in fact celebrate the widespread availability of sexual encounters in Cuba (including liaisons with possibly underage youths) — "pleasures" listed along with the spectacular beaches, good rum, and fine cigars; the esprit of these travelers is notably different from my own, as the following passage from *Hombres Latinos* by Oscar Montoya, a member of a gay American tour group, amply shows: "There is laughter, there is a good time of no consequence as we indulge in the vacuous activities of ordinary tourists. . . . Then we return to our hotel, one last night with *our Cuban admirers*."[7]

I will refrain from a thorough deconstructive analysis of such travel narratives, but I invite readers to do their own. Suffice it to say that, in this brief description, euphemism is key to avoiding an actual confession of exchanging money for sex; taking advantage of a dire economic situation to obtain pleasure is presented in a rather matter-of-fact, justifiable way. It is no coincidence that Montoya compares Havana to Bangkok, a notorious capital of the international sex circuit.

As nonpolitically motivated queer travel to Cuba has become more and more popular, numerous accounts in mainstream publications and on the Internet have analyzed the nuances of personal exchanges with queer Cubans (particularly sexual ones with men) and have talked about the gay public "scene," principally as it relates to beaches and evening entertainment, especially parties in private homes. Negative critical accounts include Jonathan Lerner's denunciatory article in the cyberjournal *Salon,* which provoked angry responses in the queer New York Latino/a listserv "Mano-a-Mano," and G. Derrick Hodge's groundbreaking yet problematic piece in the *NACLA Report on the Americas,* which presents a somewhat sexist, prorevolutionary Marxist critique of the way capitalist commodification on the island manifests itself through *pinguerismo* (male sex work) — specifically, how this type of prostitution transforms men's "fluid" sex and gender identities into what the author claims are rigid ones. Hodge feels that *pingueros* nevertheless maintain revolutionary Cuban masculinity far more than *maricones,* an argument he bases on the claim that they are the ones that "penetrate" their clients and thus assert their dominance. (In a 2005 follow-up article, the author once again disarticulates pingueros from homosexuality, except for the "gay" status of their customers, focusing on their relationships with girlfriends and on their insertion into an increasingly class-stratified society divided on the basis of access to material goods such as clothes and shoes; he also indicates that police repression and incarcerations of pingueros have increased dramatically since 2000.)[8]

Middle-of-the-road or mainstream accounts of gay tourism include Corey Sabourin's travel column in *Out,* Reed Ide's feature article with Ezequiel de la Rosa's photographs in the queer travel magazine *Passport* (which even features a view of Havana on its cover), and "Pacho's" interesting chronicle at the cyberspace site *Gay Wired.*[9] Homoerotic photographs of Cuban men are found in Benno Thoma's book *Somos Cubanos*[10] and in "Cruisin' in Cuba: A Special Pictorial," in the February 2001 issue of *Machismo,* which also notes that American film companies have started to shoot gay porn in Cuba.[11] Knowledge about the lesbian experience (e.g., that lesbians also partake of jineterismo or that in the past they served as intermediaries for heterosexual prostitution, as *chulos* or *proxenetas* [pimps]) can be obtained only in fragmentary form from most widely available sources.[12]

A distinction should be made between general queer travel and the return trips of lesbian and gay Cuban exiles or the lesbian, gay, bisexual, and transgender (LGBT) children of exiled Cubans, voyages in which personal and familial investments are much more profound; the cases of the poet Lourdes Casal (who helped to establish the Antonio Maceo Brigades) and of the playwright Jorge Ignacio Cortiñas (whose play *Abrázame fuerte* was performed in Havana in 2004, and who has organized trips to Cuba with Maria Irene Fornés) come to mind. In addition to Tropicana's piece *Milk of Amnesia/Leche de amnesia,* return trips have been explored in Reinaldo Arenas's novella *Viaje a La Habana* (Trip to Havana), in which a returning exiled father unwittingly commits incest with his own, now fully grown son, who then temporarily steals all of his father's possessions; in Sonia Rivera-Valdés's story "La más prohibida de todas" ("The Most Forbidden of All"), in which the return trip of an older, exiled woman to visit her new, younger (nonexiled) female lover signals national and affective completion or reconciliation; and in Eduardo Machado's autobiographic play *Havana Is Waiting* (2001), in which Federico, an exiled gay Cuban who was airlifted out of the island as a child during the Catholic Church-led Operation Peter Pan in the early 1960s, returns as an adult with his straight Anglo friend Fred, an extremely sensitive actor who accompanies the protagonist while he experiences a crisis of hysteria.[13] In José Quiroga's "Amargos Daiquirís (crónica de cristal)" (Bitter daiquiris: Crystal chronicle), we have the fascinating case of an extremely beautiful and complex travel account by an exiled Cuban visiting Havana, in which the sexual identity of the author is never revealed (contrary to what happens in Quiroga's *Tropics of Desire*), but where the writing has the strong and unmistakable mark of a queer textuality, culture, and — why not? — sensibility.[14] "Bitter Daiquiris" presents a clear case of the rich possibilities of reading "between the lines" for queer meaning.

A different case is that of Cuban American lesbian author Achy Obejas. In her interview with Jorjet Harper, she discusses her return trip to Cuba and offers a thorough analysis of the activist/political strategies and postures possible in the United States and Cuba; she also expresses frustration at what she perceives to be Cuban lesbians' resignation to their political oppression, and acknowledges that, while she may be profoundly familiar with all things Cuban, she is no longer essentially from there; she does not quite belong.[15] Curiously, Obejas does not portray return trips for the lesbian Cuban American protagonists in her own fiction; rather, she presents several examples, specifically in "We Came All the Way from Cuba So You Could Dress like This?" and *Memory Mambo,* of women who desire but cannot attain such a return.[16]

"De un pájaro las dos alas" reflects my disillusionment with a revolution that I had held up as a model of social development, in spite of its notorious persecution of homosexuals, such as Virgilio Piñera and Reinaldo Arenas (the latter having left as part of the Mariel boat lifts in 1980), and its forced-labor camps, known as UMAP (Unidades Militares de Ayuda a la Producción, or Military Units to Aid Production), which were active in the mid- to late 1960s and had as their objective the "re-education" of homosexuals, understood principally as effeminate men. While I was fully aware of the serious problems endured in Cuba since the beginning, in 1990, of the "Special Period," caused by the end of Soviet and Eastern-bloc economic subsidies and by the intensification of the U.S. embargo, I was unprepared physically and mentally for the experiences I had. It is my impression that most tourists (queer or straight) do not experience this type of close encounter with the actual living conditions of Cubans, do experience them but prefer (out of solidarity) not to discuss it in public unless prompted, or simply don't care about them — especially if the prime motive for their trip is precisely to take advantage of this situation and the relatively cheap prostitution it offers. Cuba has become, since the early 1990s, one of the prime global locations for sexual tourism.[17]

There are also those who negotiate these difficulties with greater ease or feel that it is unfair to single out Cuba for criticism when so many other places (especially in Latin America) have grave problems of social injustice but do not face the same adverse treatment from the United States.[18] I also recognize that my experience was profoundly marked by my economic situation at the time as a limited-budget, debt-encumbered graduate student; by my excessive sense of largesse, which led to my constantly being taken advantage of; by my personal sexual neuroses; by my experiences as an island-born Puerto Rican who lived in New York City; and by the fact that I was often read as gay or especially foreign because of my fair complexion, light-colored hair, mannerisms, clothing and accoutrements, tone of voice, loud laugh, accent, and clearly visible tattoos and piercings (these last markers still not common in Cuba in 1998).[19]

The particularities of a Puerto Rican's experience in Cuba have to do with specific historical and cultural links between the two islands, links well synthesized in the following metaphor by the Puerto Rican poet and patriot Lola Rodríguez de Tió (1843–1924): "Cuba y Puerto Rico son / de un pájaro las dos alas" (Cuba and Puerto Rico are / of a bird, the two wings); this image is taken up by the gay Puerto Rican writer Manuel Ramos Otero (1948–90) in the opening of his second book of poetry, *Invitación al polvo* (Invitiation to the dust), which focuses on his relationship with a Cuban house painter named José (see epigraph).[20] Rodríguez de Tió's two verses are the refrain of a revolutionary poem that urges the two Antillean islands to join forces in their struggle against colonialism, which at the time (pre-1898) was against Spain, and, furthermore, to become a single nation, in the style of the pan-Caribbean confederacy advocated by Eugenio María de Hostos (who echoed Ramón Emeterio Betances's revolutionary fervor) or the Latin American union proposed by Simón Bolívar.[21] The importance of Rodríguez de Tió rests in great part on her involvement in the pan-Caribbean liberatory movement, for she composed the revolutionary lyrics of the Puerto Rican national anthem, "La Borinqueña."[22] It has also been suggested that she was, or at least looked like, a lesbian, since she dressed in men's clothes (a sartorial practice Luisa Capetillo would later emulate); the profound tone of affect in her letters to her niece also gives ample cause for speculation.[23]

As the only remaining Spanish colonies in the Americas in the late nineteenth century, Cuba and Puerto Rico waged wars of independence that eventually proved successful for the former but not the latter, which partly explains why Puerto Rico remains a U.S. colony. Nevertheless, different types of solidarity between the islands have remained constant ever since. For example, numerous Puerto Rican intellectuals, artists, and labor- and leftist-oriented political groups have maintained relations with Cuba in open defiance of the U.S.-imposed embargo; they have sent their children to summer camps and have gone on study tours and vacations there. In Havana there is even a nonofficial Puerto Rican "embassy" (Misión de Puerto Rico en Cuba) sponsored by the independence movement; it serves as a cultural center and clearinghouse for information, organizing, and solidarity.[24]

Links of a different nature have been forged by the post-1959 migration of Cubans to Puerto Rico. Only Florida and the New York–New Jersey area have received more Cubans since the revolution. Cubans have become assimilated in Puerto Rico much faster than in the United States, which is not surprising, given the similar cultural, linguistic, racial, and religious backgrounds of the two islands' populations; there have still been ethnic tensions regarding politics and class.[25] Dominant pro-statehood and pro-commonwealth sectors in Puerto Rico, caught up in a cold war anticommunist mentality since 1959, have used the fear of "becoming another Cuba" as one of several justifications for their anti-independence policies, which have included illegal surveillance and harassment of those perceived as friendly to this position and even state-sponsored assassinations, as in the notorious case of Cerro Maravilla in 1978.[26]

But the meanings of the metaphor of a bird and its two wings for a gay Puerto Rican go well beyond mere anticolonial politics and cultural affinities, as the epigraph by Ramos Otero reveals. In Cuba, *pájaro* (bird) and *pajarito* (little bird), along with *mariposa* (butterfly), are common, somewhat derogatory terms for male homosexuals, similar to *pato* (duck) in Puerto Rico.[27] The "bird" constructed in "De un pájaro las dos alas" had, as its two wings, two gay individuals of disparate racial and class backgrounds. Josué and his family — referred to as "laterals," which we can perhaps associate with the twisted or queer — were of a more popular (lower) class provenance, were darker-skinned, and were more openly defiant of the regime and participated fully in the informal sectors of the economy, principally through jineterismo. Abraham and his family — indexed as "vertical," that is, straight or correct — had a higher level of education and more "respectable" positions, were lighter-skinned, suffered greater material privation because of their lack of sustained contact with foreigners, and exhibited more racist and classist behavior.[28]

I was particularly struck by the limited gay and transgendered public sphere I witnessed, which is dominated by the sexual trade; my lack of exposure to other spaces might have overdetermined my interpretation of what I saw, as other visitors such as Richard Ammon describe what he identifies as "a discrete community" of (middle class, more closeted) gay people who do things such as attend the ballet at the Teatro Nacional and run *casas particulares* (small bed and breakfast-type hotels in their own homes);[29] the poet and playwright Norge Espinosa has organized Semanas del Arte Homoerótico (Homoerotic Art Weeks) in Havana for at least three years. Lesbian visibility is also somewhat limited; I have since heard interesting stories by lesbian travelers about their (fairly similar) interactions and am aware of the documentation available from sources such as Kelly Anderson's and Sonja de Vries's films on lesbianism on the island.[30] What I found most remarkable was the (apparently) completely closeted existence of most gay expression and organizing that is not in some way related to the tourist trade or the arts.[31] Abraham, for example, was openly gay with his family and had a boyfriend whom he had met at the university, if memory serves me right, but he did not hang out — and had never had any contact — with the jineteros or drag queens who frequent the notorious gay area of La Rampa around the Coppelia ice cream parlor (where *Strawberry and Chocolate* was filmed), the Habana Libre Hotel, and the Yara Theater, or that of the Fiat dealership by the Malecón. It was as though they lived in different Havanas. Abraham's gay world was a strictly private one, in part because disclosure of his sexual orientation could have jeopardized his job but also because there are, as far as I am aware, few if any officially sanctioned gay organizations or spaces in Cuba, where every single organization must be approved by the government to operate legally.[32] Abraham's relationship with his boyfriend was also not dependent, to my knowledge, on economic exchange, although there did seem to be a slight age difference between them.

The world of Josué and his family, in contrast, was enormously privileged; they greatly benefited from numerous contacts with foreigners, who provided them with hard currency. However, Josué's affective and sexual relationships with other men were predominantly based on economic exchange, which is becoming difficult to sustain as more and more tourists and young, sexually active Cubans become involved in the sexual economy; this pattern of money for sex reflects more common practices in poor, working class, rural, and traditional Latin American environments. As such, we can say that (male-to-male) sexual tourism not only affects relations between Cubans and foreigners but also affects relations between Cubans themselves, favoring the maintenance of older models of payment for sex (especially for working class men) while possibly impeding the expansion of other types of relations based on the establishment of stable, egalitarian bonds (a phenomenon evinced more clearly among middle class men and among lesbians of diverse class backgrounds).

There was also widespread mention of Europeans, Canadians, and, to a lesser degree, Latin Americans coming to Cuba to have unprotected sex with minors or others under the impression that they were safe from contracting AIDS. Ironically, this misperception is a consequence of the revolutionary government's past policies of restricting the movement of AIDS patients to sanatoriums. These policies, arguably, had the effect of keeping transmission rates low; however, they have been severely modified since 1994 as a result of the acute economic crisis, and it is not surprising that rates of the transmission of AIDS and other sexually transmitted diseases (STDs), such as syphilis and gonorrhea, are growing exponentially in Cuba, particularly among prostitutes who have sex with foreign tourists. This practice seriously affects men, for "the historical trend has been for more men than women to be infected with STDs."[33]

While female jineteras and their relationship to the international sexual tourism circuit have received enormous attention — in books by Tomás Fernández Robaina, Rosa Miriam Elizalde, and Rodolfo G. Almaguer; in songs by the exiled singer Willy Chirino; in the Cuban Mexican experimental documentary film *Who the Hell Is Juliette?*; and in articles by Coco Fusco and others — scant attention has been paid to "gay" or male jineteros, now also known as pingueros, for *pinga* (penis).[34] Ian Lumsden and Oscar Montero have commented on historical precedents for male prostitution that date to before the revolution; indeed, it was widely practiced and acknowledged in the nineteenth century and was even studied by Benjamín de Céspedes in his infamous *La prostitución en la ciudad de la Habana* (1888);[35] Lourdes Argüelles and B. Ruby Rich also make much of the preponderance of prostitution before the revolution.[36] Lumsden resists identifying current-day jineterismo with (exploitative) prostitution per se; rather, he argues against the general view, asserting that it is a benign and fruitful type of exchange. This view is somewhat consistent with the declarations of the self-identified jineteros documented by Fernández Robaina, who insist that they are *luchadores*: people struggling to make a living.[37] Others argue that the jineteros engage in sex or other practices for material gain to obtain not basic necessities but consumer goods; there is a fine line between the two, however, when staples such as meat are rare luxuries without hard currency (i.e., American dollars, at least before these were banned in November 2004) and when a new pair of shoes might cost months of savings. One also hears little discussion about how the clandestine (European and Canadian) trade in hormones has affected male-to-female transgendered individuals or how the transfer payments of gay Cuban sexual workers off the island have impacted gay social formations or family perceptions of homosexuality in Cuba.[38] All of these subjects require more intensive research.

The *fiestas particulares* or private house parties, which have received some attention, are not an exclusively tourist phenomenon, although they do depend on people's access to hard currency (at least in the past).[39] The interaction in these environments is markedly different from what occurs in middle class gay bars and discos in Latin America, perhaps coming closer to working class (popular) or rural environments, but really constituting a phenomenon all of their own. There is a heightened feeling of camaraderie and a sense of transgression, which comes in part from the knowledge that at any moment the party might be raided by the police; this sense of risk is similar to what I experienced in Argentina in 1989 in the "underground" scene and is, unfortunately, still the norm in places like Peru, even in legitimate commercial establishments. It is also curious to see families pile all of their furniture and belongings into one room to prepare the rest of the space for the "public" event. Most people arrive in couples, usually comprising a jinetero and his or her customer or companion for the night. There are other couplings, too, as well as individuals and groups of friends. I never went to any of the more "official" nightclubs periodically favored by gays (for example, El Periquitón), which often change or are closed by the police, so I do not know what interactions occur there.

In this type of environment, all tourists are seen as potential customers, and interpersonal relationships that are not based on economic exchange are rare. In this respect, my experience in Cuba differed markedly from what I have witnessed in other Latin American countries. The extreme economic disparities were also noticeable in the segregation of spaces according to the possession of dollars; this phenomenon is not exclusive to the gay world, but it definitely impacts the formation of a gay public sphere.

Hispanic queer cultural productions (be they national or foreign) have reverberated among the gay population in Cuba. In his interactions with me, Josué seemed to imitate scenes from Tomás Gutiérrez Alea and Juan Carlos Tabío's film rendition of Senel Paz's story "El lobo, el bosque y el hombre nuevo" (The wolf, the forest, and the new man), that is, *Strawberry and Chocolate*.[40] Josué's gesture of pulling a novel by Gabriel García Márquez out of a bag and offering to lend it to me, or inviting me to his home to have tea, can be seen as references to this film.[41] There are a couple of possible interpretations for these acts: that Josué was taking cues from the movie as to how a gay man should act, for instance, or that he thought I would be charmed by these gestures because of their referentiality — that they were a sort of cultural code legible by people in the know. I have the impression that it was a little of both, yet it has been pointed out that drinking tea has become more popular, not because of the film, but because of the scarcity of coffee for local consumption.

The sphere of the arts, and of theater in my case, affords other types of contact with gay Cubans or with Cubans who explore and develop the work of gay artists. My acquaintance in 1998 with the young director Raúl Martín, who specializes in the work of the Cuban playwright Virgilio Piñera, is an example.[42] Martín is one of several theater practitioners (including the well known Carlos Díaz) who have rescued Piñera's plays from the oblivion in which they existed for many years after his death; the Latin American theater critic Camilla Stevens has observed that a "rehabilitation" of the formerly banned playwright has resulted in a boom of productions of his work.[43] Piñera invented such characters as Electra Garrigó and Clitemnestra Pla, Cubanized versions of the heroines of classical Greek tragedy, characters who nicely contrast with the semicloseted Puerto Rican playwright Luis Rafael Sánchez's notorious Antígona Pérez.[44]

It should not escape notice that one gay couple I met (referred to jokingly as "Electra Garrigó" and "Clitemnestra Pla") lived together thanks to the efforts of one of their mothers, who had moved from her apartment to a smaller one on the outskirts of the city so that her son and "son-in-law" would have a more favorable living situation.[45] Their above-average living standard was also the result of both the Cuban state's preferential treatment of artists and the opportunities they have to gain hard currency during trips abroad or from contact with visiting arts professionals in Cuba, like me.

In my writing I have not explored the possibility that gay and lesbian tourism or travel in Cuba has significant benefits apart from the economic well-being of individuals engaged in the sex trade or, more broadly, of those who form any type of friendship with foreigners (especially, but not exclusively, gay men).[46] Several such benefits may be conjectured: (1) Increased contact with foreigners (or with exiled Cubans) who have different, more open or militant viewpoints about homosexual identities and politics may be beneficial to those who lack clear models at home for this type of identity formation and positioning, while also providing all island residents with a firsthand chance to exchange ideas, debate, and define their position. Foreign visitors also have a chance to experience and learn about a sexual system that possibly operates differently from their own (or that may be very similar, in the case of Latin American visitors), and which might challenge their ideas of "universal" gay identities and practices. (2) Foreign tourism allows people outside Cuba to learn firsthand about the actual political, economic, and socio-cultural conditions on the island, and this exposure may have a short- or long-term effect on general (global) perceptions of Cuba and on the foreign policy of the tourists' countries of origin (particularly that of the United States). (3) There seems to be an underground network for smuggling hormones for gender reassignment and AIDS medicines that is greatly facilitated by tourism, although pharmaceutical drug transfers are also conducted through more formal channels, such as the Miami-based Cuba AIDS Project and the New York-based AID FOR AIDS. The negative impacts of this contact may include the importation or adoption of consumption-based sexual and identity politics, the reification of payments for sex for working class men or for those involved in jineterismo and pinguerismo, as well as the more worrisome possibility of increasing HIV and other STD transmission rates.

Some of the benefits of queer tourism or travel in Cuba have clear antecedents in the experiences of leftist, gay-liberationist North Americans of diverse racial and ethnic backgrounds who participated in the early 1970s Venceremos Brigades, some of which radically challenged both the Cuban government's sexism and homophobia and the brigade organizers' own biases and complicity with queer oppression.[47] Documents from the "Responses by the Gay Liberation Party and the Gay Committee of Returned Brigadistas" to the patently homophobic 1971 "Declaration of the Cuban First National Congress on Education and Culture," which banned homosexuals from teaching and participating in arts institutions, show not only that queer progressive travelers have gone to Cuba for decades but that their difficult experiences there have led them to demand social change.[48] The Venceremos Brigade's "Policy on Gay Recruitment" (1972), in turn, shows how both the Cuban government and U.S. leftist sympathizers have tried to prevent radical U.S. gays and lesbians from traveling to the island and spreading their "subversive" liberationist message.[49]

Allen Young has written extensively about how his travels in Cuba as a gay man affected his understanding and appraisal not only of the Cuban Revolution but of leftist politics broadly defined. His early essay "The Cuban Revolution and Gay Liberation" (1972) describes the experiences of a socially committed leftist traveling on the island in 1969, months before the Stonewall revolt, and later on, in 1971.[50] He is candid about his personal experiences (sexual and otherwise) and ambiguous about the contradictions he observes. In his later book, *Gays under the Cuban Revolution* (1981), written as thousands of gay Cubans who had emigrated through the port of Mariel were resettled in the United States, he is more willing to condemn the abuse he witnessed.

"De un pájaro las dos alas" was not written with the idea of gay tourism in mind; rather, it attempted to see the intersection of gay-cultural travel with the political and material conditions of the Cuban people through Puerto Rican eyes. What struck (and continues to strike) me most about Cuba was how profound the political and economic crisis is and how it affects all spheres, including the gay and transgendered one. At such moments I always remember Carmelita Tropicana's *Milk of Amnesia/Leche de amnesia,* particularly when, at the end of her performance, she quotes the renowned singer-songwriter Pedro Luis Ferrer, who affirms, "El embargo nos está matando" (The embargo is killing us), and whose lyrics proclaim:

> Todos por la misma cosa,
> entre las páginas del colonialismo:
> Capitalistas, homosexuales, ateos, espiritistas, moralistas
>
> [Everybody for the same thing
> between the pages of colonialism:
> Capitalists, homosexuals, atheists, spiritualists, moralists].[51]

The motives for and results of Tropicana's (Troyano's) trip to Cuba as an exiled, Cuban American lesbian performance artist in search of her childhood memories and some understanding of contemporary Cuban society are different from and similar to my own and those of others such as Juani, the lesbian Cuban American protagonist of Obejas's novel *Memory Mambo,* who never returns to the island, or the author herself, who does.

I am profoundly ambivalent about the results of my trip to Cuba. It is partly with melancholy that I repeat the verses of the Puerto Rican patriot Rodríguez de Tió, who uttered her sentiments in exile, having found a welcoming home in Cuba, where she would die and be buried. I, too, live in a sort of exile, in the United States, far from the Puerto Rico where I was born and raised; for me, Cuba was not a welcoming place — a *nido* or nest, as Rodríguez de Tió repeats in her poetry — but a site of grave anxiety. What is the responsibility of a traveler who voyages to a previously unknown location? How do different queer Puerto Ricans experience Cuba? Am I justified in portraying my experience in the terms that I have used, when it is well known that Cubans face enormous privation every day? I would like to think that my chronicle and interpretive effort are not just denunciations but texts that allow nuanced, contradictory readings that escape me but may hint at a greater truth. Let these pages serve as an effort to remedy the problems and difficulties faced in Cuba and to foster greater bonds of understanding; let them also serve as a reflection of some of the implications and results of queer tourism, both for the traveler and for the location visited.

NOTES

Earlier versions of this essay appeared in "Queer Tourism: Geographies of Globalization," ed. Jasbir Kaur Puar, special issue, *GLQ* 8, no. 1–2 (2002): 7–33; and (in Spanish) in *La Habana Elegante* 17 (2002), http://www.habanaelegante .com/Spring2002/Febrero2002.html. I wish to thank Jasbir Puar, Carolyn Dinshaw, Chris Mazzara, and Francisco Morán for their editorial suggestions and encouragement in the writing (and translating) of this piece; Thomas Glave, for the Caribbean recognition; Oscar Montero, for unlocking the mysteries of Sarduy; Carmelita Tropicana, because she makes us laugh and cry; and José Quiroga, *porque fue el único que me advirtió que ir a Cuba no era fácil.*

1 La Fountain-Stokes, "Maéva y su maravilloso muñeco: El performance lésbico-homosexual nuyorican de Arthur Avilés y Elizabeth Marrero" (paper presented at the conference "La crisis de los post: El discurso teatral latinoamericano ante el siglo XXI," Casa de las Américas, Havana, May 4–8, 1998); published as "Dancing la Vida Loca: The Queer Nuyorican Performances of Arthur Avilés and Elizabeth Marrero," in *Queer Globalizations: Citizenship and the Afterlife of Colo-*

nialism, ed. Arnaldo Cruz Malavé and Martin F. Manalansan IV (New York: New York University Press, 2002), 162–75.

2 La Fountain-Stokes, "Bolero, memoria y violencia," *Conjunto,* no. 106 (1997): 68–69; José O. Rosado, "Seis piezas 'liminales' de la 'nueva' nueva dramaturgia puertorriqueña," *Conjunto,* no. 106 (1997): 50–54. An expanded version of my piece on Merced was published more recently as "Entre boleros, travestismos y migraciones translocales: Manuel Ramos Otero, Jorge Merced y *El bolero fue mi ruina* del Teatro Pregones del Bronx," *Revista Iberoamericana* 71, no. 212 (2005): 887–907.

3 I am hesitant to use the term *gay* because it is culturally and historically specific and does not have universal currency outside the United States. An extensive bibliography distinguishes between homosexual, men-who-have-sex-with-men, gay, and a myriad of other terms in the Latin American context. See Tomás Almaguer, "Chicano Men: A Cartography of Homosexual Identity and Behavior," in *The Lesbian and Gay Studies Reader,* ed. Henry Abelove, Michèle Aina Barale, and David M. Halperin (New York: Routledge, 1993), 255–73; Roger N. Lancaster, *Life Is Hard: Machismo, Danger, and the Intimacy of Power in Nicaragua* (Berkeley: University of California Press, 1992); and Stephen O. Murray, ed., *Latin American Male Homosexualities* (Albuquerque: University of New Mexico Press, 1995).

4 Numerous sources on political, historical, and socio-cultural aspects of homosexuality in Cuba (including the sometimes severe repression of it) offer varying appraisals of the Cuban gay experience and varying critiques of the revolution. More favorable portrayals of the island experience include Ian Lumsden, *Machos, Maricones, and Gays: Cuba and Homosexuality* (Philadelphia: Temple University Press, 1996); and Lourdes Argüelles and B. Ruby Rich, "Homosexuality, Homophobia, and Revolution: Notes towards an Understanding of the Cuban Lesbian and Gay Male Experience," pt. 1, *Signs* 9 (1984): 683–99; pt. 2, *Signs* 11 (1985): 120–36. This article created significant controversy, including Roger N. Lancaster's response, "Comment on Argüelles and Rich's 'Homosexuality, Homophobia, and Revolution: Notes towards an Understanding of the Cuban Lesbian and Gay Male Experience, Part II,'" *Signs* 12 (1986): 188–92, which provoked Argüelles and Rich's "Reply to Lancaster," *Signs* 12 (1986): 192–94. I have strong objections to Argüelles and Rich's analysis, which privileges a type of "revolutionary closeting" in the interest of Cuban national sovereignty and also tries to discredit the gay Mariel refugees as principally economic migrants. Other assessments include Emilio Bejel, *Gay Cuban Nation* (Chicago: University of Chicago Press, 2001); Víctor Fowler, *Historias del cuerpo* (Havana: Editorial Letras Cubanas, 2001) and *La maldición: Una historia del placer como conquista* (Havana: Editorial Letras Cubanas, 1998); Marvin Leiner, *Sexual Politics in Cuba: Machismo, Homosexuality, and* AIDS (Boulder, Colo.: Westview, 1994); José Quiroga, *Tropics of Desire: Interventions from Queer Latino America* (New York: New York University Press, 2000); and Allen Young, *Gays under the Cuban Revolution* (San Francisco: Grey Fox, 1981). For extensive discussion of queer Cuban American culture, see José Esteban Muñoz, *Disidentifications: Queers of Color and the Performance of Politics* (Minneapolis: University of Minnesota Press, 1999); and Ricardo

Ortíz, *Cultural Erotics in Cuban America* (Minneapolis: University of Minnesota Press, 2007). Juana María Rodríguez's *Queer Latinidad* (New York: New York University Press, 2002) also has interesting reflections on Cuban American lesbian identities.

5 See Alina Troyano, *I, Carmelita Tropicana: Performing between Cultures* (Boston: Beacon, 2000), 52–71.

6 See esp. Gloria Anzaldúa, *Borderlands/La frontera: The New Mestiza* (San Francisco: Aunt Lute, 1987); Cherríe Moraga, *Loving in the War Years: Lo que nunca pasó por sus labios,* expanded ed. (Cambridge, Mass.: South End, 2000); and Chela Sandoval, *Methodology of the Oppressed* (Minneapolis: University of Minnesota Press, 2000).

7 Emphasis added; Oscar Montoya, "Five Days in Havana," *Hombres Latinos* (San Francisco) 6 (1996): 23. "This holiday in Havana," Montoya states, "was designed for the gay male, one who not only loves Latino men, but also is an aficionado of cigars and rum" (20). The article concludes by encouraging readers interested in such a trip to write to the offices of *Hombres Latinos* for information on future tours. (Curiously, according to the magazine's editors, this issue of *Hombres Latinos* was censored by many newsstands and vendors, who refused to sell it because of a cover pictorial on frat-house "water sports" [urination].)

8 Jonathan Lerner's less well known but sensationalist account of queer travel appeared under the catchy rubric "Whorehouse of the Caribbean," *Salon,* January 4, 2001, www.salon.com/sex/feature/2001/01/04/havana/index.html. Lerner, who seems to have been more restrained than Montoya and his cohorts, asserts that he never had sex in Cuba. He nevertheless gave money to two Cuban males: one, who propositioned him, received five dollars for flirting; the other, a much younger man, got fifteen dollars to go back to his town of origin, which we eventually learn he did not do. When this article circulated on Mano-a-Mano, it generated at least two negative responses from the readership. Andrés Duque, the listserv's editor, presented the article under the following heading: "Incredibly myopic column by American travel writer . . . ugh" ("[News] 'Salon' Article: Prostitution in Cuba," January 11, 2001, mano_mano_ny@yahoogroups .com). This in turn provoked a response from a pseudonymous subscriber, "Gran Plátano," a gay Latino college student just returned from three months in Havana, who severely criticized Lerner ("[Response] 'Salon' Article: Prostitution in Cuba," January 16, 2001, mano_mano_ny@yahoogroups.com). I did not become aware of G. Derrick Hodge's piece, "Colonization of the Cuban Body: The Growth of Male Sex Work in Havana," *NACLA Report on the Americas* 34, no. 5 (2001): 20–28, until after I had finished my (original) article. Hodge's piece is the result of interviews with over fifty pingueros. One of his main contributions is the sharp distinction he makes between pingueros and jineteros; he is among the first persons to write of this significant semantic and epistemological shift, which had been registered earlier by "Señor Córdova" in *A Man's Guide to the Caribbean '98/'99* (Beverly Hills: Centurion Press, 1998). At no moment does Hodge mention his own sexual orientation (which I understand to be gay), or his motivation for this research, except for what can be understood as an interest in the way the Cuban body becomes commodified under capitalism; his piece is

principally a critique of globalization and the present-day economic and political world order as it affects Cuba. In Hodge's article there is no mention of any positive effects of the gay rights movement. Also see G. Derrick Hodge, "Sex Workers of Havana: The Lure of Things," *NACLA Report on the Americas* 38, no. 4 (2005): 12–15; and Henry E. Scott, "Cuba Libre? Guess Again!," *Gay City News*, January 17–23, 2003, http://www.globalgayz.com/cuba-news03–06.html (accessed September 13, 2007).

9 Corey Sabourin's column, in the section "Essentials: Gay Travel," is identified on the cover of the magazine as "Havana: The New Gay Hot Spot"; in the index it is referenced as "Havana: Why Has It Become the New American A-Gay Hot Spot?"; and it appears in the body of the magazine as "Cuba Libre?" See *Out,* February 2001, 70–72. See also Reed Ide, "Discovering Havana," *Passport,* June 2001, 48–55; and Pacho, "Welcome to Havana: The Cuban Gay Underground," *Gay Wired,* February 1997, www.gaywired.com/travelcolumn1.html. *Cuba Libre* is also the name of a trendy new restaurant on Eighth Avenue in Chelsea, Manhattan's gay neighborhood; such upscale restaurants are displacing the older, traditional, inexpensive Cuban and Chino Latino (Cuban Chinese) restaurants once common in the neighborhood. For a more recent mainstream appraisal of gay tourism in Cuba, see Michael Luongo, "Sleeping with the Enemy? Tourism and Gay Cuba's Changing Face," *Gay City News*, February 14–20, 2003, http://www.globalgayz.com/cuba-news03–06.html (accessed September 13, 2007). Richard Ammon's "Gay Cuba 2003" attempts to offer a general overview and balanced portrayal; see http://www.globalgayz.com/g-cuba2.html (accessed February 11, 2005).

10 The experience of the German photographer Benno Thoma and his traveling companion, C. Pister, indicates greater ambivalence about gay travel. In a wonderful afterword to *Somos Cubanos,* Thoma's book of explicitly homoerotic male images, including several nudes, Pister narrates the problems that they had with the police for photographing scantily clad youths in Old Havana. It is unclear from the text what financial remuneration the models received. Pister only vaguely hints that he, Thoma, and the models engaged in other "untraditional" activities beyond the photo shoots: "We went through more adventures with all of them, but to go on and on about that would give the wrong image of the pleasure we had in the course of making *Somos Cubanos*" ("Somos Cubanos," in Benno Thoma, *Somos Cubanos* [Berlin: Gmünder, 1998], n.p.). The foreigners seem to have shared a sense of relief when they left the country. José Quiroga's book *Tropics of Desire* has a colorized photograph from Thoma's book on its cover.

11 This segment is also referred to in the magazine as "Cruizin' in Cuba" and "Cruzin' for Cubans." See Ron Rico and Ricardo Mann, "Travel Report," *Machismo,* February 2001, 34–37.

12 For example, a drag queen interviewed by Tomás Fernández Robaina explains that lesbians do participate in jineterismo:

Ah, espera cariño, no vayas a pensar que las tortas, que las lesbianas, se han quedado fuera de esto; ellas siempre se están quejando de que no las mencionan, que no aparecen en la literatura, que son más discriminadas que los gays. Ellas tienen

también su mercado, ahora todo tiene salida en este mercado estelar donde todo se
vende y todo se compra; pero no, no es particular a nosotros, eso es general,
carísimo, general.

[Oh, wait, dear, I don't want you to think that lesbians aren't involved; they are always complaining that they don't get mentioned, that they don't appear in the literature, that they are more discriminated against than gays. They also have their market
— nowadays everything is available in this stellar market where everything is bought
and sold — but no, it is not exclusive to us; it is a general phenomenon, my dear]
(*Historias de mujeres públicas* [Havana: Editorial Letras Cubanas, 1998], 130–31).

See Rodolfo González Almaguer, *Yemayá las bendice, jineteras* (Elizabeth, N.J.:
Majestic, 1997), for a fascinating anecdote on a lesbian pimp called Nelson Nedé,
"una lesbiana de baja estatura que en oportunidades nos había conseguido turis-
tas provenientes de Montreal" (a lesbian of short stature who at times had gotten
us tourists from Montreal), also referred to as "la diminuta proxeneta," the tiny
pimp (96–97).

13 See Reinaldo Arenas, *Viaje a La Habana: Una novela en viajes* (Mexico: Grijalbo/
Mondadori, 1991); and Sonia Rivera-Valdés, "La más prohibida de todas," in *Las
historias prohibidas de Marta Veneranda* (Havana: Casa de las Américas, 1997),
101–40, translated by Alan West-Durán as *The Forbidden Stories of Marta Veneranda* (New York: Seven Stories Press, 2000), 93–131. In her book *Caribe Two
Ways: Cultura de la migración en el Caribe insular* (San Juan: Ediciones Callejón,
2003), Yolanda Martínez-San Miguel analyzes Arenas's and Rivera-Valdés's stories in the context of diaspora and national reunification. On Machado, see
Matthew Murray, "Havana Is Waiting," http://www.talkinbroadway.com/ob/
10_24_01.html; Corey Sabourin, "Havana Is Waiting: A Review," http://
www.thegully.com/essays/cuba/011109_machado_havana.html; and Kristin
Sterling, "The Return to Cuba Helps Eduardo Machado Find Home and Inspiration," http://www.columbia.edu/cu/news/01/10/eduardoMachado.html
(accessed September 13, 2007). See also Ricardo Ortíz, "Beyond All Cuban
Counterpoints: Eduardo Machado's *Floating Island* Plays," *Cultural Erotics in
Cuban America* (Minneapolis: University of Minnesota Press, 2007), 156–89.

14 José Quiroga, "Amargos Daiquirís (crónica de cristal)," *La Habana Elegante*, no.
11 (2000), http://www.habanaelegante.com/Fa112000/Ronda.htm. See also
Quiroga's more recent work on Cuba, particularly *Cuban Palimpsests* (Minneapolis: University of Minnesota Press, 2005).

15 Jorjet Harper, "Dancing to a Different Beat: An Interview with Achy Obejas,"
Lambda Book Report 5, no. 3 (1996): 1, 6–7.

16 Achy Obejas, "We Came All the Way from Cuba So You Could Dress like This?"
in *We Came All the Way from Cuba So You Could Dress like This?* (Pittsburgh:
Cleis, 1994), 113–31; and Obejas, *Memory Mambo* (Pittsburgh: Cleis, 1996).
Kate McCullough reminds us that other lesbian and bisexual characters in *Memory Mambo* do visit the island, such as Patricia, a U.S.-born Cuban American
whose parents left before the revolution, and Gina, the protagonist's Puerto
Rican ex-girlfriend ("'Marked by Genetics and Exile': Narrativizing Trans-
cultural Sexualities in *Memory Mambo*," *GLQ* 6 (2000): 577–607).

17 The following quote is one indication: "A survey carried out in 1995 by the Italian tourist magazine *Viaggiare* classed Cuba as the most attractive destination for sex tourists. The publication described the island as a true paradise for men, women, and homosexuals traveling alone" (Dalia Acosta, "Cuba: Pimps and Prostitutes Expelled from 'Blue Paradise,'" *Inter Press Service*, June 11, 1996. Worldwide distribution via the APC Networks).

18 This is one of "Gran Plátano's" main objections to Lerner's article. I, too, was accused of being antirevolutionary (and thus reactionary) and anti-Puerto Rican when I read "De un pájaro las dos alas" at the Educational Testing Service's advanced placement Spanish grading session at Clemson University in June 1999; one woman simply found homosexuality immoral and loudly denounced me as nothing more than a "maricón" (faggot).

19 The "marked" nature of my self-presentation and person makes me very aware of the challenges in conducting supposedly objective ethnographic work outside one's immediate community. I was struck by this conundrum as it applies to the experience of the gay researcher in an environment where this subject identity might be stigmatized while reading Roger N. Lancaster's otherwise insightful article "Guto's Performance: Notes on the Transvestism of Everyday Life," in *The Gender/Sexuality Reader*, ed. Roger N. Lancaster and Micaela di Leonardo (New York: Routledge, 1997), 559–74. Lancaster assumes that his sexuality is ambiguous and potentially discreet ("non-readable"), while I more often assume that people can read me as gay right away. The same consciousness of the importance of the researcher's marked identity (as a white American woman) is evident in Louisa Schein, "The Consumption of Color and the Politics of White Skin in Post-Mao China," in *The Gender/Sexuality Reader*, 473–86; and (as an African American woman) in Jacalyn D. Harden, "The Enterprise of Empire: Race, Class, Gender, and Japanese National Identity," in *The Gender/Sexuality Reader*, 487–501. Of course, a fundamental difference between these works and my own is that I was not ostensibly an anthropologist conducting research in Cuba but an interested traveler participating in a type of "educational" or highbrow cultural tourism. See Jasbir Kaur Puar's insightful discussion of this type of travel in her essay "Circuits of Queer Mobility: Tourism, Travel, and Globalization," *GLQ* 8 (2002): 101–138. Puar's essay is also relevant in the sense that my negative experience in Cuba was the result of my being interpellated in a certain way (as a white, foreign, well-off, gay tourist), as a subject of whom certain behaviors were expected.

20 Rodríguez de Tió's verses begin the next to last stanza of the poem "A Cuba" ("To Cuba"), which originally appeared in her third book of poetry, devoted entirely to that island: *Mi libro de Cuba* (My book of Cuba; 1893). The poem is Rodríguez de Tió's lament of her situation of exile from Puerto Rico, coupled with her admiration and praise for her new home. The stanza reads:

> "Cuba y Puerto Rico son / de un pájaro las dos alas, / reciben flores o balas / sobre un mismo corazón. / ¡Qué mucho si en la ilusión / que mil tintes arrebola, / sueña la musa de Lola / con ferviente fantasía, / de esta tierra y de la mía: / hacer una patria sola!"

[Cuba and Puerto Rico are / of a bird, the two wings; / they receive flowers or bullets / over the same heart. / How grand if in the illusion / that a myriad inks redden, / the muse of Lola dreams / with fervent fantasy / of this land and of mine: / to make one single nation!] (Cesáreo Rosa Nieves, ed., *Aguinaldo lírico de la poesía puertorriqueña,* vol. 1 [Río Piedras: Edil, 1971], 210).

The opening of Ramos Otero's poem reads (in translation): "Cuba and Puerto Rico are / the two ephemeral wings of the angel of love. / Cuba and Puerto Rico are / two sweaty men exiled in the sun" (Ramos Otero, *Invitación al polvo* [Río Piedras: Plaza Mayor, 1991], 9).

21 Rodríguez de Tió's two verses are often erroneously attributed — among others, by the Cuban singer-songwriter Pablo Milanés and possibly by Fidel Castro himself — to the Cuban poet and revolutionary leader José Martí. Pablo Milanés cites Rodríguez de Tió's verses in his song "Son de Cuba a Puerto Rico," included in the collective album *Viva Puerto Rico Libre* [*Viva Free Puerto Rico*] (New York: Paredon Records, 1978). "De un pájaro las dos alas" was also the name of a concert that Milanés offered with the pro-independence, Puerto Rican lesbian singer Lucecita Benítez on August 20, 1987, at the Theater of the University of Puerto Rico's Río Piedras campus.

22 See José Luis González, *Literatura y sociedad en Puerto Rico* (Mexico City: Fondo de Cultura Económica, 1976), 135–38; and Francisco Manrique Cabrera, *Historia de la literatura puertorriqueña* (Río Piedras: Editorial Cultural, 1986), 212–15.

23 See, for example, Daniel Torres, "An AIDS Narrative," *Centro Bulletin* 6 (1994): 178–79. César Salgado's research into the correspondence between Rodríguez de Tió and her niece is a ripe field for lesbian analysis. See Salgado, "Archivos suprimidos del 1898: Cuba y Puerto Rico en el epistolario de Lola Rodríguez de Tió" (paper presented at the Fourth Puerto Rican Studies Association Conference, University of Massachusetts, Amherst, October 2000).

24 Cuba is one of the few countries that has consistently supported Puerto Ricans' rights to self-determination and independence, as evidenced by the Cuban participation in the United Nations's Decolonization Committee on behalf of Puerto Rico.

25 See José A. Cobas and Jorge Duany, *Cubans in Puerto Rico: Ethnic Economy and Cultural Identity* (Gainesville: University Press of Florida, 1997); Yolanda Martínez-San Miguel, *Caribe Two Ways* and "Cartografías pancaribeñas: Representaciones culturales de los enclaves caribeños en Puerto Rico y Estados Unidos," *Revista de estudios hispánicos* (Puerto Rico) 25, nos. 1–2 (1998): 65–90; and Yeidy M. Rivero, "Beyond U.S. Dominance: Cuban and Local Influences on the Origins of Puerto Rican Commercial Television," *Centro Journal* 13 (2001): 60–77 and *Tuning Out Blackness: Race and Nation in the History of Puerto Rican Television* (Durham, N.C.: Duke University Press, 2005).

26 See Manuel Suárez, *Requiem on Cerro Maravilla: The Police Murders in Puerto Rico and the U.S. Government Coverup* (Maplewood, N.J.: Waterfront, 1987).

27 For extensive linguistic analysis of Cuban jargon used to describe homosexuality, see Carlos Paz Pérez, *La sexualidad en el habla cubana* (Madrid: Agualarga, 1998); and Marlene García and José R. Alonso, *Diccionario ilustrado de voces eróticas*

cubanas (Madrid: Celeste Ediciones, 2001). For extensive discussion of homosexuality in Puerto Rico, see La Fountain-Stokes, "Culture, Representation, and the Puerto Rican Queer Diaspora" (PhD diss., Columbia University, 1999); "Cultures of the Puerto Rican Queer Diaspora," in *Passing Lines: Sexuality and Immigration*, ed. Brad Epps, Keja Valens, and Bill Johnson González (Cambridge: David Rockefeller Center for Latin American Studies and Harvard University Press, 2005), 275–309; and "Queer Ducks, Puerto Rican *Patos*, and Jewish *Feigelekh*: Birds and the Cultural Representation of Homosexuality," *CENTRO: Journal of the Center for Puerto Rican Studies* 19, no. 1 (2007): 192–229.

28 Critics have pointed out the irony of the widespread return of prostitution in Cuba, given that the revolutionary government went to great lengths to eliminate it (and "re-educate" its practitioners) in the 1960s. Under the current Cuban penal code, prostitution is not illegal, although profiting indirectly from it (i.e., through pimping) is. Alma Guillermoprieto notices that it is precisely the sectors previously labeled "lumpen" and "scum" by the government that are now the most active in jineterismo and that thus have the greatest contact with foreigners ("Love and Misery in Cuba," *New York Review of Books,* June 11, 1998, 10–14).

29 Ammon, "Gay Cuba 2003."

30 Documentary films on lesbians and gays in Cuba include: Néstor Almendros and Orlando Jiménez-Leal, *Improper Conduct* (New York: Cinevista, 1984); Kelly Anderson, *Looking for a Space: Lesbians and Gay Men in Cuba* [*Buscando un espacio: Los homosexuales en Cuba*] (New York: Filmmakers Library, 1993); Sonja de Vries, *Gay Cuba* (San Francisco: Frameline, 1995); and Graciela I. Sánchez, *No porque lo diga Fidel Castro* (San Francisco: Frameline, 1988).

31 I did not have a chance to meet individuals involved in, or to see shows such as those presented in Margaret Gilpin's and Luis Felipe Bernaza's documentary *Mariposas en el andamio* [*Butterflies on the Scaffold*] (Charlottesville, Va.: Water Bearer Films, 1995), which was shot in La Güinera and does indicate limited space for gay and transgendered community organizing and social interaction in Cuba. I am not sure whether the practice of Santería, the Yoruba-based religious tradition, is as open and welcoming of homosexuals in Cuba as it is in other places, such as Puerto Rico and New York. See Tomás Fernández Robaina, "Cuban Sexual Values and African Religious Beliefs," in Lumsden, *Machos, Maricones, and Gays,* 205–7.

32 Lumsden includes the 1994 "Manifesto of the Gay and Lesbian Association of Cuba" as an appendix in *Machos, Maricones, and Gays* (211–14); this anonymous text documents the organization's clandestine existence. People have told me in conversation that this group basically consisted of one man.

33 See Dalia Acosta, "Population-Cuba: Rise in Prostitution Causes STDs to Soar," *Inter Press Service,* November 20, 1998. Worldwide distribution via the APC Networks.

34 Robaina, *Historias de mujeres públicas*; Rosa Miriam Elizalde, *Flores desechables: ¿Prostitución en Cuba?* (Havana: Ediciones Abril, 1996) and *Jineteros en La Habana* (Havana: Pablo de la Torriente Editorial, 1996); Almaguer, *Yemayá las bendice, jineteras*; Willy Chirino, "La jinetera," *Asere* (New York: Sony International, 1995); and Carlos Marcovich, *¿Quién diablos es Juliette?* [*Who the Hell is*

Juliette?] (Mexico: El Error de Diciembre, 1997). See also Coco Fusco, "Hustling for Dollars: *Jineteras* in Cuba," in *The Bodies that Were Not Ours* (London: Routledge, 2001): 137–53; Amalia Lucía Cabezas, "Discourses of Prostitution: The Case of Cuba," in *Global Sex Workers: Rights, Resistance, and Redefinition,* ed. Kamala Kempadoo and Jo Doezema (New York: Routledge, 1998), 79–86; Georgetown University Institute for the Study of Diplomacy, "Sexploitation? Sex Tourism in Cuba," www.georgetown.edu/sfs/programs/isd/files/cases/nhma.htm (accessed July 28, 2000); and Julia O'Connell Davidson, "Sex Tourism in Cuba," in *Race and Class* 37, no. 3 (1996): 39–48. See, finally, Lerner, "Whorehouse of the Caribbean"; and Paz Pérez, *Sexualidad en el habla cubana.*

35 See Oscar Montero, *Erotismo y representación en Julián del Casal* (Amsterdam: Rodopi, 1993). According to Reinaldo Arenas, both Virgilio Piñera and José Lezama Lima favored sexual encounters with male hustlers: the former liked big, strong black men and the latter young boys reminiscent of Greek ephebi (*Before Night Falls,* trans. Dolores M. Koch [New York: Viking, 1993], 79–87).

36 Argüelles and Rich, "Homosexuality, Homophobia, and Revolution."

37 Lumsden, *Machos, Maricones, and Gays,* 140–41; Fernández Robaina, *Historias de mujeres públicas.*

38 More recent sources indicate that the Cuban Health Ministry's National Center for Sex Education, under the direction of Fidel Castro's niece, Mariela Castro Espín, "has identified 23 people in Cuba as transsexuals and another 62 cases are under study" and is also offering "free psychological counseling and hormonal treatments"; see Andrea Rodríguez, "Cuba's Transsexuals Get Powerful New Friend," *Associated Press,* September 5, 2004, http://www.globalgayz.com/cuba-news03-06.html (accessed September 18, 2007). The center's website, however, describes transsexuality in pathological terms as "un trastorno de la identidad sexual y de género" (an ailment of sexual and gender identity), referring to it as gender dysphoria and as a "problema de salud" (health problem). See http://www.cenesex.sld.cu/webs/diversidad/diversidad_sexual.htm (accessed December 18, 2004).

39 Lumsden identifies these events as "fiestas de diez pesos" (ten-peso parties). See *Machos, Maricones, and Gays,* 141–43.

40 Senel Paz, *Fresa y chocolate* (Navarra, Spain: Txalaparta, 1994); Tomás Gutiérrez Alea and Juan Carlos Tabío, *Strawberry and Chocolate* [*Fresa y chocolate*] (Havana: El Instituto Cubano de Arte e Industria Cinematográfico [ICAIC], 1994).

41 In the film the main gay character (Diego) entices his object of desire (David) with Mario Vargas Llosa's *Conversations in the Cathedral.* For an analysis of the film and its relation to culture and nostalgia, see José Quiroga, "Homosexualities in the Tropic of Revolution," in *Sex and Sexuality in Latin America,* ed. Daniel Balderston and Donna J. Guy (New York: New York University Press, 1997), 133–51.

42 See Raúl Martín and Adolfo de Luis, "La boda: Una conversación a tres voces," interview by Bárbara E. Rivero, *Tablas,* nos. 3–4 (1994): 27–33.

43 Camilla Stevens, pers. com., June 2000. See also Lumsden, *Machos, Maricones, and Gays,* 195.

44 See Luis Rafael Sánchez, *La pasión según Antígona Pérez* [*The Passion According to Antígona Pérez*] (Hato Rey, P.R.: Ediciones Lugar, 1968).

45 She, in fact, carried out a *permuta,* the trading of one or more properties for another. She exchanged one big property for two smaller ones (one for herself and one for her son and his companion).

46 Referring to male prostitution in the United States, John Preston argues that being a "male hustler" offers numerous benefits. His assertion relies on the assumption that freely chosen prostitution is one of many lucrative sources of employment (*Hustling: A Gentleman's Guide to the Fine Art of Homosexual Prostitution* [New York: Kasak, 1994]).

47 I have heard anecdotal evidence that the LGBT participants in the late 1970s — those in early 1980s Antonio Maceo Brigades, which included many Cuban American young adults who had emigrated as children or had been born outside Cuba — encountered difficulties when they tried to bring up LGBT issues during their trip to Cuba; subsequent Maceo Brigades, similar to the Venceremos Brigades, dissuaded gay individuals from participating or forced them to keep quiet. According to José Quiroga, who participated in the brigades, vegetarians were also harassed, because they seemed too nonconformist (pers. com., March 2001).

48 "Responses by the Gay Liberation Party and the Gay Committee of Returned Brigadistas," in *We Are Everywhere: A Historical Sourcebook of Gay and Lesbian Politics,* ed. Mark Blasius and Shane Phelan (New York: Routledge, 1997), 409–10; "Declaration of the Cuban First National Congress on Education and Culture," *Casa de las Américas* 11, no. 65–66 (1971): 4–19.

49 Venceremos Brigade, "Policy on Gay Recruitment," in Blasius and Phelan, *We Are Everywhere,* 411–12.

50 Allen Young, "The Cuban Revolution and Gay Liberation," in *Out of the Closets: Voices of Gay Liberation,* ed. Karla Jay and Allen Young, 2d ed. (New York: New York University Press, 1992), 206–28. This volume also includes a transcript of a forum held by gay Venceremos Brigade participants who had returned from Cuba, as well as all of the documents included by Blasius and Phelan in *We Are Everywhere.*

51 Troyano, *I, Carmelita Tropicana,* 71.

AUDRE LORDE

Of Generators and Survival:
Hugo Letter (1990)

DECEMBER 1989

Dear Friend:

Those who do not learn from history are doomed to repeat their mistakes. It is necessary to remember the nightmare experience and extraordinary heroisms of the hurricane. But it is also important that we remember those lessons, both immediate and long term, learned in the bleak days afterward.

No one who experienced it will ever forget that night when the hurricane winds rode us down to a stand and the trees gave up their leaves and the land almost gave up her name. Sometimes at night the wind blows and the storm sounds start to howl and whistle from the sea and I am still afraid.

SEPTEMBER 18, 1989 — DAY ONE

We venture forth, wet, trembling, exhausted, and relieved to be alive. The sky over our wrecked and roofless rooms is sodden and wet. The front door is blocked with fallen timbers from the roof. All the glass doors have been blown in and the porch is totally gone except for only a concrete slab. The living room is completely open on two sides.

The house is a heartbreaking shambles of almost unrecognizable wreckage, with the kitchen, workroom, dining room, and living room a mass of splintered wood, shattered glass, and jumbled-up sodden papers and foodstuffs. It looks like some mean-spirited and powerful monster has gone on a jealous rampage through our home. Couches are blown end-up against the wall, chandeliers fallen, kitchen cabinets down, their doors stoven in and their contents strewn everywhere. The refrigerator has been wrenched away from the wall.

But parts of our roof held, and the back rooms of the house are only flooded. Our cisterns have water which is fairly clean, since through Gloria's foresight we had covered the overflow pipes to prevent groundwater fouling.

We were lucky. Ninety percent of the island's dwellings are gone or damaged. We step outside to look around, and all our landscapes are different and unfamiliar, as if we had been transported to an entirely different part of the island. We can now look straight out to sea. The coconut grove that once stood between us and the water is almost completely gone, and what few trees are left tilt in crazy angles almost to the ground. Nothing green is visible, except for the battered, wind-chewed collard greens at the back of our once-garden. Later I wonder at their hardiness. There are no leaves left on the trees, no flowers, no bushes. Everywhere, burned, blasted landscapes of sparse and tortured broken trees.

Monday was the stun of relief. Sweeping out glass and water, digging through the debris for a pot, a spoon, the camera. Listening to the rain fall into our house, and trying to get dry. We find a semi-soaked can of Sterno, boil some water for tea in the back washroom, and fall into sodden beds in the back of the house.

Tuesday we start the cars. Both have windshields broken, and rats have chewed the wires in Char's truck. We cut the brush away from the driveway, and try to make a short run to estimate the neighboring damage, but the roads are impassable. Char, the tri-athlete who shares our household, and I collect as many coconuts as we can from the fallen trees along the shore, knowing food will be in short supply. We pick up roof boards littering the roadside. Maybe we can find some way to get them back onto the house. We move like zombies, in the never-ending rain.

Under the fallen shelves in the workroom, we find our six bottles of stored water. From the size of this disaster we realize immediately they will not be enough for any length of time. There is water in the cistern which we think is usable. But we have no workable pump. No word to or from our friends in other parts of the island, inaccessible because of blocked roads. One radio station broadcasts in English from St. Thomas, extending sympathy to us, the people of St. Croix, and urging us to be of good cheer, help is on the way. We do not know what kind, nor from where. This is the first we hear that St. Croix was in the eye of Hugo and the worst hit of all the storm's targets. These words of encouragement help. They seem to mean we are not totally isolated and alone.

But the batteries in our portable radio are starting to fail.

There is little time to think about anything other than physical safety and survival.

We have stepped out into a world forever altered.

Three days pass in rain, coping and rally, but no help comes from the outside. The stored food is running out. If I have ever been addicted to excitement before, I just OD'd with Hugo. It is hard to believe that it is Wednesday somewhere in the ordinary world, and lights go on, faucets work, toilets flush, soap operas unfold, and it is not raining.

It has been an exhausting day of cutting bush and hauling out debris and storm rubbish in the rain. Our refrigerator conked out today, Hugo's battering was too much. Using the last of our salvageable supplies, Gloria prepares a scrumptious pot of stir-fry onions and potatoes and eggs. We have just had a quiet intimate little dinner for three by candlelight, cooked outdoors over a driftwood fire, under freshly washed stars. Because our roof is gone, our furniture and kitchen appliances are gone, our telephone and radio and porches and doors are gone, and the Sterno has run out.

The promised help is a long time in coming. On the third day the navy and the gunboats arrive in St. Croix. U.S. Marshals with M-16s they shove into anybody's face at the first hint of any disagreement with any of their orders. Army Military Police, army transport planes with command vehicles and armored trucks, but no blankets, no cots, no emergency rations. Even the Red Cross is running out of water. Food, water, batteries, Sterno, diapers, medical supplies, nonexistent. The generators in the hospital blow up. M.A.S.H. tents, known as deployable medical facilities, are put up in a field next to the evacuated hospital. The first supermarket with food for sale will not open for another month.

On the fourth day rain starts again at 6 a.m. We race out in relief to stand naked under the overhanging timbers of the broken roof. The cascading water is cold, but it feels great to be clean again. One of the hardest parts of the bleakness is the absolute lack of color — no flowers, no leaves, no color on our beautiful island, except for the multicolored patches of clothing spread over the bare bushes to dry, the only joy for weary eyes.

For the first week we drag out fallen timber, wet stinking debris, and the twisted remains of our past lives. Char hauls out truckload after truckload of sodden cut-up rugs, broken furniture, and appliances and other wreckage. By hand, we fill the tubs with water from the fetid, earth-laden pool to flush the toilets, and haul up buckets of water on a rope out of the cistern to boil for drinking.

We learn in quick order, after the Sterno goes, how to chop damp wood, build driftwood fires between cement blocks in the driveway, make lamps out of scrap oil and waxed string, wash ourselves under downspouts and go to sleep at sundown.

And think about the 60 percent of the rest of the world that live like this much of their lives. Some of whom still show up in the morning clean and well-combed and smiling at counters and kitchens every day in Johannesburg and New Delhi and Antigua and Tunica, Mississippi.

Usually there are friends in and out of our house constantly, but it is the end of the first week after Hugo before our first island visitors can make their way to our house. Adjoa comes by, and then Lipia, with the children, and Cassie, in her truck. It is wonderful to see friendly faces. We greet each other with tears of relief and joy. We share stories of survival, and whatever else we have that the other needs — batteries, flashlights, plastic bags. This pattern of mutual sharing, once so much an everyday part of island life, will be re-learned and repeated many times among many of us over the next few months.

WEDNESDAY, SEPTEMBER 27, 1989 — DAY TEN

The most horrible thing this past week has not been the nightmare of Hurricane Hugo, or even the terrible heart-wrenching devastation of the land and the dwellings, or the absence of any green. People are beginning to rally, beyond the material losses. Sun shines amid the rainy days more and more, and now the brown bruised hills are beginning to peep a faint green. Yesterday I saw a banana tree unfurling its first pale green flag.

What is most horrible in these days is the man-made ugliness, the extreme images haunting my nightmares. Army hippos driven by blond men rolling down Coconut Grove Beach, the backs filled with black and white soldiers, guns drawn.

The depressed horses in Cathy's Fancy wreckage, standing with their heads drooping, bloody haunches gashed to the bone by flying galvanized roofing, hooves hopelessly trapped by fallen telephone wires. The thick black oil covering the sands of Pelican Cove, relentlessly washing in on waves all along the North Shore's once beautiful beaches.

Hurricane Hugo was a terrible natural disaster, but nature heals herself. It is what we inject into her like tumors that fester and grow loathsome without constant attention, refusing to self-destruct, because out of our twisted wisdom — some fantasy of bloodless immortality — we have created them as if they would last one thousand years. But wind is our teacher.

The only way so many people could have existed in the fashion we have existed on this small island is with a superstructure created by extreme development. Now that the structure has been ripped apart, it becomes apparent that to sustain life under current circumstances — and these are circumstances which anyone living here must always keep in mind as imminently possible — to sustain life under post-Hugo circumstances requires more than many are prepared to deal with. And so they leave. Evacuated in those huge grim triple-decker C-140s, the first military planes onto St. Croix that brought armored trucks and rifles and military police, but no blankets, no cots, no food. It reminds me of lines in Billy Joel's song "I Saw the Lights Go out on Broadway":

> They sent a carrier up from Norfolk
> and took the Yankees off for free . . .

Maybe they will tell their friends not to come. On the other hand, maybe they will be followed by something worse.

Word slowly begins to leak out across the stunned island. This one survived in the car. That one crouched down between a washing machine and a wall, the only thing left standing of the house. This family jumped into their cistern. Another woman clung for six hours to the fender of a VW bus wrapped around a fallen tree, after she was caught outside in the eye of the storm when her house collapsed. The stories of heroism and survival are endless, and inspiring.

Because 14,500 of 16,000 powerline poles are destroyed, no power for at least 6 months, no telephones until next spring. Spring? Spring? Is there any other season but dreary?

We have a little generator, bought last year after Hurricane Gilbert, which provides just enough electricity to run a refrigerator. It needs to be filled with two gallons of gas every five hours, and gasoline is almost as impossible to get as fresh water. We siphon some out of one of our cars.

The bees and the jack-spaniels, yellow-jackets, are everywhere, stinging and furious. All their natural homes are gone, and no flowers and few trees survived for them. They sting everything, even plastic tablecloths. It is eight days before I see my first live flower after Hugo, coming up through the mud and ruins of a downed house in town.

The second week, gasoline starts being available, but scarce. Long waits on longer lines. Sometimes to be turned away, if the gas runs out or the generator running the pump gives out, sometimes to pay four dollars a gallon. We try to get someone to help us put the roof back on. In an effort to shield our few usable cooking utensils, we stretch plastic sheeting over places in the roofless kitchen, near the useless sink, to keep our canned goods and pots and dishes, our jugs of boiled water. Against the wall with a marker, Gloria carefully labels each area according to use, in an attempt to bring some semblance of order into our shattered lives.

The candles are running out. The batteries are going. We use the precious generator to recharge an old camp-lantern from happier days.

We have still not been able to communicate off-island. Eight days after Hugo, a bank of twenty-four emergency phones are established in Christiansted, and we stand on line to make five-minute calls to our families. They swing into action immediately, gathering foodstuffs, tools, other necessities. Two days later, a dear friend, Bob, appears from up north with supplies collected from our families and friends: batteries, a chain saw, canned and dried foods, first aid supplies, and a delicious home-cooked meal.

For the next month or so we share our collard greens, which is the only vegetable in the garden not destroyed by Hugo, along with the food, supplies, and care-packages sent to us from the mainland by our families, friends, and strangers, all of whom respond to our plight with heartwarming acts of generosity and support. These gifts of food help to sustain many worse off than we are.

Since not one visible banana tree survived the storm here, the Caribbean island of St. Lucia sends the gift of a boatload of ripe bananas to the people of St. Croix. On Saturday the wharf at Gallows Bay is filled with people picking up their bunches of bananas, many seeing each other for the first time since Hugo.

"How did you-all make out? Where were you during . . . Well, thank God for life . . ."

Remembering how that first yellow banana from St. Lucia tasted, three weeks after Hugo, still brings tears to my eyes.

MONDAY, OCTOBER 2, 1989 — DAY FIFTEEN

Dan and Ernie, Gloria's brother and nephew, have come down to help us clear the place. Things should be getting easier and easier, but they're not. Life seems harder and harder. Thank God for life, as we say here, but we'd all like it to be normal again.

Up at 5:45 a.m. Flush the toilet with a bucket of water from the tub. Pour water from the cistern bucket into the sink to wash. Ernie knocks, needs some water. Find a cistern bucket for him. Wash out the towels left soaking on the porch overnight. Organize the water Char has hauled from the cistern into chlorinated and nonchlorinated buckets. Get Ernie to pull some more buckets from the pool to flush the johns. Gas up the generator, noting we must find some more gas today. Start the generator after several tries. The carburetor sounds like it needs cleaning.

Back indoors, plug the refrigerator into the generator cord which runs through a hole cut into the front door. After being off all night the freezer compartment is cold, but unfrozen. Make juice, cut the last grapefruit that Dan and Ernie brought down. Make tea on the Sterno, sit down to have breakfast. 8:45. Char and her friend Colin want to borrow the generator to do some work over at the Queens Quarter house. We decide Dan should go with them. Help load Char's truck. Clear the table and pull some water to rinse the cups. Gloria takes the dishwater out to the hybrid hibiscus plant she is trying to reclaim from the effects of Hugo. We head out at 9:30 a.m.

Lots of people at the post office, but the doors are closed. Generator out. No mail. We pick up disaster-notification cards, then on to the Work and Rest house. Our friend Glenda from Fredericsted is staying in one part since her house collapsed. She is drying out her things in the yard. We leave a note for Curtis, who lives on the other side, asking him to come by tomorrow so he can help Dan and Ernie haul debris at Queens Quarter. Communication is a real problem.

We go on, first to one insurance agency and then across town to another, gathering up various insurance forms to be filed for the houses and the cars. The last one is doing business from a desk near the door, their generator out also. On to the chiropractor to make an appointment for my back, which is aching. Dr. Menzies isn't there, but we find out the health club has a working shower, and decide to come back later with soap and shampoo. The idea of a shower is a great lift.

On to Queens Quarter where we pick up Dan and the generator, and pull back into our yard at 12:30 p.m. The carpenter pulls in right behind us. He has tentative estimates for work to be done at Work and Rest, Queens Quarter, and Judith's Fancy. We will need these to begin filing insurance claims, and to decide where we must start repairs, until some money comes in. We discuss what still needs to be covered, and he takes the estimates back. Will try to return near the end of the week. Purify some cistern water, pumping it by hand through a tube anchored in a charcoal filter. Enjoy a glassful, and put the rest to cool in the refrigerator.

2:00 p.m. Exhausted. Bruce and Mary, an elderly couple from Estate Welcome, come by for a glass of cool water. They get their water from the army trucks at the wharf. It must be boiled, and they have no cooler or refrigerator. We light the Sterno, sit down on the steps, and have a cup of broth. They leave. Ernie comes in. He's cut himself on a tree branch. Spray and bandage his arm. Realize I never finished washing the towels. Fetch another bucket of chlorinated water, rinse, and hang them out on the make-shift line stretched across where the porch used to be. Wash out the buckets. We gather our soap and shampoo and head back out to the health club.

The shower and shampoo are glorious.

Make appointments with the chiropractor, then home. Out of kindling for our makeshift fireplace in the driveway. Back down to the beach to collect driftwood. Sort out the driest for kindling and build a fire for dinner. I grate a beet, the others fix the hamburger meat that's been thawed since Sunday. We rush to get dinner ready before sundown since sunset is 5:45 p.m. and no one wants to have to wash dishes in the dark. I remember that we have forgotten to pick up gas for the generator in the morning. Or was that Tuesday? I forget. The days go by so fast.

Slowly the island re-greens itself. We are rebuilding. This is our home. We pass from the stun of crisis to the interminable frustrations of long-range coping within a profit-based economy. Gas lines, bank lines, insurance lines, potable water lines, food lines, disaster relief lines, debris removal lines, etc. The growing fury when what is promised or owing is not delivered. The most ordinary errand takes three times as long as usual. It takes two to negotiate the littered roads. No traffic lights. No phones to check if this or that survived or is functioning. Many roads still impassable. We arrive to find a heap of timber.

Driving into town is like looking into a mirror while recuperating from an almost fatal disease. You are so glad to be alive, yet you can't help mourn-ing the destruction. On every trip out of the house, the constant visual reminders of the true extent of the devastation around the island saps even more energy.

Stress is telling upon everybody. People in town look brave but harried, and older. Many of our elders develop severe, delayed-reaction, physical conditions and have to leave, or be hospitalized. And all we can offer them here is a field-hospital in army camouflage tents, like in the movie *MASH*. Tempers are frayed. Even close friends become impossibly cross with each other.

We come back from a short generator gas run completely exhausted. It seems we stay tired all the time.

I sense a deep well of fury in many people that underlies the courageous coping. It is an anger, largely unexpressed, stoked by the way St. Croix has been treated, by government agencies and in the U.S. media, as a naughty, irresponsible, and irritating stepchild deserving of correction. In the critical and chaotic early days after Hugo, more immediate U.S. military attention is given to policing local activists feared as dissidents than is given to proper identification — let alone burial — of those who lost their lives when the hospital failed. Frantic relatives seeking their dead, no time for grieving, must sort out stories of common, unlabeled graves.

The people of St. Croix are totally unprepared for being viewed as a hostile population, particularly after surviving a disaster of Hugo's magnitude. Our first encounter with the U.S. version of immediate disaster response is not a pleasant one. Obviously, the first and primary mission of the U.S. military upon arrival is to protect property.

No matter what.

Drawn guns barring the road to the airport. Drawn guns protecting the road to Hess Oil, a private company with government contracts. Drawn guns in the hospital lot. A U.S. military M-16 shoved into her face stops my friend as she tried to go to her aged and disoriented mother, who is crying out for one scrap of familiarity, dignity, or help as she is being abruptly rushed into a military ambulance for evacuation to who knew where. She calls to her daughter, who cannot run to comfort her because of the M-16s barring her way.

The navy and the National Guard and the U.S. Marshals are joined by the FBI, the marines, and the military police. Army vehicles in camouflage, their squat ugly bodies filled with grim, slightly embarrassed young men, holding in their hands M-16s or bags of Kentucky Fried Chicken. Patroling our streets and roads. Holding old women at gunpoint in the airport, chatting with girls on the beach. St. Croix begins to remind me more and more of Grenada, 1983, another U.S. invasion of a Caribbean island.

Ninety percent of the dwellings on St. Croix were damaged or destroyed. Most of these houses lost their roof. Yet the first plastic tarpaulins shipped to the island for temporary roofing by the Federal Emergency Management Agency went — not to senior citizens, not to families with children huddled under oilcloth in the post-Hugo rains — but to tourist hotels. The rapidity with which much privately constructed, state-aided housing literally melted before Hugo's winds, left countless local people homeless, bewildered, and infuriated. Before long, insurance companies not properly supervised by local authorities begin to fail.

Workers and linesmen from power companies, some as far away as Guam, come to help rewire our island, and they are welcomed.

One month later, another terrible natural disaster, an earthquake, hits northern California. The level of concern and outpouring of aid to that community is in such marked contrast to the treatment deemed acceptable for St. Croix that few could miss this costly lesson of what it really means to be in a colonial relationship to a superpower, no matter what we want to call that relationship.

The same forces which brought us army transports filled with guns and armed personnel instead of food and water immediately after the hurricane, flood the mainland media with stories of looting, but none of the countless acts of heroism and survival. St. Croix after Hugo comes to be seen in the continental U.S. as a dangerous and lawless place, deserving of whatever happened to it and not much other attention, rather than as the site of the worst natural disaster in U.S. history.

The V.I. [Virgin Island] government imposes a curfew on all three islands: 8:00 p.m. for St. Thomas and St. John, but 6:00 p.m. in St. Croix, even though the effects of Hugo make life much more difficult here than on the other islands. Originally this was for security reasons, because of the lack of any streetlights after dark and the huge amounts of fallen debris still on the roads.

But the curfew is imposed selectively in St. Croix. Well-to-do East Enders have little difficulty leaving the one restaurant that re-opened in Gallows Bay. But the curfew begins to work genuine hardship upon those Virgin Islanders living inland, slowly reclaiming their lives and returning to work. There is no refrigeration, so food must be bought every day after work. The schools are not open, so children must be picked up from relatives or friends after work. Local people caught on the road after curfew are frequently subjected to rough treatment, fines, and even jailing. Friends report several scuffles with the police. Suit is finally brought against the government to have the curfew extended in St. Croix.

But we are rebuilding.

A lively business in generators springs up all around the island. They are the only sources of power, both real and symbolic. We realize we must try to get a larger one if we want to pump water from our cistern, or to do anything electrical other than run the refrigerator. But generators are at a premium, scarce as hensteeth, and monstrously overpriced, whenever available. A 3500-watt generator that sells for $800 stateside, and cost about $1,500 here pre-Hugo, now goes for $3,000, if you can beg, hustle, or wrangle one.

Questions in town shift from "How did you stay alive?" to "Do you know where I can get a generator?" The stunned and birdless silence that followed

Hugo is being replaced by the constant abrasive noise of generator motors of all sizes and conditions. Old friendships between neighbors are being strained to the utmost by resentments concerning how many hours each runs their generator and how late into the night. Where does he get all that gas from, anyway?

There is a prevailing and insistent language of the generators that we all begin to learn. No matter what else is going on, in the midst of every conversation, one ear is always attuned to the coughs and spits that might mean the generator is struggling, or missing, or about to run out of gas. Quick, quick, throw the switch before it stalls, or else it will be twice as hard to get started again! And then, of course, since they were never meant to be run constantly, the overworked generators soon begin to fail. The frantic quest begins to find someone with the expertise and time to repair your generator, not to mention trying to locate necessary but unavailable parts.

Quite quickly, an influx of mainland workers, more and less qualified, begins. Some are hired by state-aided private companies at wages 30 percent higher than local workers earn doing the same job. Some of these new arrivals are skilled and dedicated workers who lend a genuine helping hand in rebuilding. Others acquire a hammer and a bag of nails, and become construction workers, snapped up by new and indiscriminate contractors. Brash and noisy, eternal beer cans in hand, these "construction crews" are often the lately unemployed of depressed southern mainland cities, continental roustabouts seeking any opportunity, who float from disaster area to disaster area. Nakedly disregarding local culture, their social impact is unavoidable.

There is an enormous amount of work and restoration to be done. Qualified builders in other Caribbean islands cannot help us rebuild because of immigration and work permit quotas, but anyone with proof of American citizenship can call herself or himself a contractor. And do. Construction companies spring up overnight and vanish as quickly. Even some local contractors take on more work than they can handle, promising what they cannot deliver, and disappearing for weeks on end. Complaints about shoddy work and dishonored contracts sprout like guinea grass across the island.

The nights are hardest. Even though the mangled landscapes are less visible after dark, there is more time to think and feel the true impact of this experience, to cry and to marvel at all our varied powers of survival in the face of disaster.

I try to write in my journal as often as I can before weariness overtakes me. I am sitting at my desk by a flickering glass lamp from Mexico with a bowl of rose-colored lamp oil that sheds a warm light. A warm breeze blows from the sea. At any other time it would be quite an idyllic scene. Now I could give it all up IN A MINUTE!

DECEMBER 17, 1989

Twelve weeks and many crises in other parts of the world later, and we still do not have electrical power, telephones, rapid communication, a permanent roof, or glass in our boarded-up windows. But we do have a gas stove, brought to us by Curtis from out of his own kitchen, and a temporary roof and a larger generator that runs the refrigerator lent to us by Mary Mingus, and some lamps and a water pump. The island is green again, the sun is more brilliant than ever. We see spectacular sunsets, and even the flowers are returning, covering over the mangled, broken trees in the rainforest, and the mounds of twisted galvanize heaped alongside every roadway, waiting for the Army Corps of Engineers to come haul it away.

We are rebuilding, more wisely if we can, those of us who claim this island as home. With determination and will, as well as courage and style. For those of us who live in the Caribbean, hurricanes are natural occurrences that we must be prepared to experience as we experience the beauty and other benefits of living in this region. But we must also learn to live in such a way that the effects of these natural events are minimized, and the aftereffects of such occurrences are absorbed by realistic preplanning that includes all members of our society.

When the next hurricane season comes, will there still be unfortunate people displaced by Hugo still living under blue temporary tarpaulins that are decaying from overlong use in our tropical sun? We are a territory of the most powerful country on earth, supposed to be. Why are there almost seven hundred families still homeless? If we do not learn the lessons of Hurricane Hugo, we are doomed to repeat them. Because Hugo will not be the last hurricane in this area.

Our earth is healing herself. Again. And we pay a price for the violence we have done to her in the name of scientific progress. I am determined to pay my part of that price here, in the best way I can.

In west Africa the vodun say it is at the crossroads that we must leave our problems for other travelers to find and seek solution. I do not want to indulge in magical thinking as an excuse for avoiding action. But I do know that hurricanes are a way of cooling off the earth, and I also know we are burning down the rain forests, polluting the atmosphere, and heating up the oceans and the earth, not to speak of tearing jagged holes in her protective ozone layer.

The earth is telling us something about our conduct of living, as well as about our abuse of this covenant we live upon. Not one of us can believe himself or herself untouched by these messages, no matter where she or he lives, no matter under what illusion of safety or uninvolvement we may pretend to hide. Each one of us has some power that can be used, somewhere, somehow, to help save our earth. And the next time you think choosing a rub-on deodorant instead of an aerosol is the only thing you can do to make a difference, just feel what kind of ecological violence it does to hurl forty tons of revolving plutonium up into the sky over our heads and call it scientific progress, which is what the U.S.A. has just done. In our name. With our money.

And remember Hurricane Hugo.

My friend, I wish you were living down the road. Rocky as it may be, it is still also the most beautiful. Gloria and I would take our walking sticks after a long day's work, and the three little bluefish Curtis just brought by, and go clean them down on the beach, throwing the guts to the seabirds. We'd bring the fish over to your house, and all sit around and have a fish-fry over driftwood coals, swapping stories of how it was, and how it is, and how it is surely going to be.

May 1, 1990
St. Croix, USVI

From *Zami: A New Spelling of My Name* (1982)

I have always wanted to be both man and woman, to incorporate the strongest and richest parts of my mother and father within/into me — to share valleys and mountains upon my body the way the earth does in hills and peaks.

I would like to enter a woman the way any man can, and to be entered — to leave and to be left — to be hot and hard and soft all at the same time in the cause of our loving. I would like to drive forward and at other times to rest or be driven. When I sit and play in the waters of my bath I love to feel the deep inside parts of me, sliding and folded and tender and deep. Other times I like to fantasize the core of it, my pearl, a protruding part of me, hard and sensitive and vulnerable in a different way.

I have felt the age-old triangle of mother father and child, with the "I" at its eternal core, elongate and flatten out into the elegantly strong triad of grandmother mother daughter, with the "I" moving back and forth flowing in either or both directions as needed.

Woman forever. My body, a living representation of other life older longer wiser. The mountains and valleys, trees, rocks. Sand and flowers and water and stone. Made in earth.

Grenadians and Barbadians walk like African peoples. Trinidadians do not.

When I visited Grenada I saw the root of my mother's powers walking through the streets. I thought, this is the country of my foremothers, my forebearing mothers, those Black island women who defined themselves by what they did. "Island women make good wives; whatever happens, they've seen worse." There is a softer edge of African sharpness upon these women, and they swing through the rain-warm streets with an arrogant gentleness that I remember in strength and vulnerability.

My mother and father came to this country in 1924, when she was twenty-seven years old and he was twenty-six. They had been married a year. She lied about her age in immigration because her sisters who were here already had written her that americans wanted strong young women to work for them, and Linda was afraid that she was too old to get work. Wasn't she already an old maid at home when she had finally gotten married?

My father got a job as a laborer in the old Waldorf-Astoria, on the site where the Empire State Building now stands, and my mother worked there as a chambermaid. The hotel closed for demolition, and she went to work as a scullery maid in a teashop on Columbus Avenue and 99th Street. She went to work before dawn, and worked twelve hours a day, seven days a week, with no time off. The owner told my mother that she ought to be glad to have the job, since ordinarily the establishment didn't hire "Spanish" girls. Had the owner known Linda was Black, she would never have been hired at all. In the winter of 1928, my mother developed pleurisy and almost died. While my mother was still sick, my father went to collect her uniforms from the teahouse to wash them. When the owner saw him, he realized my mother was Black and fired her on the spot.

In October 1929, the first baby came and the stockmarket fell, and my parents' dream of going home receded into the background. Little secret sparks of it were kept alive for years by my mother's search for tropical fruits "under the bridge," and her burning of kerosene lamps, by her treadle-machine and her fried bananas and her love of fish and the sea. Trapped. There was so little that she really knew about the stranger's country. How the electricity worked. The nearest church. Where the Free Milk Fund for Babies handouts occurred, and at what time — even though we were not allowed to drink charity.

She knew about bundling up against the wicked cold. She knew about Paradise Plums — hard, oval candies, cherry-red on one side, pineapple-yellow on the other. She knew which West Indian markets along Lenox Avenue carried them in tilt-back glass jars on the countertops. She knew how desirable Paradise Plums were to sweet-starved little children, and how important in maintaining discipline on long shopping journeys. She knew exactly how many of the imported goodies could be sucked and rolled around in the mouth before the wicked gum arabic with its acidic british teeth cut through the tongue's pink coat and raised little red pimples.

She knew about mixing oils for bruises and rashes, and about disposing of all toenail clippings and hair from the comb. About burning candles before All Souls' Day to keep the soucouyants away, lest they suck the blood of her babies. She knew about blessing the food and yourself before eating, and about saying prayers before going to sleep.

She taught us one to the mother that I never learned in school.

Remember, oh most gracious Virgin Mary, that never was it known that anyone who fled to thy protection, implored thy help, or sought thy intercession, was ever left unaided. Inspired with this confidence I fly unto thee now, oh my sweet mother, to thee I come, before thee I stand, sinful and sorrowful. Oh mother of the word incarnate, despise not my petitions but in thy clemency and mercy oh hear and answer me now.

As a child, I remember often hearing my mother mouth these words softly, just below her breath, as she faced some new crisis or disaster — the icebox door breaking, the electricity being shut off, my sister gashing open her mouth on borrowed skates.

My child's ears heard the words and pondered the mysteries of this mother to whom my solid and austere mother could whisper such beautiful words.

And finally, my mother knew how to frighten children into behaving in public. She knew how to pretend that the only food left in the house was actually a meal of choice, carefully planned.

She knew how to make virtues out of necessities.

Linda missed the bashing of the waves against the sea-wall at the foot of Noel's Hill, the humped and mysterious slope of Marquis Island rising up from the water a half-mile off-shore. She missed the swift-flying bananaquits and the trees and the rank smell of the tree-ferns lining the road downhill into Grenville Town. She missed the music that did not have to be listened to because it was always around. Most of all, she missed the Sunday-long boat trips that took her to Aunt Anni's in Carriacou.

Everybody in Grenada had a song for everything. There was a song for the tobacco shop which was part of the general store, which Linda had managed from the time she was seventeen.

> 3/4 of a cross
> and a circle complete
> 2 semi-circles and a perpendicular meet . . .

A jingle serving to identify the store for those who could not read T O B A C C O.

The songs were all about, there was even one about them, the Belmar girls, who always carried their noses in the air. And you never talked your business too loud in the street, otherwise you were liable to hear your name broadcast in a song on the corner the very next day. At home, she learned from Sister Lou to disapprove of the endless casual song-making as a disreputable and common habit, beneath the notice of a decent girl.

But now, in this cold and raucous country called america, Linda missed the music. She even missed the annoyance of the early Saturday morning customers with their loose talk and slurred rhythms, warbling home from the rumshop.

She knew about food. But of what use was that to these crazy people she lived among, who cooked leg of lamb without washing the meat, and roasted even the toughest beef without water and a cover? Pumpkin was only a child's decoration to them, and they treated their husbands better than they cared for their children.

She did not know her way in and out of the galleries of the Museum of Natural History, but she did know that it was a good place to take children if you wanted them to grow up smart. It frightened her when she took her children there, and she would pinch each one of us girls on the fleshy part of our upper arms at one time or another all afternoon. Supposedly, it was because we wouldn't behave, but actually it was because beneath the neat visor of the museum guard's cap she could see pale blue eyes staring at her and her children as if we were a bad smell, and this frightened her. *This* was a situation she couldn't control.

What else did Linda know? She knew how to look into people's faces and tell what they were going to do before they did it. She knew which grapefruit was shaddock and pink, before it ripened, and what to do with the others, which was to throw them to the pigs. Except she had no pigs in Harlem, and sometimes those were the only grapefruits around to eat. She knew how to prevent infection in an open cut or wound by heating the black-elm leaf over a wood fire until it wilted in the hand, rubbing the juice into the cut, and then laying the soft green now flabby fibers over the wound for a bandage.

But there was no black-elm in Harlem, no black oak leaves to be had in New York City. Ma-Mariah, her root-woman grandmother, had taught her well under the trees on Noel's Hill in Grenville, Grenada, overlooking the sea. Aunt Anni and Ma-Liz, Linda's mother, had carried it on. But there was no call for this knowledge now; and her husband Byron did not like to talk about home because it made him sad, and weakened his resolve to make a kingdom for himself in this new world.

She did not know if the stories about white slavers that she read in the *Daily News* were true or not, but she knew to forbid her children ever to set foot into any candystore. We were not even allowed to buy penny gumballs from the machines in the subway. Besides being a waste of precious money, the machines were slot machines and therefore evil, or at least suspect as connected with white slavery — *the most vicious kind,* she'd say ominously.

Linda knew green things were precious, and the peaceful, healing qualities of water. On Saturday afternoons, sometimes, after my mother finished cleaning the house, we would go looking for some park to sit in and watch the trees. Sometimes we went down to the edge of the Harlem River at 142nd Street to watch the water. Sometimes we took the D train and went to the sea. Whenever we were close to water, my mother grew quiet and soft and absent-minded. Then she would tell us wonderful stories about Noel's Hill in Grenville, Grenada, which overlooked the Caribbean. She told us stories about Carriacou, where she had been born, amid the heavy smell of limes. She told us about plants that healed and about plants that drove you crazy, and none of it made much sense to us children because we had never seen any of them. And she told us about the trees and fruits and flowers that grew outside the door of the house where she grew up and lived until she married.

Once *home* was a far way off, a place I had never been to but knew well out of my mother's mouth. She breathed exuded hummed the fruit smell of Noel's Hill morning fresh and noon hot, and I spun visions of sapadilla and mango as a net over my Harlem tenement cot in the snoring darkness rank with nightmare sweat. Made bearable because it was not all. This now, here, was a space, some temporary abode, never to be considered forever nor totally binding nor defining, no matter how much it commanded in energy and attention. For if we lived correctly and with frugality, looked both ways before crossing the street, then someday we would arrive back in the sweet place, back *home*.

We would walk the hills of Grenville, Grenada, and when the wind blew right smell the limetrees of Carriacou, spice island off the coast. Listen to the sea drum up on Kick'em Jenny, the reef whose loud voice split the night, when the sea-waves beat upon her sides. Carriacou, from where the Belmar twins set forth on inter-island schooners for the voyages that brought them, first and last, to Grenville town, and they married the Noel sisters there, mainlander girls.

The Noel girls. Ma-Liz's older sister, Anni, followed her Belmar back to Carriacou, arrived as sister-in-law and stayed to become her own woman. Remembered the root-truths taught her by their mother, Ma-Mariah. Learned other powers from the women of Carriacou. And in a house in the hills behind L'Esterre she birthed each of her sister Ma-Liz's seven daughters. My mother Linda was born between the waiting palms of her loving hands.

Here Aunt Anni lived among the other women who saw their men off on the sailing vessels, then tended the goats and groundnuts, planted grain and poured rum upon the earth to strengthen the corn's growing, built their women's houses and the rainwater catchments, harvested the limes, wove their lives and the lives of their children together. Women who survived the absence of their seafaring men easily, because they came to love each other, past the men's returning.

Madivine. Friending. Zami. How Carriacou women love each other is legend in Grenada, and so is their strength and their beauty.

In the hills of Carriacou between L'Esterre and Harvey Vale my mother was born, a Belmar woman. Summered in Aunt Anni's house, picked limes with the women. And she grew up dreaming of Carriacou as someday I was to dream of Grenada.

Carriacou, a magic name like cinnamon, nutmeg, mace, the delectable little squares of guava jelly each lovingly wrapped in tiny bits of crazy-quilt wax-paper cut precisely from bread wrappers, the long sticks of dried vanilla and the sweet-smelling tonka bean, chalky brown nuggets of pressed chocolate for cocoa-tea, all set on a bed of wild bay laurel leaves, arriving every Christmas time in a well-wrapped tea-tin.

Carriacou which was not listed in the index of the *Goode's School Atlas* nor in the *Junior Americana World Gazette* nor appeared on any map that I could find, and so when I hunted for the magic place during geography lessons or in free library time, I never found it, and came to believe my mother's geography was a fantasy or crazy or at least too old-fashioned, and in reality maybe she was talking about the place other people called *Curaçao,* a Dutch possession on the other side of the Antilles.

But underneath it all as I was growing up, *home* was still a sweet place somewhere else which they had not managed to capture yet on paper, nor to throttle and bind up between the pages of a schoolbook. It was our own, my truly private paradise of blugoe and breadfruit hanging from the trees, of nutmeg and lime and sapadilla, of tonka beans and red and yellow Paradise Plums.*

---

*Years later, as partial requirement for a degree in library science, I did a detailed comparison of atlases, their merits and particular strengths. I used, as one of the foci of my project, the isle of Carriacou. It appeared only once, in the *Atlas of the Encyclopedia Britannica,* which has always prided itself upon the accurate cartology of its colonies. I was twenty-six years old before I found Carriacou on a map.

Out on Main Street (1993)

1

Janet and me? We does go Main Street to see pretty pretty sari and bangle, and to eat we belly full a *burfi* and *gulub jamoon*, but we doh go too often because, yuh see, is dem sweets self what does give people like we a presupposition for untameable hip and thigh.

Another reason we shy to frequent dere is dat we is watered-down Indians—we ain't good grade A Indians. We skin brown, is true, but we doh even think 'bout India unless something happen over dere and it come on de news. Mih family remain Hindu ever since mih ancestors leave India behind, but nowadays dey doh believe in praying unless things real bad, because, as mih father always singing, like if is a mantra: "Do good and good will be bestowed unto you." So he is a veritable saint cause he always doing good by his women friends and dey chilren. I sure some a dem must be mih half sister and brother, oui!

Mostly, back home, we is kitchen Indians: some kind a Indian food every day, at least once a day, but we doh get cardamom and other fancy spice down dere so de food not spicy like Indian food I eat in restaurants up here. But it have one thing we doh make joke 'bout down dere: we like we *meethai* and sweetrice too much, and it remain overly authentic, like de day Naana and Naani step off de boat in Port of Spain harbor over a hundred and sixty years ago. Check out dese hips here nah, dey is pure sugar and condensed milk, pure sweetness!

But Janet family different. In de ole days when Canadian missionaries land in Trinidad dey used to make a bee-line straight for Indians from down South. And Janet great grandparents is one a de first South families dat exchange over from Indian to Presbyterian. Dat was a long time ago.

When Janet born, she father, one Mr. John Mahase, insist on asking de Reverend MacDougal from Trace Settlement Church, a leftover from de Canadian Mission, to name de baby girl. De good Reverend choose de name

Constance cause dat was his mother name. But de mother a de child, Mrs. Savitri Mahase, wanted to name de child sheself. Ever since Savitri was a lil girl she like de yellow hair, fair skin and pretty pretty clothes Janet and John used to wear in de primary school reader—since she lil she want to change she name from Savitri to Janet but she own father get vex and say how Savitri was his mother name and how she will insult his mother if she gone and change it. So Savitri get she own way once by marrying this fella name John, and she do a encore, by calling she daughter Janet, even doh husband John upset for days at she for insulting de good Reverend by throwing out de name a de Reverend mother.

So dat is how my girlfriend, a darkskin Indian girl with thick black hair (pretty fuh so!) get a name like Janet.

She come from a long line a Presbyterian school teacher, headmaster and headmistress. Savitri still teaching from de same Janet and John reader in a primary school in San Fernando, and John, getting more and more obtuse in his ole age, is headmaster more dan twenty years now in Princes Town Boys' Presbyterian High School. Everybody back home know dat family good good. Dat is why Janet leave in two twos. Soon as A-Level finish she pack up and take off like a jet plane so she could live without people only shoo-shooing behind she back . . . "But A A! Yuh ain't hear de goods 'bout John Mahase daughter, gyul! How yuh mean yuh ain't hear? Is a big thing! Everybody talking 'bout she. Hear dis, nah! Yuh ever see she wear a dress? Yes! Doh look at mih so. Yuh reading mih right!"

Is only recentish I realize Mahase is a Hindu last name. In de ole days every Mahase in de country turn Presbyterian and now de name doh have no association with Hindu or Indian whatsoever. I used to think of it as a Presbyterian Church name until some days ago when we meet a Hindu fella fresh from India name Yogdesh Mahase who never even hear of Presbyterian.

De other day I ask Janet what she know 'bout Divali. She say, "It's the Hindu festival of lights, isn't it?" like a line straight out a dictionary. Yuh think she know anything 'bout how lord Rama get himself exile in a forest for fourteen years, and how when it come time for him to go back home his followers light up a pathway to help him make his way out, and dat is what Divali lights is all about? All Janet know is 'bout going for drive in de country to see light, and she could remember looking forward, around Divali time, to the lil brown paper-bag packages full a *burfi* and *parasad* that she father Hindu students used to bring for him.

One time in a Indian restaurant she ask for parasad for dessert. Well! Since den I never go back in dat restaurant, I embarrass fuh so!

I used to think I was a Hindu *par excellence* until I come up here and see real flesh and blood Indian from India. Up here, I learning 'bout all kind a custom and food and music and clothes dat we never see or hear 'bout in good ole Trinidad. Is de next best thing to going to India, in truth, oui! But Indian store clerk on Main Street doh have no patience with us, specially when we talking English to dem. Yuh ask dem a question in English and dey insist on giving de answer in Hindi or Punjabi or Urdu or Gujarati. How I suppose to know de difference even! And den dey look at yuh disdainful disdainful — like yuh disloyal, like yuh is a traitor.

But yuh know, it have one other reason I real reluctant to go Main Street. Yuh see, Janet pretty fuh so! And I doh like de way men does look at she, as if because she wearing jeans and T-shirt and high-heel shoe and makeup and have long hair loose and flying about like she is a walking-talking shampoo ad, dat she easy. And de women always looking at she beady eye, like she loose and going to thief dey man. Dat kind a thing always make me want to put mih arm round she waist like, she is my woman, take yuh eyes off she! and shock de false teeth right out dey mouth. And den is a whole other story when dey see me with mih crew cut and mih blue jeans tuck inside mih jim-boots. Walking next to Janet, who so femme dat she redundant, tend to make me look like a gender dey forget to classify. Before going Main Street I does parade in front de mirror practicing a jiggly-wiggly kind a walk. But if I ain't walking like a strong-man monkey I doh exactly feel right, and I always revert back to mih true colors. De men dem does look at me like if dey is exactly what I need a taste of to cure me good and proper. I could see dey eyes watching Janet and me, dey face growing dark as dey imagining all kind a situation and position. And de women dem embarrass fuh so to watch me in mih eye, like dey fraid I will jump up and try to kiss dem, or make pass at dem. Yuh know, sometimes I wonder if I ain't mad enough to do it just for a little bacchanal, nah!

Going for a outing with mih Janet on Main Street ain't easy! If only it wasn't for burfi and gulub jamoon! If only I had a learned how to cook dem kind a thing before I leave home and come up here to live!

2

In large deep-orange Sanskrit-style letters, de sign on de saffron-color awning above de door read "Kush Valley Sweets." Underneath in smaller red letters it had "Desserts Fit For The Gods." It was a corner building. The front and side was one big glass wall. Inside was big. Big like a gymnasium. Yuh

could see in through de brown tint windows: dark brown plastic chair, and
brown table, each one de length of a door, line up stiff and straight in row
after row like if is a school room.

Before entering de restaurant I ask Janet to wait one minute outside with
me while I rumfle up mih memory, pulling out all de sweet names I know
from home, besides burfi and gulub jamoon: meethai, *jilebi*, sweetrice (but
dey call dat kheer up here), and *ladhoo*. By now, of course, mih mouth
watering fuh so! When I feel confident enough dat I wouldn't make a fool a
mih Brown self by asking what dis one name? and what dat one name? we
went in de restaurant. In two twos all de spice in de place take a flying leap in
our direction and give us one big welcome hug up, tight fuh so! Since den
dey take up permanent residence in de jacket I wear dat day!

Mostly it had women customers sitting at de tables, chatting and laughing, eating sweets and sipping masala tea. De only men in de place was de
waiters, and all six waiters was men. I figure dat dey was brothers, not too
hard to conclude, because all a dem had de same full round chin, round as if
de chin stretch tight over a ping-pong ball, and dey had de same big roving
eyes. I know better dan to think dey was mere waiters in de employ of a
owner who chook up in a office in de back. I sure dat dat was dey own family
business, dey stomach proudly preceding dem and dey shoulders throw back
in de confidence of dey ownership.

It ain't dat I paranoid, yuh understand, but from de moment we enter de
fellas dem get over-animated, even armorously agitated. Janet again! All six
pair a eyes land up on she, following she every move and body part. Dat in
itself is something dat does madden me, oui! but also a kind a irrational envy
have a tendency to manifest in me. It was like I didn't exist. Sometimes it
could be a real problem going out with a good-looker, yes! While I ain't
remotely interested in having a squeak of a flirtation with a man, it doh hurt
a ego to have a man notice yuh once in a very long while. But with Janet at
mih side, I doh have de chance of a penny shave-ice in de hot sun. I tuck mih
elbows in as close to mih sides as I could so I wouldn't look like a strong man
next to she, and over to de l-o-n-g glass case jam up with sweets I jiggle and
wiggle in mih best imitation a some a dem gay fellas dat I see downtown
Vancouver, de ones who more femme dan even Janet. I tell she not to pay de
brothers no attention, because if any a dem flirt with she I could start a fight
right dere and den. And I didn't feel to mess up mih crew cut in a fight.

De case had sweets in every nuance of color in a rainbow. Sweets I never
before see and doh know de names of. But dat was all right because I wasn't
going to order dose ones anyway.

Since before we leave home Janet have she mind set on a nice thick syrupy curl a jilebi and a piece a plain burfi, so I order dose for she and den I ask de waiter-fella, resplendent with thick thick bright-yellow gold chain and ID bracelet, for a stick a meethai for mihself. I stand up waiting by de glass case for it but de waiter/owner lean up on de back wall behind de counter watching me like he ain't hear me. So I say loud enough for him, and everybody else in de room to hear, "I would like to have one piece a meethai, please," and den he smile and lift up his hands, palms open-out motioning across de vast expanse a glass case, and he say, "Your choice! Whichever you want, Miss." But he still lean up against de back wall grinning. So I stick mih head out and up like a turtle and say louder, and slowly, "One piece a meethai — dis one!" and I point sharp to de stick a flour mix with ghee, deep fry and den roll up in sugar. He say, "That is koorma, Miss. One piece only?"

Mih voice drop low all by itself. "Oh ho! Yes, one piece. Where I come from we does call dat meethai." And den I add, but only loud enough for Janet to hear, "And mih name ain't 'Miss.'"

He open his palms out and indicate de entire panorama a sweets and he say, "These are all meethai, Miss. *Meethai* is 'sweets.' Where are you from?"

I ignore his question and to show him I undaunted, I point to a round pink ball and say, "I'll have one a dese sugarcakes too, please." He start grinning broad broad like if he half-pitying, half-laughing at dis Indian-in-skin-color-only, and den he tell me, "That is called chum-chum, Miss." I snap back at him, "Yeh, well back home we does call dat sugarcake, Mr. Chum-chum."

At de table Janet say, "You know, Pud [Pud, short for Pudding; is dat she does call me when she feeling close to me, or sorry for me], it's true that we call that 'meethai' back home. Just like how we call 'siu mai' 'tim sam.' As if 'dim sum' is just one little piece a food. What did he call that sweet again?"

"Cultural bastards, Janet, cultural bastards. Dat is what we is. Yuh know, one time a fella from India who living up here call me a bastardized Indian because I didn't know Hindi. And now look at dis, nah! De thing is: all a we in Trinidad is cultural bastards, Janet, all a we. *Toutes bagailles!* Chinese people, Black people, White people. Syrian. Lebanese. I looking forward to de day I find out dat place inside me where I am nothing else but Trinida-dian, whatever dat could turn out to be."

I take a bite a de chum-chum, de texture was like grind-up coconut but it had no coconut, not even a hint a coconut taste in it. De thing was juicy with sweet rose water oozing out a it. De rose water perfume enter mih nose and get trap in mih cranium. Ah drink two cup a masala tea and a lassi and still de rose water perfume was on mih tongue like if I had a overdosed on Butchart Gardens.

Suddenly de door a de restaurant spring open wide with a strong force and two big burly fellas stumble in, almost rolling over on to de ground. Dey get up, eyes red and slow and dey skin burning pink with booze. Dey straighten up so much to overcompensate for falling forward, dat dey find deyself leaning backward. Everybody stop talking and was watching dem. De guy in front put his hand up to his forehead and take a deep Walter Raleigh bow, bringing de hand down to his waist in a rolling circular movement. Out loud he greet everybody with "Alarm o salay koom." A part a me wanted to bust out laughing. Another part make mih jaw drop open in disbelief. De calm in de place get rumfle up. De two fellas dem, feeling chupid now because nobody reply to dey greeting, gone up to de counter to Chum-chum trying to make a little conversation with him. De same booze-pink alarm-o-salay-koom-fella say to Chum-chum, "Hey, howaryah?"

Chum-Chum give a lil nod and de fella carry right on, "Are you Sikh?"

Chum-chum brothers converge near de counter, busying deyselves in de vicinity. Chum-chum look at his brothers kind a quizzical, and he touch his cheek and feel his forehead with de back a his palm. He say, "No, I think I am fine, thank you. But I am sorry if I look sick, Sir."

De burly fella confuse now, so he try again.

"Where are you from?"

Chum-chum say, "Fiji, Sir."

"Oh! Fiji, eh! Lotsa palm trees and beautiful women, eh! Is it true that you guys can have more than one wife?"

De exchange make mih blood rise up in a boiling froth. De restaurant suddenly get a gruff quietness 'bout it except for a woman I hear whispering angrily to another woman at de table behind us, "I hate this! I just hate it! I can't stand to see our men humiliated by them, right in front of us. He should refuse to serve them, he should throw them out. Who on earth do they think they are? The awful fools!" And de friend whisper back, "If he throws them out all of us will suffer in the long run."

I could discern de hair on de back a de neck a Chum-chum brothers standing up, annoyed, and at de same time de brothers look like dey was shrinking in stature. Chum-chum get serious, and he politely say, "What can I get for you?"

Pinko get de message and he point to a few items in de case and say, "One of each, to go please."

Holding de white takeout box in one hand he extend de other to Chum-chum and say, "How do you say 'Excuse me, I'm sorry' in Fiji?"

Chum-chum shake his head and say, "It's okay. Have a good day."

Pinko insist, "No, tell me please. I think I just behaved badly, and I want to apologize. How do you say 'I'm sorry' in Fiji?"

Chum-chum say, "Your apology is accepted. Everything is okay." And he discreetly turn away to serve a person who had just entered de restaurant. De fellas take de hint dat was broad like daylight, and back out de restaurant like two little mouse.

Everybody was feeling sorry for Chum-chum and Brothers. One a dem come up to de table across from us to take a order from a woman with a giraffe-long neck who say, "Brother, we mustn't accept how these people think they can treat us. You men really put up with too many insults and abuse over here. I really felt for you."

Another woman gone up to de counter to converse with Chum-chum in she language. She reach out and touch his hand, sympathy-like. Chum-chum hold the one hand in his two and make a verbose speech to her as she nod she head in agreement generously. To italicize her support, she buy a takeout box a two burfi, or rather, dat's what I think dey was.

De door a de restaurant open again, and a bevy of Indian-looking women saunter in, dress up to weaken a person's decorum. De Miss Universe pageant traipse across de room to a table. Chum-chum and Brothers start smoothing dey hair back, and pushing de front a dey shirts neatly into dey pants. One brother take out a pack a Dentyne from his shirt pocket and pop one in his mouth. One take out a comb from his back pocket and smooth down his hair. All a dem den converge on dat single table to take orders. Dey begin to behave like young pups in mating season. Only, de women dem wasn't impress by all this tra-la-la at all and ignore dem except to make dey order, straight to de point. Well, it look like Brothers' egos were having a rough day and dey start roving 'bout de room, dey egos and de crotch a dey pants leading far in front dem. One brother gone over to Giraffebai to see if she want anything more. He call she "dear" and put his hand on she back. Giraffebai straighten she back in surprise and reply in a not-too-friendly way. When he gone to write up de bill she see me looking at she and she say to me, "Whoever does he think he is! Calling me dear and touching me like that! Why do these men always think that they have permission to touch whatever and wherever they want! And you can't make a fuss about it in public, because it is exactly what those people out there want to hear about so that they can say how sexist and uncivilized our culture is."

I shake mih head in understanding and say, "Yeah. I know. Yuh right!"

De atmosphere in de room take a hairpin turn, and it was man aggressing on woman, woman warding off a herd a man who just had dey pride publicly cut up a couple a times in just a few minutes.

One brother walk over to Janet and me and he stand up facing me with his hands clasp in front a his crotch, like if he protecting it. Stiff stiff, looking at me, he say, "Will that be all?"

Mih crew cut start to tingle, so I put on mih femmest smile and say, "Yes, that's it, thank you. Just the bill please." De smartass turn to face Janet and he remove his hands from in front a his crotch and slip his thumbs inside his pants like a cowboy 'bout to do a square dance. He smile, looking down at her attentive fuh so, and he say, "Can I do anything for you?"

I didn't give Janet time fuh his intent to even register before I bulldoze in mih most un-femmest manner, "She have everything she need, man, thank you. The bill please." Yuh think he hear me? It was like I was talking to thin air. He remain smiling at Janet, but she, looking at me, not at him, say, "You heard her. The bill please."

Before he could even leave de table proper, I start mih tirade. "But A A! Yuh see dat? Yuh could believe dat! De effing so-and-so! One minute yuh feel sorry fuh dem and next minute dey harassing de heck out a you. Janet, he crazy to mess with my woman, yes!" Janet get vex with me and say I over-reacting, and is not fuh me to be vex, but fuh she to be vex. Is she he insult, and she could take good enough care a sheself.

I tell she I don't know why she don't cut off all dat long hair, and stop wearing lipstick and eyeliner. Well, who tell me to say dat! She get real vex and say dat nobody will tell she how to dress and how not to dress, not me and not any man. Well I could see de potential dat dis fight had coming, and when Janet get fighting vex, watch out! It hard to get a word in edgewise, yes! And she does bring up incidents from years back dat have no bearing on de current situation. So I draw back quick quick but she don't waste time; she was already off to a good start. It was best to leave right dere and den.

Just when I stand up to leave, de doors dem open up and in walk Sandy and Lise, coming for dey weekly hit a Indian sweets. Well, with Sandy and Lise is a dead giveaway dat dey not dressing fuh any man, it have no place in dey life fuh man-vibes, and dat in fact dey have a blatant penchant fuh women. Soon as dey enter de room yuh could see de brothers and de couple men customers dat had come in minutes before stare dem down from head to Birkenstocks, dey eyes bulging with disgust. And de women in de room start shoo-shooing, and putting dey hand in front dey mouth to stop dey surprise, and false teeth, too, from falling out. Sandy and Lise spot us instantly and dey call out to us, shameless, loud and affectionate. Dey leap over to us, eager to hug up and kiss like if dey hadn't seen us for years, but it was really only since two nights aback when we went out to dey favorite Indian restaurant for dinner. I figure dat de display was a genuine happiness to be seen wit us in dat place. While we stand up dere chatting, Sandy insist on rubbing she hand up and down Janet back — wit friendly intent, mind you, and same time Lise have she arm round Sandy waist. Well, all cover get blown. If it was even remotely possible dat I wasn't noticeable before, now Janet and I were overexposed. We could a easily suffer from hypothermia, specially since it suddenly get cold cold in dere. We say goodbye, not soon enough, and as we were leaving I turn to acknowledge Giraffebai, but instead a any recognition of our buddiness against de fresh brothers, I get a face dat look like it was in de presence of a very foul smell.

De good thing, doh, is dat Janet had become so incensed 'bout how we get scorned, dat she forgot I tell she to cut she hair and to ease up on de makeup, and so I get save from hearing 'bout how I too jealous, and how much I inhibit she, and how she would prefer if I would grow *my* hair, and wear lipstick and put on a dress sometimes. I so glad, oui!, dat I didn't have to go through hearing how I too demanding a she, like de time, she say, I prevent she from seeing a ole boyfriend when he was in town for a couple hours en route to live in Australia with his new bride (because, she say, I was jealous dat ten years ago dey sleep together). Well, look at mih crosses, nah! Like if I really so possessive and jealous!

So tell me, what yuh think 'bout dis nah, girl?

ANTON NIMBLETT

Time and Tide (2002)

Ten days after the car accident I leave New York and go to Trinidad—make a flight reservation and just leave. And from the time the plane comes in for a night landing, it's good. I see the lights sparkling on the coast of Port of Spain, splayed out into the Northern Mountain Range. These aren't the flashy, big-city-bright lights of a New York City landing at Kennedy or La Guardia. No, they're quiet, beaconing—flecks of quartz splashed deep in dark, rich stone. Good. The plane lands at Piarco and I walk out of the stale, pressurized air down the old-fashioned stairs and onto the tarmac. The tropical night air blows around my body and grabs me tight, penetrating fast though clothes and flesh, deep to the bone, wafting into my nose and deep into my lungs. Good. I think I smell sugar cane burning, and whether it's real or not, it's good.

At first I plan to go back "home." To spend time with my aunts and cousins and be pampered and fussed over, having them cook my favorite meals. I picture Auntie Midge shelling pounds and pounds of fresh pigeon peas, enough to stew some for lunch one day, with still more left to curry the next. And I see Aunt Phyllis and me in the backyard my first morning in Couva— even before breakfast—watering plants and picking guavas. I'd eat the green guavas with salt and pepper, and Aunt Phyllis would make juice and jelly with the ripe ones.

But I don't go to Couva, I check into Chaconia Inn like a tourist. I don't let my aunts know I am in Trinidad. I can't let them know that their "only nephew" is staying anywhere but with one of them, or with all of them in turn—a week here and a couple nights there.

The first day there're no guavas, but there's also no damned phone to answer, or to ignore as messages are left on the machine. "Hey, you okay? Holler back . . . we wanna make sure everything's all right." How could I be? I could say, "Yeah, I'm okay." Or maybe even, "Not so good, but I'm hanging in there." But definitely not "No, I'm not all right." "Everything" is not just the accident. I know that my friends are worried about my behavior after the accident, but I'm worried about my behavior before. The physical jolt of the crash forced me out of orbit. But how long would I have continued seeing Leigh "on the side" if we hadn't run off the road in his boyfriend's car? What did it mean that I was so easily caught up with someone who wasn't mine for the taking? The questions mount one on top of the other.

But the first day in Trinidad, the only question is, "Yuh want the maid to straighten yuh room this morning, or later?" Good and easy. And the second day, another easy question: "Ey boy! Ey, what you doing down here?" Ronald is flowing out of a store on Frederick Street, with one hand on the hip of his linen drawstring trousers and the other pulling down his shades for effect. Good. That question doesn't need an answer. It isn't the inquiry "Why are you here?" but rather the statement "It's nice to see you." And the next statement is, "You ain' going back before we have a chance to lime?" Yes, that's another easy one. I answer with, "Nah man, I just reach."

So on my third day "home" I'm liming with Ronald — practicing that special Trini art of passing time without a set activity. "Listen man, don't stay at nobody's hotel, " he'd said. "Yuh coming with me . . . I'm going up to Maracas to escape my many admirers and temptations . . . and try to finally finish some sewing I have to do." I'm comfortable around Ronald, and Maracas Bay, nestled amidst the hills of the north coast, is far from Couva, so there is no chance of my aunts finding me out. And liming is easier than trying to figure out why I've spent weeks convincing myself that I wasn't doing anything wrong; that I wasn't having an affair with someone else's man.

And just as I expect, Ronald fills the morning with talk of politics and his latest fashion project and good juicy gossip about no one in particular. There's no need to talk about me. We walk on the beach and a man playing football catches my eye. He looks just like the other fellas running the ball — dressed in a beat-up pair of shorts, barefoot and barebacked with a rag sticking out of his back pocket. Except, he's working some fancy footwork on the ball, moving with the ease of a coconut palm's branch in a breeze. The grin on his face matches the sweep and run of his legs as he puts those wicked beats on the ball. Light reflecting off the sweat on his back mirrors the sun flashing off the water on the bay. And as he runs, his calf muscles seem to ripple in time with the rhythm of the cresting waves. Yeah, he is beautiful.

"See that one, that specimen there?" Ronald asks. "That's Glen Moore."

I wonder if he's telling me this because he's caught me staring, or just as a point of interest. Ronald is liming partner and modern day griot — drinking at Smokey's and talking some slackness about a nice, nice man one minute, and explaining the next minute that the root of the old calypso refrain *"sanie mani te"* is the French phrase *"sans humanité."*

Whatever the reason, he begins, "That's a real Trini kinda *commess* story, yuh know. His family are the Moores who own Moore Building Equipment and Contracting down south. But for the past few years he's living in the woods somewhere 'round here with some woman in a shack."

Before I can tell Ronald that I went to school with a boy named Glen Moore, the fellas finish up the game. This Glen Moore walks right past me, and as my grandmother used to say, our "eyes make four." He walks another few feet, turns around, and stares again. And I know that he's the same Glen Moore from my class at Presentation College — more than twenty years ago.

Ronald continues with the story, but it's lost between the crashing waves, and the counterpoint of blood drumming on my ears. The look on Glen's face asks, "Don't I know you?"

I answer with a pointed finger, and a smile at him that says, "Yeah, I know you."

I feel Ronald's eyes boring into me, almost saying, "Ay, ay."

And Glen says, "Pres, right? Lemme see . . . you used to sit . . . behind me, in form two."

Later, Ronald and I sit on his gallery. It gets dark — night, fast and hard, races past dusk. We've had a dinner of fried shark from one of the stalls down the bay, and now Ronald's applying beads to a gown, his current project. A desk lamp attached to an extension cord bathes him in a spotlight as though he's on stage. I smell lime on my hands from the juice I made earlier, and the mosquito repellant coil adds a smoky musk to the ocean breeze.

"Boy, I ain' used to seeing you without a stiff drink," I tease him.

"Dear, you just haven't seen the industrious side of me before," he flips back. "Drinking and driving — maybe. But drinking and sewing — never."

We trade lines back and forth, as I again avoid talking about me, and my life. And Ronald lets me get away with it. It's hard to say how long we sit there accompanied by the ocean sounds in the background. When Glen comes walking up the path, Ronald's arched eyebrows and tilted head reflect my surprise.

"Company," he says, making the word sing. "Com-pah-nee."

"Behave yourself," I tell him.

And by the time Ronald gives me a response of mock innocence and an "I-don't-know-what-you're-talking-about" look, Glen is just feet from us, close enough for us to notice the crisp whiteness of his short-sleeved shirt. Glen throws his arms out from his sides in a simple announcement of his presence.

As I fumble for something cool to say, Glen says, "Oh Gawd, all yuh don't have to watch me like I just land from outer space. Yuh didn't believe I was going to pass by?"

"Nah, we believe yuh," Ronald says, "and you don't look like you land from outer space. Yuh just look like yuh walking into assembly at Presentation College in you nice white shirt."

I suck my teeth and laugh. "Don't bother with him, man. Come and sit down."

Glen laughs with us. "I'll tell you one thing, I never walked into Pres' with a bottle of *babash*." He pulls a flask from his back pocket.

"Yeah, Brother Michael would never stand for that," I say.

Glen sits on the brick banister. "And Brother Michael didn't miss anything," he says.

"Not anything," I agree.

If I were in my Brooklyn apartment, I'd have put on a soul CD and lighted a scented candle. But the natural sounds and light and smells — waves and stars, citrus and smoke — are all we need as we sit and talk. Sit and "old talk."

But soon Ronald says, "Fellas, is work I working here, so all yuh better take that babash and go and lime down on the beach."

Glen and I walk toward the surf and I hear different sections of the ocean orchestra: the booming bass of the big waves yards away from shore, the swooshing *shack-shack* beat as the water laps against the sand, sending it gently shifting; the flittering high notes as foamy bubbles burst and rejoin the salty night air.

Glen is just ahead of me, leading the way, on his own turf. I watch his back, a man's back now, but I remember the boy's back on the bench in front of me in form two. The back that held my attention while Mr. Mungal read to us on a lazy Friday afternoon, or while Brother Timothy explained the physical principles of polarity, attraction and repulsion.

We sit on a piece of driftwood and talk about those days when we did wear white shirts and go to assembly. Days when we made up nicknames for our teachers: Brother Timothy, always in a hurry, was BT Express, like the disco band with the hit song "Express"; Mr. Williams, our fanatic Spanish master, was *todos,* because he knew it all. I ask about Rambachan, the teacher's pet. I ask if Cole, the smartest guy in the class, became the doctor we all expected he would. And what ever happened to Jacobs, the saga-boy of form three? But I keep to myself that Jacobs was the first boy to make me feel that way, that "first-sign-of-puberty-way," just by standing over me on a bus trip to an inter-college football match. But Jacobs wasn't in my class, he didn't sit in front of me, so it was Glen's back that I'd let my pen graze across, once, then twice; Glen's back that my finger brushed against. Glen's back that the white cotton moved against, while I enjoyed the sensation of his male flesh. I keep that to myself too.

"Tell me about your wife," I say.

He takes a big swig from the flask and turns to me. "So you've heard the story about me, eh? Yuh want to know how it is that I end up living here instead of in a posh house like the rest of the boys from school? Or living the American dream like you?"

In the silent moment that follows I want to explain that that's not what I mean. I search for a way to explain that I'd left New York feeling out of control. Explain that I don't live the American dream, and I'm not sure what my own dreams are anymore. But that's too much to try to say now.

"Nah, man, nah. I'm just asking how you doing?"

Maybe I should ask those other fellas how they've ended up living perfect little lives. I reach over for the flask, which is wedged in the sand at his feet, touching his back with my other hand for balance. How is it that I have ended up here on this beach tonight?

"No, just tell me about your wife."

Glen tells me first that, yes, she is his wife, even though some of the stories say they're just living together. He tells me that she's from Paramin, where they don't mix with outsiders. He met her the year after his parents died within a month of each other. He tells me that they were married in a tiny little church because neither family approved: her family didn't want an "outsider," and his older brothers wanted him to meet a "proper" girl at university.

"That was when they still thought I was going to be just like one of them," he laughs.

He tells me that only his wife cuts his hair. No barber in the world can touch it. "But boy, you shoulda see the first time she put a scissors in my head . . . she *zug* up the thing so bad, I had to walk around with a cap for a week."

I think about how Leigh lets only his sister cornrow his hair. For the first time, I think about him with a calm, clear view — without the panic that set in after the accident and didn't seem to leave. I take a big swig of the home brew, and I take the time to feel the clean wet liquid in my mouth, feel the sharp burn as it spreads down my throat to my stomach. Inhaling slowly through my mouth, I savor the difference between the night air and my breath. I accept the difference.

Glen tells me that now I have to meet his wife, since I've heard so much about her, and oh yeah, the babash we're drinking is her uncle's recipe. Her uncle is her only relative who still talks to her. His two brothers don't talk to him anymore, but they don't talk to each other either, except to fight over the family business. Fitting the parts together, he's told me how he has ended up living here, turning his back on the conflict, turning toward a different coast of the island and a new family — creating a new dream. I'm glad that I didn't run into Cole or Jacobs or one of our other classmates. Glen weaves a tapestry of his life, the same story that he knows people tell behind his back; the details are the same ones that his brothers sneer at, and that her parents have cried about; details that in the telling from Paramin to Maracas to Ronald sound either crazy or like just a local joke. But Glen tells them with a simple pride — a calm contentment.

I'm outside of this scene looking in. I'm looking at me sitting here, cradled in the rich, jade hills, swigging clear strong fire from the same bottle with this man, viewing his life through his own eyes and enjoying the moment. This is so close to a scene I have wished for, even conjured over the years; a scene, imagined in lonely moments — with a different end. But I laugh, happy with this just the way it's been, not wanting more; not needing to be carried off on some other current.

"Let's walk back," I say.

"All right," he says, "and I'll stop talking about me and you can talk about you."

Yes, now I can talk about me. Soon enough I'll listen to my messages and answer my phone. And for right now as we walk beside the surf, I'll tell Glen about how my apartment in Brooklyn feels like home, and how the people at work sometimes remind me of the boys from school. And I know that I'll wake up tomorrow in a beach house on Maracas Bay, not like a piece of driftwood swept in on a rogue tide, but because I've decided that this is my time to be here.

We Came All the Way from Cuba So You Could Dress Like This? (1994)

For Nena

I'm wearing a green sweater. It's made of some synthetic material, and it's mine. I've been wearing it for two days straight and have no plans to take it off right now.

I'm ten years old. I just got off the boat—or rather, the ship. The actual boat didn't make it: We got picked up halfway from Havana to Miami by a gigantic oil freighter to which they then tied our boat. That's how our boat got smashed to smithereens, its wooden planks breaking off like toothpicks against the ship's big metal hull. Everybody talks about American ingenuity, so I'm not sure why somebody didn't anticipate that would happen. But they didn't. So the boat that brought me and my parents most of the way from Cuba is now just part of the debris that'll wash up on tourist beaches all over the Caribbean.

As I speak, my parents are being interrogated by an official from the office of Immigration and Naturalization Services. It's all a formality because this is 1963, and no Cuban claiming political asylum actually gets turned away. We're evidence that the revolution has failed the middle class and that communism is bad. My parents—my father's an accountant and my mother's a social worker—are living, breathing examples of the suffering Cubans have endured under the tyranny of Fidel Castro.

The immigration officer, a fat Hungarian lady with sparkly hazel eyes and a perpetual smile, asks my parents why they came over, and my father, whose face is bright red from spending two days floating in a little boat on the Atlantic Ocean while secretly terrified, points to me—I'm sitting on a couch across the room, more bored than exhausted—and says, We came for her, so she could have a future.

The immigration officer speaks a halting Spanish, and with it she tells my parents about fleeing the Communists in Hungary. She says they took everything from her family, including a large country estate, with forty-four acres and two lakes, that's now being used as a vocational training center. Can you imagine that, she says. There's an official presidential portrait of John F. Kennedy behind her, which will need to be replaced in a week or so.

I fold my arms in front of my chest and across the green sweater. Tonight the U.S. government will put us up in a noisy transient hotel. We'll be allowed to stay there at taxpayer expense for a couple of days until my godfather— who lives with his mistress somewhere in Miami—comes to get us.

Leaning against the wall at the processing center, I notice a volunteer for Catholic Charities who approaches me with gifts: oatmeal cookies, a plastic doll with blond hair and a blue dress, and a rosary made of white plastic beads. She smiles and talks to me in incomprehensible English, speaking unnaturally loud.

My mother, who's watching while sitting nervously next to my father as we're being processed, will later tell me she remembers this moment as something poignant and good.

All I hold onto is the feel of the doll—cool and hard—and the fact that the Catholic volunteer is trying to get me to exchange my green sweater for a little gray flannel gym jacket with a hood and an American flag logo. I wrap myself up tighter in the sweater, which at this point still smells of salt and Cuban dirt and my grandmother's house, and the Catholic volunteer just squeezes my shoulder and leaves, thinking, I'm sure, that I've been traumatized by the trip across the choppy waters. My mother smiles weakly at me from across the room.

I'm still clutching the doll, a thing I'll never play with but which I'll carry with me all my life, from apartment to apartment, one move after the other. Eventually, her little blond nylon hairs will fall off and, thirty years later, after I'm diagnosed with cancer, she'll sit atop my dresser, scarred and bald like a chemo patient.

Is life destiny or determination?

For all the blond boyfriends I will have, there will be only two yellow-haired lovers. One doesn't really count—a boy in a military academy who subscribes to Republican politics like my parents, and who will try, relatively unsuccessfully, to penetrate me on a south Florida beach. I will squirm away from underneath him, not because his penis hurts me but because the stubble on his face burns my cheek.

The other will be Martha, perceived by the whole lesbian community as a gold digger, but who will love me in spite of my poverty. She'll come to my one-room studio on Saturday mornings when her rich lover is still asleep and rip T-shirts off my shoulders, brutally and honestly.

One Saturday we'll forget to set the alarm to get her back home in time, and Martha will have to dress in a hurry, the smoky smell of my sex all over her face and her own underwear tangled up in her pants leg. When she gets home, her rich lover will notice the weird bulge at her calf and throw her out, forcing Martha to acknowledge that without a primary relationship for contrast, we can't go on.

It's too dangerous, she'll say, tossing her blond hair away from her face.

Years later, I'll visit Martha, now living seaside in Provincetown with her new lover, a Kennedy cousin still in the closet who has a love of dogs, and freckles sprinkled all over her cheeks.

At the processing center, the Catholic volunteer has found a young Colombian woman to talk to me. I don't know her name, but she's pretty and brown, and she speaks Spanish. She tells me she's not Catholic but that she'd like to offer me Christian comfort anyway. She smells of violet water.

She pulls a Bible from her big purse and asks me, Do you know this, and I say, I'm Catholic, and she says that, well, she was once Catholic, too, but then she was saved and became something else. She says everything will change for me in the United States, as it did for her.

Then she tells me about coming here with her father and how he got sick and died, and she was forced to do all sorts of work, including what she calls sinful work, and how the sinful work taught her so much about life, and then how she got saved. She says there's still a problem, an impulse, which she has to suppress by reading the Bible. She looks at me as if I know what she's talking about.

Across the room, my parents are still talking to the fat Hungarian lady, my father's head bent over the table as he fills out form after form.

Then the Catholic volunteer comes back and asks the Colombian girl something in English, and the girl reaches across me, pats my lap, and starts reading from her Spanish-language Bible: Your breasts are like two fawns, twins of a gazelle that feed upon the lilies. Until the day breathes and the shadows flee, I will hie me to the mountain of myrrh and the hill of frankincense. You are all fair, my love; there is no flaw in you.

Here's what my father dreams I will be in the United States of America: A lawyer, then a judge, in a system of law that is both serious and just. Not that he actually believes in democracy — in fact, he's openly suspicious of the popular will — but he longs for the power and prestige such a career would bring, and which he can't achieve on his own now that we're here, so he projects it all on me. He sees me in courtrooms and lecture halls, at libraries and in elegant restaurants, the object of envy and awe.

My father does not envision me in domestic scenes. He does not imagine me as a wife or mother because to do so would be to imagine someone else closer to me than he is, and he cannot endure that. He will never regret not being a grandfather; it was never part of his plan.

Here's what my mother dreams I will be in the United States of America: the owner of many appliances and a rolling green lawn; mother of two mischievous children; the wife of a boyishly handsome North American man who drinks Pepsi for breakfast; a career woman with a well-paying position in local broadcasting.

My mother pictures me reading the news on TV at four and home at the dinner table by six. She does not propose that I will actually do the cooking, but rather that I'll oversee the undocumented Haitian woman my husband and I have hired for that purpose. She sees me as fulfilled, as she imagines she is.

All I ever think about are kisses, not the deep throaty kind but quick pecks all along my belly just before my lover and I dissolve into warm blankets and tangled sheets in a bed under an open window. I have no view of this scene from a distance, so I don't know if the window frames tall pine trees or tropical bushes permeated with skittering gray lizards.

It's hot and stuffy in the processing center, where I'm sitting under a light that buzzes and clicks. Everything smells of nicotine. I wipe the shine off my face with the sleeve of my sweater. Eventually, I take off the sweater and fold it over my arm.

My father, smoking cigarette after cigarette, mutters about communism and how the Dominican Republic is next and then, possibly, someplace in Central America.

My mother has disappeared to another floor in the building, where the Catholic volunteer insists that she look through boxes filled with clothes donated by generous North Americans. Later, my mother will tell us how the Catholic volunteer pointed to the little gray flannel gym jacket with the hood and the American flag logo, how she plucked a bow tie from a box, then a black synthetic teddy from another and laughed, embarrassed.

My mother will admit she was uncomfortable with the idea of sifting through the boxes, sinking arm-deep into other people's sweat and excretions, but not that she was afraid of offending the Catholic volunteer and that she held her breath, smiled, and fished out a shirt for my father and a light blue cotton dress for me, which we'll never wear.

My parents escaped from Cuba because they did not want me to grow up in a communist state. They are anti-communists, especially my father.

It's because of this that when Martin Luther King Jr. dies in 1968 and North American cities go up in flames, my father will gloat. King was a Communist, he will say; he studied in Moscow, everybody knows that.

I'll roll my eyes and say nothing. My mother will ask him to please finish his *café con leche* and wipe the milk moustache from the top of his lip.

Later, the morning after Bobby Kennedy's brains are shot all over a California hotel kitchen, my father will greet the news of his death by walking into our kitchen wearing a "Nixon's the One" button.

There's no stopping him now, my father will say; I know, because I was involved with the counterrevolution, and I know he's the one who's going to save us, he's the one who came up with the Bay of Pigs — which would have worked, all the experts agree, if he'd been elected instead of Kennedy, that coward.

My mother will vote for Richard Nixon in 1968, but in spite of his loud support my father will sit out the election, convinced there's no need to become a citizen of the United States (the usual prerequisite for voting) because Nixon will get us back to Cuba in no time, where my father's dormant citizenship will spring to life.

Later that summer, my father, who has resisted getting a television set (too cumbersome to be moved when we go back to Cuba, he will tell us), suddenly buys a huge Zenith color model to watch the Olympics broadcast from Mexico City.

I will sit on the floor, close enough to distinguish the different colored dots, while my father sits a few feet away in a La-Z-Boy chair and roots for the Cuban boxers, especially Teófilo Stevenson. Every time Stevenson wins one — whether against North Americans or East Germans or whomever — my father will jump up and shout.

Later, when the Cuban flag waves at us during the medal ceremony, and the Cuban national anthem comes through the TV's tinny speakers, my father will stand up in Miami and cover his heart with his palm just like Fidel, watching on his own TV in Havana.

When I get older, I'll tell my father a rumor I heard that Stevenson, for all his heroics, practiced his best boxing moves on his wife, and my father will look at me like I'm crazy and say, Yeah, well, he's a Communist, what did you expect, huh?

In the processing center, my father is visited by a Cuban man with a large camera bag and a steno notebook into which he's constantly scribbling. The man has green Coke-bottle glasses and chews on a pungent Cuban cigar as he nods at everything my father says.

My mother, holding a brown paper bag filled with our new (used) clothes, sits next to me on the couch under the buzzing and clicking lights. She asks me about the Colombian girl, and I tell her she read me parts of the Bible, which makes my mother shudder.

The man with the Coke-bottle glasses and cigar tells my father he's from Santiago de Cuba in Oriente province, near Fidel's hometown, where he claims nobody ever supported the revolution because they knew the real Fidel. Then he tells my father he knew his father, which makes my father very nervous.

The whole northern coast of Havana harbor is mined, my father says to the Cuban man as if to distract him. There are *milicianos* all over the beaches, he goes on; it was a miracle we got out, but we had to do it — for her, and he points my way again.

Then the man with the Coke-bottle glasses and cigar jumps up and pulls a giant camera out of his bag, covering my mother and me with a sudden explosion of light.

In 1971, I'll come home for Thanksgiving from Indiana University where I have a scholarship to study optometry. It'll be the first time in months I'll be without an antiwar demonstration to go to, a consciousness-raising group to attend, or a Gay Liberation meeting to lead.

Alaba'o, I almost didn't recognize you, my mother will say, pulling on the fringes of my suede jacket, promising to mend the holes in my floor-sweeping bell-bottom jeans. My green sweater will be somewhere in the closet of my bedroom in their house.

We left Cuba so you could dress like this? my father will ask over my mother's shoulder.

And for the first and only time in my life, I'll say, Look, you didn't come for me, you came for you; you came because all your rich clients were leaving, and you were going to wind up a cashier in your father's hardware store if you didn't leave, okay?

My father, who works in a bank now, will gasp — ¿*Qué qué?* — and step back a bit. And my mother will say, Please, don't talk to your father like that.

And I'll say, It's a free country, I can do anything I want, remember? Christ, he only left because Fidel beat him in that stupid swimming race when they were little.

And then my father will reach over my mother's thin shoulders, grab me by the red bandanna around my neck, and throw me to the floor, where he'll kick me over and over until all I remember is my mother's voice pleading, Please stop, please, please, please stop.

We leave the processing center with the fat Hungarian lady, who drives a large Ford station wagon. My father sits in the front with her, and my mother and I sit in the back, although there is plenty of room for both of us in the front as well. The fat Hungarian lady is taking us to our hotel, where our room will have a kitchenette and a view of an alley from which a tall black transvestite plies her night trade.

Eventually, I'm drawn by the lights of the city, not just the neon streaming by the car windows but also the white globes on the street lamps, and I scamper to the back where I can watch the lights by myself. I close my eyes tight, then open them, loving the tracers and star bursts on my private screen.

Up in front, the fat Hungarian lady and my father are discussing the United States's many betrayals, first of Eastern Europe after World War II, then of Cuba after the Bay of Pigs invasion.

My mother, whom I believe is as beautiful as any of the palm trees fluttering on the median strip as we drive by, leans her head against the car window, tired and bereft. She comes to when the fat Hungarian lady, in a fit of giggles, breaks from the road and into the parking lot of a supermarket so shrouded in light that I'm sure it's a flying saucer docked here in Miami.

We did this when we first came to America, the fat Hungarian lady says, leading us up to the supermarket. And it's something only people like us can appreciate.

My father bobs his head up and down and my mother follows, her feet scraping the ground as she drags me by the hand.

We walk through the front door and then a turnstile, and suddenly we are in the land of plenty — row upon row of cereal boxes, TV dinners, massive displays of fresh pineapple, crate after crate of oranges, shelves of insect repellent, and every kind of broom. The dairy section is jammed with cheese and chocolate milk.

There's a butcher shop in the back, and my father says, Oh my god, look, and points to a slab of bloody red ribs thick with meat. My god my god my god, he says, as if he's never seen such a thing, or as if we're on the verge of starvation.

Calm down, please, my mother says, but he's not listening, choking back tears and hanging off the fat Hungarian lady who's now walking him past the sausages and hot dogs, packaged bologna and chipped beef.

All around us people stare, but then my father says, We just arrived from Cuba, and there's so much here!

The fat Hungarian lady pats his shoulder and says to the gathering crowd, Yes, he came on a little boat with his whole family; look at his beautiful daughter who will now grow up well-fed and free.

I push up against my mother, who feels as smooth and thin as a palm leaf on Good Friday. My father beams at me, tears in his eyes. All the while, complete strangers congratulate him on his wisdom and courage, give him hugs and money, and welcome him to the United States.

There are things that can't be told.

Things like when we couldn't find an apartment, everyone's saying it was because landlords in Miami didn't rent to families with kids, but knowing, always, that it was more than that.

Things like my doing very poorly on an IQ test because I didn't speak English, and getting tossed into a special education track, where it took until high school before somebody realized I didn't belong there.

Things like a North American hairdresser's telling my mother she didn't do her kind of hair.

Like my father, finally realizing he wasn't going to go back to Cuba anytime soon, trying to hang himself with the light cord in the bathroom while my mother cleaned rooms at a nearby luxury hotel, but falling instead and breaking his arm.

Like accepting welfare checks, because there really was no other way.

Like knowing that giving money to exile groups often meant helping somebody buy a private yacht for Caribbean vacations, not for invading Cuba, but also knowing that refusing to donate only invited questions about our own patriotism.

And knowing that Nixon really wasn't the one, and wasn't doing anything, and wouldn't have done anything, even if he'd finished his second term, no matter what a good job the Cuban burglars might have done at the Watergate Hotel.

What if we'd stayed? What if we'd never left Cuba? What if we were there when the last of the counterrevolution was beaten, or when Mariel harbor leaked thousands of Cubans out of the island, or when the Pan American Games came? What if we'd never left?

All my life, my father will say I would have been a young Communist, falling prey to the revolution's propaganda. According to him, I would have believed ice cream treats came from Fidel, that those hairless Russians were our friends, and that my duty as a revolutionary was to turn him in for his counterrevolutionary activities — which he will swear he'd never have given up if we'd stayed in Cuba.

My mother will shake her head but won't contradict him. She'll say the revolution uses people, and that I, too, would probably have been used, then betrayed, and that we'll never know, but maybe I would have wound up in jail whether I ever believed in the revolution or not, because I would have talked back to the wrong person, me and my big mouth.

I wonder, if we'd stayed then who, if anyone — if not Martha and the boy from the military academy — would have been my blond lovers, or any kind of lovers at all.

And what if we'd stayed, and there had been no revolution?

My parents will never say, as if somehow they know that their lives were meant to exist only in opposition.

I try to imagine who I would have been if Fidel had never come into Havana sitting triumphantly on top of that tank, but I can't. I can only think of variations of who I am, not who I might have been.

In college one day, I'll tell my mother on the phone that I want to go back to Cuba to see, to consider all these questions, and she'll pause, then say, What for? There's nothing there for you, we'll tell you whatever you need to know, don't you trust us?

Over my dead body, my father will say, listening in on the other line.

Years later, when I fly to Washington, D.C., and take a cab straight to the Cuban Interests Section to apply for a visa, a golden-skinned man with the dulled eyes of a bureaucrat will tell me that because I came to the U.S. too young to make the decision to leave for myself — that it was in fact my parents who made it for me — the Cuban government does not recognize my U.S. citizenship.

You need to renew your Cuban passport, he will say. Perhaps your parents have it, or a copy of your birth certificate, or maybe you have a relative or friend who could go through the records in Cuba for you.

I'll remember the passport among my mother's priceless papers, hand-written in blue ink, even the official parts. But when I ask my parents for it, my mother will say nothing, and my father will say, It's not here anymore, but in a bank box, where you'll never see it. Do you think I would let you betray us like that?

The boy from the military academy will say oh baby baby as he grinds his hips into me. And Martha and all the girls before and after her here in the United States will say ooohhh ooooohhhhh ooooooooohhhhhhhh as my fingers explore inside them.

But the first time I make love with a Cuban, a politically controversial exile writer of some repute, she will say, *Aaaaaayyyyyyaaaaaayyyyaaaaay* and lift me by my hair from between her legs, strings of saliva like sea foam between my mouth and her shiny curls. Then she'll drop me onto her mouth where our tongues will poke each other like wily porpoises.

In one swift movement, she'll flip me on my back, pillows falling every which way from the bed, and kiss every part of me, between my breasts and under my arms, and she'll suck my fingertips, and the inside of my elbows. And when she rests her head on my belly, her ear listening not to my heart-beat but to the fluttering of palm trees, she'll sit up, place one hand on my throat, the other on my sex, and kiss me there, under my rib cage, around my navel, where I am softest and palest.

The next morning, listening to her breathing in my arms, I will wonder how this could have happened, and, if it would have happened at all if we'd stayed in Cuba. And if so, if it would have been furtive or free, with or without the revolution. And how — knowing now how cataclysmic life really is — I might hold on to her for a little while longer.

When my father dies of a heart attack in 1990 (it will happen while he's driving, yelling at somebody, and the car will just sail over to the sidewalk and stop dead at the curb, where he'll fall to the seat and his arms will somehow fold over his chest, his hands set in prayer), I will come home to Florida from Chicago, where I'll be working as a photographer for the *Tribune*. I won't be taking pictures of murder scenes or politicians then but rather rock stars and local performance artists.

I'll be living in Uptown, in a huge house with a dry darkroom in one of the bedrooms, now converted and sealed black, where I cut up negatives and create photomontages that are exhibited at the Whitney Biennial and hailed by the critics as filled with yearning and hope.

When my father dies, I will feel sadness and a wish that certain things had been said, but I will not want more time with him. I will worry about my mother, just like all the relatives who predict she will die of heartbreak within months (she has diabetes and her vision is failing). But she will instead outlive both him and me.

I'll get to Miami Beach, where they've lived in a little coach house off Collins Avenue since their retirement, and find cousins and aunts helping my mother go through insurance papers and bank records, my father's will, his photographs and mementos: his university degree, a faded list of things to take back to Cuba (including Christmas lights), a jaundiced clipping from *Diario de las Américas* about our arrival which quotes my father as saying that Havana harbor is mined, and a photo of my mother and me, wide-eyed and thin, sitting on the couch in the processing center.

My father's funeral will be simple but well attended, closed casket at my request, but with a moment reserved for those who want a last look. My mother will stay in the room while the box is pried open (I'll be in the lobby smoking a cigarette, a habit I despised in my father but which I'll pick up at his funeral) and tell me later she stared at the cross above the casket, never registering my father's talcumed and perfumed body beneath it.

I couldn't leave, it wouldn't have looked right, she'll say. But thank god I'm going blind.

Then a minister who we do not know will come and read from the Bible and my mother will reach around my waist and hold onto me as we listen to him say, When all these things come upon you, the blessing and the curse . . . and you call them to mind among all the nations where the Lord your God has driven you, and return to the Lord your God, you and your children, and obey his voice . . . with all your heart and with all your soul; then the Lord your God will return your fortunes, and have compassion upon you, and he will gather you again from all the peoples where the Lord your God has scattered you.

There will be a storm during my father's burial, which means it will end quickly. My mother and several relatives will go back to her house, where a TV will blare from the bedroom filled with bored teenage cousins, the women will talk about how to make picadillo with low-fat ground turkey instead of the traditional beef and ham, and the men will sit outside in the yard, drinking beer or small cups of Cuban coffee, and talk about my father's love of Cuba, and how unfortunate it is that he died just as Eastern Europe is breaking free, and Fidel is surely about to fall.

Three days later, after taking my mother to the movies and the mall, church and the local Social Security office, I'll be standing at the front gate with my bags, yelling at the cab driver that I'm coming, when my mother will ask me to wait a minute and run back into the house, emerging minutes later with a box for me that won't fit in any of my bags.

A few things, she'll say, a few things that belong to you that I've been meaning to give you for years and now, well, they're yours.

I'll shake the box, which will emit only a muffled sound, and thank her for whatever it is, hug her and kiss her and tell her I'll call her as soon as I get home. She'll put her chicken bone arms around my neck, kiss the skin there all the way to my shoulders, and get choked up, which will break my heart.

Sleepy and tired in the cab to the airport, I'll lean my head against the window and stare out at the lanky palm trees, their brown and green leaves waving goodbye to me through the still coming drizzle. Everything will be damp, and I'll be hot and stuffy, listening to car horns detonating on every side of me. I'll close my eyes, stare at the blackness, and try to imagine something of yearning and hope, but I'll fall asleep instead, waking only when the driver tells me we've arrived, and that he'll get my bags from the trunk, his hand outstretched for the tip as if it were a condition for the return of my things.

When I get home to Uptown I'll forget all about my mother's box until one day many months later when my memory's fuzzy enough to let me be curious. I'll break it open to find grade school report cards, family pictures of the three of us in Cuba, a love letter to her from my father (in which he talks about wanting to kiss the tender mole by her mouth), Xeroxes of my birth certificate, copies of our requests for political asylum, and my faded blue-ink Cuban passport (expiration date: June 1965), all wrapped up in my old green sweater.

When I call my mother — embarrassed about taking so long to unpack her box, overwhelmed by the treasures within it — her answering machine will pick up and, in a bilingual message, give out her beeper number in case of emergency.

A week after my father's death, my mother will buy a computer with a Braille keyboard and a speaker, start learning how to use it at the community center down the block, and be busy investing in mutual funds at a profit within six months.

But this is all a long way off, of course. Right now, we're in a small hotel room with a kitchenette that U.S. taxpayers have provided for us.

My mother, whose eyes are dark and sunken, sits at a little table eating one of the Royal Castle hamburgers the fat Hungarian lady bought for us. My father munches on another, napkins spread under his hands. Their heads are tilted toward the window which faces an alley. To the far south edge, it offers a view of Biscayne Boulevard and a magically colored thread of night traffic. The air is salty and familiar, the moon brilliant hanging in the sky.

I'm in bed, under sheets that feel heavy with humidity and the smell of cleaning agents. The plastic doll the Catholic volunteer gave me sits on my pillow.

Then my father reaches across the table to my mother and says, We made it, we really made it.

And my mother runs her fingers through his hair and nods, and they both start crying, quietly but heartily, holding and stroking each other as if they are all they have.

And then there's a noise—a screech out in the alley followed by what sounds like a hyena's laughter—and my father leaps up and looks out the window, then starts laughing, too.

Oh my god, come here, look at this, he beckons to my mother, who jumps up and goes to him, positioning herself right under the crook of his arm. Can you believe that, he says.

Only in America, echoes my mother.

And as I lie here wondering about the spectacle outside the window and the new world that awaits us on this and every night of the rest of our lives, even I know we've already come a long way. What none of us can measure yet is how much of the voyage is already behind us.

The Hunter (1999)

Compact powder is a mild comfort on the cheeks. Creamy and reliable, its scent dominates the sense of smell, and for an instant he almost forgets to dab the powder puff gently on this shadow under the eyes to blot out the bad night and the persistent traces of juvenile acne from a childhood already gone by. Something somewhat ghostly remains on his face when he looks at his reflection in the mirror. The eyebrow pencil, barely a little stub, is difficult to handle, it's so small. He moistens the rough, black charcoal pencil with saliva and only then starts to draw it across the left eyelid, which becomes taut outlining the roundness of the eye, giving it a graceful Chinese shape. And then the right eyelid. Now he darkens his eyebrows, the pencil passing back and forth, creating a slight yet provocative angle pointing upward, forming a sustained wink. Faint music arrives from the living room while he paints his face and mentally sings every song from that fabulous Simon and Garfunkel concert in Central Park. The Chinese-made air conditioner is running on high, stirring his robe, but nothing bothers him more than an unexpected, furtive drop of sweat unpityingly marking the makeup that he takes great pain in perfecting. Sky-blue shadow now covers the eyelids—he adores blue, it's always been his color—which move rapidly, dazzling the eyes that look at the image of those same eyes in the oval of the mirror. With rouge he starts to outline his lips in a burning scarlet, but stops. Delicately, he also shades the highest region of his cheekbones, and it's as if he had blushed. Then he returns to his mouth, painstakingly works on it, and puts the charcoal pencil into its case. With a natural and precise gesture he brings his lips together, presses one against the other, and when he returns them to their original position, the mouth is a red rose, open, perfumed, warm. With his thin and spatulate fingers, he musses his just-washed hair, which falls softly, as if carelessly, across his forehead. Now is when he stops singing "Mrs. Robinson" in his head; now, he only has the eyes and the mind to admire himself in the mirror: the eyelids delineated and covered by a blue cloud; the smooth and lightly flushed cheeks; the reddened, mature lips. He feels, rejoices in, and enjoys the beauty of his face, the tangible reality of his conquered loveliness, the desire to please men and feel love, masculine heat and rugged lips like Anselmo's that from the first kiss swallow the makeup.

Before he starts to cry, he dips a ball of cotton into the cream and starts to rub away the work in which he invested twenty minutes of learned skills and repressed desires, and while he recovers his original eyes, lips, and cheeks, he asks himself why life gave him what he didn't want.

Outside, the night is full of promises. He adores these clear and fresh April nights, so good for walking around in La Habana. While he puts on his pants, adjusts his belt, places his keys and money in his pockets, he thinks about where he'll go. Deciding is always difficult and he doesn't know why it's even more so now. He has a presentiment that this could be a special night and he fears that a wrong choice perhaps will thwart an encounter that is already written in the stars. In reality, every night that he doesn't feel depressed he thinks that something is going to happen, and afterward, when nothing has happened, it's worse in the solitude of his unshared bed. He finishes dressing, likes how his shirt looks tucked inside his pants, and goes into the kitchen of his apartment. He takes out a quart of milk and pours a small amount in his cat's dish, asking himself, "Where is that bandit hiding?" He takes a piece of cloth, wipes away the wet imprint left by the quart on the table and once again the kitchen is immaculate, the way he likes it.

"El Vedado or La Habana?" he asks himself. If it's destiny, then destiny already knows. Before going out, he looks at himself in the mirror for the last time and places a few drops of perfume on his neck. On the street he walks slowly toward the bus stop without stepping on the lines in the sidewalk. Now he starts to get nervous, as his future depends on the first bus that destiny sends, bound for Vedado or old Havana. Were it his choice, he would prefer the surroundings of Vedado, even though, truthfully, the street has changed tremendously and it's now difficult to meet someone classy among all the crazy, bitchy men. In La Habana Vieja, he's annoyed by those depressed people who hang around El Capitolio and La Fraternidad, with their aggressive desperation and insulting vulgarity. Six minutes later, destiny sends him an almost empty bus — given the state of transportation this has to be destiny — which travels along a route that ends at El Prado, the major hunting grounds of Havana.

Night was made for hunting, and prey roams through the city jungle.

Anyone can be attacked, but not everyone falls into the traps. One has to have a sense of smell and know what to make of the shots, avoid scandalous failures and possible misunderstandings that don't help anyone. He learned these lessons from Ever, the friend who initiated him in the most sophisticated pleasures of love and the mysteries of the hunt. But Ever had a special grace that he lacked, and that he was sure he would never attain.

The yellowish lights of El Prado, the intense traffic noise, and the unrestrained persecution of tricks in search of a stranger and a dollar have taken away all the charm this area once had; now it's worked only by desperate men who accept anything and risk suffering the worst consequences at the hands of professional hustlers. Nevertheless, he walks slowly toward Parque Central, appraising every look, weighing every gesture, studying every possibility. He's still euphoric; the nine o'clock cannon shot has barely sounded and there are many hours ahead; the good couplings occur around eleven. As he walks, he takes in his surroundings; he imagines how things could be. He's tired of short-lived relationships, often so traumatic, which end in premature disillusionment or abandonment. His regular friends, with their cups of sweet-smelling tea, selections of classical music, familiar gossip, and usual sentimentality, have never been able to satisfy him completely. He needs to find a man like Anselmo again, a male from head to toe, who is also capable of understanding why one could fall in love with him and capable, for that same reason, of returning love. Those never-to-be-repeated months he lived with Anselmo have marked him forever; three years later, his heart still beats wildly and his skin becomes cold when he sees the dark face, the full mustache, and the pair of eyes that evoke the person he has loved the most in his life. He would like never again to remember the terrible days that followed their breakup; Anselmo told him he had met a woman and thought he was in love with her. It was then that he knew loneliness had crawled into his bed again, that their nights of clean and unbridled love were ending, their unforgettable afternoons in the most discreet reaches of the beach, when they played naked in the ocean, when he felt Anselmo's lukewarm fluid falling on his hands despite the cold water, dissolving into a wave, infertile just like him. Damn, how he had loved him! Depressed, what foolish things he'd done to stun himself with the crazy whores from Coppelia, those unstable, wandering, unrestrained pleasure-seekers who give it all up to the hazard of a public bathroom, the risk of a dark stairway, the uncertainty of shelter in some park bush, forgoing the plenitude of a clean, well tended bed and, in the morning before work, a shared breakfast and a deep kiss with the taste of a man.

But it's much too early for El Prado, he thinks when he arrives at the end of the avenue. He'll return later and maybe Lady Luck will favor him; after all he's a Capricorn, he tells himself. He crosses Neptuno and enters Parque Central, trying to find an empty bench. In front of him there are two lines of people on the sidewalk: one is for the pizzeria and the other is for taxis for the tourists. He doesn't see anyone who could interest him, though. There is an empty bench along the main path of the park, and he rushes to claim it. The truth is, it's a beautiful night, and he's prepared to wait, watch, and scrutinize.

In one corner of the park there is a group of more than twenty men, who are discussing baseball. They're all talking at the same time; he barely hears a few shouts that dominate the solid chatter. On the other side of the street the lobby of the theater is now empty. The ballet began at 8:30 and he imagines the euphoria of the aficionados — I can't stand them — who have come to see Josefina and Aurora, and are so eager to feel like them: slender, languid, praised. Surely they've put on their best garb, and, totally moved by each formidable gesture their dance goddesses make, they grab at each other's sweaty hands so that they can then scream, "Dyke," with an irreverent and unbearable unfurling of feathers thrust in the air. My God, he can't stand them.

If only he weren't so shy. He's going to be thirty-eight and he can count the meaningful relationships he's had on the fingers of both hands. In reality, he can count them on ten fingers because he has never wanted to include the crazy flings he had after Anselmo left him. What would really be incalculable is the number of platonic loves he's had and which his timidity impeded him from developing into full romance. At his job, he has loved three co-workers to tears, but for sure this never crossed their minds. The worst of his infatuations was with Wilfredo, chief of propaganda. He'll never know what he saw in that skinny, pale, obsessive man who still possessed that peasant look and clothes so outdated that they went out of style in 1970. Maybe Wilfredo's helplessness and listlessness were indications of a love never solidified because of his own unredeemable timidity. He could have ensnared Wilfredo with a couple of invitations to dine on his spaghetti carbonara and go to the theater, but for some reason he couldn't pursue him at work. Neither deep down nor on the surface did he want the rest of his co-workers to know the truth — although a few of them must know already. The fear of possible reprisals had turned him into a clandestine hunter and street rambler who only went out into the city at night thinking that the man of his dreams — who looked so much like Anselmo — would appear in some park, movie theater, or maybe even on a bus.

He knew that if only he weren't so timid, one day he would go out into the street with his best makeup on and scream out what he wanted to feel; he would be prettier and crazier than the craziest crazy woman. But he just can't stand them.

Couples, unaccompanied men and women, and the most daring tricks — who are willing to do anything for those magic, yearned-for dollars that are capable of turning into shiny Adidas sneakers, Levi's, Ocean Pacific T-shirts in a thousand garish colors, and even bottles of whiskey for those with more exotic taste — are walking on the main path in the park. Old people, policemen, newspaper vendors, and students still in their school uniforms are also walking there. Any one of them could be the one he has been waiting for, so he eyes discreetly each potential candidate and sometimes, when the presentiment grows stronger, gives a subtle nod.

Nothing happens, but there is no reason to become impatient either. He decides to go by the Payret movie theater, because — as Ever always says — like everything in life, one has to hunt down the prey. At the movie theater, the lit marquee announces that the present film will also be shown at midnight. It is past ten o'clock and there are a few night owls waiting for the midnight show line to form. He eliminates everyone who is accompanied by a woman, appraises the rest one by one, and then as if absentminded, walks among them while they wait on line. He looks at them, asks one of them for matches, another one about the movie, and one more for the time, because his watch is slow.

"Mine is too," says the young man regretfully.

He is eighteen and dressed discreetly, and carries a briefcase underneath his arm. His eyes are green, and a distinctive forehead predicts premature baldness.

He feels his heart beat faster, but tells himself no, things never repeat themselves. That young man looks too much like Juan Carlos, he met him in the same place he had encountered Juan Carlos, and he asked him the same questions he had asked Juan Carlos. He knows he can't be so lucky twice. Before Anselmo, Juan Carlos had been his most intense and important relationship. Juan Carlos was barely twenty-one when they met and he became Juan Carlos's teacher in the ways of love, just as he himself had once been Ever's student. But Juan Carlos turned out to be a disappointment: he became a raging, crazy bitch, like the kind who goes around in gangs; the original purity of their relationship became lost forever.

He looks at the young man's briefcase and asks him if he has just gotten out of school.

"The School for Languages," the young man replies, "on Manzana de Gomez."

"English?" he asks.

"No, German," the young man says, smiling. "I'm a biochemist, and a great deal of the reading material is in German."

"But do you like that language?" he asks.

"I don't know about liking it, but I still have to learn it to get it, and you know what that's like," says the young man.

"And why are you going to the movies so late?" he asks.

"There's no alternative," says the young man. "I work during the day, go to school at night, and my weekends are always busy."

"My God, how boring!" he exclaims, and offers the young man a cigarette.

"Thanks, but I don't smoke," says the young man.

His heart is beating uncontrollably. Juan Carlos didn't smoke either, and going to the movies was what he liked to do most in the world. Like the Juan Carlos he once knew, this is a handsome, normal, shy young man whose green eyes can weaken one's knees with one look. He imagines him in his apartment, asking to hear a certain cassette, approving of the taste of the fritters, letting himself drop, tired, onto the sofa, and then talking and talking; asking him to stay the night, his hand on his thigh, remarking how late it is and the buses. . . . Will he go to bed with him? Will he kiss that young man with those green eyes, visibly shy, caress and embrace him to asphyxiation and then finally mount him, let him enjoy a stranger's hardness driven into his innards?

"Excuse me," says the young man, "but I have to make a phone call. My wife should have been here at ten o'clock."

"Don't worry about it," he says, and almost feels like hitting him.

He returns to the Parque Central where nothing has changed, although the discussion about baseball has ended and car noise filters through the air. It is now past eleven and there are more empty benches, but he doesn't want to sit down. He is furious and weary and refuses to spend another night alone. No sooner is he in El Prado than he comes across the persistent tricks who are pursuing some Italians and a few couples kissing indiscreetly, just to make them jealous.

The last time he saw Anselmo he was with his wife and he was carrying a child who was a year and several months old. They were walking along number 23 when he spotted and recognized them from more than a block away. He didn't feel the usual wild beating of his heart, nor his skin turning cold: this time it really was Anselmo, and his presence was so forceful he thought that he would faint on the spot. He couldn't talk, let alone have the strength to move. Anselmo had shaved off his mustache, and his wife was blonder than he had imagined, with wide hips and a face that was becoming more beautiful the closer she approached. His mind was a cyclone of jealousies, romances, memories, nostalgia, and the renewed hatred of an abandoned person. Eventually, he managed to make a half turn and left before Anselmo could see him.

He returns along Louvre Street. The pizzeria is closed, but the line of taxis is still there ready for service. No sooner has the theater let out than a small group of crazy balletomaniacs in the lobby begins to comment on the performance, coloring the dialogue with a few little screams, short pauses, and a pitiful *fouetté*. They're such queers! Once again he feels the urge to hit somebody, to hurt and humiliate them. He crosses the street and heads toward Parque Central.

He doesn't stop to look toward the benches. He crosses Zulueta Street and goes through the No Admittance doors of the Centro Asturiano. The stench of dry urine accumulated over the years assaults him, but he endures the sudden onslaught until he comes out on Floridita, which is closed for repairs. He turns right, jumps over puddles of more recent urine, and finds himself in the dark, where an enormous black man, leaning against a pillar, his legs flexed, is attempting to penetrate a young woman who is repressing her wails of pleasure — or pain?

He doesn't want to go by the Payret movie theater again. He feels empty, yet full of hatred, lust, and desperation. He can no longer endure the loneliness that gnaws at the weeks and months. It hurts him to know that there are happy people, and he almost wants to be like the crazy, bitchy men and scream that he needs a man, a man, a man.

He doesn't want to do it, but he walks to the end of Capitolio and positions himself on a short staircase, prepared to wait, to hunt. It is now past midnight and there's always prey at that hour, although it isn't hunting down an Anselmo, a Juan Carlos, an Ever, nor even a fickle egocentric like Niño Antonio. Two couples, a soldier, and three women who look like cheap whores pass by, looking at him, soliciting. Two young men, one white and one black, also pass by and go into the corner of an old building to smoke very quickly a tiny cigarette that has a foul smell, like wet grass. Then he sees him approaching. He is the one: he is eighteen, clean-shaven, and caresses his chest while he walks. There are many like him, although it is strange that he is alone. Perhaps he's been abandoned, like me, he thought. No, he doesn't want to call out to him, he tells himself, he doesn't want to go back to the staircases, the half-demolished buildings, and the fear. He isn't interested in that perverted and arrogant kid who exhibits his precocious homosexuality like a coat of arms.

Nor can he continue being alone, hunting unsuccessfully every night, smelling like masturbation, waiting for the miracle of love. He needs to give himself over to someone or have someone give himself over to him.

"Listen, kid, do me a favor," he tells him. He closes the door and slides the bolts. He places his shirt on the sofa and takes off his shoes without untying his shoelaces. He goes to the bathroom and looks at himself in the mirror before he washes his injured hands. The usual dark circles under his eyes have grown into enormous bulbs that are about to come loose. He tries to spit out the bitter taste that tortures his mouth, and the vomit surprises him. It is a deep retch coming from the pit of his stomach that pushes open his lips. When it is over, the dark circles have gotten bigger. He hates his reflection in the mirror and hates his hands that, unexpectedly, had begun to hit that young man who had quite shamelessly offered himself to him. It was an unforeseen yet logical impulse, like the retching, something that had occurred in a simple manner and that he couldn't stop. The young man, without screaming and barely protecting his face, ended up looking like an aborted fetus underneath that staircase where they had made love.

He undresses and sits on the toilet bowl. While he is urinating, he starts to cry, almost without tears, but with a few deep, sorrowful snorts. He doesn't recognize himself, nor does he know who he is or what he did. He also doesn't want to go into the bedroom and see the empty bed where he will sleep alone again, again, and again. And then he thinks he should end it all.

He had been beset by suicidal impulses for a long time: they come when he feels ill and is afraid to suffer alone; when he feels good and wants to share his euphoria and doesn't have anyone to share it with; and when he goes out to hunt and returns home alone. He knows that because he wants to do it so badly, one day he will, and thinks that this morning must be that day.

Naked, he walks into the kitchen. He looks for the sharpest knife in one of the drawers and notices that the cat's milk dish is still full. "Where is that cat hiding?" he wonders, and looks out the window, trying to find some trace of his cat, considering how much it likes milk. "That one is roaming around nearby, in love, hunting." He looks at the knife with which he is going to cut his wrists. It's going to be a complete relief; the memory of Anselmo will end, the shyness, the successful and unsuccessful hunts, and above all, the loneliness and the double life that deplete his energy, and even his happiness.

Sitting on the edge of the bed—empty, empty—he studies his arms. He clenches his fists and sees the blue—his favorite color—of his veins rise slightly. He thinks that perhaps Anselmo will never know about his death, that his father will be happy to be rid of him, that he doesn't have anyone he can write a goodbye letter to, and while his weeping comforts him and the snorts are ending, he thinks that it was all the work of destiny. He looks at his blue veins again, opens his right hand, and then the knife clanks to the floor like a bell out of tune.

"Oh, Anselmo," he says, and lays himself to rest upon the mattress.

Translated by Harry Morales

VIRGILIO PIÑERA

The Face (1956)

One morning I got a phone call. The person on the other end said he was in grave danger. To my obvious question "With whom do I have the pleasure of speaking?" he replied that we had never seen each other and never would. What does one do in a situation like this? Tell the caller he's dialed the wrong number, of course, then hang up. That's what I did, but a few seconds later, the phone rang again. I told the persistent caller to please dial the number he wanted carefully and even added that I hoped not to be bothered again, since it was too early to start joking around.

Then he told me in a voice full of anguish not to hang up, that this wasn't any kind of joke, that he hadn't dialed the wrong number, that it was true we didn't know each other, for he had picked my name at random from the phone book. And, as if to anticipate any further objection, he told me that all of this was happening because of his face; that his face had a power of seduction so strong that people would shun him — disturbed, as if fearing irreparable harm. I confess that this business interested me; at the same time, I told him not to lose heart, for everything in this world has a cure. . . .

"No," he told me. "It's an incurable affliction, an aberration without remedy. Mankind has shunned me; even my own parents abandoned me some time ago. I only deal with the lowest of the human species, that is, with servants. . . . I'm reduced to the solitude of my house. I hardly ever go out anymore. The telephone is my only consolation, but people have so little imagination. . . . Without exception, everyone takes me for a lunatic. There are those who hang up, uttering unpleasant phrases; others let me speak and my reward is an outburst of laughter; there are even those who call people over to the phone so they, too, can enjoy the poor lunatic. And so, one by one, I lose them all forever."

I was moved, but I was also thinking that I was talking to a lunatic. Nevertheless, his voice had such a tone of sincerity, sounded so pained, that I refrained from bursting out laughing, from shouting and hanging up without further explanation. A new doubt struck me. Could he be a prankster? Or could it be a joke by one of my friends trying to spark my imagination? (I'm a novelist.) Since I'm an outspoken person, I let it all out.

"Well," he said philosophically, "I can't get that idea out of your head. It's reasonable for you to be suspicious, but if you have confidence in me, if pity moves you to stick this out, you'll soon be convinced of the sad truth I have just confided to you." And without giving me time to object again, he added: "Now I await the sentence. You have the final word. What's it going to be?" he whispered in terror. "A burst of laughter, shouting?"

"No," I hastened to say. "I won't forsake you. You've gotten me interested. However," I added, "You can call me. I'll only speak with you twice a week. I have thousands of things to do. Unfortunately, my face is one that everyone — or almost everyone — wants to see. I'm a writer, and you know what that entails."

"Praise the Lord!" he replied. "You stopped me at the edge of the abyss."

"But," I interrupted, "I'm worried that our conversations will have to be suspended for lack of anything to talk about. Since we don't have anything in common, neither friends nor common circumstances; since furthermore, you aren't a woman (you know how women like to be courted over the phone), I think we'll be yawning out of boredom within five minutes."

"I've thought of that," he replied. "It's the risk people take who can't see each other face to face. . . . Well," he sighed, "there's no harm in trying."

"But," I objected, "if we fail, you're going to feel bad. Don't you see that the cure could be worse than the disease?"

I couldn't dissuade him from his strange idea. Then an even more peculiar idea occurred to him: he suggested that we attend various shows in order to exchange impressions. This proposition, which at first rather annoyed me, ended up sounding interesting. For example, he told me he'd be attending the opening of a certain movie at a certain hour. . . . I didn't fail to attend. I hoped to make out that face, seductive and dreadful, among the hundreds of people filling the movie theater. At times, my curiosity was so intense that I imagined the police blocking the exits, determining if there was a person with a seductive and dreadful face in the theater. But would this be an infallible method for the police? Both the enchanting youth and the fiendish assassin can have a seductive and dreadful face. With these reflections I calmed down, and when we returned to our telephone meetings and I told him of these rebellions, he begged me in a sobbing voice never to dare to see his face, not even in jest; that I could be sure that as soon as I saw his "astonishing" face once, I would refuse to see him again. That he knew I would go on about my business, but that I should think of all he would lose. That if I cared at all about him as a defenseless human being, I would not try to see his face. And at that point, he became nervous and asked that in the future we not attend the same shows.

"Fine," I told him. "Granted. If you prefer it that way, we'll no longer be 'together' anywhere. But under one condition. . . ."

"One condition . . . ," he repeated feebly. "You're placing conditions and requirements on me. I can imagine what the request is going to cost me."

"The only thing that you wouldn't accept is for us to see each other face to face. . . . And no, I would never insist on that. You interest me enough that I would never box you in."

"Well, what condition is it then? Whatever situation you might imagine will be foolhardy. Think about it," he begged me. "Think about it before you make matters worse. Anyway," he added, "we're so safe on the telephone."

"The hell with your telephone!" I nearly shouted. "I absolutely have to see you. No, please!" I apologized, for I sensed that he'd nearly fainted. "No, I don't mean to say that I have to see your face! I would never dare to look at it; I know that you need me, and even when I'm literally dying to contemplate your face, I'll sacrifice that desire for your safety. Rest assured. No—what I mean to say is that I'm also suffering. You aren't the only one your face plays tricks on—it plays tricks on me, too. . . . You want to make me see it; you want me to leave you, too."

"I hadn't expected that," he replied in a voice as thin as a thread. "Damned face, playing tricks on me even when it's hidden! How could I imagine you'd be desperate to see it?"

There was a long pause; we were too moved to speak. Finally, he broke the silence: "What are you going to do now?"

"Resist as long as I can, as long as is humanly possible . . . as long . . ."

"Yes, until your curiosity can't bear it any longer," he interrupted with pronounced irony. "It can bear more than your mercy can."

"Neither one nor the other," I nearly shouted at him. "Neither one nor the other is true! . . . I haven't been moved 'exclusively' by pity for you. There has also been a lot of sympathy on my part," I added bitterly. "And as you see, now I feel as wretched as you do."

Then he thought it a good idea to break the tension with a joke of sorts, but its effect was to depress me. He told me that since his face had the power to make me "lose control," he considered our conversations over, and that in the future he would look for a person who didn't have that unhealthy curiosity to see his face. "Never!" I implored him. "If you did do such a thing, I would die. Let's continue as we have up until now. Only," I added, "make me forget my desire to see your face."

"I can't do anything about it," he replied. "If I fail with you, it will be the end."

"But at least let me be near you," I begged. "For example, I suggest you come to my house. . . ."

"Now you've got to be joking. Now it's your turn to be the joker. Because that's a joke. Right?"

"What I'm proposing to you," I explained, "is that you come to my house, or I go to yours, so we might speak face to face in the darkness."

"I won't do it for anything in the world!" he said to me. "If you're already going crazy on the telephone, how will it be when we're within inches of each other?"

But I convinced him. He couldn't refuse me anything, nor could I refuse him anything. The "encounter" took place at his house. He wanted to be sure that I wouldn't play any tricks on him. A servant who came to meet me in the hall searched me carefully.

"By order of the master of the house," he informed me.

No, I wasn't carrying a flashlight or matches: I never would have resorted to such desperate measures, but he was so afraid of losing me that he couldn't gauge how ridiculous and offensive his precautions were. Once the servant was sure that I wasn't carrying any kind of light, he led me by the hand and at last seated me in an armchair. The darkness was so complete that I couldn't see my hand in front of my face. I felt a little immaterial, but was nevertheless doing fine in the dark. In any case, I was finally going to hear his voice without having to use the phone, and — even more moving — he would be within inches of me at last, seated in another armchair, invisible but not disembodied. I was burning with the desire to "see" him. Could it be that he was already seated in his armchair or would he be long before making his entrance? Had he changed his mind, and would the servant be returning now to tell me this? I began to get anxious. Finally, I said:

"Are you there?"

"Long before you came," his voice replied, which I sensed was a short distance from my armchair. "I've been 'watching' you for a while."

"I've also been 'watching' you. Who would dare offend heaven by asking for any greater happiness than this?"

"Thank you," he replied in a trembling voice. "Now I know you understand me. There's no longer room in my heart for suspicion. You'll never try to break through this darkness."

"That's right," I said. "I prefer this darkness to the darkness of your face. And as for your face, I think the time has come for you to explain a little about it."

"Why, of course!" and he shifted in his seat. "The story of my face has two periods. When I was its ally, and when I became its mortal enemy. During the first period, together we committed more horrible deeds than an entire army. Because of my face, knives have been buried in hearts and poison sunk in guts. Some have gone to remote countries just to be killed in unequal combat; others have lain in their beds until death carried them off. I must stress the following peculiarity: all those wretches expired blessing my face. How is it possible that a face that everyone runs from in horror might at the same time be an object of final blessings?"

He was silent for a good while, like someone trying in vain to find an answer. At last, he continued with his story:

"This bloody sport" (in the beginning, passionate) "was little by little becoming a terrible torture to my very soul. Suddenly, I knew I was isolating myself. I knew that my face was my atonement. The ice of my soul had been melted; I wanted to redeem myself, but my face, on the other hand, tightened even more, its ice grew thicker. While I aspired with all my soul to possess human tenderness, my face was proliferating its crimes with redoubled passion until I was reduced to the state in which you find me now."

He got up and began to walk around, I had to tell him to calm down, for in this darkness he would soon be flat on the floor. He explained to me that he knew the room by heart, and as proof of this, he would perform the "tour de force" of inviting me to have coffee in the dark. I heard him moving cups around. A weak glow told me he was just putting a pot of water on an electric burner. I looked at that luminous point. I did it as a simple reflex; furthermore, he was so well positioned that such a weak glow couldn't reveal his silhouette. I joked that I had the eyes of a cat, and he replied that when a cat doesn't want to see a dog, its eyes are like those of a mole. . . . Receiving a human being in his house and offering him the sacred civilities of hospitality, in spite of his face, made him so happy that he expressed his pleasure with a joke: he said that since the coffee would take a little while, I could amuse myself "by reading one of the magazines sitting within reach on the red table with black legs. . . ."

Days later, reviewing the visit in my mind, I realized that it was characterized by a great emptiness. But I didn't want to see things too darkly, and I imagined it was just because I was unaccustomed to the situation. In fact, I told myself, everything is happening as if that ultimate prohibition on seeing each other's face didn't exist. What importance is there, after all, in a mere physical abnormality? On the other hand, if I did see his face, I would probably lose my sanity and lose him in the process. But as far as that's concerned, if his soul isn't in conflict with his face at the moment, I don't see what power his face could have over anyone else's face. Let's suppose that I finally see his face, that his face tries to demolish mine. It wouldn't succeed, for isn't his soul there, ready to stop his face's assault? Isn't it there, ready to defend me, and — what is more important — to hold on to me?

At our next meeting, I presented this whole line of reasoning to him — reasoning which seemed to me so convincing that I didn't doubt for a moment that he would get up to flood his dark room with light. But instead, I was surprised to hear him say:

"You've thought of all the possibilities, but have forgotten the only one that couldn't be rejected. . . ."

"What?" I yelled. "Is there still one more possibility?"

"Of course. I'm not sure that my soul would defend you against the attacks of my face."

I felt like a ship that has almost been grazed by another ship. I sank into the armchair; farther than the armchair, I sank into the thick mud of that horrible possibility. I said to him:

"Then your soul isn't pure?"

"It is. I have no doubt. But if my face reveals itself? Now then, if my face should show itself, I don't know whether my soul would come out for or against it."

"Do you mean to say," I yelled, "that your soul is dependent on your face?"

"If that weren't the case," he replied sobbing, "we wouldn't be sitting here in the dark. We'd be looking at each other's faces under a dazzling sun."

I didn't reply. It seemed useless to add another word. On the other hand, in my mind, I accepted the challenge of that seductive face. I now knew how to defeat it. It would neither lead me to suicide nor to leaving him. On my next visit, I would remain permanently at his side; at his side, without the darkness, his room full of light, the two of us facing one another.

There is little more for me to add. A while later, I returned to his house. As soon as I was seated in my armchair, I told him I had poked my eyes out so his face wouldn't separate our souls, and added that since the darkness was now superfluous, the lights could very well be turned on.

Translated by Mark Schafer

PATRICIA POWELL

Dale and Ian (1994)

(from *A Small Gathering Of Bones*)

Ian was over again the following week. That afternoon, Dale was sitting in the swivel chair in the room him take over as study. Him'd repaint it himself off-white with peach trimmings, and it was big and wide and full of plenty sunshine along with just the faintest smell of burning incense. Through mail order, him did send away to England for the lace peach curtains that match perfect with a pastel but floral couch from country. It was in here, spot with hibiscus, croton, chrysanthemums, and ferns, where him keep in an oak bookcase and on wooden shelves evenly aligned against the wall, books from high school and the ones him was using now up at the university, in addition to other solemn-looking volumes of classics bound in dark cloth his mother received one by one each month for two years from a subscription to a place based in England; the scrapbook with the poems him set down now and again; subscription to *National Geographic;* clothes; and the folder with newspaper clippings of extraneous happenings. Whenever it wasn't a story about the faceless baby born to the nine-year-old girl up at Spauldings General, it was one about the stoning to death of the university professor due to his immoral acts with young calves.

The black schoolteacher desk with faded etchings of "Jesus Saves," "Batty-man," and "One Love Jamaica" sat near two large glass windows that over-look, from one side, the green-skin mango tree outside, and the way its branches, thick and crooked, cast themselves confidently into Mrs. Morgan's backyard; the row of houses on his street that all looked the same; across Red Hills Road where higglers line both sides selling over-ripe June plums, roast corn, and sky juice; and way up into Stony Hill where all the houses have swimming pools around the back and the winding driveway leading up to the verandahs have pruned weeping willows on either sides. Pasted along the painted white walls were religious quotations taken from "The Lord's Prayer," Psalm 100, and Psalm 23, outlined in a very elaborate and gothic lettering that had taken him days upon days to accomplish.

The other window look out on the large expanse of red dirt — the play field belonging to Villa Road All Age School, the stained glass windows of St. Luke's, Crew Corner bus stop and the parking lot of Exodus Gallery and Mall. Arranged on his desk, in meticulous order, in a specially made hand-carved wooden frame (baptism gift from his godfather), varying by color, type, and print size, was his collection of fountain pens. Forty-eight in all. Pass the bathroom, down the hall and around the corner was where him sleep when night come down. Back around that way, him couldn't hear who was coming and going and from which room.

Dale was sitting at the desk, the geography text for his class open wide in front him. It was about two or three the afternoon. Outside schoolchildren shriek loud and laugh heavy as them romp and kick pebbles on the way home. The door handle downstairs rattle and turn, and before Dale could make it downstairs, Ian appeared in the doorway.

"Ian Kaysen!"

"Ah, Dale Singleton." Ian glide up the stairs, shoes whispering against the carpet, long, slender fingers caressing the banister.

"You didn't go to work?" Dale seat himself back round the desk. "Yes," Ian nod, as him finger the combination on the briefcase and take out the golden cigarette case the lawyer man, Bill, buy him the last birthday.

Dale wait till him take the first three puffs, find a hanger for his jacket, and ease himself on to the couch. Him learn from practice that nothing atall budge from Ian's lips till him comfortable.

"I take half day. Tired of the blasted hot office, balance sheet, and tax statements." Him cross his legs, tilt head backwards, and blow the smoke to the ceiling, lips slightly pouted. Manicured fingernails stretch taut against the shoulder of the couch. "Me go downtown. You know me, always look-ing for what I don't put down."

"Anything good."

Ian pause for a while, eyes far off. The light dusting of face powder soak up all speckles of sweat, leaving his face cool and calm. "You know how it is with the upcoming election."

Dale shake his head. "I can't wait for it to be over. For now you have to be extra careful who you talk to, what you say, the color clothes you wear. You hear on the radio this morning how them shoot this poor man on his way to work for wearing a red shirt? The gunman assume him was a member of the National Party."

Ian shake his head. "Yesterday, it take me almost three hours to reach home from the office. Everyone of the major roads block-off with old car and burning tyre and oil drums. I just hope them don't bother with the curfews again like last election. Police just slap-slap you with batons as them have a mind. Anyway, bad news aside, I see the loveliest man at the bus stop, though." Ian's face break down into a grin, eyes deep, mysterious.

"Oh yeah?" Dale ease back in his chair, arms folded behind his head.

Ian stop and shudder, voice husky, heavy with emotions. "Big shoulders, face coarse and rough-looking. Just the way I love them." Him inhale more of his cigarette and exhale slowly, lips tunnel-shaped. "I was walking past, but I couldn't help meself. I had to stop." Him get up from off the couch and walk towards the window, brushing imaginary balls of dust off grey pin-striped trousers that flow from his narrow hips like a gown. Him loosen the cuff links of his silk shirt, drop them in his pocket, and turn up the sleeves, revealing thin hairy arms.

"Mechanic or something. You can tell. Stink of car oil. Tractor-trailer boots that drag, for him don't lace them up. Finger nails bite-up bite-up and dirty. Cap turn backwards. Shirt wide open, and not a single solitary hair on that man's chest." Ian sigh loud, voice distance. "Smooth just like baby's skin. You could see the waist of the white underpants before it sink inside the tear-up dungarees.

"So of course, I had to take a seat next to him." Ian bat his eyes, pause, take a deep breath, make sure his nostrils flare, spit on his finger then bend down and rub dirt from off the tip of his black shoes and continue on.

Dale watch from across the room, a grin flirting with the edges of his mouth.

"So I put on my best man walk. You know . . ." Ian thrust his fists inside the pants pockets and start to strut around the room, each foot step heavy. "And prop up myself next to him." Ian sit back down in the couch, legs open wide, right hand gripping his crotch.

Dale start to laugh.

"Don't laugh. It's a serious thing. That's what you have to do to get them attention. Act just like them. None of this prim and proper business. Them would never even stop to glance at you. And in my deepest man's voice, I ask him which horse was winning at Caymanas Park today. For that's what them do with them money. Pay child's support and gamble the rest. But him wasn't friendly atall." Ian's face take on a gloominess, as him resume a more comfortable pose back on the couch. "Just mumble out Shining Star or something or other."

"What you know about horse racing, anyway? Suppose him did start to engage you?"

"Me love, you have to grab the horse by the collar. Can't wait around and wonder if and but. I figure maybe him smoke. So I put the briefcase on my lap and start to unlock it. Lo and behold, my tube of Vaseline Intensive Care was sitting right on top."

"Serve you damn right," Dale burst out, voice agitated, laughter gurgling in his throat. "You think him see it?"

"Of course, him see it. Those lovely beady eyes wouldn't miss a thing. I mumble something about sunburn, or cold sore, I can't quite remember which, but lucky thing the bus pull up and him board it."

Dale shake his head, smiling, "I can't understand what you find in them, you know. Bill look after you well, but that don't satisfy you. You want the tough, ugly, ignorant man who more than quick to call you names and burst up your head."

"But if him nice looking, what I must do?" Ian grin. "I see some lovely color TV downtown on sale too. I want to buy one for my mother, for Mother's Day. What you think?"

The grin slide off Dale's face and harden the lines around his mouth. Him didn't say anything. Him take his eyes off Ian and lodge them somewhere over his head top. And from the wings them catch sight of a spider building a nest in one corner of the wall.

"Decent sale, too," Ian continue on, voice raising-up with excitement. "Thirty and forty percent off. I know that she would like that. She could give away the old one she have now. For as you cough, that thing break down. She could set it down next to the organ and maybe put one or two figurines on top . . ."

Still, Dale didn't say anything. Ian's two eyes did take on a gloss him never see before, as him sprawl back in the couch, legs cross over one another, shirt unbuttoned halfway down for it was a warm afternoon. Dale wonder if Ian didn't remember how the mother send back the silk frock him buy last Christmas. The one him save up two whole months for. How she not even did open the box, for when it came back, the wrapping paper didn't even have a scratch, not even a crinkle.

"What size you think I should get, Dale? One of the big ones that sit down on the floor or the normal size ones?"

But him didn't even wait for Dale's answer. Him continue on. "I know she would like the big one. My mother likes things big and ostentatious. And I am just like her."

"You think that's the right thing?" Dale ask him quietly, face stern, shiny from the heat outside. Him did only have on shorts and a pair of push-toe slippers. Beads of sweat start to gather up on his wide chest. Dale wasn't a hairy man. And even the little that grow on his head was thinning out quick-and-brisk. Now and again, as him feel the sweat starting to trickle down towards his navel, him use the back of his hand to wipe it dry.

"Because she send back the frock, Christmas?"

Dale didn't answer. Him could see the light fading from Ian's face, and his shoulders that did raise up a little, starting to melt back down into his belly.

"That's because she have one just like it."

"But what about graduation, Ian?" Dale try to calm his voice, but him could hear it rising. "Is not everyday you graduate from university? On top of that, she the first person you send invitation. You did even have seat reserve up front for her. And still she didn't show her foot."

Ian pause before him answer. "She say she couldn't find the invitation. Say she did put it on the dresser in her room. But my sister, with her touch-touch self, probably moved it when she was cleaning. She say she really wanted to come . . ."

From over where him sit down around the desk, legs stretch out in front and fold at the ankles, Dale wanted to reach over and hold Ian. Put Ian's head next to his chest and just hold it right there against his heart. But him didn't move. That was one cross him couldn't help Ian carry. Other things him would interfere in, but not family. Blood thicker than water his mother used to say. Instead him watch Ian sink down lower into the couch.

The room did take on a sudden glumness. Dale get up from the desk and walk towards the window. Him push it open. The warm air from outside brush against his face. Him inhale it. The laughing from outside draw his attention. It was a raucous horse laugh, ringing loud amidst the noise of Red Hills Road traffic; the kind of a laugh a woman give out when the man she with tell her which position him enjoy most last night, or about which river basin him would swim across and which mountain top him would climb over just to find her if she ever left him.

Outside the window, Dale could see Rose picking up clothes from off the line that run from one branch of the mango tree to the electric lightpost. Him couldn't see her face, her steel-rod back was to him, but now and again she would take the clothes pin prop between her lips and fling it to the side of her where Barry, the long-haired Rastafarian man she have two miscarriages for, was sitting down on a piece of dry wood peeling a grapefruit. Back in the room, Dale hear the matches strike as Ian light up another cigarette. Him listen to the shoes clip-clop as him get up walk downstairs.

As far as Dale could see, Ian shouldn't've said a word to Miss Kaysen about the lawyer man, Bill. No matter how much him love the mother and want to tell her things. For him could tell right off, from all him hear about her, that when she take away her loving, she didn't plan to give it back next week. Now and again, she attend services at St. Luke's. His own eyes had never blessed her, or not that him know of, but from what him gather, people never glad to see her. Them say she love to find fault and keep malice. Can hold grudge longer than anybody them know. Love to cause contention. Them claim that her contribution to the collection plate was always next to nothing. That she never have a welcoming smile to offer anyone, only several hard lines that crease her mouth corners and a hard gleam in her eyes.

But Ian love his mother to distraction. Not so much the father. Not when him was alive or even now since him pass on, going thirteen months. Ian have eyes only for the mother. From every paycheque, each month, a portion always send off registered mail to the mother. On top of that, she get hat and crockery every Easter, jewelry Independence time, and a one-week paid vacation to Miami every birthday. But sometimes when a thing make you happy, you don't feel good just keeping it to yourself. You want everybody to know. You want them face to widen out with glee, them eyes brim over with merriment, them belly shake with excitement same way your own. Well, Miss Kaysen didn't have any merriment left in her heart when she find out Easter gone the lawyer she used to hear so much about was starting to court Ian.

Nevin did tell Dale the story. For it started around the time Nevin and Ian were just starting to know each other. It was Miss Kaysen's birthday. Enclosed in the same gift-wrapped box with the snow-white silk evening dress, pearl earrings, and matching necklace sent certified mail, was a type-written letter to the mother explaining the state of his heart where men were concerned.

Two days later when Nevin arrive 7:00 sharp at Ian's apartment to feast upon the four-course, candle-light meal Ian plan was to prepare, him find Ian seated, back hunched over, on the emerald green rug in the middle of the living room, dress-up from head to toe in his mother's white silk frock, earrings clip to the lobes of his pinna, necklace tumbling down his hardened chest-plate. Him was whimpering softly, thumb and forefinger tenderly caressing ashes from a small white envelope that had his name scrawled on with a piece of charcoal. It was the letter the mother burn to cinders and send back.

That same evening, Ian beg Nevin please to drop him by the mother's house. Him have to talk to her desperately.

"You sure, Ian?" Nevin did ask, not really wanting to drive all the way over to Spanish Town Road. "I mean it look as if she mad as hell with you. I mean, look." Nevin stretch out his hands, empty, at the envelope with the ashes.

"You dropping me or not?"

And Nevin did have to put on back his heavy black cloak, for it was raining like hell outside, first rain storm in over two months, and drive the forty-eight minutes to the mother's house in silence, Ian's hands, cold with fear, locked tight inside his.

Nevin say him waited outside in the car, watching from the window cloudy with steam while Ian scale the gate, chain-up with a steel padlock. On the verandah, Ian fumble in his pocket for the house key to the front door. Him slip it inside the lock and turn one way, then another. Nevin say him could sense the frustration just by looking at his shoulders, the way them sag heavy like laden crocus bags around him. Then all of a sudden, Ian start to pound on the solid wooden door with his fist, hollering out "Mama" on top of his voice, for it was raining, and with the water hitting hard against the galvanized zinc roofs and dropping clamorous inside the gutters by the side of the house, and then making its way boisterous into corrugated steel drums that collect water for the chickens around the back, she probably couldn't hear him, especially if she have wads of cotton stuff-up in the holes of her ears to keep out the sounds of evil.

Finally the door open up with such force that it pull Ian headlong inside. Fifteen, twenty minutes passed. And still Ian didn't come back. Inside the car, the heat grow insufferably. Finally Nevin say him put on back the cloak and leap out the car, dancing his way over puddles of water that settle themselves all over the road, and scale the gate into her yard. The rain was beating down mercilessly on her rose bush whose baby shoots were just starting to sprout. The verandah door was locked, but one of the wooden louvres was half open, so Nevin prise it wider with a piece of stick that Miss Kaysen had mounted to the vine of a spider plant, probably to help it spread.

According to Nevin the living room was in complete darkness. Him could spot only the silver tips of Ian's shoes and the white paws of a cat or young puppy walking around in circles by his feet, but that was all.

"But why you have to change the lock, Mama? Why you have to send back . . ."

"I am not your mother."

Nevin say him jump back from the window, for her voice was so close, almost as if she was speaking right behind him, right in his neck.

"I don't know who you are. So please go."

"But, Mama."

"Don't come back. Go. Go now."

The tips of the shoes jumping backwards as if she was chucking him in the chest.

"Mama, you just can't disown me so. You just can't . . ."

"I never did like you from the beginning. Miss Iris couldn't get you out. Twist up yourself inside me womb like you plan was to stay. Them did have to force cow-itch tea down me throat to get you to budge. Even then you were no damn good. Should've followed me heart and put a blasted end to you then."

Nevin say him couldn't listen anymore. Him close the window and walk back to the car. Him wait several minutes, then slowly pull away from the kerb, circling the square several times before driving back to the house to pick up Ian who was walking in the middle of the road towards the lighted eyes of the car, head bent, shoulders drooped, hands deep inside his pockets, the rain pouring off his tall, slender frame, for the mother refuse to lend him a piece of plastic to throw over his head so him wouldn't catch a cold.

As Dale continue to think about Ian and Miss Kaysen, all of a sudden his nose started to sweat. It was the retching and heavy wheezing him hear first. Him wanted to cover his ears, block out the sound, but Ian call out his name same time, and him rush out the room and down the stairs two at a time, heart thumping out loud. Him didn't want to look to see how Ian's eyes had turned red, or how the foam, white and thick, would have curdled at the edges of his moustache. Instead him run pass the figure doubled-over on the couch, hands press against chest, the cigarette burning by the winged-tip shoes, and into the kitchen for the roll of paper towel on the counter to wipe up the phlegm Ian was spitting out. One after the other. Some brown. Purple. Others pinkish.

KEVIN EVEROD QUASHIE

Genesis (2003)

1:7

there he is: a seven year old boy wearing purple shorts
on the screened-in end of his parents' porch,
twirling in the frame of afternoon sun.
hot stuff playing off of a record, his sisters, older,
squealing at the sultry strip tease.

he's dancing, a poet, a black boy
in a culture where masculinity is code. his
father is tall, beautiful, man; he has two
(soon three) sisters, an adoring mother,
and a grandmother whose love is water.

deep-lilac hot-pants: a sliver of polyester blend
that grips tight to his thick thighs, shorts
too short for his ample body but right
for the boy he is, in flair, his ass and arms articulating
the feel of saturday, this rare moment of sibling

play. his t-shirt is purple or white and he is
dancing. *looking for some hot stuff baby*
this evening falls from summer's lips.
he's a mime, a twirling mimicry, gesturing
gawdily, becoming more grand as his sisters, older,
laugh, clap, smile. he's a dervish,
spinning until his eyes meet his father's,

eyes that betray the stammering maleness about
to leave lips and then hands.
          summer stops, music fades,
the sisters know their lesser transgression;

he, the boy, is sweaty and shirtless,
lilac synthetic pealing brighter,
holding his thighs tighter. his father
is six foot three. masculinity is code.

hot stuff baby tonight.

he will not remember anything else.

he is a seven year old boy, a poet and
a dancer under a self-imposed
moratorium.

2:14

things happen in sevens, remarkable signs of karmic
undoing, the age he was when the itch
to be loved by older boys, to be welcomed
into the fraternal order and rumble
yielded unrequited nakedness. young bodies

were not meant for sex: the misapplication
of vaseline, the awkward torque
of arms and legs, the tears of anticipation. his
wondering if they would like him after, which they
didn't, which they couldn't.

this is what he remembers seven years later:
two boys fumbling, their able and aright
penises pointing through unzipped trousers,
their clothes surprisingly still in place;
his own naked, plump boyish body
clean, scared, hopeful.

he cannot, will not, remember
what the absence of kiss
or embrace must have felt like,
or if it was an absence — if he even
knew it was a thing to be missed.

he remembers through his want —
affection, camaraderie,
not a mis-anointed desire, another

inauguration into masculinity capped by a
too long bus ride back home,
the mark of pain to linger for days,
and its attendant question:
is this my sole inheritance?

for a long while he does not hear music
except for that one sad melody
carried on karen carpenter's
perfect voice, the one
his mother used to sing when

she had something to miss:
*can't help myself i just fall
in love with you*. the arc
is all desperation. this is
his soundtrack.

3:21

my lips tremble, a keen
and perceptible flutter. i
have seen my father's lips
in similar flight
before moments of anger. i wonder
what his lips must be like now,
how much more soft and patient. he
is older and maybe he misses me.
i am thinking of butterfly wings
and of his death, not coming soon
and not wished for, but inevitable. this
grand old beautiful man, his code
reverend and in decay.

and this my tremor: in the capable grip
of a man, the chosen surrender,
his flesh entering mine. nothing is forgotten
or healed but this loving is my own
emergent code, my
sweet (un)becoming.
              oh, i have been afraid

of drowning: looking again at his
body, tan-hued brown, the
sinew of his arms, the curves and
round of flesh, surging and powerful and
impressive and furious and falling . . .
like waves . . . i remember
water and another version of what
it means to concede uprightness, frightfully.

oh.

there is no music this time
and i need no anchor. just his
kiss, his arms, his urgent breath; just
my eyes closed, locked in prayer,
not despair, not perpetuity, just this
laying down
and laying on
of hands.

starlight starbright.

i am a poet.

Bayamón, Brooklyn y yo (1987)

When I was eight years old I immigrated to the United States with my sister and my mother. It was 1961. The Puerto Rican migration after World War II affected my family (meaning my mother's side) by splitting it right down the middle. Until recently, my mother's brother, four of her sisters, and all of their children lived in Bayamón, Puerto Rico, while my mother's mother, her other seven sisters, and all of their children lived in Brooklyn, New York.

Travel back and forth, especially during the earlier years of the immigration in the 1950s and 1960s, was frequent. Some of the sisters, who eventually reclaimed Puerto Rico as their permanent home, lived in Brooklyn. One of my aunts who had lived in Bayamón until she was in her fifties immigrated later on.

My mother and all of her siblings have worked either as factory workers or as cooks, and sometimes as both.

When my mother, my sister, and I arrived in the United States we also went to live in Brooklyn with one of my aunts. For the next nine years my sister and I would spend the summers in Puerto Rico with my father, his mother, and my mother's siblings.

All I remember about the time when we left the island is missing my fourth grade friends and my father's mother, whose favorite grandchild I had always been. I don't remember missing my father. In fact, I felt relief at not having to deal with his overbearing presence in my life.

My sister and I were enrolled in Catholic school, just as we had been in Puerto Rico. I don't remember how the process of learning to speak English took place. I know that by the time we immigrated I already understood some English because all the books in the school I had attended in Puerto Rico were in English! It wasn't that we were enrolled in a special school on the island, but rather that Catholic schools in Puerto Rico during the twentieth century were one of the institutions promoting the "Americanization" of Puerto Ricans.

The way this process of Americanization manifests itself in Puerto Rico is that you grow up valuing those characteristics associated with the United States, such as blond hair, blue eyes, white skin, North American culture, and the English language, and despising those characteristics associated with Puerto Rico, such as dark skin, nappy hair, the Spanish language, and Puerto Rican culture.

Americanization, which has been an integral part of the colonization of the island by the United States since 1898, has been promoted not only in the Catholic school system, but also in public schools, the mass media, and all major social institutions in Puerto Rico. One of the tragic consequences of the attempts to wipe out any consciousness that we are a distinct national entity can be seen in the public discussions which take place in Puerto Rico from time to time as to whether Puerto Ricans have a culture or not!

I grew up hearing such arguments every time my sister and I spent our summers on the island. Grandmother would speak about how she disliked North American whites intensely because they were racist and arrogant, but she liked their form of government—meaning "free" elections, a congress, etc., as opposed to the widespread military regimes that abound in Latin America. It never occurred to her that those military regimes were many times supported and sustained by the United States itself. In any case, when I was a child I bought a lot of what my grandmother said about the U.S. government because she was the most educated woman I knew. It was a bit unclear to me how you could like someone's government and not like them, but I didn't voice my reservations to anyone.

The more Americanized I became, the more inadequate and inferior I felt as a Puerto Rican. My line of thinking was: who wants to be something everyone despises? During this time I also felt this way about being a girl. I remember saying that I wished I was a man, because men were free to do as they pleased while girls always had to follow someone else's rules.

My feelings of inadequacy were complicated by the fact that whenever my sister and I went to Puerto Rico, our friends and relatives would tell us that we were not like Puerto Ricans on the island. After all, we lived in New York, and when we did not speak English to one another, we spoke Spanish with an "English" accent. At the same time we were called "different" we were told we were not North Americans, and should speak Spanish while in Puerto Rico. The confusion created by these experiences led me to question whether I was Puerto Rican or "American."

The process of reaffirming my Puerto Rican heritage was a very painful one. The price to pay for defining myself either way seemed high, and there were things about both cultures I liked. I liked the warmth and friendliness my people are known for. At the same time, I liked the greater freedom the United States seemed to offer women. I loved the Spanish language and the English language as well. I was trying to define myself culturally without being aware that Puerto Ricans in the United States would *never* be allowed to become part of that great "melting pot" I had heard about in school. Not unless we could pass for white North Americans and were willing to give up our Puerto Rican identity.

Slowly I began to realize that the "American Dream" was more like a nightmare for Blacks and Puerto Ricans, not to mention Native Americans, the group lowest in the economic and social scale of the country. The awakening of my political consciousness was facilitated by the creation of the Young Lords and ASPIRA in the late 1960s.[1] It was the time of Malcolm X, the Black Panther Party, the civil rights movement, and the Vietnam War, yet I was so preoccupied with my own cultural identity crisis that I would not take full advantage of the support offered by the Black Power movement at the time.

During this time I was a teenager and led a very sheltered and isolated life. I took refuge, as I had all through elementary school, in studying, reading books at home, and playing music. I was going to a Catholic school in the "ghetto" where we did not have a single Black or Puerto Rican teacher. All my role models were North American, white middle class teachers. They were very much into the "U.S.-is-the-best-of-all-possible-worlds-for-everyone" philosophy. For years I had no one to offer me an alternative interpretation for what was happening to me as a Puerto Rican. The only thing I had heard in and outside my home was that if I didn't "make it" out here it was solely my own fault.

All of a sudden I became aware of the Young Lords and the Puerto Rican-identity-flowering which took place at the end of the sixties. I was proud to say hello to Puerto Ricans displaying Puerto Rican flags on their coats, cars, homes, etc. Seeing other Puerto Ricans being so public about their national identity had the same positive impact on me that the slogan "Black is Beautiful" had on many Blacks during this same period of time. It allowed me to be able to say, "Yes, I am Puerto Rican and proud," and mean it.

It was in this spirit that in 1969, at the age of sixteen, I was part of a group of students who helped form the first ASPIRA club in our high school. I joined ASPIRA in the hopes of finding other Puerto Ricans my age who were tackling the same kinds of identity issues as I was. Two years later I dropped out of ASPIRA when I couldn't find anyone in the organization to discuss these issues with. I know now that there were other people there engaged in the same kind of quest, but I never connected with them, and as a result, my feelings of frustration and isolation increased.

The feelings were complicated by the fact that during the summer of 1969, a few months before I joined ASPIRA in the U.S., I had begun to deal with another aspect of myself which had remained hidden inside me until then — my emotional attachment and sexual attraction to women. During my childhood and adolescence I had always been very attached to my girl-friends in school, but I had not consciously felt sexual attraction towards them. I had always felt sexually attracted to boys and still thought that I would get married one day.

Then, during my summer vacation in Puerto Rico at the age of sixteen, one of my cousins told me about her childhood and adolescent sexual in-volvement with another girl. From the moment she told me, it seemed totally natural to me that she should have had these experiences. After all, my cousin was not the kind of person who would do anything wrong. She had always been my idol and I fell madly in love with her.

I spent that whole summer hanging around with my cousin, as I did every summer on the island, and meeting some of her lesbian friends. I also spent a lot of time flirting with her next-door neighbor, a married woman who, from time to time, had affairs with women.

Finding myself in the middle of these new experiences I did not, at first, have any expectation about how I should behave. I was just trying to take in all the information I could about this new lifestyle which offered me the possi-bility of sharing both an emotional and a physical closeness with women.

Suddenly, I was cast into the role of a "butch" by the women around me, and I was expected to assume the behavior that went along with the role. My cousin's married friend led me to believe that being a lesbian, in my case, meant not only imitating the behavior of men, but also wanting to be one. Not knowing how to take the initiative in lesbian relationships, and feeling that I had to want to be a man physically in order to relate to women, the initial feelings of acceptance I felt when my cousin had come out to me turned to disgust. I began to feel I was a very sick person.

At the same time that I felt this disgust, I also really wanted to experience sexual relationships with women. Confronted with the notion that I could only express these feelings by choosing a "butch" or a "femme" role, I ac-cepted the label of butch. It allowed me the greatest amount of indepen-dence and control over my own life and those of other women. As a femme I would have been expected to accept all the oppressive subordinate roles society has assigned women and which I began to reject as a child.

When I returned to New York City at the end of the summer, I was more determined than ever not only to continue reclaiming my Puerto Rican identity, but also to learning what being a butch entailed.

Two years later at the age of eighteen, I came to the conclusion that the best way to deal with my sexual identity crisis and accelerate the process of reclaiming my Puerto Rican identity was to move to Puerto Rico. There I could attend the University of Puerto Rico where I could learn all I needed to know about Puerto Rican history and culture. I also hoped that moving there would strengthen the emotional ties between me and my cousin, and maybe one day, she and I would become lovers. Puerto Rico was the only place where I had gotten to know any lesbians, and so I moved there full of hopes and dreams.

In 1973, after two years in Puerto Rico, I read the book *The Colonizer and the Colonized*.[2] A whole new world opened up to me as I finally understood why I had become so confused about my cultural identity. I realized that the colonization and Americanization of all Puerto Ricans, whether they lived in Puerto Rico or the United States, was meant to foster the kind of confusion I had gone through for years. The object of the oppressor, the yankee, was to get us to a point where we would accept his definition of what Puerto Ricans are and should be. I realized that I did not have to feel guilty because I was confused, and that people in Puerto Rico, who had never visited the United States, were also going through a similar identity crisis.

Even though I was aware that I would never be accepted in Puerto Rico as a "true" Puerto Rican, that is, one who is both born and raised there, I resigned myself to that fact and felt secure in the knowledge that I had done all in my power to find out what was going on and fought to maintain and strengthen my Puerto Rican identity. I became a supporter of the Puerto Rican independence movement, and adopted a radical interpretation of history, which is still intellectually acceptable to me in many ways.

However, the more I identified as a radical, the more I felt alienated from myself as a lesbian. The supporters of the Cuban Revolution, at the time the model for all Latin American revolutionaries in "good standing," said that people like me were bourgeois counter-revolutionaries. The Puerto Rican male–dominated Left, on the other hand, found it understandable that I should have experienced a cultural identity crisis, but told me that I was sick for being a "homosexual." I got support on the one hand, but it was taken away from me with the other. Yet, the Puerto Rican Left was the only place I knew I could turn to for support as a Puerto Rican.

Though I was barely aware of the growing feminist movement, I felt the traditional Left prejudice towards feminism: that it was a white, middle class women's movement which divided the struggle of the masses along gender lines. I felt Puerto Ricans could not afford one more division in our struggle for national liberation. I was therefore not inclined to take advantage of the discussions on male/female roles which were taking place then, and which would have allowed me to question a lot of the butch/femme confusion I felt.

I was also not aware of the Stonewall Rebellion[3] which had, ironically enough, taken place in New York City during the summer of 1969 while I was in Puerto Rico confronting the lesbian issue for the first time. As a result, I could not take refuge in the growing support systems lesbians and gay men were creating during the early 1970s.

When I finished my undergraduate studies in Puerto Rico in 1975, I moved to Chicago to get my master's degree. On returning to the United States, I brought with me anger towards the oppressor that I did not know I had bottled up inside me. I had felt anger while I was in Puerto Rico, but I was not aware of its extent till I had to confront the yankee face-to-face every day once again, especially as an instructor. I also brought with me the pain of feeling sexually sick. I had settled one identity crisis only to find out that I had another one to deal with. The pain I felt led me to constant drinking, depression, suicidal thoughts, self-hatred, and shame. My response was to isolate myself from practically everything and everyone around me. I became obsessed with trying to be bisexual.

When I finished my studies in Chicago in 1978, I moved to New York to begin my PhD. After only six days in New York I did something which was totally out of character for me at the time: I joined El Comité Homosexual Latinoamericano (COHLA; the Latin American Homosexual Committee), a group of Latin American lesbians and gay men who were dealing with the issues of coming out, relating to families, lovers, etc. By the time I joined COHLA I knew I could not deal with the homophobia around me alone, though I was still not aware how I was oppressing myself. All I knew was that I needed help and I was ready to look for it. I was able to take this step because I became aware that things were a little more complicated than the traditional Left had led me to believe.

Shortly after joining COHLA, I became an active member of the New York City Coalition for Lesbian and Gay Rights and joined the 1979 National March on Washington for Lesbian and Gay Rights. With these organizations providing a new support system for me, I was able to fully embrace my lesbianism and come out as a lesbian within the Puerto Rican and U.S. Left. I learned that I did not have to push aside my concerns as a lesbian in order to have the "right" to be a part of the people's movement for a socialist society.

However, it was within the lesbian and gay rights movement that I became increasingly aware of the sexism which permeates male-female relations in our society. I also became more conscious of how racism and middle class prejudices prevent our movement from becoming a truly democratic one.

Searching for a place in which I would finally be accepted for who I am, I joined the feminist movement. It was then that I came to understand why and how women are expected to play a subordinate role in our society in order to ensure the privilege of men. I realized that the butch/femme role models I had been offered when I first came out served to perpetuate hetero-sexual stereotypes and the domination of one human being by another — this time within a lesbian context.

But in the feminist movement, once again I experienced disappointment as racism and middle class prejudices, as well as the homophobia of some sisters, interfered with our ability to work together.

After many years of searching for "a" movement where all parts of me would be accepted, I finally realized that each of these movements could not *by themselves* bring about the kind of society which would ensure the eventual elimination of all forms of oppression. This is because each of them tries to force us to prioritize issues and, in this manner, to highlight some parts of our identity at the expense of others. I do believe these groups *must interact* with one another.

I, on the other hand, *must* take the responsibility of standing up for my rights and those of other oppressed people as well. I can only take this responsibility when I have come to terms with my past. After many years of struggling to be someone else's image of who I am supposed to be, I am coming to accept myself as I am. And I am the better for it.

NOTES

Thank you to Roz Calvert for the title.

1 Young Lords is a Puerto Rican political organization which advocates, among other things, self-determination for Latinos/as and all poor and oppressed people of the world; bilingual education; equality of the sexes, and an end to all imperialist wars.

ASPIRA is a non-profit organization geared towards the needs of Puerto Rican and Latino/a youth, particularly in the areas of educational retention programs designed to lower the dropout rate in schools.

2 Albert Memmi, *The Colonizer and the Colonized* (Boston, Mass.: Beacon Press, 1967).

3 On June 27, 1969, the police made a routine raid on the Stonewall Inn, a lesbian and gay bar on Christopher Street, in Greenwich Village in New York City. This time patrons of the bar responded with a three-day riot which led to the rise of the modern lesbian and gay rights movement.

COLIN ROBINSON

The Mechanic (1998)

Long strokes,
He urges, between breaths,
Gently guides my touch
Along his rigid spine.
All the way down.
Down, my fingers think,
Clambering over the dense tufts where
His legs separate:
With a splash,
His muscles rise
Naked in the tub,
Push against my yearning
Sponge.
We both blink
Ourselves back from
This daily brink.

His grease has crawled up under
My raveled fingernails:
He comes here each day,
After hours of work
Fingering engines to life
In the shed next door,
Sits in the tub;
Tells stories of his wife
And three children back in Carriacou,
The two sons here,
The goats.

He would smile
Whenever he caught me staring
At him from the house.
You does like to watch me work?
He asked last May —
Our first words in a year;
In silence polishes the fender he had
Straightened that morning,
The oversize blue overalls
Sliding back and forth
Over each contour of his unclothed body.
Long strokes,

He winks at me,
Sharing the secret to the gleaming shine.
Suddenly he turns toward me;
My eyes, still locked
On the troubling movement in his trousers,
Dart quickly upwards.
Sheepishly he clasps his hand
Over his loose, hardening dick,
Eye to eye, grins:
You see I need to pee real bad.
I open the door,
Silently shepherd him into the narrow hallway,
My flank brushes
His blue surface.

He opens the door wide,
Stands over the bowl,
Raising his voice over his noisy stream:
It doh even have a standpipe in de shed.
He offers a wet hand in thanks,
Stumbles for language,
Fumbling in an inner pocket for
An immigration form and an old Bic.
Is so much books you have . . .
You does like to read . . .
Hesitates, releases the thought:
You could help me write something?

He makes some halting letters on the page,
Staring into my eyes for guidance,
Pauses;
My left hand, like a child's, grasps
The leathery back of his
To form in cursive: I pledge.
Long strokes,
I smile up at him,
Tonight come back
And clean up;
We can finish then
— my betrothal.

The rest is ritual:
Every day he comes,
Just once,
Without knocking;
I notice the sound of his
Frothing piss,
The faucet running,
The moan of his torso against the hot water,
The scrub brush struggling
Through the coarse hair on his chest.

Hearing me stir,
He talks loudly
Through the always ajar doorway —
Some story about home
— Or people from home here.
I enter, without knocking,
To listen,
Sit on the unflushed bowl;
Lazily pick up the sponge:
You back still black.
He shudders:
Long strokes;
Lies in the blackened water,
Eyes closed;
Will not move,
Waiting

Until I reach down
Below his waist —
He rises with a splash:
Without words,
Dries, dresses,
Wraps his arms around me,
Calls me son,
While his overgrown fingers stuff a dollar
All the way into my front pocket,
Slip a quarter in my back,
Scraping his stubbled chin
Against my forehead.

Pulling them out with sweaty palms,
I protest.
Use it for soap,
He insists,
Squeezing all the air out of me.

Haiti: A Memory Journey (1996)

Early Friday morning, February 7, 1986, drinking champagne and watching televised reports of Haitian President-for-Life Jean-Claude "Baby Doc" Duvalier fleeing for his life aboard a U.S. Air Force plane, I can't help but reminisce about my childhood experiences, and reflect on the current political and social situation, along with my expectations as a gay man who was born and grew up there.

Having seen, so many times during this AIDS crisis, Haitian doctors and community leaders deny the existence of homosexuality in Haiti; having heard constantly that the first afflicted male cases in Haiti were not homosexual, but alas, poor hustlers who were *used* by visiting homosexual American tourists who infected them and thus introduced the disease into the country; having felt outrage at the many excuses, lies, denials, and apologies — I am duty-bound to come out and speak up for the thousands of Haitians like me, gay and not hustlers, who, for one reason or another, struggle with silence and anonymity yet don't view ourselves as victims. Self-pity simply isn't part of my vocabulary. Haunted by the future, I'm desperate to bear witness and settle accounts. These are trying times. These are times of need.

For years now, Haiti has not been a home but a cause to me. Many of my passions are still there. Although I did my best to distance myself from the homophobic Haitian community in New York, to bury painful emotions in my accumulated memories of childhood, I was politically concerned and committed to the fight for change in my native land. It's not surprising that the three hardest yet most exhilarating decisions I have faced had to do with balancing my Haitian roots and gay lifestyle. The first was leaving Haiti to live in the United States. The second was going back to meet my father for the first time. The third, tearing up my application to become a U.S. citizen. Anytime one tries to take fragments of one's personal mythology and make them understandable to the whole world, one reaches back to the past. It must be dreamed again.

I was born on October 2, 1957, one week after François "Papa Doc" Duvalier was elected President. He had been a brilliant doctor and a writer of great verve from the *Griots* (*Négritude*) movement. Until that time, the accepted images of beauty in Haiti, the images of "civilization," tended to be European. Fair skin and straight hair were better than dark and kinky. Duvalier was black pride. Unlike previous dictators who had ruled the country continuously since its independence from the French in 1804, Duvalier was not a mulatto and did not surround himself with mulattoes, a mixed-race group which had long controlled the economy. Duvalier brought vodun to the forefront of our culture and, later in his reign, used it to tyrannize the people.

I grew up in Les Cayes, a sleepy port city of twenty thousand in southwest Haiti, where nothing much happened. Straight A's, ran like a girl, cute powdered face, silky eyebrows — I was the kind of child folks saw and thought quick something didn't click. I knew very early on that I was "different" and I was often reminded of that fact by schoolmates. "*Massici*" ("faggot" in Creole), they'd tease me. That word to this day sends shivers down my spine, but, being the town's best-behaved child, a smile, a kind word, were my winning numbers.

We — Mother (a registered nurse anesthetist), Grandfather (a lawyer who held, at one time or another, each of the town's top official posts, from mayor on down), Grandmother, and I — lived in a big, beautiful house facing the cathedral. The Catholic Mass, especially High Mass on Sundays and holy days, with its colorful pageantry, trance-inducing liturgy, and theatrical ceremony, spellbound me. And that incense — that incense took me heaven-high each time. I was addicted and I attended Mass everyday. Besides, I had other reasons. I had developed a mad crush on the parish priest, a handsome Belgian who sang like a bird.

I must have been seven when I realized my attraction to men. Right before first communion, confused and not making sense, I confessed to this priest. Whether he understood me or not, he gave me absolution and told me to say a dozen Hail Marys. Oh Lord, did I pray. Still, girls did nothing for me. Most of my classmates had girlfriends to whom they sent passionate love poems and sugar candies, and whom they took to movies on Sunday afternoons. All I wanted to do with girls was skip rope, put makeup on their faces, and comb their hair. I was peculiar.

Knowing that I probably would never marry, I decided that I wanted to be a priest when I grew up. For one, priests are celibate, and I had noticed that many were effeminate. Some even lisped, like me. I built a little altar in my bedroom with some saints' icons, plastic lilies, and colored candles, and dressed in my mother's nursing uniform and petticoat. I said Mass every night. The Archbishop of Haiti, François W. Ligondé, a childhood friend of my mother and uncles, even blessed my little church when he once visited my family. I was so proud. Everybody felt that I'd be the perfect priest, except my mother, who I later found out wanted me to become a doctor like my father — who I never met, never saw pictures of, never heard mention of, and accepted as a nonentity in my life.

I used to believe that I was born by Immaculate Conception, until one day I was ridiculed in school by my science teacher, who had asked me for my father's name. When I told him of my belief, he laughed and got the entire class to laugh along. Until then, I had never questioned the fact that my last name was the same as that of my mother, who was not married. It was then that I smelled foul play and suspected that I was the result of sexual relations between my mother and grandfather. I didn't dare ask.

In the early 1960s, Papa Doc declared himself President-for-Life, and things got worse and worse. I remember hearing of anti-Duvalier suspects being arrested. I remember hearing of families being rounded up and even babies being killed. I remember the mysterious disappearances at night, the mutilated corpses being found by roads and rivers the next day. I remember the public slayings, adults whispering and sending my cousins and me to another room so they could talk. Rumors of invasions by exiled Haitians abounded. Some of these invasions were quickly stopped by government forces. The *tontons macoutes* (boogeymen) were everywhere, with their rifles slung over their shoulders and their eyes of madness and cruelty.

Poverty was all around me and, in my child's mind, I had accepted this. Some had, some had not. Fate. Cyclones, hurricanes, floods came and went. Carnival was always a happy time, though. Dressed in a costume, I, along with thousands, took to the streets each year with our favorite music bands. Grandmother died during Mardi Gras '65. I was miserable for weeks and kept a daily journal to her. Soon after, Mother left for Switzerland and I moved in with my Aunt Marcelle and her husband.

In 1968, my aunt had her first and only child. Was I jealous! I had been quite comfortable and so spoiled for three years that when she gave birth to Alin, it was difficult for me to accept that I was not her real child, a fact I'd at times forgotten. That year she gave me a beautiful birthday party. My schoolmates were making fun of me more than ever. I still wanted to be a priest. I said a Mass for Martin Luther King Jr. and Bobby Kennedy, when each was assassinated. Duvalier declared himself the flag of the nation and became more ruthless. I took long walks on the beach by myself. It was a year of discovery.

One afternoon, I saw Pierre swimming alone. He called me to join him. I was surprised. Although we went to the same school and we had spoken to each other once or twice, we were not buddies. Three or four years older, tall and muscular, Pierre was a member of the volleyball team and must have had two or three girlfriends. I didn't have a swimsuit, so I swam naked. I remember the uneasiness each time our eyes met, the tension between us, my hard-on. We kept smelling each other out. He grabbed me by the waist. I felt his hard dick pressing against my belly. Taut smiles. I held it in my hand and it quivered. I had never touched another boy's dick before. I asked him if he had done this with other boys. He said only with girls. Waves.

He turned me around and pushed his dick in my ass. Shock. I remember the pain. Hours later, the elation I felt, knowing that another person who was like me existed. In Les Cayes, there had been rumors about three or four men who supposedly were homosexual, but they all were married. Some had no less than seven children. Knowing Pierre was a turning point for me. The loneliness of thinking that I was the only one with homosexual tendencies subsided.

In 1969, man walked on the moon. I was happy. Pierre and I met each other three or four times (once in my grandfather's study, and he almost caught us). I didn't say anything about this to anyone, not even in confession. I didn't pray as much. I passed my *certificat,* which was like graduating from junior high school in the U.S. Mother moved from Geneva to New York City, where I visited her in the summer of 1970. To me, New York was the Empire State Building, the Statue of Liberty, hot dogs and hamburgers, white people everywhere, museums, rock music, twenty-four-hour television, stores, stores, stores, and subways.

I remember the day I decided to stay in the U.S. A week before I was to go back to Haiti, my mother and I were taking a trip to Coney Island. Two effeminate guys in outrageous short shorts and high heels walked onto the train and sat in front of us. Noticing that I kept looking at them, my mother said to me that this was the way it was here. People could say and do whatever they wanted; a few weeks earlier thousands of homosexuals had marched for their rights.

Thousands! I was stunned. I kept thinking what it would be like to meet some of them. I kept fantasizing that there was a homosexual world out there I knew nothing of. I remember looking up in amazement as we walked beneath the elevated train, then telling Mother I didn't want to go back to Haiti. She warned me of snow, muggers, homesickness, racism, alien cards, and that I would have to learn to speak English. She warned me that our lives wouldn't be a vacation. She would have to go back to work as a night nurse in a week, and I'd have to assume many responsibilities. After all, she was a single mother.

That week I asked her about my father and found out that they had been engaged for four years while she was in nursing school and he in medical school. She got pregnant and he wanted her to abort. A baby would have been a burden so early in their careers, especially since they planned to move to New York after they got married. Mother wouldn't abort. She couldn't. Though the two families tried to avoid a scandal and patch things up, accusations were made, and feelings hurt. Each one's decision final, they became enemies for life.

ANDREW SALKEY

Johnnie, London, 1960 (1960)

(from *Escape to an Autumn Pavement*)

It was Christmas Eve. Ten-thirty in the morning. My mother's Christmas card and a letter had arrived about a quarter of an hour before. I had re-read it for the fourth time and was about to read it again when Laura, our flat-keeper, walked in, slightly winded and, as I expected, extremely talkative.

"My Lord! Those stairs! They'll be the death of all of us, one day. Up and down, up and down, and at my age it'll never do. And what do you get out of it in the long run? Nothing!" Pause. Staccato breathing. Final disgorging exhalation. "Letter from home, love?"

"Yes, Laura. From my mother."

"Nice and hot over there, I bet. All those white sand beaches, no blooming smog, and what's the place called . . . ?"

"What place?"

"Monty . . . Montygo . . . ?"

"Montego Bay, you mean?"

"Yes. One of my nieces went out there. Married to an engineer, you know. Nice boy. Steady and shrewd. Very shrewd. Clever but nice, mind you."

She rummaged in her shopping basket and brought up her indispensable packet of Weights.

"Want one, love?"

"Thanks."

"I can never understand why your people come over here. I mean to say, it doesn't make sense; all that lovely climate, and being among your own kind. You can't ask for more than that now, can you?"

"I suppose not."

"What sort of answer's that? 'I suppose not?' You ought to more than 'suppose not' about a thing like that. I mean to say who should miss the sun more than you? Who knows his own kind more than you?"

"Yes, Laura. You're right about that."

"Anyway, there must be reasons, mustn't there? We all have our problems. Take your Mr. Snape, for instance. A real nice young man, he is. Well brought up and well schooled from the sound of him. And where's he got? What's he got himself out of it? Nothing. Now I ask you, with looks and education as he's got he should be commanding a real big position somewhere. I'm telling you, love, that this country is turning sour for all of us. Canada is the place! Or even America. Those are the countries in the lead nowadays. I can see a lot of things from where I stand, you know. A lot of things!"

"I don't suppose Dick would like to go to either of those two places, Laura. D'you think so?"

"Mr. Snape is a young man, love. And all young men benefit from a bit of foreign travel, that's what I say."

She picked up her shopping basket and sighed slightly theatrically. I looked away. She mumbled something else and walked towards the kitchen.

I fumbled with the air-letter form, spread it out on my knees, and read it again:

My dearest Son,

Your letters tell me that there's something troubling you. You must remember that I'm good at reading between the lines. I've had enough experience; first your father, and now you. I sense a certain unrest. A certain, shall I say, nervousness and anxiety? Yes?

Whatever is the matter, my son? Can't you tell your own mother? I've always been your confidante. Ever since you were a child, you've always come to me with all your little problems; and haven't I helped you to solve them?

You're spending yet another Christmas away from home, and I suppose you've made plans for the holidays. Have you? Where will you have Christmas dinner? Remember to go to church on Christmas Eve night. You've never missed a midnight Mass while you were at home; don't start slipping now, son. Please.

I'm glad that you've received your pudding intact. One can never tell about the Parcel Post these days, can one, my love? They throw things around so ruthlessly that the parcels I've sent abroad have arrived on only my prayers, if you know what I mean. I worry and worry until I hear they've arrived safely. I'm still the old worrier you left behind; as you can see by this letter. I've never been able to relax; not properly, anyway. There has always been something to occupy my mind — some private anxiety, some insoluble or near insoluble problem.

I do worry a great deal about you, Johnnie. There's no use your telling me not to. You're so much a part of my life that I'm unable to live one whole day without thinking about your progress in England.

Do, son, try to make friends and not enemies of the people with whom you come in contact. You're always being watched and criticized. It's only natural that you will want to spread your wings a bit — you know the sort of things I mean — attend dances, go out drinking with your pals, take out girls, that sort of conduct may be innocent enough, but you can't exactly see around corners so be on "the best" as I've always preached, son. Don't let down my grey hairs at this late stage.

Do everything in moderation. And above all, watch your health. Do not take unnecessary risks. Wear the appropriate clothing for the season and do not go shedding your woollen things because of freak days. That's a temptation, a great temptation, especially for someone like yourself who's so accustomed to going about dressed scantily.

I shan't preach anymore.

Write soon and tell me all.

With all my love,

Mother

P.S.

Your father sends his regards, and so do a number of your friends.

My Christmas will be uneventful as usual. If only you were with me. Christmas dinner won't be the same. It hasn't been the same since you left, and won't be until you return. God bless you, my son. God bless you and keep your path safe and steady.

When things aren't going too well, do try to remember that I love you with all my heart, very, very much, and always will. Bless you, again.

*   *   *   *   *

The rest of the morning cruised by me nervously, even a bit jerkily.

I escaped Laura by going for a walk in Trafalgar Square. I visited the National Gallery, stared at two Goyas, admired their sudden white lights and hurried back to the flat. Laura buttonholed me again. I escaped once more and bolted into a news theater in Leicester Square. I emerged an hour after that and went back to the flat to find a card from Fiona. She had enclosed a note:

My Darling Johnnie,

I haven't seen you since you left me in October. I got your address from a girl who works at your club. I think she said her name was Biddy.

I came to see you last Tuesday but unfortunately it was your night off. I would have come straight along to see you, but I thought better of it.

I miss you terribly, more than you'd ever imagine. I often cry over you. Indeed, even at this moment. I never thought that I'd ever be able to cry over a man. But there you are!

Can you come up to see me at about one to one-thirty on Christmas Eve day? Gerald won't be at home.

Do try to come. No ties. Purely, as they say, a social visit.

Love, Fiona

I tore up the envelope and her note. I threw away the envelope but kept the bits of the note, which I rearranged and pasted together fifteen minutes later. I placed her card on the mantelpiece and looked at the time. It was ten minutes to one.

I asked myself: why do I want to keep her note? Why? I got no answer. I don't suppose I really wanted one. I don't suppose I'd ever admit my own confusion.

I looked at the time, again, and left the flat. The stairs seemed to creak more loudly than ever before. A kind of warning I imagined. A rebuke. I felt like the child about to steal sugar from a very tall cupboard which he has to climb to reach. I was descending. That was the difference, and I knew it.

As I walked to Piccadilly Circus, I kept squeezing and relaxing Fiona's note in my overcoat pocket and wondering what I'd tell Dick if he found out what I had done to him in a moment of confused loyalties; in a moment of confused selfishness was more like it, I thought. I bought a train ticket for Finchley Road.

I suddenly realized that everything would be all right. Fiona could never get me to betray Dick's confidence in me. She could never make Dick take second place. She could never make me do what I didn't want to do. I was positive about that. I was adamant. The rhythm of the train seemed to help to convince me: *you know you're right; you know you're right; you know you're right.* And of course, I felt as if I knew that everything was working out satisfactorily for Dick and myself.

I began, after that, to look forward to my visit; I'd say such and such a thing, and I'd answer her questions in such and such a way. I had it all planned. We were all going to have a very happy Christmas; nobody would be hurt; Fiona wouldn't be hurt; Dick and I would be together; and the smooth surface of our individual lives would remain unruffled. Calm. Calm for all in a suspect sea of submarine fears and anxieties.

I knew it would be that way; after all's said and done, I knew what to expect of Fiona, despite her warning that it would be "purely a social visit." Perhaps that's why I was on my way to see her. She'd try to trap me. She'd implore. And I'd refuse. Not reject, mind you. Just gently refuse to comply. Maybe even a little bit slightly firmly if it came to that. I knew all this.

I was prepared for Fiona, the siren of a thousand loves. And this made me feel free and easy. The rhythm of the train continued to reassure me. I grabbed at it. Wallowed in it. Never wanted it to stop, in fact.

Finchley Road looked moth-eaten and raw. Very raw. After the bright lights of the West End, the old, friendly road seemed desperately sick and passive. The street lamps were too slender; the pavement was damp and dirty; the plane trees were skinny and battered.

The front door was open. Her sitting-room door was unlocked. I walked in and stood by the first armchair. There she was, in front of me, fresh and a little flushed with expectancy.

She rose and said: "I'm glad you could make it, Johnnie. Come and sit next to me."

To the point and warm, all at the same time. She sat beside me, turned slowly to my left, and stared at me intently. Her eyes rested on my clenched fist. I felt exposed. She had seen through me, as usual. She had unearthed my secret plan, my plan of power over her, my petty strength, my ineffectual false pride.

Everything that had given me courage on the train journey slipped away from me suddenly. I hoped I wasn't showing my terror too plainly. In one sentence, "Come and sit next to me," she had established her position. She had established her assurance. She had proved her knowledge of my eggshell resistance. I was uncomfortable and I tried, for all it was worth, not to show it. Even the clenched fist was my way of not proving her right.

"You're just as nervous, just as tense, aren't you?" she said casually, scoring her point like a professional, restrained and assured, assured of her charm and intention to get to the point. A trace of a smile darted between us. She was playing her part with enviable competence. "Now, what about something to drink?"

"What have you got?"

"A roomful. Rum, Scotch, gin, vodka, wine, sherry, port, beer."

"Scotch'll do fine."

She moved about quietly.

"Soda?"

"No. Straight."

She sat beside me and threw back her head. Addressing the ceiling, she said slowly, almost tasting each word: "Got you!" She paused for about five seconds and continued: "So I've actually got you to come, and, I suppose, much against your better judgment?"

"What?" Stupidly, I pretended not to understand.

"I've got you, at last, Johnnie. I've got you to come and see me, I mean."

I said nothing. I drained my Scotch with an exaggerated sucking noise. She lowered her head and smiled.

"Another?"

"Please."

I'm going to enjoy every moment of this, I thought idly, playing with the idea of upsetting Fiona's plans for a one-woman show of grit and glamour.

I sipped my drink slowly this time.

"I don't suppose we're exactly strangers?"

"'Course we aren't, Fiona. Why do you ask?"

She eased herself down beside me. Her thighs felt large and hard. Her hair was perfumed delicately. She knew, at once, that her whole body was being appreciated, being acknowledged; the perfume of her hair, everything about her thighs, her breathing, her manner, had become a force outside herself. She knew that they could work for her in a kind of quick magic upon my numb senses; they could take the place of words of entreaty, words of revenge, words of bitterness, words of love, even.

The room had a sad stillness about it, a stillness of brooding and resentment, a stillness that carried a message of shock and bewilderment.

"I'm pregnant, Johnnie."

She was still all grit and glamour, despite the nature of her news. Her thighs felt a trifle harder and larger as she shifted her position to face me. She could afford to look majestically down on her captive, I thought quickly, as if in retaliation.

If only she had realized that her low cunning would be useless, impotent, I'm certain she would have tried another tack. Poor fool! She imagined she had trapped her witch doctor all over again! Joseph had returned to be sacrificed.

I knew it was now time for her to say something else; the pause had been long enough for her purpose. I hadn't offered anything. Silence worked wonders on Fiona. She hated it. It unnerved her. I toyed with the second Scotch and sipped it appreciatively.

She smiled sweetly. Her performance was admirable. She had eaten the entire book of rules. She was going to win, once and for all.

"Well, my darling, how're you going to explain this to Dick?"

"I don't think he'll be interested. D'you?"

"I can't say. I don't live with him."

Claws well-bared, she sprang at that one from a great height. At last, she began to show signs of anticipation. Anticipation of victory. Very bad for her position; very good for mine. After all, this was a kind of Good versus Evil demonstration.

Her calm was going, too. She fidgeted about and her breathing had become noticeably jerky and irregular. Her wonderful poise was going. I can't be sure that she knew that I was aware of all this, but I was, and that was what really counted in our little farce of a contest of wits.

"I'm nearly three months pregnant, Johnnie." Not exactly blurted out, but with a hint of passion behind it.

"Time does go quickly, doesn't it?" It was going to be like this the whole way through, and I was prepared to play my game as nastily as possible, as cautiously as possible.

"I'm pregnant!"

"By whom?"

"You, obviously!"

"Or Trado, or most of his friends, or the new tenant, or the ghost of Joseph come back to thrill you, or — "

"Stop it!"

"Why? Don't you want to hear how pregnant you really are? I'm willing to tell you; so listen. Listen carefully, my dearest, artful bitch! You're no more pregnant than the old dragon upstairs. You're as pregnant as you'd like me to believe, which means I don't believe, therefore you aren't. Now that we've settled that ruse, perhaps we can tackle plan number two. What else is there?"

"You black bastard!"

Obviously a personal, highly personal, translation of "Merry Christmas to you, Johnnie." "And Many Happy Returns" I was tempted to reply, but thought better of it.

"Another Scotch?" Wonderful recovery.

"Please."

She cooled rather smartly. Plan number two was in operation. And I was ready for it. I knew that I'd have to watch her closely this time. Just how far she'd go I wasn't certain.

"What's your life with Dick like?"

Here's my cue, I thought. Here's my time to play her silly; to play her like a die across a vast floor area, I comforted myself. I waited for her to return; she was taking a long time over the third drink. I hoped I'd get a drink of Scotch and nothing else. I chuckled at the thought.

She came up to me slowly. The glass was nearly full. I knew and she knew.

It was too obvious. We both smiled. Huge thighs grazed against me for the third time. Must have been intentional.

"Well, Fiona, life with Dick is very uneventful. It's steady. It's relaxing and it's happiness nearly all the time."

"A pack of lies!"

Just as I had expected. Yet, I ignored it like a bad smell in select company.

"It's simple and straightforward at the worst of times. And what's more we're free and able to lead the life we most desire."

"Sounds entirely false to me."

"But it would, dear, grasping Fiona. It most certainly would. Especially how relentless you are in your own miserable, greedy, over-sexed world."

"You always rose to my greedy, over-sexed moments, Johnnie. Or have you forgotten?"

"And probably will again, if you behave nicely."

That stung her as planned. Stung her way deep down. The large-thighed parasite!

"Johnnie, listen to me."

"I'm listening."

"I want to save you from making a fatal mistake."

"You do, do you?"

"I want to give you what's really yours."

"Yes?"

"I want to give you everything. I want to be everything that Dick is to you and more."

"What d'you think Dick is to me?"

"He's your lover, isn't he?"

"He's my best friend."

"What d'you mean?"

"Just that."

"Don't you make love to each other?"

"I'm sorry to disappoint you, Fiona, but we don't."

"Don't you sleep together in the same bed, like lovers?"

"Of course we do not!"

"But aren't people like Dick supposed to be . . ."

"Some are, I would, imagine."

"Are you trying to tell me that Dick's fidelity isn't based on some sort of sex or the other? I suppose he's different, is he?"

"He may not be. All I'm trying to tell you is that we do not make love to each other."

"I don't understand."

"Of course you don't."

"Explain it to me, then. Tell me why you left here and went off like a honeymoon couple. Tell me that!"

"I thought you knew."

"No, I do not!"

"All right, I'll tell you. I left here to be rid of you; to be rid of your overpowering passion; to be rid of your depressing sexuality; to be rid of the old lady upstairs; to be rid of your blasted Gerald; to be rid of one bloody tenement room!"

"Is that really all?"

"No. Above all, I left here because I couldn't stand being Joseph's gap-filler. I left because I wanted my freedom. Satisfied?"

"I should ask you that, darling."

"And my answer is yes. Yes! Yes! Yes!"

"So if the truth be known, Dick and yourself are merely sharing a flat. Is that it?"

"Yes, Fiona." I was firm about that, perhaps too firm, too passionately firm. But I would hit back nicely. I paused. She stared at me vacantly. I was waiting for that. "Now that's settled, are you still pregnant, Fiona?"

She must have been expecting it. She smiled graciously and nodded sheepishly: "No, Johnnie. No."

She wasn't even ashamed. She beamed at the hopeful views and moistened her lips. She didn't ask me this time; she refilled my glass, a good double shot. We were all going to have a very happy Christmas and no doubt about it. We were simmering in it: she wasn't pregnant, and I wasn't homosexual! At least one of her needs had been satisfied. She felt all woman again. Her pride had been restored to its dizzy eminence. Her belly was crying out once more for the hot coals of a man's pummelling embrace. Her thighs were warming up dynamo-style. The agony had begun in a new vein.

We sat and talked about Shakuntala, the old lady, Trado, ourselves. Then she introduced the first positive sign of her infernal greed: she asked me whether I remembered how happy I had made her that morning on Hampstead Heath.

Well, even if I wanted to forget, I suppose it would have been impolite not to remember in the circumstance. So I remembered. Abdication is almost impossible! And she, too, remembered the whole affair as if it had happened yesterday. And off she went in an orgy of recollection. Her thighs were nervous, now. Reckless. She fanned them carelessly; she crossed them;

she lowered one and raised the other boldly; she shook them; she banged them together; and she banged me with them. She was having a wonderful time; not hers, the way of tranquil recollection. Oh, no! She was alive once more, and she agreed to celebrate her dingy rebirth like a carnival clown.

She was prepared, fully prepared, for her invasion; throbbing limbs, and all. I was not, however, willing to be invaded. But this didn't interfere with Fiona's progress. She warmed up with great gusto.

"You haven't kissed me, d'you know that?"

"You might become just a little bit pregnant if I do. Aren't you afraid?"

"Be serious, darling."

"I am being serious, Fiona. Dead serious."

She made an earnest grab at something or other, missed and collided with my left knee-cap. She wasn't, hurt, however. She giggled wickedly, rather like a six-year-old who's after buried treasure at the bottom of the garden. She swiftly changed position and made another earnest grab. She got it that time. How happy she seemed!

I didn't resist.

She worked diligently. I watched her impassioned progress and admired her economy of movement. She brought to her activity a certain intelligence, a certain private know-how; alarming to me at first, but to which I grew accustomed as she continued on her recklessly romantic way.

At least one person's Christmas Eve had begun with a sort of a bang. There was no denying it.

"You have come back to me, really and truly, darling? Say you have. Please."

"I most certainly have not."

"Don't spoil it. Please, Johnnie! Don't! For my sake!"

"Aren't you tired?"

"No. Never."

"Aren't you uncomfortable?"

"No. Are you?"

"Slightly."

And plan number two came into operation. I was almost whisked into the adjoining room where she'd prepared the battle-bed.

Perhaps to be too weak is a very bad thing. Perhaps to be only slightly weak is a very attractive thing: it generates hope of conquest. Fiona's animal energy thrived on it. It grew, expanded, and was bolstered by it.

Trado's battle-bed was more than adequate. Almost triumphal.

Until this day I never blamed the Scotch.

And so, amid a shower of promises to return; to love her forever; to make savage love to her *ad nauseam*; to be a man and not a mouse; to face up to reality *ad infinitum*; I left Fiona on Christmas Eve at about four o'clock, and got back to Piccadilly Circus by half past or thereabouts.

The flat looked appealing. Laura had gone out.

There was a splash of mail on the mat. I sank into a chair and opened the envelopes to me; I gathered up Dick's and put them aside.

There was one from Dick. Not a simple card in good taste as I would've expected from him but a rather gay and funny one. He had signed it: *With fondest regards from Dick*. I looked at the cover again. It was very funny indeed.

I laughed aloud.

Then, suddenly, I knew that I had to tell Dick about Fiona. Awkward. But admission of failure has always been an awkward exercise at the best of times, I consoled myself. Dick, I was sure, would be let down. After all, he had been trying his best to be my friend; to be an anchor; to be a bulwark against my attacks, my frequent attacks of escapism. I had let him down, and I had let myself *way deep down*; splendidly *way deep down*, and liked it, or at least the last half of it, anyway.

But I didn't feel somehow that Fiona had conquered. She had given me a lift, if you like, a cunning strength which I needed badly. She had given me something (call it resistance, call it experience), an independence. I had given in to her but had not been destroyed, as Dick would tell me when he found out what I had done. I felt that I could manage her assaults in the future. Take it or leave it was the result of our vulgar reunion.

I took out her note and placed it on the narrow ledge of the mantelpiece, the only uncluttered part left after Laura's Christmas card display. Dick would know that I wanted him to read it. He would know it was my way of making confession easy, without the usual mawkishness and waste. He would understand.

I had a scented bath, warm and bracing after the chilling time of preparing my confessional. I dressed and left the flat. I hoped that the atmosphere of the club would act as a distraction. I sincerely hoped so; the first time I ever had.

We were all going to have a through-train to happiness. We were all going to have an enjoyable festive season: a very merry Christmas, all round.

LAWRENCE SCOTT

I Want to Follow My Friend (1994)

1

Mrs. Wainwright kept an eye on the two boys. She held them within her orbit with the affectionate touch of a restraining hand, guiding their inhibited play, as they both leant out of the window of the school bus. She watched them and smiled, parting their hair with her fingers, musing on how quickly they had grown. The smaller boy was her son, Christopher, the other was his best friend, David.

David was coming to spend the Easter holidays with them.

"Christopher?" He tugged away from her, the breeze in his face. "Christopher, darling, why do you want to go to school at Mount Saint Maur?" Christopher did not turn to answer.

He shouted his reply to the wind, "I want to follow my friend." He shouted across the cane fields, swishing past, bringing the smell of burnt cane. His words were lost to his mother, but enjoyed by his companion.

The boys resisted her, not out of malice, but because of their instinct for play. They linked their arms around each others' shoulders, holding each other in their laughing eyes.

Eventually, when they were tired of leaning out of the bus, they rested back in their seats, their eyes watering from the wind in their faces. Mrs. Wainwright dabbed them with her handkerchief. And still the boys pulled back, squirming in their seats to avoid her attention. They were like small calves, all arms and legs.

Then, quite suddenly, as if by a miracle, their energy subsided and she was able to catch their attention. "Now, Christopher, I want you to tell me why you're so keen to go to Mount Saint Maur?"

Christopher, his mother's "little bearer of Christ," as she liked to call him, looked up into his mother's face and repeated seriously, "I want to follow my friend."

Mrs. Wainwright listened and stared, startled by the unusual seriousness of her young son.

"Yes, because I'm there," David said.

"I see," said Mrs. Wainwright, accepting what seemed an understandable response, yet nevertheless pondering her son's tone of voice.

The bus put them down near the Chapel of the Holy Innocents.

"Sybil, have you seen the boys?" Mrs. Wainwright called out to her cook the following day after lunch.

"No, madam, I think those boys in the fields playing."

Indeed, from her bedroom window, Mrs.Wainwright caught sight of Christopher and David disappearing from her sight, as they entered a field of young cane which was not to be burnt this year.

They would be safe, she thought. They would play and then be back at teatime.

Christopher and David ran on, deeper and deeper into the field of young cane. They felt that they were lost. When they looked up, they saw only the vivid blue sky, open and high, and the sun beating down.

They had been playing all morning nearer the house, in the yard itself, and climbing trees just beyond the hedge. Their play evolved, each making their demands and feelings known, bargaining for power, now David had it, now Christopher.

A whole imaginary world had been constructed in the sand-bank on the side of the bungalow. Losing themselves in this world, the two boys drove their toy cars and played at what they saw adults do. The struggle for a balance of power could go wrong here. It brought tears. Anger arose, and the kicking in of these self-created worlds.

After lunch they returned to their sand-bank, but the game no longer held its allure. In the heat, they sat on a bench and threw stones, seeing who could throw the farthest. But soon they were bored with this as well.

Then, a kind of silence fell between them. Then they had butterflies in their stomachs. They exchanged looks and brushed against one another, feeling the skin on their arms tingle with an excitement which was different from throwing stones, or playing with dinky cars, or even climbing to the top of the tamarind tree, hanging on for dear life in the high wind.

"Let's go to the cane fields," said Christopher.

"Yea, let's," David answered almost at once, as if they had had the same idea at the very same moment.

The field sloped increasingly. Eventually, they found themselves at the bottom of a gully. They were now quite far away from the bungalow.

No one would find them here.

They stopped running and sat down on the loose earth in the furrows between the rows of young cane. The wind sang through the serrated sugarcane grass. They each knew why they had come here. They did not talk. Without any suggestion from the other, each boy began to take off his clothes.

They were barefooted and forgot about what Christopher's father said about catching giggers.

Then they wrestled a little, laughing and tugging at each other's pants until they both fell on the ground. They pulled off their merino jerseys and squirmed in the soft, grainy earth, which stuck to their skin. Their small penises grew hard.

From farther down the gully, a train clanged along the line.

It was as if they were blind and feeling without seeing, touching each others' "totees," rubbing them in their hands, cupping the tight, small balls. Nothing happened, just this tingling feeling—a feeling to go on and on. But nothing happened. It felt as if something might, but it didn't. Finishing this game like their others, they began putting on their clothes again and tied their jerseys round their necks.

Out of the gully, they entered an orchard of fruit trees. They climbed, picked and sucked grapefruit, the juice dribbling down their chests.

When they got back to the bungalow, Mrs. Wainwright said, "Ah, there you are. Run along and have a shower."

That Easter holiday ended and Christopher looked forward to their August holiday together before he joined David at Mount Saint Maur.

2

"You'll have to be up at the crack of dawn." His father spoke with relish, remembering his school. "A cold shower."

Christopher smiled, trying to be brave. His mother ran her fingers through his hair soothingly.

"Sports, plenty of sports, young man," his father continued. "Make a man of you."

"Give him the present," his mother said.

Mr. Wainwright went off and returned with a long parcel. As it was presented to Christopher, both his parents looked on eagerly for his reaction.

No sooner had Christopher unpacked the cricket bat than his father took it from him. "Got to stay in your crease, and you have to watch for the ball as it leaves the bowler's hand." Mr. Wainwright knocked the bat gently on the tiles of the verandah. *Pock, pock.* "So," he said, looking like a batsman waiting for the ball. He kept tightening his grip on the handle of the bat and looking up again at the imaginary ball. He feigned a stroke, going out a little from the imagined crease to meet the imaginary cork ball. He then settled back into his crease again. He ran his hand along the smooth side of the bat. "You have to keep this well oiled, my man. We'll have to get you some linseed oil." He handed the bat to Christopher, holding it firmly in the middle with the handle towards his son. "You have a try."

Christopher's mind was filled with the terror of the imaginary cork ball. He had watched the Indian boys on the savannah. He had heard the hard knock of the leather on the wood. He had seen the ball speed through the grass to the boundary. He looked down at the bat. It felt heavy and awkward in his hand.

"Well, you'll have to learn fast, young man."

He heard his father. Young man.

His mother smiled encouragingly, but looked a little disappointed that he had not entered into his father's game.

Christopher put the bat in the spare room.

The house became filled with reminders of Christopher's imminent departure for boarding school. The Singer sewing machine was forever humming in the spare room. The floor was covered with threads and scraps of khaki and grey uniforms.

Christopher had to stand, to be measured and then for fitting. Pants and shirts were made a little too big. "He'll grow into them," Mrs. Wainwright said to Miss Sing, the seamstress.

Christopher heard his mother and father.

Make a man of you.

He'll grow into them.

At siesta, when his father had gone back to work, Christopher lay next to his mother on the big bed. He looked at her face. It was changing. When she had fallen asleep he tiptoed out of the room. At the door, he looked back at her. Her face looked sad. Then he thought what she might look like if she was dead. He did not want her to die. He did not want to go away. He did not want anything to change.

Christopher tiptoed downstairs to one of the servants' rooms which was used as a junk room. He closed the door behind him. The only light came through the cracks in the jalousies.

In the corner of the room, there was an old trunk with old clothes and old carnival costumes. Christopher took off his clothes. He rummaged around in the trunk for his favorite costume. It was made of muslin, hand painted. Yellow and black. A butterfly costume. It was encrusted with sequins and beads. He stood in the half light transformed by the costume. His body tingled.

This was his game.

Play was like a deep soft bed into which to climb. A warm pool in which to swim.

Then, at last, David arrived for the end of the August holidays.

They played their usual games, but then they crept into the junk room at siesta when the house was asleep.

They took off their clothes and dressed and undressed. Butterfly. Bat. Emperor. Red Devil. They changed and changed into funny hats and wire masks.

They played in the half dark with the cracks of light, piercing shafts laden with dust.

The rains were heavy. They played in the rain and in the canals at the bottom of the gully. They swam naked. Dried off in the rain.

Siesta. They had their twilight world, in from the blinding sun. It seemed that something would happen, but nothing did. It could go on and on.

On the last day of the holidays, Christopher and David went as usual to the junk room. The dressing-up trunk was not there. The room had been tidied up. The shutters were open. It was a dull room.

They soon found out why.

In the spare room, where all of Christopher's clothes and equipment for boarding school were accumulating, the boys found the trunk. It was empty. There were little sachets of mothballs and cuscus grass lying at the bottom. It stood on the floor empty. Waiting. Soon, Mrs. Wainwright would be packing the school uniforms, towels, linen, blanket, cardigans, and shoes. There was a new toothbrush and toothpaste, soap. They were all heaped up on the bed. All his shirts and pants, towels, and linen had a number, 59, sewn on with his name, Christopher Wainwright, in red.

The cricket bat with a tin of linseed oil and shiny red cork ball lay next to the clothes.

On the top shelf of the press the boys found their costumes neatly stacked away.

The boys stared.

Christopher heard his mother and father.

Make you a young man.

He'll grow into them.

3

Christopher watched his father's car from the portico of the school, round the bend, move along the avenue of casuarinas. He followed it with his eye until it became a dot.

He imagined his mother and father driving over the plains alone.

He continued to look out, long after their car had disappeared.

The horizon was different from here.

The first night he could not fall asleep. David was somewhere else in the dormitory. He was one year ahead. He didn't know the boy next to him. There was a dim nightlight outside Father Benedict's room, which would stay on all night. Next to his bed, the cricket bat leaned up against his locker. He touched it and smelt the linseed on his fingers.

As the first term continued, Christopher and David saw less and less of each other. At first they had held together, a new boy with his more experienced friend, then, without understanding what it was, some force was pulling them apart. David was chosen by other boys. He moved around in a gang. They weren't the boys Christopher liked. It was not safe to be on your own or to be with a single friend. There were loyalties and rivalries.

Boys who did not take part were sissies.

"Sissy, sissy," a boy called. Christopher's eyes burnt, but he would not show that he wanted to cry. His hurt was deep. His anger, furious. He did not know what it meant, this change, but it felt like they wanted him to disown something quite close and precious to him. Or, to give them something. He sensed what it might be.

Why did some boys belong to one gang and others to another? Why couldn't he belong to David's gang? Why couldn't he be alone with David?

Their games in the holidays were a secret. They had always been a kind of secret. But here, they were definitely not to be spoken about. In a way, what they did was a secret from themselves.

They avoided each other when other boys were around.

One afternoon, Christopher straggled behind the other boys back from the refectory after tea. He stood near a bonfire outside the woodwork shop. He was absorbed, kicking bits of wood into the fire and watching the shavings curl into the flames. Then he heard crunching footsteps on the gravel path. He turned to look. It was an older boy.

Christopher continued to throw bits of wood on to the fire. He watched the resin bubbling off the bark in the heat. Then he felt the older boy right next to him. The boy spoke softly. "I want to kiss you like if you were a girl." Then he walked away.

Christopher turned to say something. What should he say? "Wait."

The boy was well ahead of him. He began running up the steep, stony path to the college.

"Wait," Christopher shouted again, trying to catch up. Confused, but wanting to say something. "Wait." Christopher slipped on the gravel. The boy had lost him.

Christopher felt dejected. Something had stirred in him. He thought of how he had lost David. He turned back from where he had fallen and took the lower path into the forest behind the college. This was out of bounds, but he decided to risk it.

He felt like he used to feel when he was smaller and had climbed to the top of the tamarind tree. Dangerous. Quite quickly he was climbing into the hills, looking down on the college. He could see the other boys like little dots, running around. He kept from where other boys might be climbing themselves, finding secret places to smoke. He skirted the old scout's den with the list of measurements scratched forcibly into the wooden walls. *Timothy de Freitas has the biggest cock.*

Christopher found himself running now, slipping and grabbing hold of the young saplings. His heart was pounding in his chest. He had a stitch in his side. He was beginning to cry. His lips were trembling.

He reached a clearing where it was different from the shadows of the forest. The light was streaming down from the afternoon sky.

High in a blue sky, he saw a flock of green parrots. Then, suddenly, the air was full of their screams.

He was thirsty. He decided to head down to the valley where the river flowed over large rocks.

Suddenly, he saw it. His heart was in his mouth. A pink and black coral snake was entwined on a branch which lay across the track. He knelt down quietly and picked up a stone and a stick. He hit the branch with the stick and the snake slithered to the ground. But before it could slide away into the grass, Christopher threw his stone and then another and another, a large one falling on the snake. It was crushed.

Long after he knew that he must have killed it, Christopher continued to heap stones upon the snake, crushing its head. He was deliberate. He wanted it dead.

When he was finished he felt exhausted. He sat down and dried his eyes. Then he realized that all the while he had been crying.

Christopher found the river and drank from his cupped hands, lying on his belly across a rock.

In the days which followed, Christopher still wanted to talk to the boy who had said that he wished to kiss him. He didn't get a chance. He wrote him a letter, keeping it in his pocket. It burnt his leg with its presence.

Then he tore it into small pieces and threw it on the bonfire one afternoon, where he stood on the gravel path, straggling behind the other boys.

Waiting.

MAKEDA SILVERA

Man Royals and Sodomites:
Some Thoughts on the Invisibility of
Afro-Caribbean Lesbians (1992)

I will begin with some personal images and voices about woman-loving. These have provided a ground for my search for cultural reflections of my identity as a Black woman artist within the Afro-Caribbean community of Toronto. Although I focus here on my own experience (specifially, Jamaican), I am aware of similarities with the experience of other Third World women of color whose history and culture has been subjected to colonization and imperialism.

I spent the first thirteen years of my life in Jamaica among strong women. My great-grandmother, my grandmother, and grand-aunts were major influences in my life. There are also men whom I remember with fondness — my grandmother's "man friend" G., my Uncle Bertie, his friend Paul, Mr. Minott, Uncle B., and Uncle Freddy. And there were men like Mr. Eden who terrified me because of stories about his "walking" fingers and his liking for girls under age fourteen.

I lived in a four-bedroom house with my grandmother, Uncle Bertie, and two female tenants. On the same piece of land, my grandmother had other tenants, mostly women and lots and lots of children. The big veranda of our house played a vital role in the social life of this community. It was on that veranda that I received my first education on "Black women's strength" — not only from their strength but also from the daily humiliations they bore at work and in relationships. European experience coined the term *feminism*, but the term *Black women's strength* reaches beyond Eurocentric definitions to describe the cultural continuity of my own struggles.

The veranda. My grandmother sat on the veranda in the evenings after all the chores were done to read the newspaper. People — mostly women — gathered there to discuss "life." Life covered every conceivable topic — economic, local, political, social, and sexual: the high price of salt-fish, the scarcity of flour, the nice piece of yellow yam bought at Coronation Market,

Mr. Lam (the shopkeeper who was taking "liberty" with Miss Inez), the fights women had with their menfolk, work, suspicions of Miss Iris and Punsie carrying on something between them, the cost of school books. . . .

My grandmother usually had lots of advice to pass on to the women on the veranda, all grounded in the Bible. Granny believed in Jesus, in good and evil, and in repentance. She was also a practical and sociable woman. Her faith didn't interfere with her perception of what it meant to be a poor Black woman; neither did it interfere with our Friday night visits to my Aunt Marie's bar. I remember sitting outside on the piazza with my grandmother, two grand-aunts, and three or four of their women friends. I liked their flashy smiles and I was fascinated by their independence, ease, and their laughter. I loved their names — Cherry Rose, Blossom, Jonesie, Poinsietta, Ivory, Pearl, Iris, Bloom, Dahlia, Babes. Whenever the conversation came around to some "big 'oman talk" — who was sleeping with whom or whose daughter just got "fallen" — I was sent off to get a glass of water for an adult, or a bottle of Kola Champagne. Every Friday night I drank as much as half a dozen bottles of Kola Champagne, but I still managed to hear snippets of words, tail ends of conversations about women together.

In Jamaica, the words used to describe many of these women would be *man royal* and/or *sodomite*. Dread words. So dread that women dare not use these words to name themselves. They were names given to women by men to describe aspects of our lives that men neither understood nor approved.

I heard "sodomite" whispered a lot during my primary-school years; and tales of women secretly having sex, joining at the genitals, and being taken to the hospital to be "cut" apart were told in the schoolyard. Invariably, one of the women would die. Every five to ten years the same story would surface. At times, it would even be published in the newspapers. Such stories always generated much talking and speculation from "Bwoy dem kinda gal naasti sah!" to some wise old woman saying, "But dis caan happen, after two shutpan caan join" — meaning identical objects cannot go into the other. The act of loving someone of the same sex was sinful, abnormal — something to hide. Even today, it isn't unusual or uncommon to be asked, "So how do two 'omen do it? . . . What unoo use for a penis? . . . Who is the man and who is the 'oman?" It's inconceivable that women can have intimate relationships that are whole, that are not lacking because of the absence of a man. It's assumed that women in such relationships must be imitating men.

The word *sodomite* derives from the Old Testament. Its common use to describe lesbians (or any strong, independent woman) is peculiar to Jamaica — a culture historically and strongly grounded in the Bible. Although Christian values have dominated the world, their effect in slave colonies is particu-lar. Our foreparents gained access to literacy through the Bible when they were indoctrinated by missionaries. It provided powerful and ancient stories of strength, endurance, and hope which reflected their own fight against oppression. This book has been so powerful that it continues to bind our lives with its racism and misogyny. Thus, the importance the Bible plays in Afro-Caribbean culture must be recognized in order to understand the his-torical and political context for the invisibility of lesbians. The wrath of God "rained down burning sulphur on Sodom and Gomorrah" (Genesis 19:24). How could a Caribbean woman claim the name?

When, thousands of miles away and fifteen years after my school days, my grandmother was confronted with my love for a woman, her reaction was determined by her Christian faith and by this dread word *sodomite* — its meaning, its implication, its history.

And when, Bible in hand, my grandmother responded to my love by sitting me down, at the age of twenty-seven, to quote Genesis, it was within the context of this tradition, this politic. When she pointed out that "this was a white people ting," or "a ting only people with mixed blood was involved in" (to explain or include my love with a woman of mixed blood), it was a strong denial of many ordinary Black working class women she knew.

It was finally through my conversations with my grandmother, my mother, and my mother's friend five years later that I began to realize the scope of this denial which was intended to dissuade and protect me. She knew too well that any woman who took a woman lover was attempting to walk on fire — entering a "no man's land." I began to see how commonplace the act of loving women really was, particularly in working class communities. I realized, too, just how heavily shame and silence weighed down this act.

A conversation with a friend of my mother:

Well, when I was growing up we didn't hear much 'bout woman and woman. They weren't "suspect." There was much more talk about "battyman businesses" when I was a teenager in the 1950s.

I remember one story about a man who was "suspect" and that every night when he was coming home, a group of guys use to lay wait for him and stone him so viciously that he had to run for his life. Dem time, he was safe only in the day.

Now with women, nobody really suspected. I grew up in the country and I grew up seeing women holding hands, hugging-up, sleeping together in one bed, and there was no question. Some of this was based purely on emotional friend-ship, but I also knew of cases where the women were dealing, but no one really suspected. Close people around knew, but not everyone. It wasn't a thing that you would go out and broadcast. It would be something just between the two people.

Also one important thing is that the women who were involved carried on with life just the same; no big political statements were made. These women still went to church, still got baptized, still went on pilgrimage, and I am thinking about one particular woman name Aunt Vie, a very strong woman, strong-willed and everything; they use to call her "man royal" behind her back, but no one ever dare to meddle with her.

Things are different now in Jamaica. Now all you have to do is not respond to a man's call to you and dem call you sodomite or lesbian. I guess it was different back then forty years ago, because it was harder for anybody to really conceive of two women sleeping together and being sexual. But I do remember when you were "suspect," people would talk about you. You were definitely classed as "different," "not normal," a bit of a "crazy." But women never really got stoned like the men.

What I remember is that if you were a single woman alone or two single women living together and a few people suspected this . . . and when I say a few people I mean like a few guys, sometimes other crimes were committed against the women. Some very violent; some very subtle. Battery was common, especially in Kingston. A group of men would suspect a woman or have it out for her because she was a "sodomite" or because she act "man royal" and so the men would organize and gang rape whichever woman was "suspect." Sometimes it was reported in the newspapers; other times it wasn't — but when you live in a little community, you don't need a newspaper to tell what's going on. You know by word of mouth and those stories were frequent. Sometimes you also knew the men who did the battery.

Other subtle forms of this was "scorning" the women. Meaning that you didn't eat anything from them, especially a cooked meal. It was almost as if those accused of being "man royal" or "sodomite" could contaminate.

A conversation with my grandmother:

I am only telling you this so that you can understand that this is not a profession to be proud of and to get involved in. Everybody should be curious and I know you born with that, ever since you growing up as a child, and I can't fight against that, because that is how everybody get to know what's in the world. I am only telling you this because when you were a teenager, you always say you want to experience everything and make up your mind on your own. You didn't like people telling you what was wrong and right. That always use to scare me.

Experience is good, yes. But it have to be balanced; you have to know when you have too much experience in one area. I am telling you this because I think you have enough experience in this to decide now to go back to the normal way. You have two children. Do you want them to grow up knowing this is the life you taken? But this is for you to decide . . .

Yes, there was a lot of women involved with women in Jamaica. I knew a lot of them when I was growing up in the country in the 1920s. I didn't really associate with them. Mind you, I was not rude to them. My mother wouldn't stand for any rudeness from any of her children to adults.

I remember a woman we use to call Miss Bibi. She lived next to us — her husband was a fisherman, I think he drowned before I was born. She had a little wooden house that back onto the sea, the same as our house. She was quiet, always reading. That I remember about her because she use to go to the little public library at least four days out of the week. And she could talk. Anything you wanted to know, just ask Miss Bibi and she could tell you. She was mulatto woman, but poor. Anytime I had any schoolwork that I didn't understand, I use to ask her. The one thing I remember though, we wasn't allowed in her house by my mother, so I use to talk to her outside, but she didn't seem to mind that. Some people use to think she was mad because she spent so much time alone. But I didn't think that because anything she help me with, I got a good mark on it in school.

She was colorful in her own way, but quiet, always alone, except when her friend come and visit her once a year for two weeks. Them times I didn't see Miss Bibi much, because my mother told me I couldn't go and visit her. Sometimes I would see her in the market exchanging and bartering fresh fish for vegetables and fruits. I use to see her friend, too. She was a jet Black woman, always her hair tied in bright colored cloth, and she always had on big gold earrings. People use to say she lived on the other side of the Island with her husband and children and she came to Port Maria once a year to visit Miss Bibi.

My mother and father were great storytellers and I learnt that from them, but is from Miss Bibi that I think I learnt to love reading so much as a child. It wasn't until I move to Kingston that I notice other women like Miss Bibi . . .

Let me tell you about Jones. Do you remember her? Well she was the woman who lived the next yard over from us. She is the one who really turn me against people like that and why I fear so much for you to be involved in this ting. She was very loud. Very show-off. Always dressed in pants and man-shirt that she borrowed from her husband. Sometimes she use to invite me over to her house, but I didn't go. She always had her hair in a bob haircut, always barefoot and tending to her garden and her fruit trees. She tried to get me involved in that kind of life, but I said no. At the time I remember I needed some money to borrow and she lent me, later she told me I didn't have to pay her back, but to come over to her house and see the thing she had that was sweeter than what any man could offer me. I told her no and eventually paid her back the money.

We still continued to talk. It was hard not to like Jonesie—that's what everybody called her. She was open and easy to talk to. But still there was a fear in me about her. To me it seem like she was in a dead end with nowhere to go. I don't want that for you.

I left my grandmother's house that day feeling anger and sadness for Miss Jones—maybe for myself, who knows? I was feeling boxed in. I had said nothing. I'd only listened quietly.

In bed that night, I thought about Miss Jones. I cried for her (for me) silently. I remembered her, a mannish-looking Indian woman with flashy gold teeth, a Craven A cigarette always between them. She was always nice to me as a child. She had the sweetest, juiciest Julie, Bombay, and East Indian mangoes on the street. She always gave me mangoes over the fence. I remember the dogs in her yard and the sign on her gate. "Beware of bad dogs." I never went into her house, although I was always curious.

I vaguely remember her pants and shirts, although I never thought anything of them until my grandmother pointed them out. Neither did I recall that dreaded word being used to describe her, although everyone on the street knew about her.

A conversation with my mother:

Yes, I remember Miss Jones. She smoke a lot, drank a lot. In fact, she was an alcoholic. When I was in my teens she use to come over to our house—always on the veranda. I can't remember her sitting down—seems she was always standing up, smoking, drinking, and reminiscing. She constantly talked about the past, about her life. And it was always women: young women she knew when she was a young woman, the fun they had together and how good she could make love to a woman. She would say to whoever was listening on the veranda, "Dem girls I use to have sex with was shapely. You shoulda know me when I was younger, pretty, and shapely just like the 'oman dem I use to have as my 'oman."

People use to tease her on the street, but not about being a lesbian or calling her sodomite. People use to tease her when she was drunk, because she would leave the rumshop and stagger down the avenue to her house.

I remember the women she use to carry home, usually in the daytime. A lot of women from downtown, higglers and fish-women. She use to boast about knowing all kinds of women from Coronation Market and her familiarity with them. She had a husband who lived with her and that served her as her greatest protection against other men taking steps with her. Not that anybody could easily take advantage of Miss Jones; she could stand up for herself. But having a husband did help. He was a very quiet, insular man. He didn't talk to anyone on the street. He had no friends so it wasn't easy for anyone to come up to him and gossip about his wife.

No one could go to her house without being invited, but I wouldn't say she was a private person. She was a loner. She went to the rumshops alone, she drank alone, she staggered home alone. The only time I ever saw her with somebody were the times when she went off to the Coronation Market or some other place downtown to find a woman and bring her home. The only times I remember her engaging in conversation with anybody was when she came over on the veranda to talk about her women and what they did in bed. That was all she let out about herself. There was nothing about how she was feeling, whether she was sad or depressed, lonely, happy. Nothing. She seemed to cover up all of that with her loudness and her vulgarness and her constant threat — which was all it was — to beat up anybody who troubled her or teased her when she was coming home from the rumshop.

Now Cherry Rose — do you remember her? She was a good friend of Aunt Marie and of Mama's. She was also a sodomite. She was loud too, but different from Miss Jones. She was much more outgoing. She was a barmaid and had lots of friends — both men and women. She also had the kind of personality that attracted people — very vivacious, always laughing, talking, and touching. She didn't have any children, but Gem did.

Do you remember Miss Gem? Well, she had children and she was also a barmaid. She also had lots of friends. She also had a man friend name Mickey, but that didn't matter because some women had their men and still had women they carried on with. The men usually didn't know what was going on, and seeing as these men just come and go and usually on their own time, they weren't around every day and night.

Miss Pearl was another one that was in that kind of thing. She was a dressmaker; she use to sew really good. Where Gem was light complexion, she was a very black Black woman with deep dimples. Where Gem was a bit plump, Pearl was slim, but with big breasts and a big bottom. They were both pretty women.

I don't remember hearing that word sodomite *a lot about them. It was whispered sometimes behind their backs but never in front of them. And they were so alive and talkative that people were always around them.*

The one woman I almost forgot was Miss Opal, a very quiet woman. She use to be friends with Miss Olive and was always out of her bar sitting down. I can't remember much about her except she didn't drink like Miss Jones and she wasn't vulgar. She was soft-spoken, a half-Chinese woman. Her mother was born in Hong Kong and her father was a Black man. She could really bake. She use to supply shops with cakes and other pastries.

So there were many of those kind of women around. But it wasn't broadcast.

I remembered them. Not as lesbians or sodomites or man royals, but as women that I liked. Women whom I admired. Strong women, some colorful, some quiet.

I loved Cherry Rose's style. I loved her loudness, the way she challenged men in arguments, the bold way she laughed in their faces, the jingle of her gold bracelets. Her colorful and stylish way of dressing. She was full of wit; words came alive in her mouth.

Miss Gem: I remember her big double iron bed. That was where Paula and Lorraine (her daughters, my own age) and I spent a whole week together when we had chicken pox. My grandmother took me there to stay for the company. It was fun. Miss Gem lived right above her bar, and so at any time we could look through the window and on to the piazza and street, which was bursting with energy and life. She was a very warm woman, patient and caring. Every day she would make soup for us and tell us stories. Later on in the evening she would bring us Kola Champagne.

Miss Pearl sewed dresses for me. She hardly ever used her tape measure — she could just take one look at you and make you a dress fit for a queen. What is she doing now, I asked myself? And Miss Opal, with her calm and quiet, where is she — still baking?

What stories could these lesbians have told us? I, an Afro-Caribbean woman living in Canada, come with this baggage — their silenced stories. My grandmother and mother know the truth, but silence still surrounds us. The truth remains a secret to the rest of the family and friends, and I must decide whether to continue to sew this cloth of denial or break free, creating and becoming the artist that I am, bringing alive the voices and images of Cherry Rose, Miss Gem, Miss Jones, Opal, Pearl, and others. . . .

There is more at risk for us than for white women. Through three hundred years of history we have carried memories and the scars of racism and violence with us. We are the sisters, daughters, mothers of a people enslaved by colonialists and imperialists.

Under slavery, production and reproduction were inextricably linked. Reproduction served not only to increase the labor force of slave owners but also, by "domesticating" the enslaved, to facilitate the process of social control. Simultaneously, the enslaved responded to dehumanizing conditions by focusing on those aspects of life in which they could express their own desires. Sex was an area in which to articulate one's humanity, but because it was tied to attempts "to define oneself as human," gender roles, as well as the act of sex, became badges of status. To be male was to be the stud, the procreator; to be female was to be fecund, and one's femininity was measured by the ability to attract and hold a man and to bear children. In this way, slavery and the post-emancipated colonial order defined the structures of patriarchy and hetero-sexuality as necessary for social mobility and acceptance.

Socioeconomic conditions and the quest for a better life have driven steady migration from Jamaica and the rest of the Caribbean to the United States, Britain, and Canada. Upon my arrival, I became part of the "visible minorities," encompassing Blacks, Asians, and Native North Americans in Canada. I live with a legacy of continued racism and prejudice. We confront this daily, both as individuals and as organized political groups. Yet for those of us who are lesbians, there is another struggle: the struggle for acceptance and positive self-definition within our own communities. Too often, we have had to sacrifice our love for women in political meetings that have been dominated by the "we are the world" attitude of heterosexual ideology. We have had to hide too often that part of our identity which contributes pro-foundly to the whole.

Many lesbians have worked, like me, in the struggles of Black people since the 1960s. We have been on marches every time one of us gets murdered by the police. We have been at sit-ins and vigils. We have flyered, postered; we have cooked and baked for the struggle. We have tended to the youths. And we have all at one time or another given support to men in our community, all the time painfully holding on to, obscuring, our secret lives. When we do walk out of the closet (or are thrown out), the "ideologues" of the Black communities say "Yes, she was a radical sistren, but I don't know what happened; she just went the wrong way." What is implied in this is that one cannot be a lesbian and continue to do political work and, not surprisingly, it follows that a Black lesbian/artist cannot create using the art forms of our culture. For example, when a heterosexual male friend carne to my house, I put on a dub poetry tape. He asked, "Are you sure that sistren is a lesbian?"

"Why?" I ask.

"Because this poem sound wicked; it have lots of rhythm; it sounds cultural."

Another time, another man commented on my work, "That book you wrote on domestic workers is really a fine piece of work. I didn't know you were that informed about the economic politics of the Caribbean and Canada." What are we to assume from these statements? That Afro-Caribbean lesbians have no Caribbean culture? That they lose their community politics when they sleep with women? Or that Afro-Caribbean culture is a heterosexual commodity?

The presence of an "out" Afro-Caribbean lesbian in our community is dealt with by suspicion and fear from both men and our heterosexual Black sisters. It brings into question the assumption of heterosexuality as the only "normal" way. It forces them to acknowledge something that has always been covered up. It forces them to look at women differently and brings into question the traditional Black female role. Negative responses from our heterosexual Black sisters, although more painful, are, to a certain extent, understandable because we have no race privilege and very, very few of us have class privilege. The one privilege within our group is heterosexual. We have all suffered at the hands of this racist system at one time or another, and to many heterosexual Black women it is inconceivable, almost frightening, that one could turn her back on credibility in our community and the society at large by being lesbian. These women are also afraid that they will be labeled "lesbian" by association. It is that fear, that homophobia, which keeps Black women isolated.

The Toronto Black community has not dealt with sexism. It has not been pushed to do so. Neither has it given a thought to its heterosexism. In 1988, my grandmother's fear is very real, very alive. One takes a chance when one writes about being an Afro-Caribbean lesbian. There is the fear that one might not live to write more. There is the danger of being physically "disciplined" for speaking as a woman-identified woman.

And what of our white lesbian sisters and their community? They have learned well from the civil rights movement about organizing, and with race and some class privilege, they have built a predominantly white lesbian (and gay) movement—a precondition for a significant body of work by a writer or artist. They have demanded and received recognition from politicians (no matter how little). But this recognition has not been extended to Third World lesbians of color—neither from politicians nor from white lesbian (and gay) organizations. The white lesbian organizations and groups have barely (some not at all) begun to deal with or acknowledge their own racism, prejudice, and biases—all learned from a system which feeds on their ignorance and grows stronger from its institutionalized racism. Too often white women focus only on their oppression as lesbians, ignoring the more complex oppression of non-white women who are also lesbians. We remain outsiders in these groups, without images or political voices that echo our own. We know too clearly that, as non-white lesbians in this country, we are politically and socially at the very bottom of the heap. Denial of such differences robs us of true visibility. We must identify and define these differences and challenge the movements and groups that are not accessible to non-whites — challenge groups that are not accountable.

But where does this leave us as Afro-Caribbean lesbians, as part of this "visible minority" community? As Afro-Caribbean women we are still at the stage where we have to imagine and discover our existence, past and present. As lesbians, we are even more marginalized, less visible. The absence of a national Black lesbian and gay movement through which to begin to name ourselves is disheartening. We have no political organization to support us, through which we could demand respect from our communities. We need such an organization to represent our interests, both in coalition building with other lesbian and gay organizations, and in the struggles which shape our future — through which we hope to transform the social, political, and economic systems of oppression as they affect all peoples.

Although not yet on a large scale, lesbians and gays of Caribbean descent are beginning to seek each other out — are slowly organizing. Younger lesbians and gays of color are beginning to challenge and force their parents and the Black community to deal with their sexuality. They have formed groups, Zami for Black and Caribbean Gays and Lesbians and Lesbians of Color, to name two.

The need to make connections with other Caribbean and Third World people of color who are lesbian and gay is urgent. This is where we can begin to build that other half of our community, to create wholeness through our art. This is where we will find the support and strength to struggle, to share our histories and to record these histories in books, documentaries, film, sound, and art. We will create a rhythm that is uniquely ours — proud, powerful, and gay. Being invisible no longer. Naming ourselves, and taking our space within the larger history of Afro-Caribbean peoples. A dream to be realized, a dream to act upon.

Jerome (1993)
(from *Spirits in the Dark*)

That evening he was sitting on the bleaching stones when his father entered the yard astride a donkey Jerome didn't know he'd acquired. He dropped his machete before dismounting, and Jerome watched him silently surveying his seated profile against the growing dusk.

Earlier that afternoon, he had told his mother that he'd had a serious quarrel with a teacher. She wanted to hear the full story, but as he looked at the deep lines under her eyes and the pain already etched in her face, he postponed telling her.

After securing the donkey, his father returned and stood towering over him. "What yo' doing home in the middle o' the week? It not no holiday."

He didn't answer.

"Look, boy, yo' see I jus' come in from the land tired and everything, don' get my spirit vex up. I ask yo' a question and I expec' a answer."

Jerome still did not answer.

"Father in heaven, give me patience."

Pongy and Millicent came out in their yard. String was in his. Comsie hurried out from the kitchen.

"Henry, leave 'im alone, please." She said it pleadingly. "He get in trouble in school today with one o' his teachers and he not ready fo' talk 'bout it."

"Woman, yo' done gone out yo' head? What yo' mean he not ready fo' talk 'bout it?" His shouting brought more people out into their yards.

He watched his father turn to look at the gathering people. His father bowed his head and walked into the hut. Yawesi started to cry then, and his father picked him up.

Jerome ate no supper. His father ate sitting on the bleaching stones and then he summoned Jerome into the hut. "Now yo' will ha' fo' tell me everything that happen, from A right down to Z. And yo' better tell me everything, cause although this two by four build 'pon Mr. Manchester land, is still me that build it, and longst as I still have breath in my body when I ask yo' a question in here I want a answer, cause, as yo' well know, two bo'rattah can't live in the same hole. Now tell me what happen today."

"Don' be too rough with him, Henry. Go easy with that boy. I never see him like this before. We don' want a nervous breakdown 'pon we hands."

"Shut up, Comsie!"

His mother already knew that he had left his books at school and that he didn't even go to Miss Dellimore's before coming to the country.

He hesitated.

His father pounded his fist on the makeshift table and it came crashing down. Henry got up and walked out of the hut. He came back very late that night.

Next morning his mother took the bus to town. She felt she should apologize to Miss Dellimore for the anxiety his absence must have caused her, and she wanted to see the principal.

He awaited her at the canal bridge. She had his books and there were scaly patches below her eyes where the tears had dried. He was deeply saddened that he had pained her. He loved her dearly. But he'd already decided to put on a brave face. He knew he didn't matter in the scheme of things. Not even Bunyan was important. Bunyan too took orders. After his classmates' parents had heard the story they would threaten to withdraw their contributions to the school or to remove Bunyan if Jerome was permitted to return. He understood that very well. Yaw had opened his eyes and set him thinking long after he left. Not about the things Yaw would have liked, but thinking nevertheless.

When Comsie got into the yard, the weight of the day's woe seemed to be upon her, and she sank onto the bleaching stones.

"Go bring Wesi let me nurse him," she said, putting the sack of books down on the stones.

He brought out Yawesi, and his mother took out one breast and later the other, and his brother noisily sucked away at her milk. When he was finished she handed him to Jerome, went into the hut, changed into her home clothes, and set about preparing supper.

When his brother had fallen asleep, he joined her in the kitchen. She shook her head, brought her bare hands up to her eyes, and wiped the tears that had begun to flow again.

"Mr. Bunyan not taking yo' back. I never think I woulda live to see the day when I would go down on my knees in front of a White man. I do that today cause I know it important fo' yo' get yo' schooling. Is yo' only hope. I didn' know yet what yo' do. When he tell me the teacher catch yo' playing with she bottom, he self had to help me get up off the floor. Jerome, I never did know yo' was so stupid. I never know that."

There was a long silence while she peeled away at the tannias and occasionally adjusted the firewood under the iron pot.

"Well, Mr. Manchester estate out there. And when no work on it yo' can help yo' father on Miss Bensie farm." She said not another word to him until his father's arrival. It was as if she'd settled the matter once and for all. He could not understand it.

His father came home sooner that day. He came into the kitchen. "Comsie, what the head teacher tell yo'?"

"Henry, Jerome finish. Jerome try fo' feel up a White woman teacher from 'merica behind."

Henry walked into the yard. He came back about five minutes later. "Tell me the rest, Comsie."

"Nothing fo' tell, just that them expel him. That mean he can' go back to school. Henry, that is one coalpit that burn to ashes. Tree waste, labour waste, everything waste. God make mouth and He provide bread; is not so the world go?"

His father went to sit on the stones outside. His mother served him his dinner there. Jerome ate his in the kitchen.

After she finished washing the dishes and nursing his brother she said to his father, "Henry, you and me and Jerome have fo' sit and talk this whole thing over. When yo' have a half-rotten onion yo' does use the piece that ain't spoil."

They sat on the makeshift bench inside the hut.

"Who name Peter?" she asked him.

"A White boy in my class."

"I didn' know yo' go to town fo' friend up with White people. I did think yo' have better sense than that."

"Peter is no ordinary White boy. It's he who pushed his friendship on me."

"Go on! Dig out me eye!" his father responded.

"Well he say fo' tell yo'," Comsie said, "that he really sorry fo' what happen. He see me when me leave the head teacher office and he come up to me and he say, 'Are you Mrs. Quashee?' I nod my head and he say, 'Tell Jerome I'm coming out to the country to see him as soon as I find out where he lives. Tell him he must come to town on Saturday and see Mr. Morrison. Mr. Morrison gave me the message and I went up the hill to look for him and the lady I met there told me she didn't see him after he left for school. I told her he got into trouble at school and she said he probably went to the country.'

"Next thing, what yo' been writing in yo' book them?"

That question surprised him.

"Well, the head teacher read some things from one of yo' book them and it really frighten me. I don' know what fo' say. I never did think anybody what win scholarship so stupid."

"What he write in the book, Comsie?"

"Yo' know the blessed are the peacemaker part in the Bible? Well, Jerome take them and add his own words to them fo' make them sound blasphemous. And the book even have in rude words too about the same White woman that he try to feel up. Henry, we can't save this. It done gone sour."

"Go bring the book."

"He don' got it. Mr. Bunyan say he keeping it."

Jerome was frightened. He'd written everything in that book. He carried it around with him because he didn't want it to fall into anyone's hands. He had written a lot about Miss Blunt in that book, his feelings about White people, his growing affection for Peter, his opinions about Mr. Bunyan, the dreams about having sex with Errol and later Peter and the big question he was asking himself. He knew he could never stare Mr. Bunyan in the face again. Would Bunyan tell all the teachers what was in the journal? Did Miss Blunt read it? Was that all he had told his mother or was she hiding part of it from his father?

He never found out how much his mother was told. Once when she asked him whether he was seeing anyone, he had become suspicious. When Hetty had started telling people that there was something between them, his mother had looked relieved. He knew she wouldn't have told his father about that part, and he was sure that if she knew, she would have hoped for a miracle.

Boy-boy, his mother's first cousin, was gay. He'd been present many times when jokes were made about him and even more than jokes. He was a constant point of reference for what the society would not accept:

"You not no man, you is like Boy-boy."

"I see yo' talking with Boy-boy. What happen? Yo' turning weird?"

"What you know 'bout 'oman? Is Boy-boy yo' interested in."

The first August he was home on holidays, his mother had sent him to the shop over in Mercy village to buy salted cod, and Boy-boy was in the shop. Alice Bolton, who boasted sometimes about all the men she had slept with, and sometimes threatened to tell their wives — her tongue never stopped going just like her fat body that rippled in the see-through fabrics she sometimes wore — was there too. She went up to Boy-boy, placed her hand on his crotch, and shouted to the men drinking and playing dominoes in the far corner, "I never taste this yet."

"What yo' wasting yo' time for? That ain't gwine raise it head for you," said Alfred Boatswain.

"It gwine raise it head if yo' promise fo' let in by the back door," said a young woman Jerome did not know.

Everyone in the shop laughed.

"It have fo' smell shit first," said another rum drinker called Hardup. "Ain't me is right, Boy-boy?"

"Yo' not saying nothing on yo' own behalf?" Alice asked him.

Boy-boy remained silent. He moved only when Alice took away her hand, and Jerome could see that he was trembling.

During the first year when he went to work in the civil service and was living on his own in the capital, there was a very handsome fellow who worked on a road repair crew who had smelled him out and used to send messages to him. He refused to speak to the messenger; he didn't like him; he didn't look careful enough. The one who sent the messages was quite different though. Jerome never knew how he found out where he lived, but one Wednesday, when he only worked half-day, Jerome had met him standing at the gate to his rooming house.

"Yo' don' take my message them, so I come in person."

His biggest fear was that someone might see him talking to this fellow; that would have been enough for them to conclude that he was that way too. He didn't answer the fellow. He walked past him and began climbing the steps to his room. The fellow began to climb the stairs too. "If you follow me," Jerome told him, "I will call the police."

The fellow stared him straight in the face and said, "Who yo' think yo' foolin'? I can see in yo' eyes that yo' love me and yo' know I love yo.' What yo' so 'fraid for? Yo' will live fo' regret this."

He said nothing more to him, but he did not climb the stairs right away. He stared at him and he remembered Boy-boy and the pain his mother and Boy-boy's cousins and sisters were living through. Never. Never will his mother ever have to face that on account of him. And he had stifled his desires over the years. Each time that he saw this fellow on the street a slight chill went through his body. It happened for others too.

For twenty-seven years he kept the promise.

If Mr. Bunyan told Mr. Morrison about it, Jerome did not know because Mr. Morrison never mentioned it. If he told Peter, Peter never mentioned it to him either. How many people knew his secret? How many people had secretly passed on his secret? Was he a deaf person wondering why the world was so silent?

Fragments of Toronto's Black Queer Community: From a Life Still Being Lived (2005)

1

Every Sunday I go to church. Church Street, that is: the heart of Toronto's gay ghetto. My church, located at a gay bar, Crews and Tango, is presided over by three black drag queens: Miss Burundi, the newest addition to black queens in Toronto; Jackae Baker, the original circuit queen;[1] and Michelle Ross, legendary and incredible. No matter how bad a day I'm having, these three queens shift my mood from somber to jubilant — and sometimes, quite frankly, to extremely exuberant. Michelle and Jackae are of Caribbean descent; Miss Burundi is from continental Africa. I am beginning with a meditation on these three because I believe that black drag queens hold an important political and emotional place in the queer community that is often not acknowledged. These days much talk focuses on hidden black queers, "down low" sex, and the like;[2] out and proud black drag queens in racist, white gay male communities have all but gone missing. Rarely are these brave black men — who are out for all to see as both gay men and imitators of black and sometimes white women — given any consideration in discussions of black or, generally speaking, queer communities. These days, when folks write about queers, especially black queers, drag queens hardly get a mention. It is almost as though, despite their crucial importance to contemporary queer communities, queer liberation depends upon denying their presence in our midst.

Michelle Ross, who has performed drag in Toronto since the early 1970s, has enduring ties to Jamaica. Jackae Baker, a performer since the early 1980s, has similar ties to Guyana. These queens, along with others, are featured in the film *Divas: Love Me Forever. Divas* chronicles their lives as drag queens in Toronto and is described by its director, Edimburgo Cabrera, and producer, Anton Wagner, as "an eighty-one-minute documentary about desire, fantasy, self-acceptance and the search for love."[3] The film attends to a range of ongoing social and cultural issues that affect the lives of the (mainly, but not exclusively) Caribbean-descended men it features. What I find most poignant about *Divas* is its illustration of the ways in which black drag queens in Toronto have impacted the queer scene without so much as a public acknowledgment from anyone that their labor has been crucial to the development of what we might actually call a community. This lack of public acknowledgment makes many of their performances on Sundays particularly piercing, as the music they lip-synch produces deeper meaning vis-à-vis the economy of race, sexuality, and gender that they occupy and labor within. Black men, straight, gay, and otherwise, can learn from these queens about how to be men in a world that continually reproduces narrowly defined roles for us to play.

2

Learning how to be a man is one of the most difficult forms of labor for black men, especially when they are gay. Black masculinity is generally a reviled and dangerous performance; at the same time, it is a much copied performance. No black man can ever be sure, in his encounters with others, which of these performances he will be called upon to play: dangerous and threatening, or possessor of the mysterious, most wanted, most "loved" body. Black men, whether we recognize it or not, constantly negotiate between love, hostility, hatred, intimacy, violence, and all possibilities in between. How we perform through these extremes often determines much about our day-to-day existence in North America: when should we be outwardly "bad," when "cool," when coolly "bad"? Black masculinity, more often than not a performance of bravado, constantly requires its performers to assess the often threatening circumstances in which they find themselves in order to configure the range of the performance. Interestingly, black gay spaces are, among others, places where the tensions between these extremes are often quite evident.

The spaces of black masculine performance in contemporary North American popular culture are actually few, despite the overwhelming impact that black popular culture has had and continues to have on North American popular culture. These spaces—largely characterized by popular musical culture, fashion, and an urban cowboy aesthetic[4]—limit black men to a small number of roles (gangster or stud, for example). Although small, these roles have a tremendous impact on how other non-black men perform their masculinity—either in concert with black men or in opposition to them. Black men who fashion identities beyond, or contradictorily, in relation to these roles are misread in all kinds of ways — at the extreme sometimes vulnerable to danger (such as violence) from all sorts of men who, in a racist society constructed on patriarchal hierarchies, perceive them as threats.

One of the prevailing demands on black men is that we must be somehow "knowable" to ourselves but — most importantly — to others. That is, we must, as black men, fit preordained racialized scripts, which we have often had little or no part in drafting but must live up to. Such demands place an enormous amount of pressure on black men to conform to the limited roles offered us. All this is not to say that many of us do not take great pleasure in performing these limited roles, while simultaneously producing new and disturbing limited roles (such as the more recent "homothug" role)[5] for ourselves to play — evidence not only of how others attempt to delimit black men, but also of our own complicity with what the black feminist Patricia Hill Collins long ago identified as "controlling images": visual representations deployed to control the perception and assessment of black women.[6] Our complicity with this practice in regard to ourselves indicates the ways in which — regarding stereotypes about black masculinity — we have internalized and performed these reductive images as the essence(s) of our identities. These images (homothug, stud, drug dealer, etc.), many of them dangerously and damagingly negative, become *us*. Partly in complicity with the ideology behind controlling images, we perform these images of ourselves in numerous spaces in North American contexts; in a queer milieu, gay bars are one such place.

I know of no free-standing black gay clubs in Toronto. As opposed to definitively black clubs, "black nights" at general population gay clubs have characterized the scene in Toronto. But once a club's black night is advertised, the venue basically becomes a black gay club. The taint of blackness means that even one black night gives a club space the reputation of being a "black club," so that the place and space become firmly associated with black bodies even if not occupied by black bodies on every night of operation. Association and affiliation with blackness always seem to blacken.

In the mid- to late 1990s, Toronto's black night place to be in was the Red Spot, in the heart of the city's gay ghetto. After that, it was the Manhattan club, on the edges of one of Toronto's ritzy 'hoods. A black night has recently returned to the gay ghetto at the renamed Red Spot, now called Papi's. These moves all followed the career of one DJ, Blackcat. The move to Manhattan, however, was organized and run by two black lesbians. Their story, which still needs to be told, complicates the story I'm about to relay.

Manhattan was in full swing when media hype about the "down low" phenomenon broke. In the summer of 2001, I was asked by the now defunct Pride Vision TV (a Canadian national gay cable station, now called OUT TV) to comment on the phenomenon and to talk about the local club — Manhattan — where black gay men congregated. Among black men interested in other men, Manhattan had long been known as a place where those who were not out of the closet could go to meet other men. The club's reputation in this regard did nothing to address the fact that many of the black men who frequented it also were out — an important reality that complicated stereotypical thinking about black men, the "down low," and constant attempts to render black men the abject "others" of gay life. Pointing out that closeted white gay men went to white gay clubs to meet other men seemed to have little impact on many of the questions being asked and the conversations taking place at that time about the "down low." And yet we have Miss Baker and Miss Ross. What is to be made of all this?

3

One of the best sites for encountering black queer life in Toronto is at Blockorama, a party held within the context of the annual gay pride celebration in June. This party was established by a group of black gay and lesbian activists, community members, and artists, under the moniker of Blackness Yes, with the aim of bringing a cultural specificity and sense of identifiable queer black life to the overwhelming whiteness of the annual pride parade and its many parties. Blockorama — attended by gays from all parts of the African disapora, especially the Caribbean — illustrates how deeply diasporic black Canadian queer life, in its practices and identification with queer life beyond white Canadian contexts, remains. In this regard, African American black gay pride celebrations and Caribbean neighborhood block celebrations alongside Canadian forms of public parade and spectator culture — each a form of cultural creolization — might be seen as cultural parallels to Blockorama. Black Canadian queer life is an excellent barometer of how black Canadian diasporic identities cross a range of political and cultural agendas and concerns that spans the local and the extra-local. Black queers in Toronto are as interested in and connected to what is happening in Zimbabwe and Jamaica as they are to what is happening in Vancouver or Halifax. Thus, organizations like GLAD (Gays and Lesbians from the African Diaspora, based in Toronto) have placed issues of sexuality in relation to contemporary continental Africa at the forefront of thinking about black queer Toronto and Canada.

4

One of my most salient memories of the black queer community in Toronto centers on a memorial held for Audre Lorde at the 519 Community Center (the LGBT community center) in 1992, the year Lorde died. The 519 Center is located squarely in the heart of the city's gay community. From what I can recall, the memorial was organized by black lesbian feminists, many of them of Caribbean descent but not exclusively so. In the packed auditorium, black women remembered Lorde from conferences, poetry readings, personal meetings, and a range of other contexts that had brought them into contact with her. I remember attending that memorial and marveling at the bravery of these black women who had confronted not only homophobia and gender prejudice but racism as well. Their politics, articulated through a feminism that refused any easy separation between race, sexuality, and gender, envisioned a truly liberatory, ethical culture and society. When I think about black queer community in Toronto, I find it difficult not to simultaneously think of this kind of feminism as well.

Since the 1980s, it has been impossible to make any claims about black queer community in Toronto without taking seriously the increasingly complex questions that black feminists have placed on the agenda for discussion, among them intricate deliberations on community, family, sexuality, and migration. Not every feminist involved in the discussions came out as a lesbian, but those who did laid the groundwork for the existence of a vast, more complex community. Those black lesbian feminists and their allies founded important institutions, such as the now defunct Toronto-based Sister Vision Press, and infiltrated and made much more equitable publishers like the Women's Press of Toronto. They participated in and broadened the scope of International Women's Day, and appeared on community radio and television to give voice and sight to black bodies as members of the Canadian queer community. Black lesbian feminists in Toronto founded my queer community.

At Lorde's memorial I read from her essay "Man Child: A Black Lesbian Feminist's Response," in which Lorde wrote not only about her son, but also about the kinds of gay black men she had been meeting.[7] She wrote of men who were articulating and practicing different ways of being men, different masculinities. "Man Child" has had a profound impact on my adult life. I read it often as a reminder that feminist politics are also about liberation from a narrow and stultifying masculinity. I wish that Lorde's essay could be a manifesto for many more black men. I would like to think that I am one of the "new" kinds of men that Lorde envisioned.

5

Lorde's obvious Caribbean connections played a role in how women in Toronto who organized the celebration of her life went about their effort. Lorde's memorial was a diasporic gathering and distillation of black and Caribbean connections across space, time, history, and, importantly, political desires. It is exactly these sorts of connections that I would say characterize black and Caribbean queer life in Canada. Links with Caribbean communities, personal contacts, experience with intimate and other relationships, and experiences with other aspects of Caribbean cultures (books, films, music, food, and other ephemera) play a crucial role in how black queer life in Canada — generally lived in moments of dislocation from the Caribbean and often with the desire to share something (such as culture or cultural memory) with those from the imagined or longed-for region — is experienced and enacted. The Red Spot and Manhattan (now Papi's) are spaces where some of these sharings and imaginings happened. These dance spaces increase the possibility of black and Caribbean queer life that complicates, but also makes much more textured and rich, the ways in which queer community might be experienced. The drag queens of African descent (Michelle Ross, Jackae Baker, Miss Burundi, and others) bring to the picture a performance of femininity and masculinity that, despite the constantly reviled masculinity of black men, opens up a space for other expressions of blackness in all of the complications that drag can put on stage.

And so on Sundays when I go to church presided over by Jackae Baker and Michelle Ross, I am reminded of (among many other things) the ways in which these two drag queens in particular suggest a kind of black feminism. Miss Baker's renditions of songs by Erykah Badu and Jill Scott reproduce a lightweight feminism; that is, one obviously woman-centered but, as seen and heard in popular lyrics, in many ways still bound to representations of idealized heterosexual romance that, by way of lyrics and music, also encourage audience identification with (the pleasure to be taken in) the popular. Miss Ross's performance almost always ends with a gospel set—more often than not, her particular rendition of "King Jesus." When she performs this song, she also does a strut around the bar, "anointing" the participants as any evangelical Pentecostal preacher might do. At that point I say a silent prayer for the black and Caribbean feminists and drag queens who have made it less complicated, and in some ways quite easy and pleasurable, to be a black, openly gay man in Toronto. These underacknowledged community makers provided—and continue to provide—examples of how to live a life still in progress and how to imagine a future that might be different from the present. The boldness and bravery of some black drag queens offer us all access to that future.

NOTES

1 *Circuit queen* is an appellation given to some drag queens known for performing at large (2,000 men or more), all-night dance parties across North America and other parts of the world. The term can also refer to gay men who exclusively attend such parties. The most famous circuit parties are Montreal's Black and Blue, Miami's White Party, the now defunct Fire Island Party, and Sydney's Mardi Gras. These parties have become controversial because of the relationship between the use of "party drugs" (such as crystal meth or methylamphetamine), "unsafe" sex (without condoms), and alleged HIV/AIDS transmission. Ms. Baker was at one point a preferred performer for many of the biggest circuit parties.

2 The *down low* is a term used primarily to refer to black men, and sometimes Latinos, who are visibly situated in relationships with women and/or assumed to be heterosexual, but are simultaneously suspected of secret sexual involvements with other men—liaisons frequently believed to involve "unsafe" sexual practices (such as anal and oral sex without condoms). These men have not historically identified themselves as either gay or bisexual. Some observers believe that their unprotected sexual practices with other men are, in part, a manifestation of an inability to acknowledge that they are actually engaging in sex with men. (Some men who do not identify or perceive themselves as "gay" or "homosexual" but have sex with other men claim to believe that it is unlikely that they will be infected with HIV from unprotected sex with other men, since HIV/AIDS, associated in the public realm largely with gay-identified men, will supposedly not affect those who do not view themselves as "gay." This belief is, of course, incorrect.) The "down low" has been blamed for some of the recent increases in HIV/AIDS occurrences among heterosexual black women and ostensibly heterosexual black men. For further discussions of the "down low," see J. L. King, *On the Down Low: A Journey into the Lives of "Straight" Black Men Who Sleep with Men* (New York: Broadway Books, 2004); Keith Boykin's responding text,

Beyond the Down Low: Sex, Lies, and Denial in Black America (New York: Carroll and Graf, 2004); and, most recently, King's *Coming Up from the Down Low: The Journey to Acceptance, Healing, and Honest Love* (New York: Crown, 2005).

3 Publicity blurb for *Divas: Love Me Forever* (Canada: Anton Wagner Productions, Inc., 2002).

4 By my use of the phrase "urban cowboy aesthetic," I mean to suggest and high-light how black men now symbolically represent another notion of the lawless cowboy, retooled for the postmodern era's highly urban contexts. When "bad-ness" is contemplated in contemporary urban scenarios, representations of black masculinities are always lurking somewhere. In many ways, many black men have come to occupy these representations as "true" representations of themselves.

5 *Homothug* refers to black gay men who have taken on the dress and attitudes of hypermasculine "gangsta" rappers and their adherents. This particular style of dress, which references aspects of prison life, manifests itself most regularly in baggy and oversized clothing. Homothugness is frequently linked, correctly and incorrectly, to genres of rap music (such as gangsta rap) that highlight violence, and is very much related to the urban cowboy aesthetic. Homothugness signifies both "badness" and hypermasculinity.

6 See Patricia Hill Collins, *Black Feminist Thought: Knowledge, Consciousness, and the Politics of Empowerment* (Boston: Unwin Hyman, 1990).

7 Lorde, "Man Child: A Black Lesbian Feminist's Response," *Sister Outsider: Essays and Speeches* (Trumansburg, N.Y.: The Crossing Press, 1984), 72–80.

GLORIA WEKKER

Mati-ism and Black Lesbianism:
Two Idealtypical Expressions of Female Homosexuality
in Black Communities of the Diaspora (1996)

There are different ways in which black women in the African Diaspora have given expression to their erotic fascination with other women. In this article two idealtypical expressions of black female homosexuality—*mati-ism* and *black lesbianism*—and the outlines of their underlying cosmologies are sketched. *Mati* (or *matisma*) is the Sranan Tongo word for women who have sexual relations with other women, but who typically also will have had or still have relationships with men, simultaneously. More often than not they will also have children.

While both types can only be understood via a constructionist view of homosexuality, the institution of mati-ism will be shown to have retained more Afrocentric, working class elements, while black lesbianism has more middle class, Eurocentric features.

INTRODUCTION

In this article I want to focus on the experience of black women and the ways their erotic interests in those of their own gender have taken shape. I shall begin by giving a résumé of the historical and social factors which enable us to think of the black female experience in the Diaspora as a unitary, though multifaceted, process. I shall then indicate that ideas about female homosexuality in black communities in the Diaspora are anything but uniform. By presenting a large excerpt from a public discussion with two black women poets, I hope to elucidate the contours of two idealtypical cosmologies as far as female homosexuality is concerned. I am assuming that their views are representative of those held by larger groups of women in black communities in the United States, Suriname, and the Netherlands. These cosmologies may be indicated as *mati-ism* and *black lesbianism*.[1] My argument will make clear that both types can only be understood via a constructionist view of homosexuality.

YOU ARE THE OFFSPRING OF SLAVES

Black women of the Diaspora share a terrible history involving the slave trade based on Africa, a history of being transported like cattle across the Atlantic Ocean, of rootlessness in the "New" World, of centuries of living under a system of slavery, of various degrees of retention in their communities of African elements, and after Abolition (Suriname, 1863; U.S., 1865), of living in sexist and racist societies, based on class.[2]

Originating from West Africa, an area which stretches from Senegal to Angola and extending far into the interior, the slaves belonged to various tribes with hundreds of different languages and dialects, different systems of family relationships, and many habits and customs. For centuries, slaves of both sexes in the Americas were forbidden to learn how to read and write and hardly had opportunities to develop their creative and artistic gifts. The list of prohibitions to which they were subjected was extensive: no marriages were permitted without the consent of their masters, nor other relations among themselves; no control over children born to such relationships — the children were the property of the mother's owner; no right to own property or to wear shoes; and no protection against cruel and unreasonable treatment by the master class.

For both the North American and the Surinamese slaves, one of the things which enabled them to maintain themselves in the new environment was their African culture, which they endeavored to keep intact in the given circumstances and which, in the unspeakable misery of their existence, gave them a sense of having something to which they belonged and which afforded them some foothold. In the days of slavery and later on, the role women played in preserving, communicating, and developing elements of African culture was of inestimable importance. Recent scholarship indicates that the principal residue of the African cultural heritage in the Diaspora should be explored in the realm of social values and orientations to reality rather than in more or less concrete sociocultural forms.[3]

Important differences between the history of black women in the United States and that of black women in Suriname can be pointed to. Some of these differences had their effect on the degree to which retentions — especially orientations to reality — were able to continue almost unharmed. One of these differences concerns the ratio of blacks to whites that existed during a great part of the eighteenth and nineteenth centuries in the (former) British and Dutch colonies. In North America there was always a considerable numerical preponderance of whites over blacks. The ratio in 1780 was, for example, 15 to 1.[4] On the estates of the Surinamese colony, on the other hand, a handful of whites endeavored to exert control over an immense number of slaves. The ratio there ranged from 1 to 25 in the urban area, to 1 to 65 in the plantation districts farther removed from the capital.[5]

It was partly due to this numerical relationship that different cultural policies towards the slaves took shape in the two colonies. The British colonists succeeded in forbidding their slaves to speak their original African languages. As a result, black English with a grammar, a syntax, and a lexicon of its own developed. In Suriname, on the other head, slaves were left free to develop their own tongue, a creole called Negro English (now Sranan Tongo), for centuries. They were also allowed to elaborate and work out their own cultures. Government policy in the colony until Abolition and after, until 1876, was aimed at creating as wide as possible a geographical, cultural, and psychological gap between the colonists and the slaves. The ban on speaking Dutch was only one of an endless series of ordinances designed with this view in end.

Generally speaking, the Surinamese slaves had more freedom than their North American partners in misfortune, and for a longer period of time they were able to cultivate their languages and their ways of life and thought, as long as these did not conflict with the interests of the planter class. That the African constituent in the Surinamese orientation to reality must have been considerable for many centuries is emphasized by the fact that the importation of so-called "saltwater Negroes" (i.e., slaves newly transported from Africa) was a continuing necessity until the official ban on the slave trade in 1808. In contrast to the situation in North America, where the capacity of female slaves to produce children was encouraged and in certain periods even subjected to coercion, the Surinamese planters preferred to force as much labor from the slaves as possible in the space of a few years. The maltreatment, undernourishment, and murder of slaves repeatedly saw to it that within a few years the entire body of slaves could be "written off." Surinamese female slaves hardly reproduced. Whereas at the end of the U.S. Civil War there were 4 million blacks, the Surinamese census only counted 50,000 ex-slaves at the time of Abolition, though roughly the same number of slaves (350,000 to 400,000) had been imported into each colony over the course of the past two and a half centuries.[6] The world the slave owners created in Suriname was one which one left as soon as one could, with one's pockets loaded with money.

Despite these differences between North American and Surinamese history, the correspondences are so marked that one can speak of a unitary, though multi-faceted, experience of black women in the Diaspora.

CONSIDERING THE ROOTS, SURINAMESE STYLE

In describing the history of black women in the Diaspora, I have made no distinction between the history of black women in general and "lesbian" women in particular. There are various reasons for this. First, black lesbian women have been, for the greater part of the time they have been in the Diaspora, an integral part of their communities; they were subject to the same orders and prohibitions as other women in these communities. Secondly — this is important as regards their position in their own circles — they often had simultaneous relationships with men and had children.

The earliest information about mati-ism in Suriname dates from 1912 and refers precisely to its being embedded in the culture of the ordinary Creole population. A. J. Schimmelpenninck van den Oye, a high ranking Dutch government official, remarks in a memorandum on the physical condition of the "underprivileged":

> Speaking about the physically weak condition of so many young women, in addition another reason should be mentioned. I am referring to the sexual communion between women themselves ("mati play"), which immorality has, as I gather, augmented much in the past decades, and, alas!, penetrated deeply into popular customs . . . It is not only that young girls and unattached women of various classes make themselves guilty of this, the poorest often going and living together in pairs to reduce the cost of house rent and food for each of them, but women who live with men, and even schoolgirls, do the same, following the example of others.[7]

Somewhat later, in the 1930s, mati culture had taken on such proportions that another reporter, Th. Comvalius, expressed his disturbance about "the unusual relationships among women in Suriname, which were not dependent on social rank, intellectual development, race or country of origin. Love(?) brought women and young girls of very different walks of life together as intimate friends . . . While this in itself . . . could be called a 'sociological misconception,' there is another, dark side to it, the discussion of which is no concern of ours. Probably it was blown over here from the French West Indies."[8]

With hindsight, it is possible to state that the institution of mati relationships did not just fall down out of the blue sky. Linguistically, two explanations for the word *mati* are offered: one would trace it to old Dutch *maatje*, meaning "buddy," or "mate"; the other one is more convincing and links it to Hausa *mata* or *mace*: "woman," or "wife." It is now known that in a number of West African regions from which slaves were taken (for example, Ashanti and Dahomey) that female homosexuality occurred in times long past and that it was not burdened with negative sanctions prohibiting it. The anthropologists Melville and Frances Herskovits reported that in Dahomey a woman could formally marry another woman and that offspring born to the one woman were regarded as the children of the other woman.[9] The women slaves who were carried off to the New World were therefore familiar with the phenomenon. Elsewhere it is stated about the Saramaka Maroons, the descendants of the runaway slaves who formed viable societies in the rainforests of Suriname from the seventeenth century on, that in Saramaka society, "Mati is a highly charged volitional relationship, usually between two men, that dates back to the Middle Passage — matis were originally "shipmates," those who had survived the journey out from Africa together . . . *Sibi* is a relationship of special friendship between two women. As with the mati relationship, the reciprocal term of address derives from the Middle Passage itself: sibi referred to shipmates, those who had experienced the trauma of enslavement and transport together."[10]

The word *sibi* does not occur with this meaning in Sranan Tongo, the coastal creole; here the term *mati* covers all modalities. It may very well be that, encapsulated in Sranan Tongo "mati," there may at one time also have been the notion of shipmates who had survived together, but at present that connotation is not there.

Features of mati culture that are mentioned in older sources have been preserved to this day. There were, for example, female couples who wore *parweri*, the same dress; women who embroidered handkerchiefs with loving texts in silk for each other, *lobi kon* (love has come) and *lobi n'e prati* (love does not go away); women who courted each other by means of special ways of folding and wearing their *anyisa*, headcloths; and finally the widespread institution of *lobi singi* (love songs). In these songs women sing the praises of their mati, in metaphorical language, and enlarge the faults of their rivals.[11] One such text is sung as follows:[12]

Roos e flauw

A de fadon

Roos e flauw

A de fadon

Ma stanvaste

Dat e tan sidon

[The rose is weak / It has fallen down / The rose is weak / It has fallen down / But "steadfast" / That stays upright.]

Mati relationships in 1990 are a very visible feature of Afro-Surinamese working class culture. Spokespersons speak of "one big family," where every-one knows each other and older women clearly predominate. But women and men of younger age groups also are present. Many female couples have a marked role division, where one partner will play a "male" role, and the other a "female" role. It is, furthermore, important to note that a mati career, for most women, is not a unidirectional path: thus it is very possible that a woman takes a man for a lover, after having had several relationships with women. It also is not unusual for a woman to have a female and a male lover at the same time. Nor does mati life necessarily imply restriction to one partner. As one 35-year-old informant told me:

I never have just one lover, at the same time. I have my *tru visiti* (steady girlfriend) and then two or three other lovers. If my "steady" is a Creole woman, I take care that the others are of different ethnic origin or just over here on vacation from Holland, because Creoles aren't likely to take this arrangement easily. I handpick my lovers, I don't take just anybody. Because it takes a lot of time to find a "Ms. Right," I can't afford to begin looking after me and my steady have broken up. So I keep them in reserve.[13]

AN AFRO-AMERICAN ANGLE

The literature of black North American women writers, which began to appear in a rich variety of forms from the beginning of the 1970s, makes it clear that the societies they describe would have been unthinkable failing the strong ties of love and eroticism among women. The literature also reveals a certain tolerance of homosexuality in the working classes, as long as it does not bear a name, and this corresponds with the situation in Suriname. I want to illustrate this by a single fragment from the biomythographical novel *Zami: A New Spelling Of My Name* by Audre Lorde. In this fragment the

North American black communities of the 1950s are discussed, and Lorde describes the attitude of Cora, a factory worker and the mother of Zami's first woman lover, Ginger:

> With her typical aplomb, Cora welcomed my increased presence around the house with the rough familiarity and browbeating humor due another one of her daughters. If she recognized the sounds emanating from the sunporch on the nights I slept over, or our haggard eyes the next day, she ignored them. But she made it very clear that she expected Ginger to get married again. "Friends are nice, but marriage is marriage," she said to me one night as she helped me make a skirt on her machine. . . . "And when she gets home don't be thumping that bed all night, neither, because it's late already and you girls have work tomorrow."[14]

LESBIANISM, SAY WHAT?

In addition to the established custom of women having relationships with other women and the degree of tolerance for this in black communities, there is another reason for my choosing not to make a sharp distinction between the history of black women in general and "lesbian" women in particular. There are strong indications that the Western categories of "homo," "bi," and "hetero" have insufficient justification in some black situations. The concept of "homosexuality" introduces an etic category that is alien to the indigenous, emic system which exists in some sections of black communities.

Sexuality cannot be considered independently from the social order in which it exists. Ellen Ross and Rayna Rapp state rightly that the biological basis of sexuality is always experienced and interpreted according to cultural values. The simple biological facts of sexuality are not self-explanatory, they require social expression. The image employed for the universal rootedness of sexuality in larger social units such as family relationships, communities, and national and world systems, is that of the union of all of these elements. One may have the illusion that by peeling off one layer after another one comes nearer to the core of sexuality, after which one realizes that all the different layers together form its essence.[15]

How societies precisely give form to sexuality remains relatively obscure. I am not claiming to describe all the different layers of the emic system of sexuality to which mati-ism belongs. I would, however, like to sketch the outlines of two idealtypical socio-historical structures, situating two differing cosmologies, as far as female homosexuality in black communities is concerned.

In the summer of 1986, black women in Amsterdam had the good fortune to be witnesses to and participants in a public discussion between two eminent women poets, true children of the black Diaspora, Audre Lorde and Astrid Roemer.[16] While many subjects were addressed during this discussion, the burning question, which also aroused a passionate interest among the audience, proved to be the matter of namegiving and nomenclature: how important is it that black women who love other women should call themselves "black lesbians"?

TWO IDEALTYPICAL EXPRESSIONS

ASTRID ROEMER: I do not call myself "lesbian" and I do not want to be called "lesbian" either. Life is too complex for us to give names not derived from us—dirty, conditioned words—to the deepest feelings within me. If I were to call myself a lesbian, it would mean that I should be allowing myself—on the most banal, biological level—to be classed as one who chooses persons who also have female genitals. If I love a woman, I love that one woman, and one swallow does not make a summer.

People have a masculine and a feminine component in them, and these two components constantly seek to come into equilibrium with each other and with the rest of the world. Who is to say whether I shall not love a man in my later life? The result of that search for equilibrium is not a constant. I should be terribly ashamed as a human being were I to know in advance that for the rest of my life I should love only women. It would, moreover, conflict with feminism, for feminism also insists that men can change.

AUDRE LORDE: First of all, I want to make clear what I understand [to be constituted] by a "lesbian." It is not having genital intercourse with a woman that is the criterion. There are lesbian women who have never had genital or any other form of sexual contact with another woman, while there are also women who have had sex with other women but who are not lesbian. A lesbian is a woman who identifies fundamentally with women, and her first field of strength, of vulnerability, of comfort, lies in a network of women. If I call myself a black, feminist lesbian, I am acknowledging by that that the roots of my strength, and of my vulnerability, lie in myself as a woman. What I am trying to achieve in the first place [are] changes in my awareness and that of other women. My priority does not lie with men.

There are two reasons only why I call myself a black lesbian. It makes me aware of my own strength and shows my vulnerability too. In the sixties we could do anything we wanted to as long as we did not talk about it. If you speak your name, you represent a threat to the powers that be, the patriarchate. That's what I want to be too. The price I pay for that and the vulnerability it makes me aware of are no greater than what I feel if I keep it a secret and let others decide what they want to call me. That also perpetuates the positions of inferiority we occupy in society.

The other reason I consider it important is that there may be a woman in my audience who, through this, may see that it is possible to speak your name and to go on living. If we, who are in a relatively more secure position enabling us to come out for what we are, if we fail to do so that will only perpetuate the vicious circle of inferiority.

ASTRID: I think your definition of a lesbian is interesting. In that sense, all Surinamese women are lesbian, because they draw their strength to carry on from women. All the same, I do not see why it is necessary to declare oneself a lesbian. In the community from which I come, there is not so much talk about the phenomenon of women having relations with other women. There are, after all, things which aren't to be given names—giving them names kills them. But we do have age-old rituals originating from Africa by which women can make quite clear that special relations exist between them. For instance, birthday rituals can be recognized by anyone and are quite obvious. Also, when two women are at a party and one hands the other a glass or a plate of food from which she has first tasted herself, it is clear to everybody and their mother what that means. Why then is it necessary to declare oneself a lesbian? It is usual there. Surinamese women claim the right to do what they want to do. They can love women, go to bed with men, have children. We distinguish between the various levels of feeling and experiencing which life has to offer and allow ourselves the opportunity to enjoy these things in a creative manner. This is different from the situation in the Netherlands, where you are shoved into a pigeon-hole and find your opportunities restricted. My not wanting to declare myself a lesbian is certainly not prompted by fear. I also want to remain loyal to the ways in which expression has been given from of old in my community to special relationships between women. Simply doing things, without giving them a name, and preserving rituals and secrets between women are important to me. Deeds are more obvious and more durable than all the women who say they are lesbian and contribute nothing to women's energy.

AUDRE: I respect your position and I recognize the need and the strength that lie behind it. It is not my position. I think it necessary for every woman to decide for herself what she calls herself, and when and where. Of course, there have always been rituals and secrets between women and they must continue. But it is important to make a distinction between the secrets from which we draw strength and the secrecy which comes from anxiety and is meant to protect us. If we want to have power for ourselves this secrecy and this silence must be broken. I want to encourage more and more women to identify themselves, to speak their name, where and when they can, and to survive. I repeat: and to survive.

Finally, I think it important to state my essential position as follows: it is not my behavior that determines whether I am lesbian, but the very core of my being.

TOWER OF BABEL

So much for the burning discussion among the black poets. The positions taken up here are shared by large groups of women in the black communities of the Diaspora and are typical of two idealtypical cosmologies where female homosexuality is concerned. The position defended by Andre Lorde is a prototype of that held by groups of black lesbians within the United States, Suriname, and the Netherlands. In the attitudes adopted by Astrid Roemer, features can be discerned of the mati paradigm, whose protagonists are also to be found everywhere in the Diaspora yet who, almost by definition, attract less attention.

Perhaps it is unnecessary to say that in practice numerous intermediate positions and hybrid forms exist. Without wishing to force people into one camp or the other, or to question the legitimacy or "political correctness" of either position, I seek to throw light on the outlines of these two idealtypes. Exchanges around the theme of namegiving often give rise to heated discussions that aren't particularly fruitful, because as in a true Tower of Babel, people speak in mutually unintelligible tongues.

Central to my thinking on the matter is the fact that orientation to reality — which includes the meaning given to and the form taken by homosexuality in black communities in the Diaspora — is more or less colored by the cultural heritage from Africa. In the cosmology of mati-ism more African elements have been preserved, while the black lesbian groups have drawn more inspiration from Western influences. Mati-ism is characterized by a *centripetal,* a comprehensive and inclusive movement, whereas in the black lesbian world a *centrifugal,* exclusive spirit seems to be present. This is reflected in the attitudes in various circles to relationships with men. While in the lives of many mati-women men play a role, among the black lesbians this must generally be excluded. Children in the lives of black lesbians are either a residue from a former lifestyle or a conscious choice within a lesbian relationship. Neither circumstance necessarily requires continued emotional or financial commitment from the father to the child or the mother. The part played by men in the life of mati-women, apart from possible economical support for children, is underscored by the fact that motherhood is regarded as a rite of initiation into adulthood and by many as a sign of being a woman.

Besides displaying a differential level of African elements, mati-ism and black lesbianism are exponents of two different *class cultures*. Mati typically are working class women, whose claims to social status lie in their capability to mobilize and manipulate kin networks. Indeed, according to Marie-José Janssens and Wilhelmina van Wetering, matisma can be seen as entrepreneurs who, through their extensive kin networks with women and men, try to build up social and real capital.[17] While, in Suriname, middle and higher class black lesbians are largely invisible, obviously not having found appropriate models to style their behavior, in the United States and in the Netherlands they have increasingly come out of the closet. Through their education, income, and often professional status, they are insulated against some of the survival hazards of working class black lesbians.

A further difference distinguishing mati relationships from black lesbian connections is the often wide *age gap* between mati partners, while in the latter circles "equality" along many dimensions, including age, seems to be an aspiration. It is not at all unusual, in the mati world, to find a twenty-year-old (*yong doifi*, young dove) having a relationship with a sixty-year-old woman. For the young woman, the emotional and financial security of the older woman, who will typically have raised her children and will get financial support from them, is an important consideration. The older woman, for her part, now as almost sixty years ago when it was first recorded,[18] will demand unconditional loyalty and faithfulness from her "young dove" in return for indulging and spoiling her with presents, notably gold and silver jewelry. Ideally, she teaches her young dove *a mati wroko* (the mati work) and she "trains" her the way she wants the young woman to be.

A further differentiation would seem to lie in the *underlying self* that organizes all life's experiences, sifts through them, and integrates them into manageable material. Though this issue awaits farther elaboration,[19] the self of matisma would seem to be a *sociocentric* phenomenon, while the self of black lesbians could be characterized as an *egocentric, individualistic* entity. Among matisma, sociocentrism is evident not only in the zeal with which human capital is constantly being mobilized, but also in the perceptions of what a person is. Linked with the folk religion "Winti," persons are perceived to be built up out of several components: *kra* (or *jeje*), *djodjo*, and several *winti* or Gods, who each have their specific characteristics.[20] Kra, with its male and female component, can be understood as the "I"; djodjo, also male and female, are like "guardian angels," gotten at birth. The different winti are divided into four pantheons: those of the Sky, the Earth, the Bush, and the Water. Male homosexuals are often believed to have a female "Aisa," the (upper-) goddess of the Earth, who is said to be frightfully jealous of real women the man would get involved with. Female homosexuals are perceived to be "carried" by a male Bushgod, Apuku, who cannot bear to see the woman connected, on a long-term basis, with a flesh-and-blood male.

Black lesbians' personhood, on the other hand, seems more aptly characterized by Western notions of individuality, persons as self-contained "islands," with their own motivations and accountabilities.

An additional distinction between matisma and black lesbians is that concentration on women for the latter is a *political issue,* aimed at male dominated society. In their own communities they often wage war on sexism and homophobia. While they experience their sexual choice as a matter of politics, matisma tend to see their behavior as a *personal issue.* A typical response is: "Mi na wan bigi uma f' mi eygi oso. No wan sma e gi mi njan" (I am a big woman in my own house. Nobody gives me food), meaning it's nobody's business but my own with whom I sleep. In a small scale society like Suriname (400,000 inhabitants), this can be seen as a rather defiant survival posture.

Lastly, one could posit that matisma display *lesbian behavior,* while black lesbians have a *lesbian identity.* I assume that matisma unwillingness to declare oneself can, functionally, be explained with reference to this point. In a society where the avenues to status for working class women are limited, it would not seem wise to declare oneself openly and thereby alienate potential personnel, men and women, from one's network.

EPILOGUE

Within black communities there are many different ways of giving expression to erotic relationships between women. The biological basis of sexual desire takes form in various socio-historical structures, underpinned by differing cosmologies. Mati-ism and black lesbianism are two of these structures. Lesbians have not always existed in black communities. In some sectors, today, they still do not exist. But this statement is not a complaint about the lack of sexuality between those of the same gender in the black communities of the Diaspora. Rather it is a statement that tells us more about the socio-historical structure of the concept "lesbian."

NOTES

1 *Mati* is the Sranan Tongo word for "friend," used both in a heterosexual and a homosexual context. It is used by and for men and women. The word *matisma* (literally "mati people") specifically connotes women who have sexual relations with other women. By mati-ism, I mean the institution of those who are mati, in this case, women. In Dutch I would use the term *matischap*.

2 Audre Lorde, "For Each of You," in *Chosen Poems, Old and New* (New York: W. W. Norton, 1982), 42–43.

3 Sidney Mintz and Richard Price, *An Anthropological Approach to the Afro-American Past* (Philadelphia: Ishi, 1976).

4 Richard Price, *The Guiana Maroons: A Historical and Bibliographical Introduction* (Baltimore: The Johns Hopkins University Press, 1976), 21.

5 Rudolf van Lier, *Samenleving in een Grensgebied*, Een sociaal-historische Studie van Suriname (Amsterdam: Emmering, 1949), 38.

6 Ibid., 92.

7 Oye, *Het Ambacht in Suriname: Rapport van de commissie benoemd bij Gouvernementresolutie van 13 januari 1910* (Paramaribo: Suriname Gouvernement, 1912), n.p.

8 Theodor A. C. Comvalius, *Krioro: Een bijdrage tot de kennis van het lied, de dans en de folklore van Suriname*, vol. 1 (Paramaribo: n.d.), 11.

9 Melville J. Herskovits, *Dahomey: An Ancient West-African Kingdom*, vol. 1 (New York: J. J. Augustin, 1938).

10 Richard Price and Sally Price, *Two Evenings in Saramaka* (Chicago: University of Chicago Press, 1991), 396, 407.

11 See Comvalius, *Krioro*; and Melville J. Herskovits and Frances Herskovits, *Suriname Folklore* (New York: Columbia University Press, 1936).

12 This text was recorded at a lobi singi performance in Paramaribo, November 1990. Stanvaste (steadfast) is the name of another flower.

13 See my dissertation, "'I am Gold Money' (I Pass through All Hands, but I Do Not Lose My Value): The Construction of Selves, Gender, and Sexualities in a Female, Working Class, Afro-Surinamese Setting" (PhD diss., University of California, Los Angeles, 1992), 281–82.

14 Lorde, *Zami: A New Spelling of My Name* (Trumansburg, N.Y.: The Crossing Press, 1982), 142.

15 Ross and Rapp, "Sex and Society: A Research Note from Social History and Anthropology," in *Powers of Desire: The Politics of Sexuality*, ed. Ann Snitow, Christine Stansell, and Sharon Thompson (New York: Monthly Review Press, 1983), 51–72.

16 This public discussion, organized by the black lesbian group Sister Outsider, took place on June 21, 1986, in the black and migrant women's center Flamboyant in Amsterdam. Astrid Roemer (born in Paramaribo in 1947) is an Afro-Surinamese poet-novelist, living in the Netherlands, while Afro-American Audre Lorde (born in Harlem in 1934) resided on St. Croix, U.S. Virgin Islands, until her death in 1992.

17 Janssens and van Wetering, "Mati en lesbiennes: Homoseksualiteit en ethnische identiteit bij Creools — Surinaamse vrouwen in Nederland," *Sociologische Gids* 32, no. 5–6 (1985): 394–415.

18 Herskovits and Herskovits, *Suriname Folklore*.

19 See Wekker, "I am Gold Money."

20 See Charles J. Wooding, *Winti: Een Afroamerikaanse godsdienst in Suriname: Een cultureel-historische analyse van de Cosmologie en het Etnomedische Systeem van de Para* (Rijswijk: C. J. Wooding, 1988), 69–70.

LAWSON WILLIAMS

On Homophobia and Gay Rights Activism in Jamaica (2000)

Jamaica is perceived to be the most homophobic Caribbean territory. It is also a badly kept secret that Jamaica has a perceptibly vibrant gay population. Navigating the choppy waters of Jamaica's renowned homophobia is a potentially confounding experience, with attitudes that range from gratuitous violence to virulent contempt to reluctant acknowledgment. This homophobia also manifests itself among gay people as internalized hate. Many gay people resort to the same hostile behavior against other gay persons in an attempt to deflect attention from themselves.

In the early 1990s, popular dancehall artist Buju Banton's song "Boom Bye Bye," a call to arms against "batty bwoy" (male homosexuals), was widely celebrated and encountered little if any disapproval from the church or other sector of society, despite its obvious support for violence. In the late 1990s, another popular dancehall artist, Bounty Killer, a declared homophobe, sang "Can't Believe Mi Eyes," a piece that expresses consternation at the specter of gayness in Jamaica in 1998: "Can't believe seh gunman and battyman a frien!" (I can't believe that gunmen and gay men are actually friends!).[1] He went on to express incredulity at the fact that so many men now adorn themselves in tight pants. To his mind, this was an effeminate tendency and a visible display of gayness. Much to Bounty Killer's shock, however, this phenomenon of gayness existed with great impunity. The singer's surprise is better understood when one examines Jamaica's recent history with anything that remotely touches the issue of homosexuality. On August 19, 1997, the commissioner of corrections, Colonel John Prescod, stated on a radio program that condoms would be distributed to prisoners and warders as part of an acquired immune deficiency syndrome (AIDS) prevention campaign — a recognition of homosexuality as a fact of life in Jamaican prisons. What ensued was nothing short of stupendous. Between August 20 and 23 of the same year, sixteen inmates were killed as prisoners rioted in reaction to the commissioner's statement. Reports of the incident indicated that there was a concerted effort by the "men" (heterosexuals) in the prisons to kill the "boys" (homosexuals).

The reactions that followed are instructive. Warders displayed apathy during and after the incident. In a television interview, trade union leader Lambert Brown of the University and Allied Workers Union (UAWU), the warders' trade union, suggested that the issue demonstrated the incompetence of the commissioner. The prevailing attitude of homophobia in the scenario was, to his mind, secondary. He indicated that the loss of life was unfortunate, but quickly added, "But I don't like homosexuals." Very few, if any, commentators addressed the issue of homophobia as having precipitated the orgy of violence.

The Jamaican government issued no direct statement against homophobia, or of the undesirability of hatred at any level. It assembled a commission of inquiry, which devoted one and a half pages of its thirty-seven page written report to the issue of homosexuality. It initiated no official program to address the levels of hatred and intolerance that led to this massacre. Subsequent to the publication of the commission's findings, the minister of national security, K. D. Knight, stated at a seminar in Portmore, parish of St. Catherine, that there should be "no fear that the government will pass any law to legalize homosexuality."[2]

Against this background, the Jamaica Forum for Lesbians, All-Sexuals and Gays (J-FLAG) was launched in December 1998 to, by its own account, "ferocious opposition from all quarters."[3] Its advent was unprecedented, as it constituted the first significant political and institutional attempt to address homosexual issues in Jamaica since the long-defunct Gay Freedom Movement (GFM), founded in Kingston in the late 1970s. The shock in the society ran high, both in straight and gay circles.

What explains the intensity of responses, from undiluted violence and strident opposition to an almost nervous ignoring of gays in Jamaica? The noted Jamaican psychologist Dr. Leachim Semaj, commenting on the foolhardiness he felt inherent in the decision to form J-FLAG, adverted to what he perceived to be a "balance" between heterosexuals and gays in Jamaica. He argued that J-FLAG, by threatening to make gayness open and visible, was upsetting this delicate "balance" that existed.[4]

In a 1998 article entitled "J-FLAG Must Cool Down Its Homosexual Heat," the *Jamaica Observer* columnist Mark Wignall raged, "Jamaicans expect homosexuals to be quiet as they indulge their 'whatchamacallit.' Jamaicans expect them to be ashamed, remorseful, penitent and retiring. None of us want them to take their song and dance routine to the National Arena or to Jamaica House."[5] In one fell swoop, Wignall captured, rather cynically, not only the views of some "tolerant" Jamaican heterosexuals on homosexuality, but also defined the parameters within which most gay Jamaicans themselves see their scope of existence. It is a common understanding that the issue of gayness must never enter the "national arena," or at least not in any way that gives the issue any political legitimacy. Homosexuality must always be dealt with conjecturally or in abstraction, but never in any tangible form. The idea of activism focused on homosexual issues is anathema to the Jamaican community. Such activism also unsettles the learned responses of gay people who perceive any homosexual visibility as doing violence to the "balance" that exists with the straight community.

It is for this reason that J-FLAG constitutes an audacious departure from convention, thus making some people extremely uneasy, if not wary, of its objectives. This suspicion amongst gay people is characteristic of the attitude of the "shy and retiring" gay person. Jamaican gays have long learned that, in Jamaica, there can be no legitimacy as a gay person or as a gay community. Legitimacy comes only from excelling in spite of, if not in denial of, one's homosexuality. Edwin Myers, in a letter to the editor of the *Daily Gleaner,* bemoaned, "As long as there are no obvious signs of homosexuality, a gay person is allowed to function as an otherwise productive member of society. It doesn't matter if making oneself invisible sexually requires lying or subterfuge."[6] There is thus an unwillingness among some gays to identify with anything that implicates them any further than a personal engagement in a private gay sexual encounter. Their sexuality is never seen in its full political context. For most gay individuals, indifference to the gay community and to any semblance of gay political activity is seen as critical to survival as a gay person in Jamaica.

The philosophical framework used to support this position is the public versus private debate. The issue of sexual orientation, it is argued by many straight and gay people, is purely a private matter and has no place in the public domain of one's life. This analysis accommodates the mental gymnastics necessary to justify abstaining from agitating for changes in — or removal of — obtrusive and outdated laws that prohibit homosexual sexual expression, or challenging the prevailing attitudes towards homosexuality fueled by the church and other sources of homophobia.

Shortly after the formation of J-FLAG, the radio talk show host Barbara Gloudon facetiously urged members of the organization not to put themselves at risk of being beaten because of their activities. In the wake of J-FLAG's much publicized formation, some letter writers to the editors of the two major daily newspapers (the *Jamaica Gleaner* and the *Jamaica Observer*) expressed the view that, until the society was more educated about homosexuality, or made aware of it, it would be best if gays kept their business to themselves and did not thrust it upon the rest of the society, since the society was already burdened with presumably more serious issues.

Michelangelo Signorile, in his seminal work *Queer in America,* argues that the notion of gayness as a private issue is a concession to the view that homosexuality is not of comparable standing as heterosexuality.[7] If there is casual reference to one's heterosexuality in everyday activities, Signorile posits, then the same should obtain for homosexuality. The failure to do so by both gay and straight people perpetuates the continued pathologizing of gayness. He argues, "If, as we've been saying all along, being gay is not about sex acts or about what we do in our bedrooms, but is a much larger matter regarding identity and culture and community, then how can the fact of a person being gay be private when being straight isn't? Sex is private . . . something that escapes most heterosexuals because they don't really see homosexuality as a full orientation equal to heterosexuality."[8] Privacy ought not to mean the right to indulge in otherwise "shameful" behavior in one's bedroom. It is instead a right to family life, sexual preference, and home environment—rights that are protected from the conflicting whim of the statistical majority.

Arguments for change in the status quo ought to be evident to gays themselves. The law in Jamaica presently prohibits male homosexual sexual expression. Section 76 of the Offences Against the Person Act prohibits the "abominable crime of buggery," even where it occurs between consenting adult males. The offence of gross indecency prevents activities of sexual intimacy between males. Justice Albie Sachs of the South African Constitutional Court, in the case of *National Coalition of Gay and Lesbian Equality v. Minister of Justice,* opined:

> It is important to start the analysis by asking what is really being punished by the anti-sodomy laws. Is it an act, or is it a person? . . . In the case of male homosexuality, however, the perceived deviance is punished simply because it is deviant. It is repressed for its perceived symbolism rather than because of its proven harm . . . it is not the act of sodomy that is denounced by law, but the so-called sodomite who performs it; not any proven social damage, but the threat that the same sex passion in itself is seen as representing to heterosexual

hegemony. The effect is that all homosexual activity is tainted and the whole gay and lesbian community is marked with deviance and perversity.[9]

Although homosexuality among females is not addressed by Jamaican law, life is no easier in Jamaica for lesbians. The notion of a gay or homosexual person is not one that has any standing worthy of protection in Jamaica. The law, of course, is merely a reflection of wider social attitudes that choose to ignore or actively suppress the realities of gay people and gay communities. The church has been instrumental in the maintenance of these views, with a steady volley of biblical references that supposedly disapprove of homosexuality.

Gayness in Jamaica is not generally seen as a human rights issue, and when it is, it runs second to issues such as general societal violence and the underperformance of the nation's economy. The tendency to deem gay rights as secondary to other, more compelling issues discloses a lack of understanding of the interconnection of rights. The factors that construct a homophobic society are the same ones that create violence in general. The inability to treat differences civilly and manage our attitudes of opposition gives rise to violence as much as it secures the continuation of homophobia or even violent homophobia.

The failure to validate persons in their difference and treat them with respect affects self-esteem, and ultimately jobs. If the quality of human resources is crucial to productivity, then clearly a diminution in value of gay employees is inimical to production. The failure to protect gay people from a hostile working environment, both physically and emotionally, also affects morale on the job and, ultimately, the quality of human capital. For these reasons, social engineering is important to effect the necessary behavioral adjustment towards homosexuality.[10] There is a profound need for Jamaica's legal and social framework to adjust to accommodate gay people as a legitimate constituency in the society. Additionally, gay Jamaicans themselves must be proactive in making their concerns heard and understood. They must set their own agenda for self-improvement. Each of these issues must be addressed not only on a personal, individual level, but nationally. Only then will acceptance of gay Jamaicans in Jamaica move toward becoming a reality.

NOTES

"Lawson Williams" is a pseudonym.

1 "Boom Bye Bye," written by Mark Myrie, *Buju Banton: The Early Years 90–95* (Kingston, Jamaica: Penthouse Record Distributors, 1992); "Can't Believe Mi Eyes," written by Dave Kelly and Rodney Price, *Next Millenium* (New York: TVT, 1998).

2 *Jamaica Observer,* "No Gay Rights for Jamaica," March 2, 1998.

3 See Rex Wockner, "Jamaican Gay Group Faces 'Ferocious Opposition,'" *Pink Ink* 2 (January 1999): n.p., http://www.khsnet.com/pinkink/9901/news2.htm.

4 Gilbert Dunkley, "Jamaica Should Make its Gay Citizens Welcome," *Caribbean Today,* January 1999, 8, 10.

5 Mark Wignall, "J-FLAG Must Cool Down Its Homosexual Heat," *Jamaica Observer,* December 21, 1998.

6 Edwin Myers, letter to the editor, *Daily Gleaner,* February 1999.

7 Michelangelo Signorile, *Queer in America: Sex, the Media, and the Closets of Power* (New York: Anchor, 1993), 79–80.

8 Ibid.

9 *National Coalition for Gay and Lesbian Equality v. Minister of Justice*, CCT 11/98; 1999 (1) SA 6 (CC); 1998 (12) BCLR 1517 (CC), at paragraphs 108–9.

10 By "social engineering," I mean the process of effecting fundamental social changes through changes in institutions, symbols, and attitudes.

GLOSSARY

Ánimo: courage, energy

Areté: virtue, bravery, great human effectiveness (as in the achievement of impressive, profound results); also, the highest human potential attainable (frequently found in Homeric Greek)

Así: so, thus; in some parts of Latin America and the Caribbean, this word is used as a coded reference to people who are perceived or known to be lesbian, bisexual, transgendered, or gay, as in "así son ellos" (literally, "that's how they are," but figuratively, "they're *that* way," meaning non-heterosexual)

Babonuco: cloth or cloths wrapped or coiled on top of a person's head to balance objects carried there

Bigetty (*biggety*, *biggerty*): acting fractiously assertive, often with little regard for the consequences, in order to be heeded, noticed, or respected by others

Cheups: the sound made by "kissing" or "sucking" one's teeth as an expression of disgust or contempt

Commess (*konmès*): scandalous gossip; also, a disturbance or a confused, unsettling, possibly illicit situation

Coolie: a person of East Indian background or descent (now generally derogatory)

Crop-over: the end of the sugar cane harvest; in Barbados, a time of national festivity in July in commemoration of the end of the sugar cane harvest

Danzón: a form of dance and music evolved from the French-Haitian contradance brought to Cuba in the eighteenth century by people fleeing the Haitian Revolution. Widely regarded as Cuba's most traditional dance music and dance form, danzón has influenced all subsequent Cuban musical forms.

Diablesse (*djablès, jablesse*): an evil spirit typically manifested in the form of a beautiful, elegant young woman, most often encountered on deserted moonlit roads, who is believed to lure men into isolated areas where she will reveal herself as an ugly old woman, often with cloven hooves, and either make her victim insane or kill him

Duppy: a ghost or evil spirit

Flamboyan (*flamboyant*): poinciana or royal poinciana tree. Synonyms include flame tree, flame-of-the-forest, cock-and-hen tree, shack-shack tree, cokyoco tree.

Jouvert (*jouvay, jouvé, j'ouvert*): Eastern Caribbean term for the pre-dawn beginning of Carnival celebrations on the Monday preceding the first week of Lent; also, the entire first day of Carnival and its celebrations. Jouvert traditionally begins with steel band music and street dancing.

Jumbie (n.): ghost, evil spirit; (adj.): something dangerous, weird, or false (as in "jumbie umbrella," the popular name for a type of inedible and possibly toxic mushroom)

Lyme (*lime*) (v.): to socialize with friends and/or family, sometimes with food and drink; (n.): an informal party or gathering, generally with food and drink

Make a cook: to have a cooked, informal meal out in the open, as part of regular socializing or as a form of celebration. The cooking is done mainly with wood or charcoal, sometimes with large stones or bricks arranged on the ground to hold a large pot of food.

Mas band: a band that performs during Carnival, usually beginning in jouvert

Miliciano: militiaman

Obatalá (*Obàtálá*; *Oxalá*, in the Brazilian Candomblé religion): an orisha (spirit-god) of the Yoruba religion, always clad in white, whose name means "the king who wears white cloth." The eldest of all the orishas, Obatalá is the father of all orishas and humanity and the creator of humankind and the earth. He is also the patron orisha of the handicapped.

Osun (*Oshun, Oschun*; *Oxum*, in Brazilian Candomblé): an orisha of the Yoruba religion who represents love, beauty, riches, intimacy, and diplomacy. The preferred wife of Shango (also Changó or Sàngó), she is the force of harmony in the universe.

Oya (*Oyá*): an orisha of the Yoruba religion who represents wind, fertility, magic, fire, and lightning, and creates tornadoes and hurricanes. She is also the guardian of the underworld, and is often associated with numerous orishas, especially Shango.

Pasodoble (*paso doble*): a style of dance originated in southern France, but modeled after the action, movement, and sounds of the Spanish bullfight; in Spanish, "two step"

Stchupsing (*cheupsing*): to make the sound of "kissing" or "sucking" one's teeth in an expression of disgust or contempt

Soucouyant (*soukouyan, sucoyan*): an evil old woman of legend who passes as an ordinary human being in daylight hours, sometimes hidden from the view of others, and at night sheds her wrinkled skin (sometimes storing it in a jar) and travels through the night in search of sleeping victims, often young children and infants, whose blood she sucks before returning to her skin

Tontons Macoutes: in Haitian Creole, "boogeyman," a frightening character from Haitian folklore, most often represented as an old man with a *macoute*, or bag, in which he puts children he has captured; also, the informal name of the Volunteers for National Security, a paramilitary group established in 1958 by Haiti's then-President François "Papa Doc" Duvalier, which was accountable only to Duvalier and later to his son President Jean-Claude Duvalier. Under the Duvalier dictatorships, thousands of members terrorized, raped, tortured, and killed with impunity any person suspected by the president of being a political adversary.

Yemayá (*Yemaja*; *Yemanjá* or *Iemanjá*, in Brazilian Candomblé): an orisha who represents the ocean and motherhood and protects children

Zami: Creole term used in some French and English Eastern Caribbean islands for women who express or are suspected of harboring sexual, romantic, or erotic interest in other women. This term is believed to have originated in the French Caribbean colonial period, deriving from the phrase "les amies," the (female) friends, who, as implied by "les amies," are more than friends.

CONTRIBUTORS

JOSÉ ALCÁNTARA ALMÁNZAR, one of the most distinguished fiction writers in the Spanish Caribbean and Latin America, was born in Santo Domingo in 1946. Among his numerous publications are *Antología de la literature dominicana* (Anthology of Dominican literature), *Callejón sin salida* (Dead-end alley), *Viaje al otro mundo* (Journey to the other world), *El sabor de lo prohibido: antología personal de cuentos* (The taste of the forbidden: A personal anthology of short stories), and *La carne estremecida* (Trembling flesh), winner of the 1989 Premio Nacional de Literatura. A co-author of the *Caribbean Writers* encyclopedia edited by Donald E. Herdeck, Alcántara has been a professor of sociology at the Universidad Autónoma of Santo Domingo and the Universidad Nacional Pedro Henríquez Ureña. He has also taught at the Instituto Tecnológico of Santo Domingo, and as a Fulbright professor (1987–88) at Stillman College in Alabama.

ALDO ALVAREZ is the author of *Interesting Monsters,* which was nominated for a 2002 Violet Quill Award and named by the *Washington Post Book World* as one of the best short story collections for fall 2001. Alvarez received an MFA in creative writing from Columbia University and a PhD in English from the State University of New York, Binghamton. He was a fiction scholar at the Bread Loaf Writers' Conference in 1998 and was featured in *Out* Magazine's *Out* 100 list of "gay success stories of 2001." In October 2004, he was presented with a Trailblazer Award. In 1997, he founded *Blithe House Quarterly: Queer Fiction Lives Here* (blithe.com), and currently serves as its executive editor, designer, and publisher. He is a professor of English at Wilbur Wright College in Chicago.

REINALDO ARENAS (1943–90), one of the Caribbean and Latin America's most celebrated writers, was born in Holguín, Cuba. As a teenager, he joined Fidel Castro's revolutionary movement against the dictator Fulgencio Batista. He briefly studied philosophy and literature at the University of Havana, and later worked at the Biblioteca Nacional José Martí, as an editor at the Cuban Book Institute, and as a writer and editor for the magazine *Gaceta de Cuba*. His increasingly anti-Castro stance throughout the 1960s and '70s, in part due to the government's intolerance of homosexuality, led to his increased isolation and alienation as a writer living in Cuba and the government's ultimate censorship of his work. In 1973, he was tried and imprisoned for "ideological deviation" and for having his works published outside of Cuba without government approval. In 1980 he left Cuba as part of the Mariel boatlift exodus. Among his most famous works are *Celestino antes del alba* (*Singing from the Well*), *Otra vez el mar* (*Farewell to the Sea*), *La vieja Rosa* (*Old Rosa*), *El color del verano* (*The Color of Summer*), and *Antes que anochezca* (*Before Night Falls*). After several years of struggle with HIV/AIDS, he committed suicide in New York City.

RANE ARROYO is a Puerto Rican poet from Chicago. He is the author of five books of poetry, the latest being *The Portable Famine*, winner of the 2004–2005 John Ciardi Poetry Prize. His book of experimental short stories about gay Latinos, *How to Name a Hurricane,* was published by the University of Arizona in 2005 in their Camino del Sol Series. He has been publishing poems and stories for over two decades, and his plays have been produced throughout the United States. Arroyo has lost friends and family to AIDS, and his drag queen uncle, Uncle Rachel, has become one of his major muses/ghosts. He earned his PhD in English and cultural studies from the University of Pittsburgh and currently teaches and lives in Toledo, Ohio. He can be contacted at RRArroyo@aol.com.

JESÚS J. BARQUET was born in Havana in 1953. He left Cuba for the United States in 1980 via the Mariel boatlift, and is presently a professor at New Mexico State University. His poetry books include *Sin decir el mar* (Without naming the sea), *Sagradas herejías* (Sacred heresies), *El libro del desterrado* (The book of the exile), *Un no rompido sueño* (A dream unbroken), *Naufragios/Shipwrecks*, and *Sin fecha de extinción* (Without expiration date). His books of literary criticism include *Consagración de la Habana* (Consecration of Havana), *Escrituras poéticas de una nación* (Poetic writings of a nation), and *Teatro y revolución cubana* (Theater and the Cuban Revolution). Barquet is also the co-editor with Rosario Sanmiguel of *Más allá de la isla: 66 creadores cubanos* (Beyond the island: 66 Cuban creators); with Maricel Mayor Marsán of *Haz de incitaciones* (Sheaf of incitations); and with Norberto Codina of *Poesía cubana del siglo XX* (Cuban poetry of the twentieth century). He has been awarded the Lourdes Casal Prize in Literary Criticism (1998), the Letras de Oro Essay Prize (1990–91), and the 19th Chicano/Latino Poetry 2nd Prize (1993).

MARILYN BOBES, born in Havana in 1955, studied history at the University of Havana, and later became a journalist. A poet as well as a prose writer, Bobes won the Casa de las Américas prize in 1995 for her story collection *Alguien tiene que llorar* (*Somebody Has to Cry*). Bobes has also published collections of poetry and, with Mirta Yáñez, co-edited an anthology of Cuban women's fiction, *Estatuas de sal* (Pillars of salt).

DIONNE BRAND was born in Trinidad in 1953 and has lived in Canada since 1970. Educated at the University of Toronto, she has taught at York University and the University of Guelph. Brand was awarded the Governor-General's Award and the Trillium Award for her writing and is the author of the novels *In Another Place, Not*

Here; *At the Full and Change of the Moon*; and *What We All Long For*. She has also written a collection of short fiction, *Sans Souci and Other Stories*, and numerous books of poetry and essays, including, most recently, *Inventory*. She has also made several film documentaries on the lives of black and immigrant working women in Canada.

TIMOTHY S. CHIN was born in Jamaica and raised in Kingston and Queens, New York. He received his PhD in English from the University of Michigan, and currently teaches courses in African American, Caribbean, and American literature at California State University, Dominguez Hills. He has written on the work of Paule Marshall, Michelle Cliff, Claude McKay, and other African American and Caribbean authors. Chin's research interests include diasporic and transnational approaches to issues of gender and sexuality in African American and Caribbean literature. He has published essays and fiction in *Callaloo*, *Small Axe*, and *Amerasia Journal*, and is currently working on a project that explores the role of Chinese Jamaicans in the reggae industry.

MICHELLE CLIFF was born in Jamaica and educated there, in New York City, and in London. She currently resides in California. Her work includes the short story collections *Bodies of Water* and *The Store of a Million Items*, the latter chosen by the *Village Voice* as one of the twenty-five best books of 1998; and the novels *Abeng, No Telephone to Heaven,* and *Free Enterprise*. From 1993 to 1999 she held the Allan K. Smith Professorship of English Language and Literature at Trinity College, Hartford. The recipient of two NEA fellowships and a fellowship from the Artists Foundation of Massachusetts, Cliff was a Fulbright Distinguished Scholar in New Zealand and the recipient of the Martin Luther King Jr.-Cesar Chávez-Rosa Parks Visiting Professorship at the University of Michigan. Her most recent work includes the novel *Into the Interior,* the essay collection *Apocalypso,* and translations of poetry by Federico García Lorca, Alfonsina Storni, and Pier Paolo Pasolini. She is presently at work on a new short story collection, entitled *Crocodilopolis*.

WESLEY E. A. CRICHLOW is an associate professor in the Faculty of Social Science at the University of Ontario Institute for Technology, Oshawa, where he teaches courses in criminal law and the Canadian justice system. He is the author of *Buller Men and Batty Bwoys: Hidden Men in Toronto and Halifax's Black Communities,* and has published widely in a variety of journals and anthologies. He holds a PhD from the University of Toronto.

MABEL CUESTA was born in Matanzas, Cuba, in 1976. A scholar and critic, she was educated at the University of Havana, and has taught literary studies and theory at the University of Matanzas. She is the author of two works of fiction, *Cuaderno de la fiancée* (The fiancée's notebook) and *Confesiones*, as well as articles published in periodicals throughout Latin America and the United States. Presently teaching Spanish at the Instituto Cervantes in New York City, she is completing a dissertation on the feminine imaginary in Cuba, archetypes, and representations of women in literature by women authors.

OCHY CURIEL has lived in Mexico, Brazil, and Colombia, and presently lives in Argentina. She has worked for many years in feminist, lesbian feminist, and women's anti-racist movements, and has authored articles on the political relationships between race, class, gender, and sexuality. Also a musician and singer-songwriter, her recordings have similarly focused on these concerns and on the lives of lesbians and all women. Curiel helped to organize two major international events: the 1992 first ever Encuentro of Black Women of Latin America and the Caribbean, out of which emerged the Network of Afro-Latin American and Afro-Caribbean Women; and the eighth Feminist Encuentro of Latin America and the Caribbean.

FAIZAL DEEN was born in Guyana in 1968 to parents from Trinidad and Guyana. He immigrated in 1997 to Canada. A 1992 graduate of Queen's University, Kingston, Ontario, he has also studied postcolonial literatures and theories at the University of the West Indies, Mona. His memoir *Land without Chocolate* was published in 1999.

PEDRO DE JESÚS was born in 1970 in Fomento, Cuba. A graduate of the University of Havana, he has published essays; two short story collections, *Cuentos frígidos* (*Frigid Tales*) and *La sobrevida* (Survival), winner of the 2006 Premio Alejo Carpentier for short stories; and a novel, *Sibilas en Mercaderes* (Fortune-tellers on Mercaderes).

R. ERICA DOYLE was born in Brooklyn to Trinidadian parents. Her work has appeared in various publications, including *Best American Poetry*, *Utne Reader*, *Ploughshares*, *Callaloo*, *Ms.*, *Bum Rush the Page*, *Gumbo*, and *Best Black Women's Erotica*. A recipient of awards from the Hurston/Wright Foundation and the Astraea Lesbian Writers Fund, Doyle has completed a poetry manuscript, *Proxy*, and is at work on a novel, *Fortune*. She teaches English and creative writing in the libraries, community centers, and public schools of New York City.

THOMAS GLAVE, born to Jamaican parents in the Bronx and raised there and in Jamaica, is a founding member of the Jamaica Forum for Lesbians, All-Sexuals and Gays (J-FLAG). He is the author of *Whose Song? And Other Stories,* the essay collection *Words to Our Now: Imagination and Dissent* (winner of a 2005 Lambda Literary Award), and the forthcoming short fiction collection *The Torturer's Wife* (2008). He teaches in the English department at the State University of New York, Binghamton.

ROSAMOND S. KING, PHD, is a writer and performer of Trinidadian and Gambian heritage. Her poetry and other writing have appeared in over a dozen journals and anthologies, among them *MaComère*, *Xcp: Cross-Cultural Poetics*, *Callaloo*, and *The Caribbean Writer.* Her reading events and performance art have been presented around the world, and her book and paper art are held in several private collections. Her scholarship focuses on Caribbean and African literature and performance. A member of the No. 1 Gold Artists' Collective, she has taught inmates, women on public assistance, and public school teachers, as well as university and high school students. In 2004, with New York University and the Organization of Women Writers of Africa, she co-organized "Yari Yari Pamberi: Black Women Writers Dissecting Globalization," the largest ever gathering of its kind. She is an assistant professor in the English department at Long Island University, Brooklyn.

HELEN KLONARIS is a Greek Bahamian writer and social activist who has worked locally for over thirteen years to raise awareness about gender inequities and gay and lesbian human rights. The author of numerous poems, essays, and a play, *The Death of Silence: A New Ceremony,* she is co-founder of the Bahamian journal for women writers and artists, *WomanSpeak,* and co-founder and leading spokesperson of a GLBT human rights organization, The Rainbow Alliance of the Bahamas. Klonaris also helped to found Zemi House, an interfaith center that houses the Bahamas' first GLBT Center. She earned a BA in religious studies from Wesleyan University in 1991, and is presently studying for an MFA in the Writing and Consciousness program at The New College of California.

LAWRENCE LA FOUNTAIN-STOKES is a Puerto Rican writer and scholar who specializes in Caribbean, Latino/a, and queer Latin American literary and cultural studies. He currently teaches Latino/a studies and Spanish in the Program in American Culture and the Department of Romance Languages and Literatures at the University of Michigan. His forthcoming book, *Queer Ricans: Cultures and Sexualities in the Diaspora,* focuses on Puerto Rican migration and homosexuality as they appear in Puerto Rican cultural productions (literature, film, cartoons, performance, dance, photography, clothing, and parades) and in political activism, both on the island and in the United States. His volume of short stories, *Uñas pintadas de azul/Blue Fingernails,* was published in 2005.

AUDRE LORDE (1934–92), one of the twentieth century's most powerful voices and a lifelong human rights activist, lived and wrote as a self-described "black, lesbian, feminist, warrior, mother, poet." Born in New York City to parents who emigrated there from Grenada and Barbados, she earned a BA from Hunter College (where, years later, she held the prestigious Thomas Hunter Chair of literature) and an MA in library science from Columbia University. Lorde authored numerous collections of poetry and prose, among them *From a Land Where Other People Live* (nominated for a National Book Award in 1974), *Sister Outsider,* and *The Cancer Journals.* While battling cancer, Lorde continued to write and teach while working as an internationally renowned activist. Not long before her death in St. Croix, she was awarded the Walt Whitman Citation of Merit and named Poet Laureate of the State of New York for the years 1991–93.

SHANI MOOTOO, born in Ireland and raised in Trinidad, is a video and visual artist whose photo-based compositions and paintings have been exhibited around the world. A published poet, Mootoo is the author of the story collection *Out on Main Street,* as well as two novels, *Cereus Blooms at Night* and *He Drown She in the Sea.*

ANTON NIMBLETT, a native of Trinidad, lives and writes in Brooklyn, New York. His fiction has appeared in *Calabash: A Journal of Caribbean Arts and Letters*, *African American Review*, and *African Voices*. He is a graduate of Carnegie Mellon University.

ACHY OBEJAS, born in 1956 in Havana, emigrated with her parents six years later, after the Cuban Revolution, to the midwestern United States, where she grew up. A return trip to Cuba years later proved profoundly important to her writing. An award-winning journalist, Obejas has written for several U.S. publications, and has worked for the *Chicago Tribune* since 1991. A two-time Lambda Literary Award winner (in 1996 for her first novel *Memory Mambo*, and in 2002 for her second, *Days of Awe*), she has also written and published poetry and short fiction.

LEONARDO PADURA FUENTES, one of Cuba's and Latin America's most well-known writers, was born in Havana in 1955. A graduate of the University of Havana (where he earned a degree in Latin American literature), he has also worked as a journalist. The author of screenplays as well as essays and detective fiction, his novel *Paisaje de otoño* (*Havana Black*) won the 1998 Premio Hammett of the Asociación Internacional de Escritores Policiacos. His work has been translated into English, German, and several other languages. Among his novels number *Adios Hemingway*, *La neblina del ayer* (Yesterday's fog), and the *Cuatro estaciones* (*Mario Conde Mystery*) detective series: *Pasado perfecto* (*Havana Blue*), *Vientos de cuaresma* (*Havana Yellow*), *Máscaras* (*Havana Red*), and *Paisaje de otoño*.

VIRGILIO PIÑERA (1912–79), author of plays, poetry collections, critical essays, and novels, is considered one of Cuba's greatest twentieth-century writers, along with José Lezama Lima, Alejo Carpentier, and Reinaldo Arenas. Among his most famous works are the novel *La carne de René* (*René's Flesh*) and the fiction collection *Cuentos fríos* (*Cold Tales*). Born in Cardenas, Cuba, he studied literature at the University of Havana. His immigration in 1950 to Argentina, where he began to publish his first works of fiction, earned him the admiration of writers like Jorge Luis Borges and Luis Bianco. He returned to Cuba in 1957 and, though an early supporter of the revolution, later encountered political difficulties with the Cuban bureaucracy because of his homosexuality and his refusal to write "socialist" literature. He died impoverished in Havana.

PATRICIA POWELL, originally from Jamaica, is the author of the novels *Me Dying Trial*, *A Small Gathering of Bones*, and *The Pagoda*.

KEVIN EVEROD QUASHIE was born in St. Kitts and grew up there and in St. Croix. An associate professor at Smith College, he is the co-editor (with Joyce Lausch and Keith D. Miller) of *New Bones: Contemporary Black Writers in America* and the author of *Black Women, Identity, and Cultural Theory: (Un)Becoming the Subject*. He is currently writing about the relationship between black culture and quiet.

JUANITA RAMOS (Dr. Juanita Díaz-Cotto) is originally from Puerto Rico. She is the author of *Gender, Ethnicity, and the State: Latina and Latino Prison Politics* and *Chicana Lives and Criminal Justice: Voices from El Barrio*, silver medal winner of *ForeWord* Magazine's 2006 Book of the Year Award for women's studies and honorable mention in the English history book category of the 2006 International Latino Book Awards. She is also the editor of the anthology *Compañeras: Latina Lesbians*. A professor of sociology, women's studies, and Latin American and Caribbean area studies at the State University of New York, Binghamton, Díaz-Cotto has been active in diverse human rights struggles for over thirty years. A co-founder of Las Buenas Amigas/Latina Lesbians of New York, she was one of the national organizers of the 1979 national march on Washington for lesbian and gay rights.

COLIN ROBINSON straddles an ethnic and cultural identity rooted in Trinidad (where he was born, raised, and came out) and the political and sexual identity he has built with other black gay men and queer people of color in New York City, where he has spent his entire adult life. In New York, he led Gay Men of African Descent's board and was the group's first director, and served nine years at Gay Men's Health Crisis in management and policy roles. He coordinated field production in New York for Marlon Riggs's 1989 film *Tongues Untied*, played editorial and leadership roles in the black gay men's writing collective Other Countries, and helped plan the 1995 historic "Black Nations/Queer Nations" conference held at the City University of New York. He hopes to bring this political and cultural work back to the Caribbean. "The Mechanic" was written in a college poetry class while finishing a degree he started sixteen years earlier.

ASSOTTO SAINT (1957–94) was born and raised in Les Cayes, Haiti, and spent his adult years in the United States, making his home in New York City where he worked with the Other Countries black gay men's writing collective and founded Galiens Press, dedicated to publishing and making more widely known the works of African-descended gay men. Poet, activist, playwright, editor, and anthologist, he authored numerous works, among them *Risin' to the Love We Need*, *New Love Song*, *Spells of a Voodoo Doll*, *Triple Trouble*, and *Black Fag*. He was featured as one of several HIV-affected men in Marlon Riggs's documentary *Non, Je Ne Regrette Rien* (*No Regret*). He died of an HIV-related illness in New York City.

ANDREW SALKEY (1928–95) was born in Colón, Panama, to Jamaican parents, and raised in Jamaica, where he attended St. George's College in Kingston. He received a BA from the University of London in 1955, and later worked as a writer and broadcast journalist for BBC radio. The author of numerous collections of poetry, short fiction, essays, plays, children's stories, and novels, Salkey taught writing at Hampshire College in Amherst, Massachusetts, from 1956 to 1976. Among his many awards number a Guggenheim fellowship and a Casa de las Américas prize.

LAWRENCE SCOTT is from Trinidad. In 1999, his novel *Aelred's Sin* was awarded a Commonwealth Writers' Prize, Best Book in Canada and the Caribbean, and hailed for its exploration of possibilities for male relationships. His first novel, *Witchbroom*, was short-listed for a Commonwealth Writers' Best First Book Prize in 1993, and was followed in 1994 with a collection of short stories, *Ballad for the New World*, including the prize winning story "The House of Funerals." His most recent novel, *Night Calypso*, was also short-listed for a Commonwealth Writers' Prize, Best Book Award, in 2005. He divides his time between writing and teaching literature and creative writing. He lives in London and in Port-of-Spain.

MAKEDA SILVERA, born and raised in Jamaica and now living in Canada, is the author of a novel, *The Heart Does Not Bend*, and two acclaimed story collections, *Remembering G.* and *Her Head a Village*. The founder of Sister Vision Press in Canada, she is the editor of *Piece of My Heart: A Lesbian of Colour Anthology* and *The Other Woman: Women of Colour in Contemporary Canadian Literature*.

H. NIGEL THOMAS, born and raised in St. Vincent, has consistently woven both Caribbean folklore and themes of male homosexuality into his novels and short fiction. He attended university in Montreal and for ten years taught with the Protestant School Board of Greater Montreal. Presently a professor of literature at the Université Laval in Québec, he is the author of the novels *Return to Arcadia*, *Behind the Face of Winter*, and *Spirits in the Dark* (finalist for the 1994 Québec Writers' Federation Hugh MacLennan Fiction Award); a story collection, *How Loud Can the Village Cock Crow*; a collection of poems, *Moving Through Darkness*; and a critical study, *From Folklore to Fiction: A Study of Folk Heroes and Rituals in the Black American Novel*.

RINALDO WALCOTT, born and raised in Barbados, is the author of *Black Like Who? Writing Black Canada* and the editor of *Rude: Contemporary Black Canadian Cultural Criticism*. He is an associate professor in the University of Toronto's Department of Sociology and Equity Studies in Education, where he holds the Canada Research Chair in Social Justice and Cultural Studies. Walcott's teaching and research have focused principally on movements and connections between cultural studies, postcolonial studies, queer theory, and performing arts, with an emphasis throughout on black diaspora studies. He is presently preparing a critical study on the work of the Barbadian Canadian author Austin C. Clarke.

GLORIA WEKKER was born in Paramaribo, Suriname, and was one of the founding members of Sister Outsider, a literary circle of black lesbians in Amsterdam (1984–87). She earned her PhD in socio-cultural anthropology at the University of California, Los Angeles; since 2001, she has held the IIAV Chair in gender and ethnicity in the Women's Studies Department at Utrecht University, the Netherlands. She also is the Director of GEM, the Expertisecenter on Gender, Ethnicity, and Multiculturality in Higher Education, at the same university. She has published in a wide range of fields, on topics including constructions of sexual subjectivity of women in the black diaspora, knowledge systems in the Dutch academy and in multicultural society, and the history of the Dutch black migrant and refugee women's movement. Her monograph *The Politics of Passion: Women's Sexual Culture in the Afro-Surinamese Diaspora* was published in 2006. Wekker has also published poetry and other prose, and is the editor of several international journals.

LAWSON WILLIAMS (pseud.) is a lawyer and the former legal/advocacy director for the Jamaica Forum for Lesbians, All-Sexuals and Gays (J-FLAG).

THOMAS GLAVE is an associate professor of creative writing and Latin American and Caribbean studies at the State University of New York, Binghamton. He is the author of *Words to Our Now: Imagination and Dissent* (winner of a 2005 Lambda Literary Award), *Whose Song? And Other Stories*, and the forthcoming fiction collection *The Torturer's Wife*.

Library of Congress Cataloging-in-Publication Data

Our Caribbean : a gathering of lesbian and gay writing from the Antilles / edited and with an introduction by Thomas Glave.
p. cm.
Includes bibliographical references.

ISBN 978-0-8223-4208-3 (cloth : alk. paper) —
ISBN 978-0-8223-4226-7 (pbk. : alk. paper)

1. Caribbean literature — 20th century — Translations into English.
2. Caribbean literature — 21st century — Translations into English.
3. Caribbean literature (English) — 20th century.
4. Caribbean literature (English) — 21st century.
5. Gays' writings, Caribbean.
6. Homosexuality — Caribbean Area.

I. Glave, Thomas.

PN849.C32O87 2008
808.8'9920664 — dc22
2007044901